The National Kitchen & Bath Association
presents

Bathroom Basics

A Training Primer for Bathroom Specialists

By Patrick J. Galvin

- Information about this book and other Association programs and publications may be obtained from The National Kitchen & Bath Association, 687 Willow Grove St., Hackettstown NJ 07840, phone (908) 852-0033, fax (908) 852-1695. email: educate@nkba.org

- ISBN # 1-887127-14-3.

- This book was produced by Galvin Publications, E. Windsor NJ.

- Graphic illustrations by Design Services Unlimited, Syracuse NY.

- Cover bathroom designed by Tom Trzcinski, CBD, CKD, Kitchen Concepts of Pittsburgh.

- Cover photo by Maura McEvoy.

Acknowledgements

American Olean Tile Co.

American Standard, Inc.

Heritage Custom Kitchens

Merillat Industries

Nevamar Div., International Paper

Robern, Inc.

Santile Distributing, Jerry Norton

Union Hardware, Charles Goldberg

Bathroom Basics

A Training Primer for Bathroom Specialists

CONTENTS

Appendices

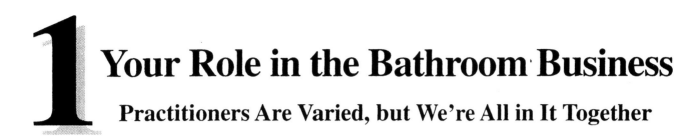

Your Role in the Bathroom Business

Practitioners Are Varied, but We're All in It Together

The bathroom remodeling business is as advanced as the kitchen business in some areas of North America, with all that entails in sophisticated space planning and design. But in other areas, sometimes as near as the next city, county or province, it still consists of little more than fixture replacement, new fittings or addition of a vanity cabinet.

Whichever it may be in your area depends entirely on the practitioners, and that includes you.

A bathroom designer and/or salesperson may work at or be any of the following:

- **Full-service bathroom showrooms.**

- **Specialized high-end plumbing, hardware and accessory showrooms.**

- **Plumbing contractors.**

- **Independent designers; architects.**

- **Remodeling and building contractors.**

- **Kitchen distributors.**

- **Plumbing wholesalers.**

- **Home centers, independent or chain.**

We'll take a broader look at each of those categories, but first you should appreciate how the bathroom business has evolved.

Historically, bathroom remodeling did not develop as a business until the mid-'50s when, here and there, some tradesman (often a plumbing contractor with vision) saw the need and opportunity in planning and designing better kitchens. With the aid of a little education, these pioneers soon extended the same principles of space planning and merchandising to the bathrooms in which they already were replacing fixtures.

Bathrooms until then had been somewhat short of ideal. They had been decreed indoors by law in the U.S. in all single-family homes shortly before the building boom of the early 1920s, and builders developed the habit of using for a bathroom whatever space they could shave from bedrooms and closets.

Thus we got the standard three-fixture 5' x 7' (more or less) bathroom that has become the golden opportunity for creative space planners of the 90s.

And golden it is—golden and silver, brass, chrome, wood, marble, granite, ceramics, fabulous plastics, brilliant colors, jets, "environment" tubs, steam, sauna, sensor venting, powered flushes, valves with temperature and pressure control, heated floors, towel warmers, and lighting that is as decorative as it is functional.

Along with the parade of products, improved dramatically in both function and aesthetics, came an awareness among homeowners that existing bathrooms were woefully inadequate and that expanding the space could improve the quality of life. This awareness was fueled by shelter magazine articles and newspaper features. Many of these pictured the bathroom as a locus for luxury, where a new "me" generation could indulge itself in steam or sauna without the guilt felt by previous generations and as a logical site for physical fitness activity.

All of this coincided with the advent of the working spouse, necessitating more order and organization of storage and activity space.

No less significant was the move of kitchen designers into the field of bathroom remodeling. It was logical, it was needed, and nobody else was doing it. Both involved the same design skills, similar product knowledge, expertise in planning space and solving problems, and professional presentation.

In 1973, *Kitchen Business* magazine (then the only trade magazine in the field, now *Kitchen & Bath Business*) ran a year-long promotion called "Operation BRACE," and **more than 3,000 kitchen dealers** sent in a coupon pledge to expand into bathroom remodeling. (BRACE was an acronym for **B**uild, **R**emodel, **A**dd, **C**reate, **E**xtend a bathroom.)

Education grew with the movement. The old American Institute of Kitchen Dealers developed bathroom schools, changed its name to National Kitchen & Bath Association, and later formalized training and bathroom design itself, for the first time, with development of the six-volume Bathroom Industry Technical Manual and formation of a professional group, the Society of Certified Bathroom Designers.

Now it all has fallen into place—consumer demand, innovative products, availability of education and training, and a growing cadre of creative design professionals who know what to do and how to do it in small or large spaces, whatever the homeowner's budget might be.

How we work, apart or together

There is a place in the bathroom business

Fig. 1.1. There might be a dozen or more complete bathroom displays, all fully accessorized, in the showroom of a full-service bath dealership.

Fig. 1.2. Independent designers often work from an office to design bathrooms.

Fig. 1.3. Luxury plumbing fixtures and decorative hardware often are displayed in showrooms by firms that specialize in these products.

for everyone who wants to learn the ropes and do it right, either as an entrepreneur or as an employee working in design or sales in any one of the types of businesses we have mentioned.

Let's look a little more closely at how these businesses operate, how you fit in and how they might help each other.

The full-service showroom (Fig. 1.1). This is operated by the total professional, usually in conjunction with a kitchen business. This pro knows how to get leads, how to follow up and qualify them, how to identify the problems in existing bathroom facilities, how to solve them, how to design bath facilities that solve the problems within the customer's budget, how to sell the job at a fair price with a reasonable profit, and then see that all is installed properly.

This dealer will have access to all of the needed products and will know how to install them. He or she will have agreements and procedures set up with any necessary subcontractors such as plumbing and electrical, but will retain full supervision of and responsibility for the installation.

Bathroom dealers see the value in having one or more **CBD**s on staff. There might also be one or more **interior designers** on staff, preferably with CBD status or in a study course aiming for it.

The dealer conducts this business in the same way he or she conducts the kitchen business. The first customer contact should be in the showroom. There should be a visit to the home where the customer is interviewed and the home is surveyed. Then plans are drawn and a contract is signed in the showroom. If there is a design retainer it should be collected at this time. *(For the complete sales process, see Chapter 8.)*

The showroom and staff might be available to customers of **building** or **remodeling contractors, interior designers** or other allied professionals, which could help build business for

Fig. 1.4. Plumbing wholesalers increasingly are opening separate bathroom showrooms for retail trade.

Fig. 1.5. Both luxury and low-end fixtures are displayed in many home centers..
played in many home centers..

This will introduce
Please extend the courtesy of your showroom.
John Jones, Designer

Fig. 1.6. Outside designers and contractors without showrooms sometimes will use a card to introduce their customers, to see your displays.

all of them. When this is done it almost always is prearranged and by appointment, and usually the customer must carry an introduction card or the allied professional must accompany the customer on the visit. The allied professional might want to do the pricing to the customer, then buy from the showroom.

Plumbing/hardware/accessory showrooms (Fig. 1.3). These have been around for a long time, but are more involved now in the luxury bathroom business because of the advent of luxury showers with multiple shower and spray heads. Their expertise is essential because a simple water supply pipe won't do it. Plumbing manifolds often are needed for proper flow to the multiple sprays, and this often is beyond the training of many plumbers.

The stores emphasize both bath and kitchen products and usually do not compete with bathroom design firms. But they can help each other. They will do well to make deals with bathroom design firms to furnish their high-end products for the bathroom displays in return for a display sign crediting them for the products. They also can agree to refer their customers to the bathroom design firms with which they are working by showing a sign which might read, for example: "See our products in use in the showroom of Bathroom Creations."

Plumbing contractors (Fig. 1.1). As noted, many of the early kitchen and bath specialist firms grew out of this category, and it is still happening. Over the years many abandoned their original plumbing businesses in favor of kitchens and bathrooms.

It has seldom worked, however, unless they set up kitchens and bathrooms as a separate department. Without this step, plumbing contracting and bathroom/kitchen design find it difficult to co-exist. Plumbing contractors are aware that kitchens and baths must be merchandised, and that is a skill they often are too busy to learn. It is more common for them to hire a manager for a separate branch.

Otherwise their role in the bathroom business is in replacement sales and installation and as subcontractors for the full-service design firm or for builders.

Independent designers, architects (Fig. 1.2). These are significant players in the bathroom business. They include professional designers, many architects who specialize in bathrooms and kitchens, some bathroom/kitchen specialists who may have sold their showrooms, and growing numbers of graduates of college bathroom/kitchen design courses. They often work from an office, frequently a home office, but many work for full-service bathroom firms.

Many sell design and plans only. Others will work with specialist firms or distributors, use their showrooms and collect a commission on product sales.

Remodeling/building contractors. Remodelers sometimes specialize in bathrooms and kitchens, but in many cases they will avoid design and do cosmetic remodeling, such as floors, walls, vanity cabinets and counters. They usually are geared for a quicker kind of sale than the multiple customer contacts required for bathroom design. When they take a bathroom job, they often will work with a full-service bathroom firm for a commission on the products.

Builders usually do bathroom remodeling only as a stopgap when housing starts are slow. When they do remodeling, bathroom jobs tend to be too small to get their attention. They'll do a bathroom only to keep a customer happy. There are some, of course, who will commit to a full-service job, and when they do they are equipped to do a very good job of it

Distributors, wholesalers (Fig. 1.4). Kitchen distributors have long been accused of selling "out the back door," rightly or wrongly, especially appliances. Plumbing wholesalers have faced the same charge. All in all it hasn't mattered much, because any consumers who wanted discounts could always find plenty of discount outlets.

Now many distributors and wholesalers are going into the retail bathroom remodeling business legitimately, the former to protect their businesses and the latter for the sake of expansion.

Distributors have been threatened by a trend among cabinet and appliance manufacturers to sell through their own sales managers rather than through independent distributors. The trend has been aggravated by mergers and acquisitions. As distributors lose their lines, the only way to stay in business has been to add retailing.

Plumbing wholesalers have seen the vast

expansion opportunity in kitchen/bath showrooms. Many of them have become multi-branch bathroom remodelers, with several regional showrooms.

This can be a welcome addition to the industry. It increases employment opportunities and it also increases the possibilities for CBDs or CKDs to lease bathroom remodeling departments at those establishments, especially those of the plumbing wholesalers to whom the concept of space planning might be more remote. It also adds greatly to the mass of bathroom advertising and promotion to homeowners. Increased advertising in any locale helps stimulate demand. It elevates consumer consciousness, makes homeowners more aware of their bathroom problems and of the fact that solutions are available, thus making business better for all bathroom remodelers.

Home centers (Fig. 1.5). These are a significant part of the industry, as they always have been. The only difference now is that some are much larger. Historically, home center chains occasionally announced big plans for design departments, but, in the past, those plans didn't work out under the in-store pressure of volume, speed and price. No salesperson could navigate from selling a pound of nails in one minute to selling and designing a bathroom over a period of days regardless of how capable the computer was. In past years, the separate design department that was planned frequently deteriorated under the pressure of the bottom line. The whole procedure now is much more sophisticated.

The home center employee knows very well how to sell products. But when the job becomes design as well as selling, it takes time, expertise and thorough knowledge of a customer's needs. There is no way around it, and present-day management apparently understands this. Otherwise, home center bath sales will consist simply of over-the-counter transactions to do-it-yourselfers.

But we must all be aware that this is a nation of **do-it-yourselfers.** After all, we built a

country this way, and without much input from experts. Now, at whatever level we are selling, we are the experts and the only intelligent approach is to be as helpful as we can to everyone who might be a potential customer.

Even if we sell from a full-service showroom, if the customer wants to buy products and do it herself the prudent course is to sell the products (if we have them and if it is within company policy), but with full information. This includes:

- **Basic information (and warnings) on plumbing, code requirements.**

- **Basic information (and warnings) on electrical work, codes and use of GFCIs.**

- **How to install a vanity, lav and faucet.**

- **How to install a countertop, with integral lav and without.**

- **How to install a surface-mounted or recessed medicine cabinet, with and without lighting.**

- **How to install specialized bath cabinets, such as those that might be fitted above the bathtub or over the water closet.**

Sales time is too valuable to do this orally, and oral information is too hard for the consumer to retain and too easy to misconstrue anyway. It is best to have simple leaflets printed that can be passed out to the do-it-yourselfers with only a minimum of talk.

Why? Because every one of these is a potential customer. Many homeowners may plan to do these things themselves, but change their minds when confronted with the actual work to be done, the code approvals and the hazards.

Those that don't change their minds this time can become bigger customers in the future. After one tussle with the pipes or wires they possibly will hesitate to try it again when, sooner or later, they discover more needs in the bathroom or kitchen.

You want them to appreciate your helpfulness when that time comes. In the meantime, when they do appreciate you for what you are doing right now, the referrals they send to you might turn out to be your best jobs of the year.

A question that persists is: Do you deal with **customers** or **clients?** When you sell over the counter, of course, you sell to a customer, and you might be laughed off the floor if you referred to your customer as a client. But when you work as a professional bathroom specialist you deal with a client. In this book, with mixed groups of readers, we tend to use the terms client and customer interchangeably.

Your role in the bathroom business might be with any of the firms we mentioned. Whichever it is, one goal always should be to expand your horizons and opportunities by becoming more of an expert and arming yourself with the status and recognition that comes with certification.

This book on Bathroom Basics is a good start. But don't stop here. If your goal is professionalism in the industry, don't stop until you become a **Certified Bathroom Designer.**

Notes:

Construction, Plumbing, Electrical
How a House Is Built; How the Bathroom Fits in

To the average homeowner a bathroom may be just another compartment in the house. You open a door and there it is.

But to a bathroom remodeler there is more to it. It is supported in space by a system of joists and studs designed to perform specific functions and support specific weight loads. It has nerve networks of wiring and piping, for lighting, ventilation and heat; for hot and cold water supply; for waste lines to carry away "used" water and other waste, and traps to protect from the backup of sewerage gases.

The remodeling expert must know what is behind the walls and under the floor before specifying new fixtures or adding a bath or half-bath in a different area of the house. And the expert must know about building codes, both general and local, that govern nearly every move.

We're not going to build a house here, but to start we have to know rudimentary facts about house construction.

Most of the houses we will work in are of "platform" construction, with multiple studs nailed together in the corners that support the platform of the second story and then the platform of the attic, and the subfloors extending all the way to the outside edges of the building. But in some older houses we will find "balloon" construction in which longer studs rise from the

foundation to the roof all the way around the perimeter. Upper floor joists rest on a ledger notched into the studs and are nailed to the studs, so we might not find the well-defined corners we find in platform construction. We might have to build up these corners before installation.

Balloon framing can have open spaces in the walls all the way from top to bottom. This makes it easy to bring pipe or wire up to a second-floor bathroom, but it can create a chimney effect in case of fire. So if you are remodeling a second-story bathroom in a balloon-framed house, and if the walls are not filled with insulation, codes require that you install a fire-stop in the wall between floors. This is a 2x4 nailed horizontally between studs, and caulked.

In remodeling a bathroom or adding a bath or half-bath, we usually will be concerned with three interior walls and possibly one exterior wall. The 2x4 studs normally will be 16" (41cm) apart, on center (o.c.). However, 2x6 studs used on the exterior wall at 24" (61cm) apart o.c., are structurally equivalent. The larger studs are used to allow more insulation in the exterior walls.

But even if a house is framed with 2x4s, either an interior or exterior wall might have 2x6s if they are "wet walls" that contain the plumbing risers and waste and vent stacks. (Vent stacks are part of the house drainage system installed to maintain atmospheric pressure, protecting trap seals from siphonage and back pressure; more on them later.)

The significance of 24" o.c. framing for you as the bathroom remodeler is that you may need to add more backing (horizontal 2x4s between studs) to support wall-hung toilets, lavatories, grab bars, soap dishes and towel bars.

Fig. 2.1 shows an overall view of platform framing so you see how it all fits together. Now let's look more closely and get into structural details as we encounter them in the bathroom. We'll be interested in a window, a door, a skylight, and installation of a tub, shower, toilet, lav, bidet, accessories such as grab bars, soap dishes and towel bars, and a medicine cabinet.

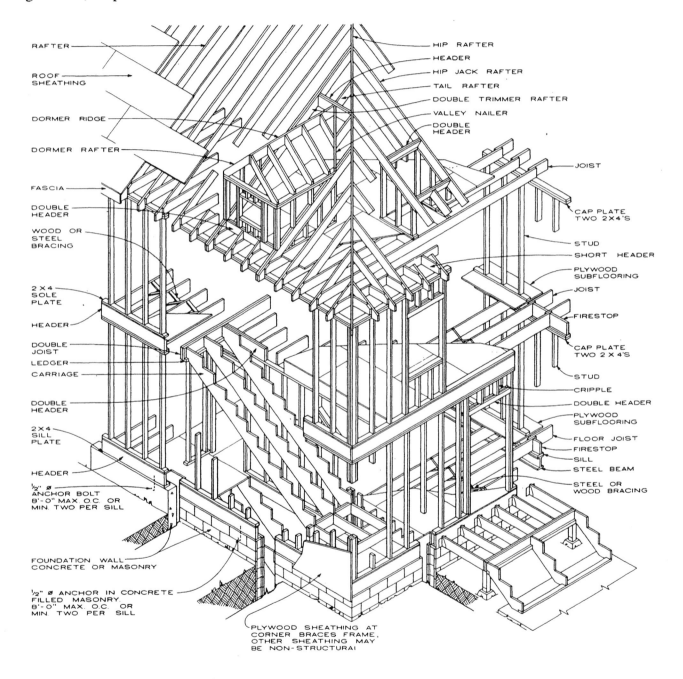

Fig. 2.1. Platform framing is the most prevalent type of framing found in the U.S. In this type, each floor becomes a platform on which that story is built. Horizontal framing members are joists, usually 2" x 10" (5 x 25cm) for load-bearing floors, 2" x 6" 5 x 15cm) in the ceiling at the attic. Vertical framing members are studs, 16" (41cm) apart o.c. Sometimes this is increased to 24" (61cm) apart.

Fig. 2.2 shows simple framing for a wall and a window, as they might exist in a typical bathroom or as you might want to install them. The parts shown are 2x4s, except for 2x6 or 2x8 double headers, depending on the span, above the window opening, laid on edge for added strength. It would be the same for a door. But remember that in a bathroom you might find 2x6s or 2x8s to allow for drain pipes in one or more of the walls. The hubbed parts of a 4" cast iron pipe for the soil stack are more than 6" across, requiring a 2x8 wall. A 3" copper or plastic pipe needs a 2x6 wall. You can determine the wall thickness by measuring at a door or window, subtracting the trim and wall covering. If there is no wall or window, you can find a stud to measure under the baseboard.

How the plumbing system works

House plumbing actually consists of two systems which work quite differently from each other (Fig. 2.6):

1. Bringing clean water into the house, which is the **water supply** system;

2. Getting rid of it after it is used, which is the drain-waste-vent (**DWV**) system.

The supply system brings water in from a city main or a well under pressure, normally from 30 to 80 pounds per square inch (psi). Because it comes in and is distributed under pressure, it can use smaller pipes than the DWV system. The typical service main that brings water into the house will be 1 1/4" galvanized iron or 1" copper. In the house, piping will range from 1" down to 1/4". A common size for supply lines in the house is 3/4" to 1/2", and 3/8" risers to lavs and toilets.

But DWV lines, because they work by gravity flow, must be larger. Commonly they will be 1 1/4" to 2", except for the waste line serving the toilet which usually is either 3"

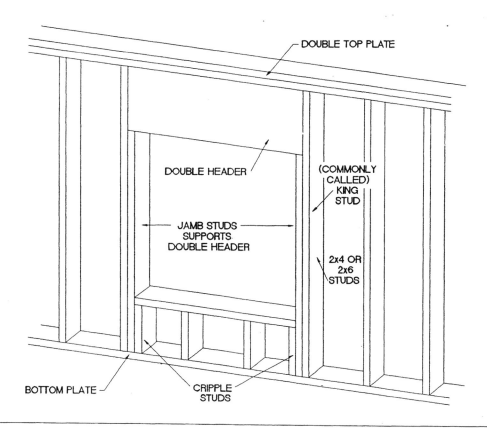

FIG. 2.2. In typical wall framing, studs are doubled for extra support at openings, such as windows and doors. Typical wall partition sits on a horizontal 2x4 wall plate with a double top plate on top of studs. Door or window takes "double header" framing at top of opening, held up by jamb studs.

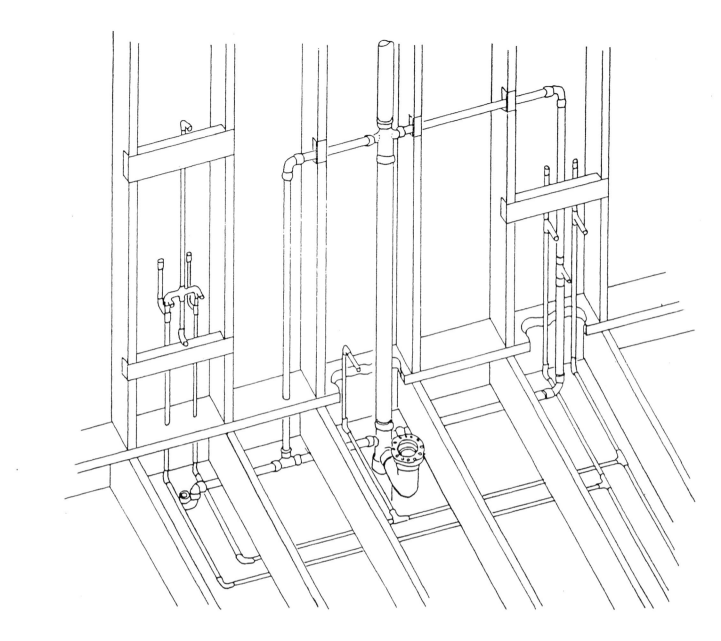

Fig. 2.3. Typical bathroom plumbing system is notched into studs with headers for, from left, tub-shower, toilet and lavatory. This is a crawl space house, so in-floor plumbing can go under the joists. If joists were between first and second story of a house, pipes parallel with joists would be routed between them or, in the other direction, through holes or notches in joists.

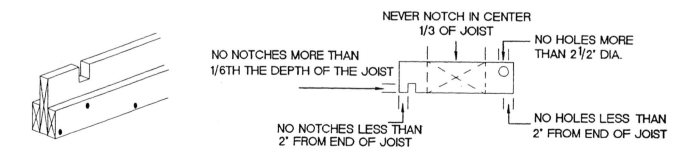

NEVER NOTCH IN CENTER
1/3 OF JOIST

NO HOLES MORE
THAN 2 1/2' DIA.

NO NOTCHES MORE THAN
1/6TH THE DEPTH OF THE JOIST

NO NOTCHES LESS THAN
2' FROM END OF JOIST

NO HOLES LESS THAN
2' FROM END OF JOIST

Fig. 2.4. Studs and floor joists often must be notched or drilled to route supply pipe or drains in confined spaces. In doing so, the integrity of the framing must be maintained. Holes and notches must not be cut in center third of a joist, and not closer than 2" from the end of the joist.

or 4". The DWV line serving the toilet is called the soil line or soil stack.

Water supply pipe must withstand pressure, heat and corrosion, and not impart any color, odor or taste to the water. The most common material is copper. Plastic pipe is inexpensive and easy to install, but it is restricted by codes in some areas. Plastics used include PVC (polyvinyl chloride) and CPVC (chlorinated PVC). PB (polybutylene) is flexible and useful in areas where access is difficult, but it has been deleted from the code for water supply. Another plastic, PE (polyethylene), is used only outdoors and under ground.

In older homes, galvanized steel is common, but you also might find brass. Many homes have been upgraded to copper or plastic.

Water supply splits into hot and cold

Before water enters the house or as it enters (unless it's from a well), it passes through the water meter. A main shut-off valve, with bleed, will be near the meter. But this main shut-off for the entire house is not enough. Every water supply line, hot and cold, to every fixture, should have a shut-off valve at the fixture to facilitate future repair and for customer convenience.

Shortly after it enters the house the supply line splits. One line goes to the water heater and/or boiler, and from that point on it provides hot

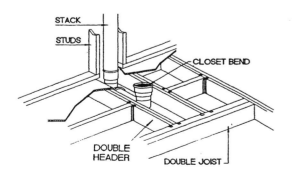

Fig. 2.5. Drain lines in floor should run parallel with joists. If a joist must be cut for a large drain, it should be framed with double header joists for added support.

Supply pipe characteristics

1. GALVANIZED STEEL
   a. Most common pipe in older homes.
   b. Rarely used now in new construction.
   c. Is rigid, requires threaded fittings at joints.
   d. Requires more time and labor for threading, installation than other types of supply pipe.
   e. Susceptible to rust and corrosion.
   f. Should not be used in conjunction with copper pipe without dielectric (nonconducting) fittings. Without such fittings there is galvanic action, a small current flow between dissimilar metals, which eventually will cause corrosion and leaks.

2. COPPER
   a. Most common now in new construction.
   b. Available either rigid, in 10' and 20' lengths, or nonrigid, in rolls of 30', 60' and 100'.
   c. Joints in copper tubing are either sweat-soldered or use compression fittings.

3. PLASTIC
   a. Includes PVC and CPVC, both very light in weight. (PB now against code.)
   b. Inexpensive and easy to install.
   c. Compression fittings are sometimes used, but joints usually are made with solvent adhesives that weld joints.
   d. Corrosion-free.
   e. Less heat loss in hot water line than with other types of supply piping.
   f. Some plastic materials prohibited by some local codes, usage restricted in others. Codes must be checked.
   g. Noisy if not properly insulated.

4. BRASS
   a. Brass piping might be found in older homes.
   b. It must be threaded, like steel, and has similar disadvantages.

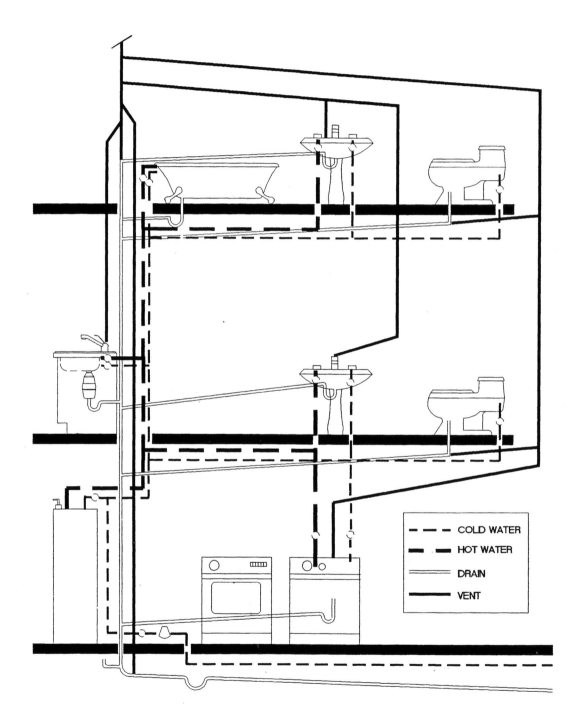

COLD WATER

HOT WATER

DRAIN

VENT

Fig. 2.6. Water supply enters house under pressure from city main and splits at water heater into hot and cold lines. DWV lines flow by gravity, so they must be angled downward at 1/4" per foot. All fixtures must connect to a vent.

water. The other line continues on to provide cold water. The hot and cold water lines usually run parallel between studs, joists, through crawl spaces or any other convenient passageway. Studs and joists often must be notched or drilled to accommodate the piping (Fig. 2.4). The twin lines branch off at distribution centers to provide hot and cold water to fixtures, as needed.

Size of piping for the hot and cold branch supply lines is determined by the number and types of fixtures supplied by the branch.

It is common to use 3/4" pipe to supply three or more fixtures, as in a complete bathroom, or 1/2" pipe for two or less fixtures, as in a powder room or half-bath. At each individual fixture supplied by the branch, however, it is customary to use a smaller pipe size to ensure proper water pressure at the fixture. This size reduction usually must be within 30" (76cm) of the water outlet. Minimum threshold pressure is critical especially with water-conserving shower heads, many of which use flexible orifices that flex into smaller diameters as pressure increases. This depends on pressure, not amount of flow.

Note, however, that while 1/2" pipe is sufficient for standard tubs and fixtures, it might not be enough for the larger tubs and whirlpool baths being sold today. 1/2" I.P.S. (iron pipe size) fittings restrict water flow to 9 (34L) gallons per minute (gpm) at the tub spout. This flow might be so slow that the hot water cools before the tub is filled. To overcome that problem, use a 3/4" branch supply line with a 3/4" I.P.S. valve and bath spout. **But always check local codes.** They can govern pipe sizes and materials.

Connecting supply pipe sizes for common fixtures are:

Bathtub	1/2"
Large tub, whirlpool	3/4"
Bidet	3/8"
Multi-head shower	3/4"
Lavatory	3/8"
Laundry	1/2"
Shower	1/2"
Water Closet	3/8"
Water Closet (1-piece)	1/2"
Dishwasher	1/2"
Kitchen Sink	1/2"

House water pressure is measured in pounds per square inch (psi) at the incoming service main. Pressure at 30 psi or lower might require installation of a booster pump. Pressure at 80 psi is high and might require installation of a pressure limiter.

Water flow is measured in gallons per minute (gpm). Factors that govern water flow:

1. **Pressure at the service main**
2. **Size and type of pipe**
3. **Length of pipe from main to fixture**
4. **Number of bends and fittings in pipe**
5. **The "head," or height to which water must rise in the building**
6. **Number of fixtures being used simultaneously**

Hot water and water heaters

The hot water supply lines must deliver water to the fixture at the rate and in the quantity needed, but they also must do it at a favorable temperature. There are three factors that affect water temperature:

1. **Distance of the using fixture from the water heater.** In some houses this distance is too far, resulting in so much heat loss that the temperature at point-of-use is too cold.

2. **Capacity of the water heater tank, how many gallons it holds.** This can be misleading. A 50-gallon tank set at 120 degrees (49 C) does not provide 50 gallons (189L) at that heat at one draining, because incoming water mixes and cools the water remaining. The tank usually will provide up to 70% of listed capacity.

3. **Recovery rate of the water heater.** This is the time required to bring stored or incoming water up to desired temperature, and the temperature of incoming water can vary widely. Recovery rate also is affected by the amount of simul-

taneous use at various fixtures. Electric water heaters have a slower recovery rate than those fueled by gas or oil.

The first factor, distance, can be corrected in four ways:

1. Install a separate insulated hot water line direct to the fixtures, a solution that often is impossible because of lack of access.

2. Install a hot water booster (a tankless heater) at any individual fixtures that need it, which requires space, access and electrical hookup.

3. Install a continuous recirculating hot water line. This solution requires access, a pump and an electrical hookup.

4. A newer system that pumps cold water out of the hot water line and into the cold water line when you turn the hot water on and off quickly, and cuts off when hot water reaches the valve. It avoids running a lot of cold water down the drain, but requires a power hookup. A newer "trickle" system leaks hot water into the line without power.

Capacity and recovery rate are related. With sufficient capacity there is no need to be concerned with recovery rate. The problem here is that the customer might not want to pay for extra capacity that is not needed. Depending on the temperature of the incoming water, a 40-gallon (151L) *electric* water heater will provide only 58.45 gallons (221L) of hot water in the first hour of use, and only 18.45 (70L) gallons each succeeding hour (if usage is continual).

A 40-gallon *gas* water heater will provide 73.61 gallons (279L) in the first hour. It will take a 52-gallon (197L) electric tank to approximate that. Solar panels sometimes are used to collect heat from the sun for heating water, but these installations nearly always are backed up by a conventional gas or electric water heater.

If 73 gallons sounds like a lot of water, consider that a family of four that takes four showers in the morning might, if they are conservation-conscious, use up 40 to 60 gallons (151-227L) of hot water in that activity alone. But if two of them take 5-minute showers they alone will use 60 gallons, possibly leaving a problem for the other two.

Those figures, however, are for older shower heads that flow freely. Newer shower heads and faucets restrict flow by 50%, so this, too, must be taken into account.

So it must start with family size and water-use habits, and the question of whether the family wants worry-free use of hot water or is willing to adapt to save money. This must be discussed thoroughly in the interview.

The somewhat higher initial cost and higher energy costs of a higher-capacity water heater must be balanced against the frustration of finding the water too cool at times of high use. It is best to give the customer all pertinent facts and then to let the customer make the decision.

Water consumption figures for appliances vary widely, especially if older models are retained. User habits vary also. But here are some common figures for **gallons per use:**

Shower, 9-30 (34-114L). Tub bath, 10-15 (38-57L). Clothes washer, 20-35 (76-132 L) each load. Dishwasher, 7.5-12 (28-45L), regular cycle. Manual dishwash, 15-25 (57-95L).

Kitchen use of hot water is a factor in the bathroom. If the family does a lot of baking the dishwasher often might be on a super-clean cycle which would use two or three gallons more. If dishes are washed manually with holding water in the sink, the figure could be much less. Usually, though, dishwashing by hand involves long periods of running water, especially for rinsing.

Oversized tubs demand special consideration. They may require a separate water heater to ensure adequate hot water, and they need a larger branch supply line or the water in the tub will cool before it is filled adequately. A 3/4" (2 cm) branch supply and 3/4" fixture connection are minimum. Two water outlets or an oversize filler may be used for faster filling. Tub fillers do not come under the legal limit of 2.5 gpm maximum flow that applies for lav faucets and shower heads.

Both hot and cold water lines should be insulated; hot lines to minimize heat loss, cold lines to control condensation.

Drains, traps and vents

Having supplied water to the various fixtures in the house, the next job is to get rid of it. That involves the drain lines, traps and vents that make up the DWV system.

All fixtures must drain through a vented trap, usually called P-traps, drum or U-traps because of their general shapes (Fig. 2.7). You also will encounter S-traps, which are no longer approved by code.

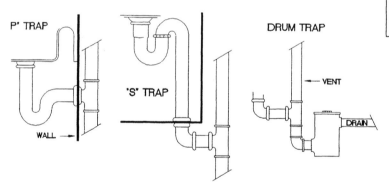
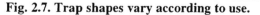

Fig. 2.7. Trap shapes vary according to use.

Waste lines in any of the above materials range from 1 1/4" to 4" (3-10cm). In some apartment and condominium units they could be up to 6" (15cm). They are larger than supply lines because they flow by gravity, not under pressure, and because they must carry some waste as well as water and air.

Because of gravity flow, horizontal waste

Characteristics of different types of DWV pipe:

1. CAST IRON
   a. Most difficult to work with because of weight and because joints must be strapped, packed with oakum and filled with hot lead. A new "hubless" pipe is available, however.
   b. Heaviest, at 700 lbs.(318 KG) per 100 feet (30 M) for 4" (10 cm) soil pipe.
   c. Has largest diameter and uses most space. 4" (10 cm) soil pipe extends to 7 1/4" (18 cm)with joints.
   d. Most common in older homes.
   e. Quietest from water action.

2. COPPER
   a. Most expensive.
   b. Lighter than cast iron. 3" (7.6 cm) soil line weighs 225 lbs. per 100 feet (103 kg per 30 M).
   c. Joints can be sweat-soldered or use compression fittings.
   d. Noisy.

3. PLASTIC
   a. Least expensive.
   b. Lightest, easiest to work with.
   c. Joints are solvent-welded.
   d. 3" (7.6 cm) soil line weighs over 140 lbs. per 100 feet (63.5 kg per 30 M).
   e. Corrosion resistant.
   f. Very noisy because of light weight. Insulate to deaden sound.

lines must have a downward pitch which will range from 1/8" to 1/2" per foot. Most desirable is 1/4" pitch. A pitch of more than 1/2" could promote clogging because the liquid could drain off too quickly and leave solids stuck in the pipe.

The **trap** at each fixture provides a water seal that prevents sewer gases from entering the home. The bend in the trap prevents water from emptying completely, providing the trap seal.

Bathtubs and showers use a P or drum trap. Lavatories and sinks use a P trap. The water you see in a toilet bowl is one end of a modified U trap that is built in.

The **vent** pipe at each fixture allows air into the system. It equalizes atmospheric pressure in the drain. Without it, the rush of water down a drain could cause a siphoning action that would pull the water seal out of the trap, permitting entry of sewer gases into the home.

All fixtures are "wet-vented" for a short distance, which means the drain pipe serves also as the vent pipe. But the vent can't be too far. Wet-vent distance relates directly to size of the drain pipe (Fig. 2.8).

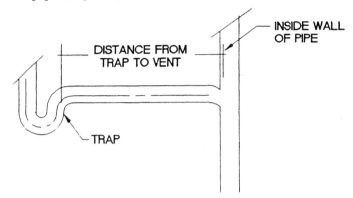

Fig. 2.8. Length of pipe for wet-venting is measured from the trap or weir of the trap (where it turns) to the vented line.

The following table shows the drain pipe size related to maximum distance from the trap to its connection with the vent pipe:

Pipe size	Distance to Vent
1 1/4"	60" (152cm)
1 1/2"	72" (183cm)
2"	96" (244cm)
3"	144"(366cm)
4"	192"(488cm)

(Note: These figures are specified by the National Standard Plumbing Code. Other codes differ. Local codes may differ from national codes. Always check local codes.)

For example, assume there is a lavatory with a 1 1/4" drain and its trap is 2'6" (76cm) from the vent. Your plan calls for moving the lavatory 6' (183cm) farther from the vent pipe. Total distance from the trap to the vent then will

be 8'6" (259cm). So the lavatory drain pipe would have to be 3" (7.6 cm) for wet-venting.

That example assumes the location of the vent stack is known. Its location sometimes can be determined by checking the attic or roof. A vent pipe will rise above its point of exit from the roof at least 6" (15cm), and it will have a 3" (7.6cm) minimum diameter (which prevents clogging by frost). If a vent stack is located within 5' (152cm) of any door, window or skylight, it must terminate at least 24" (61cm) above any such opening. (Figs. 2.9-2.11)

In that example, however, don't try to put a 3" drain pipe and trap into the customer's vanity cabinet. The answer there would be to install a **revent** pipe (Fig. 2.10) closer to the lav. It would rise vertically to a place, perhaps in the attic, where it could run horizontally, with a slight upward pitch, to join the vent stack that goes through the roof. Other new fixtures also could use this revent pipe. However, all fixtures must be revented at least 6" (15cm) above the flood level of the highest fixture.

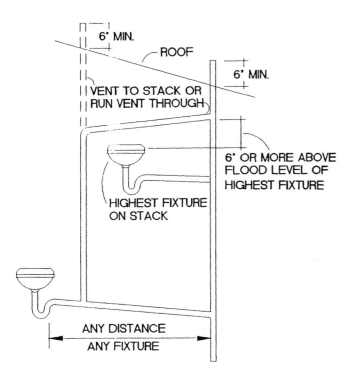

Fig. 2.9. Revent pipe must join stack at least 6" (15cm) above the flood level of the highest fixture served by stack.

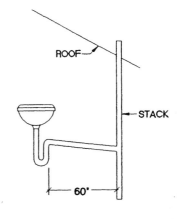

Fig. 2.11. Maximum distance from the trap of a lavatory to the stack is 60" (152.4cm).

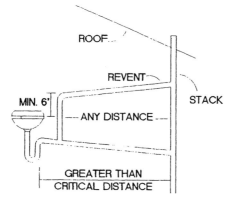

Fig. 2.10. When fixture is farther from the stack than the critical distance for wet venting, a revent pipe must rise from drain line to at least 6" above flood level of the fixture, then join stack.

The specialist may be asked to add a bath on the same floor. Simplest and least-expensive for the homeowner is to put fixtures back-to-back with an adjoining bathroom (Fig. 2.12). The supply lines can serve both groups, as can the drain if pipes are large enough. These need not be identical (Fig. 2.13). But if any of the new group exceeds critical distance for venting, a new vent must be installed and tied in (Fig. 2.14).

Before the age of low-consumption, a 3" (7.6cm) drain line could handle only two bathrooms in a home. If a third bathroom was added, the drain line had to be changed to 4" (10cm). This affected powder rooms also, because a 3" drain could not handle more than two toilets.

However, research already done at the National Institute of Standards and Technology indicates that low-consumption toilets can result in downsizing drain lines from 4" to 3", and vent stacks from 2" to 1" and possibly even to 1/2". Any action on this must wait for code writers to catch up with the technology.

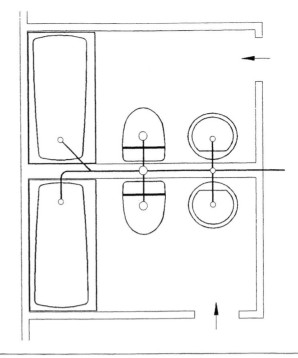

Fig. 2.12. Placing a new bathroom group back to back with an existing one can be simplest and least expensive. The drains must be large enough to serve both groups.

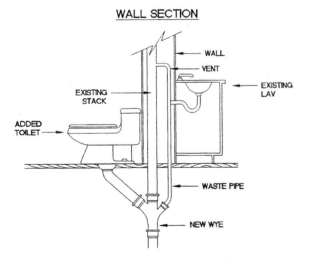

Fig. 2.13. Back-to-back groups need not be identical. Here the lav in the new group backs up to the toilet in the original. However, one-piece tub/showers cannot be installed back-to-back because there would be no access panel for plumbing.

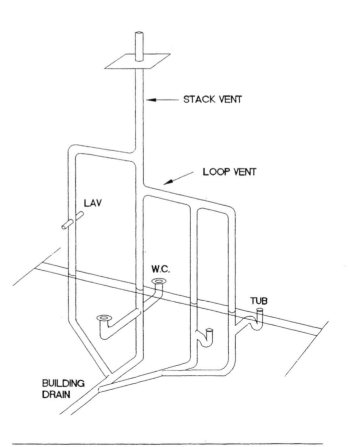

Fig. 2.14. Vent distances are critical. Here the new tub is a little too far, requiring installation of a loop vent.

Glossary of Plumbing Terms

Air Chamber—Device that reduces water pressure in a water line. These units may be installed at the individual fixtures or at the service main. They usually are simply 12" to 18" capped extensions of the water supply lines, usually in the wall near the fixtures, or plastic "bulbs" that can go in the vanity cabinet, providing air cushions for the high pressure. They belong in all pipes bringing cold and hot water to bathtubs, lavatories and showers.

Air Hammer—Hammering or pounding that can occur in a water supply line when the faucet is shut off rapidly, usually when water pressure is above 60 PSI, caused by air in the pipe. It can be eliminated by an air chamber

Backflow—Contaminated water flowing back into the potable water supply system due to negative pressure in the water supply pipe, or higher pressure than the supply.

Back Water Valve—Device to prevent backflow. A vacuum breaker also may be used.

Bathroom Group—Standard grouping of fixtures in a bathroom, consisting of water closet, lavatory and bathtub or shower stall.

Building Drain—The lowest piping in a drainage system which receives discharge from soil and other waste pipes inside a home and distributes all to a sewer system. At a distance of 5' from the foundation it becomes the house sewer.

Code—Regulations, amendments and rules formulated and enforced by federal, state, local government or designated regulatory body, to protect the health, safety and welfare of the public.

Continuous Waste— A drain from two or more fixtures connected to a single trap.

Distribution Center— Water pipe from the main distributing water to the various fixtures from various central locations.

Drain Branch—Any interior drain pipe running horizontally at an angle less than 45 degrees.

Drain Stack—Any interior drain running vertically at an angle greater than 45 degrees.

Fixture Branch—Water supply line coming from a distribution center and servicing a bathroom group.

Fixture Supply—Water supply pipe coming from a fixture branch and servicing an individual fixture.

Flood Level—The height at which water overflows a fixture.

Grade (Pitch)—Horizontal slope of a drain pipe allowing liquid waste and sewage to flow into the soil stack by means of gravity. Preferred grade is 1/4" per foot, but no less than 1/8" and no more than 1/2".

Liquid Waste— Any fixture drain not containing human waste.

Main— The principal artery supplying water, or the principal artery discharging waste.

Potable Water— Water free enough of impurities to be suitable for drinking.

Relief Valve—Safety device installed at the water heater to relieve excessive temperature or pressure.

Reventing—Running a pipe upward from a fixture waste pipe and connecting it to the stack above all waste connections. It need not be the same stack into which the fixture drains. Reventing is an alternative to putting in a new stack through the roof in cases where a new fixture is too far from the stack. (Also loop vent.)

Riser—Vertical water pipe.

Rough-in—The "behind the wall" water, drain and vent lines and fittings that must be installed before the fixtures are installed.

Soil Pipe—Pipe that carries waste from toilet bowls to the soil stack.

Soil Stack—3" or 4" main stack carrying all waste to the building drain and also extending upward to terminate above the roof for venting.

Stack Venting—Use of soil or waste stacks to vent a fixture. This also is called wet venting. All fixtures are wet vented for a short distance, but the distance is limited by code.

Trap—Plumbing fitting under any fixture that provides a water seal to prevent sewer gases from entering the house.

Trap Seal—The amount of water in the trap between the top and bottom of the bends.

Vent Pipe—Pipe allowing air into the drainage system which equalizes atmospheric pressure in the lines and prevents siphonage of water from traps.

Vent Stack—Vertical vent pipe extending through the roof and servicing any fixture except the water closet. It usually is the same size as drain pipe.

Waste Pipe—Pipe that carries waste water from all fixtures to the soil stack except waste from toilet bowls, which is carried by soil pipes.

Weir—Also crown weir, or trap weir. The top of the water seal in a trap, or point where it turns down.

Wet Venting—See stack venting.

ELECTRICITY/ELECTRONICS IN THE HOME

Electricity is becoming ever more pervasive in the home, and this includes the bathroom. Perhaps more important, the home and the bathroom are going electronic.

It has its good side. As bathroom planners we don't have to know everything about electronics. It comes in arcane chips and boxes, and does magical things. For example, we can walk into the bathroom and both the vent fan and the lights go on automatically, and turn off when we leave (see Chap. 3). We touch a button in the shower and water flows at our desired temperature, remembering how we like it (see Chap. 4).

But, of course, it starts with electricity, and we do have to know quite a lot about that.

Electrical power is supplied by the local utility company. Although there are some creative ways to produce one's own electric power, the overwhelming majority of homes use the utility company.

Power comes into the home through service conductors supplied by the utility company (Fig. 2.15). From the conductors a continuous line is extended to the meter, ground and service panel.

The meter measures how much electricity is consumed. The ground wire handles power overloads and short-circuits in the home by safely discharging them into the earth.

The service panel will use either fuses or circuit breakers (Fig. 2.16). Circuit breakers are the most common and provide the easiest maintenance.

The minimum size service panel by code is 100 ampere, or amp, which is the *amount* of current flowing at any given point. Some older homes have 60-amp panels, and they should be upgraded if extensive wiring or the code requires. Consider upgrading to a 150-amp or 200-amp service. The 200-amp service provides more available circuitry for future needs.

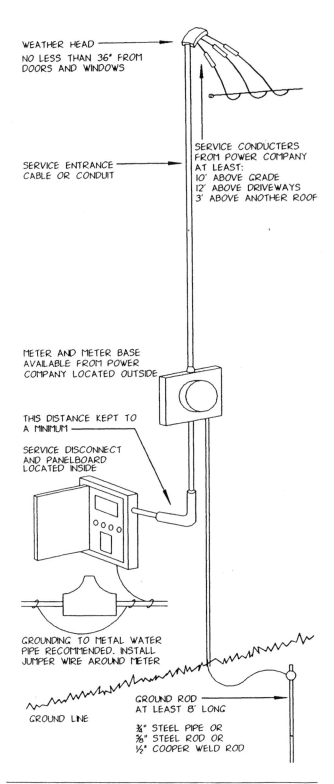

Fig. 2.15. Electricity comes to the house through service wires, either high or under ground. They connect through the meter (outside) to the service panel inside. Both the meter and the service panel are grounded.

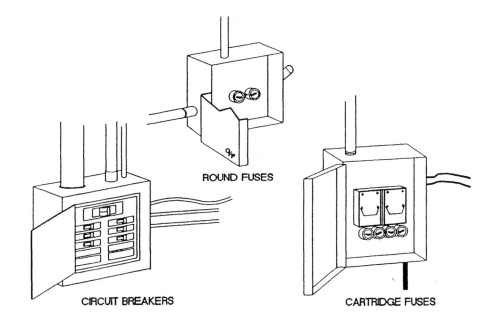

ROUND FUSES

CIRCUIT BREAKERS

CARTRIDGE FUSES

Fig. 2.16. Service panels will contain either circuit breakers or fuses. Circuit breakers are the most common, but round fuses will be found often in older houses. These are the weak points in all circuits. When a circuit is overloaded the wires heat up and the circuit is tripped by a fuse or breaker. A fuse must be replaced, a circuit breaker must be reset.

All service panels must have a main disconnect. This is a switch that cuts all power from the panel. The switch may be placed in the power line before it enters the panel or it might be on the top or bottom center of the panel itself. The switch normally will have a number on it, such as 100, 150 or 200. This number usually represents the total amps available to the home.

One way to determine the service capacity is by the gauge of the wire, which is a measure of the thickness of the wire in the cable. Most circuits use a 12-gauge (rated for 20 amps) or 14-gauge (rated for 15 amps) wire. The gauge is printed on the sheathing of NM cable, or "Romex," which is commonly used. As the gauge number goes down, wire thickness and capacity go up. Until you become familiar with cable sizes, consult an electrician if there is any question.

Each of the breakers supplies a circuit to various parts of the home. Typically, 15-amp and 20-amp circuit breakers supply 120 volts (written as 120V) of power to receptacles, switches and small appliances. Circuit breakers of 30 amp, 40 amp, 50 amp and 60 amp provide 240V connections. Sometimes a 20-amp circuit break-

er can be used for 240V connections.

A 240V circuit breaker normally occupies two slots on the service panel. A 120V breaker usually occupies one slot.

According to electrical code, all switches and receptacles in a bathroom must be out of reach when standing in the tub or shower. Also, receptacles must be GFCI type (Ground Fault Circuit Interrupter) or be controlled by a GFC breaker.

The GFCI breaker is so sensitive it can measure a difference as small as .005 amps in the current entering and leaving any device along the circuit. When it senses the difference it immediately trips the breaker and shuts down the circuit. The better GFCI receptacles have a reset switch built in.

The GFC breaker is installed in the service panel. If running new circuits to the bathroom, all should be put on a GFC breaker for maximum safety and to conform with code. A disadvantage of this practice, however, is that excessive steam and high humidity might trip the breaker. The homeowner then must go to the service panel and reset the breaker. This problem can be prevented by proper ventilation, which is part of our job in remodeling a bathroom. But GFCI receptacles in the bathroom with built-in resets also can ease this problem.

Bathroom equipment that may require separate circuits includes:

1. **Whirlpools**
2. **Saunas**
3. **Water heaters for spas**
4. **Steam generators**
5. **Vent-light-heater combinations**
6. **Infra-red heaters**

Check local codes on the need for GFCI connections for any of these that might not be in the bathroom.

The bath specialist must be aware of the common electrical symbols used in planning (Fig. 2.17). Use these symbols when designing an electrical plan, or refer to them in blueprint take-offs.

Bathrooms we remodel, like kitchens, usually are under-wired. In this era of rapid progress we should consider over-wiring, allowing for functional or convenience products that haven't been invented yet.

It is common in a bathroom to think "everything important is wired in" and to put in three switches, one for light, one for the vent fan and one for heat, plus only one duplex outlet. But when you consider all of the plug-ins people use—hair dryer, electric shaver, curling iron, electric tooth brush, etc.—it is easy to see that this is minimal. Depending on what develops in your interview, the probable need will be for at least three duplex outlets in a bathroom of normal size.

So don't be satisfied with a circuit that is barely adequate. Give the clients the power they need today and the power they probably will need a few years from now.

Glossary of Electrical Terms

Ampere—The amount of current passing a given point at a given time. An appliance has an amperage rating, and a circuit is rated for the total amperage it can carry.

Circuit—Wiring that travels through a house is divided into circuits. Each circuit is a continuous path from the service panel to various outlets and switches and back to the service panel.

Current—Movement of electricity along the circuit, measured in amperes.

Hot wire—Wire that carries current from the source. A circuit usually has two hot wires, one with black and one with red insulation, a white neutral wire and a bare ground wire. Each hot wire carries 120V into

the house, so they can supply 120V or 240V appliances.

Neutral wire—Usually has white insulation, carries current back to the service panel.

Short Circuit—Occurs when an exposed hot wire touches a neutral wire or other metal, tripping a circuit breaker or fuse that shuts off power.

Volts—Strength, or pressure, of an electrical current. In the home, circuits usually are 120V, 240V and "low." Normal circuits are 120V. Heavy duty appliances are 240V. Low voltage comes off same wiring, but voltage is cut by a transformer.

Watts—Rate at which electrical appliances and lights consume energy.

S	SINGLE POLE SWITCH	TV	TELEVISION OUTLET
S₂	DOUBLE POLE SWITCH	C	CABLE OUTLET
S₃	THREE WAY SWITCH	T L	LOW VOLTAGE TRANSFORMER
S₄	FOUR WAY SWITCH	⊗	HANGING CEILING FIXTURE
S_DM	SINGLE POLE SWITCH v/ DIMMER	⊕	HEAT LAMP
S₃DM	THREE WAY SWITCH v/ DIMMER	●	HEAT/LIGHT UNIT
S_LM	MASTER SWITCH FOR LOW VOLTAGE SWITCHING SYSTEM	HEAT/FAN LIGHT UNIT W/ OOO CFM VENT
S_L	SWITCH FOR LOW VOLTAGE SWITCHING SYSTEM	RECESSED CEILING DOWN LIGHTING
S_WP	WEATHERPROOF SWITCH	●	RECESSED CEILING VAPOR LIGHT
S_RC	REMOTE CONTROL SWITCH	BUILT-IN LOW VOLTAGE TASK LIGHT
S_D	AUTOMATIC DOOR SWITCH	BUILT-IN FLUORESCENT LIGHT
S_P	SWITCH AND PILOT LAMP	CONTINUOUS ROW FLUORESCENT LIGHTS
S_K	KEY OPERATED SWITCH	SURFACE MOUNTED FLUORESCENT LIGHT
S_F	FUSED SWITCH	WALL SCONCE
S_T	TIME SWITCH	DW DISHWASHER
Ⓢ	CEILING PULL SWITCH	GD FOOD WASTE DISPOSAL
	DUPLEX OUTLET	TC TRASH COMPACTOR
GFCI	DUPLEX OUTLET WITH GROUND FAULT CIRCUIT INTERRUPTER	R REFRIGERATOR OUTLET
S	SWITCH AND SINGLE RECEPTACLE OUTLET	H HOOD
S	SWITCH AND DUPLEX OUTLET	M MICROWAVE OVEN
B	BLANKED OUTLET	R ELECTRIC RANGE/COOKTOP
J	JUNCTION BOX	WO ELECTRIC SINGLE/DOUBLE OVEN
L	OUTLET CONTROLLED BY LOW VOLTAGE SWITCHING WHEN RELAY IS INSTALLED IN OUTLET BOX	G GAS SUPPLY
		CT GAS COOKTOP
	SINGLE RECEPTACLE OULET	WO GAS SINGLE/DOUBLE OVEN
	TRIPLEX RECEPTACLE OULET	CW CLOTHES WASHER
	QUADRUPLEX RECEPTACLE OULET	CD CLOTHES DRYER
	DUPLEX RECEPTACLE OUTLET-SPLIT WIRED	SA SAUNA
	TRIPLEX RECEPTACLE OUTLET-SPLIT WIRED	ST STEAM
C	CLOCK HANGER RECEPTACLE	WP WHIRLPOOL
F	FAN HANGER RECEPTACLE	TW TOWEL WARMER
▷◁	INTERCOM	HEAT REGISTER
◀	TELEPHONE OUTLET	
T	THERMOSTAT	
◎	SMOKE DETECTOR	

ANY STANDARD SYMBOL GIVEN ABOVE W/ THE ADDITION OF LOWERCASE SUBSCRIPT LETTERING MAY BE USED TO DESIGNATE A VARIATION OF STANDARD EQUIPMENT.

WHEN USED THEY MUST BE LISTED IN THE LEGEND OF THE MECHANICAL PLAN.

Fig. 2.17. These electrical symbols are used and understood by all professionals. They should be used on drawings.

3 Lighting, Venting & Heating

What Kinds, and How Much Is Enough?

A bathroom, like a kitchen, needs both good general lighting and good task lighting.

General lighting provides safety and security for the family. If the bathroom has light-colored ceiling, wall and countertop surfaces, mirror lighting will provide adequate general lighting for a bathroom of up to 75 sq. ft. (23M²). This should amount to 100-150W incandescent or 60W fluorescent in one to three sockets. If the bathroom is larger than 75 sq. ft. up to 120 sq. ft. (37M²), a ceiling light or wall sconces with 150W to 200W incandescent or 60W to 80W fluorescent in one to four sockets is desirable.

A super-bath of more than 120 sq. ft. requires 3/4 watts of fluorescence or 2 watts incandescence per square foot.

Task lighting is the lighting needed to perform any given task, such as shaving, hair styling or other grooming. Task lighting should be free of shadows and glare. This is especially important at a mirror. Mirror lighting should shine evenly on both sides of the face. A light-colored countertop will reflect light under the chin.

You can light a mirrored area with side lights, top lights or a combination of both, but never direct a light into a mirror. It will reflect back as glare. For side lights, use 60W to 100W of incandescence or one 20W fluorescent fixture on each side of the mirror. These fixtures should be centered 60" (152cm) off the floor and 30" (76cm) apart.

Fig. 3.1. Wall sconces are combined with down lights in this vanity arrangement. A light-colored vanity top can reflect light upward to the area under the chin.

Top-lighting a mirror requires two 75W or four 40W incandescent bulbs or two 20W fluorescent tubes.

Theatrical lighting around a mirrored medicine cabinet can produce a combination of side and top light. Theatrical lighting calls for globe-shaped (G) bulbs, preferably frosted to reduce glare. Use strips no less than 30" (76cm) long on each of the two sides and along the top, with four to six 15W to 25W G bulbs in each strip.

Theatrical is the fancy way to do it. The same lighting effect can be accomplished with wall brackets or swags on either side, 60"

(152cm) above the floor, and a center ceiling fixture.

When a separate compartment is designed into a bathroom, allow 60W to 75W incandescent light in a wall or ceiling fixture. With fluorescent lighting, use a 30W or 40W wall or ceiling fixture.

Where codes permit, a surface-mounted tub or shower light may be desirable. This is task lighting that often is neglected, but a user often needs light in the tub or shower area to read labels on shampoo or other bottles. Use a 60W or 75W incandescent bulb, and put the switch out of the bather's reach to prevent shock.

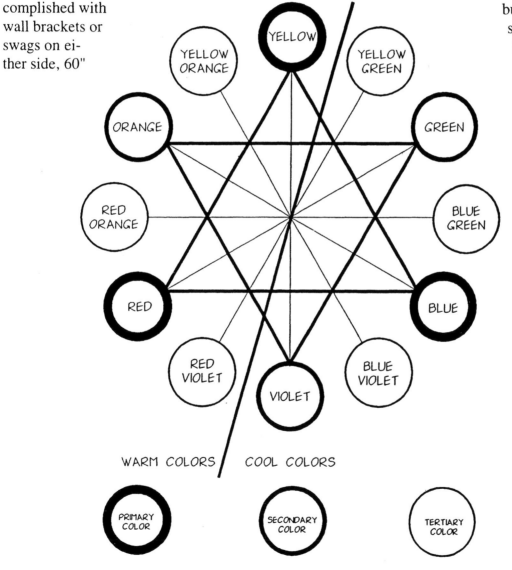

Fig. 3.2. Color wheel shows primary, secondary and tertiary hues and their relationships. Warm colors are on left, cool colors on right. For the color/light relationship, see page 28.

A recessed fixture in the tub/shower area would be a good choice, if it is workable. But these lights generate heat that must be allowed to dissipate. Recessed fixtures can't be covered with insulation because 3" (5cm) of clearance is required by code, and that space could admit moisture to the attic. In addition, there might not be sufficient clearance near outside walls because of the slope of the roof.

Incandescent or fluorescent

Knowing the quantity of light needed is the first step to a successful lighting plan. The second step is selecting the light source that best complements the colors in your design. That light source can be incandescent or fluorescent, which have different characteristics that affect the perception of color.

Colors are light waves reflecting from or passing through objects. The light waves emitted from incandescent or fluorescent lamps can enhance warm or cool colors. Choosing the wrong light can dull and gray even the best-designed rooms. Knowledge of the color wheel can help you choose the best light source (Fig. 3.2).

Colors on the left side of the wheel, from yellow to red violet, are known as warm colors. Colors on the right side of the wheel, from yellow green to violet, are known as cool colors. Your use of these colors in the bathroom will affect how people feel in the bathroom, warm or cool.

(For more on working with color and the color wheel, see Chap. 5.)

Incandescent light flatters red, orange and yellow colors and gives complexions a rosy glow because there is a lot of red in the light itself. It should be used in conjunction with a warm color scheme. It weakens blue colors.

Incandescence produces a point of light that can be directed on an object or a limited space. It is the oldest electric light source and the most popular, although it is less efficient, more expensive and produces more heat than fluorescence.

Fluorescent light can flatter cool colors. It also can flatter warm colors, depending on the color wavelengths of the tube selected.

Fluorescent tubes, because of their shape, disperse light from a larger source, therefore there are fewer shadows and the light cannot be directed to an object.

They sometimes are less attractive to homeowners who are not acquainted with newer tubes and fixtures and associate fluorescence with flickering, humming and lack of color harmony.

However, to correct older fixtures, flickering can be handled by changing the lamp or installing a newer rapid start fixture. Humming can be resolved by installing a new ballast or using a fixture with an electronic ballast or putting the ballast in a remote location. Color harmony is a matter of selecting the best tube for the job. Too often, colors are selected under lighting conditions other than those that exist in the home, and an object that looked bright red at the store under incandescence becomes a dull brown in the home under a cool white tube, resulting in a disappointed customer.

But a *cost-conscious* customer will prefer fluorescence. A 40-watt fluorescent tube will put out nearly five times as much light as a 40-watt incandescent bulb, and last 10 times longer. To put it in money terms, if you replace four 40-watt bulbs in a bath fixture with two 40-watt tubes, the savings in energy cost over the life of the lamps would be about $230 (based on 8¢ per kilowatt hour).

(In the lighting business, these aren't "bulbs" and "tubes." They are all "lamps.")

Circular fluorescent lamps are available now. Some of these can be used in incandescent sockets with adaptors. The adaptor contains the ballast.

New compact fluorescent "PL" lamps look like incandescents, but some hum constantly, flicker when turned on and don't have rapid

You can accentuate the positive with accent lighting

Lighting choices also include *low-voltage* lighting and *halogen* lamps. Both are forms of incandescence. Halogen lamps are excellent for *accent* lighting, low-voltage for general or night light.

Low-voltage lighting uses tiny bulbs working off standard house current that has been reduced to 8 to 26 volts (commonly 12V) by a small transformer. The transformer can be hidden anywhere. These are used more in the kitchen than in the bathroom, for under-cabinet task lighting or for decorative ambient light, but also are excellent for night light in a vanity kick space or behind a valance.

Halogen puts out a bright light by burning a tungsten filament, like a conventional incandescent lamp, but the filament is constantly restored by halogen gas in the lamp. It is tiny, but burns much brighter, much longer and produces less heat. A halogen lamp with reflector on regular or low voltage can be excellent for accent lighting as, for example, to light a picture or a planter in the bathroom.

start. Be sure the client is aware of these drawbacks in some of the newer compacts.

The common belief is that fluorescents can't be dimmed. They can, but this requires a special ballast and a special rheostat switch.

In planning bathroom lighting, the designer can't afford to overlook the age factor. A person 50 years old will need at least 50 percent more light to see well and for "general well-being" than a person of 30. A person 60 years old will need 100 to 200 percent more.

Fluorescent Color Chart

(Tube designations correspond with International Correlated Color Temperature, i.e.: 30=3000° Kelvin CCT)
Color temperature is measured in degrees Kelvin (K), which describes how the lamp appears when illuminated.
Low CCTs, 2700-3400 K (27-34) are considered "warm;" higher CCTs, 41-63, are "cool." Incandescent is 27-30.

Popular LAMPS	COLORS ENHANCED	COLORS GRAYED	WHITENESS OF LAMP	REMARKS
CCT30	Red, Orange	Deep Red, Blue	Yellowish	Rare-earth Phosphors
CCT35	Red, Orange, Green	Deep Red	Pale yellowish	Rare-earth Phosphors
CCT41	Red, Orange, Green, Blue	Deep Red	Pale greenish	Rare-earth Phosphors
CCT27X	Red, Orange	Blue	Warm Yellow	Rare-earth Phosphors Simulates Incandescent
CCT33X	Red, Orange Yellow	Deep Red	Pinkish White	Rare-earth Phosphors
CCT35X	Red, Orange, Yellow, Green	Deep Red	White	Rare-earth Phosphors
CCT41X	All	Deep Red	White White	Rare-earth Phosphors

(X lamps feature superior color rendition)   (Data by General Electric)

Fig. 3.3. Fluorescent lamps have different color characteristics, but observers have different perceptions. To many, "natural daylight" is ideal, but natural daylight differs from hour to hour so the term is essentially meaningless. Generally, people prefer to see themselves in warmer lighting, but cooler lighting is better for seeing and working. New lamps are being developed all the time, so a designer must keep current.

Federal law has prohibited manufacture of many common-wattage fluorescent and directional incandescent lamps for sale in the U.S. This included certain 8' types by April, 1994, and common 4' linear and U-tube fluorescents plus R30, R40 and PAR38 incandescents by October 1995.

Another factor that affects lighting is reflectance from walls, countertops and ceilings.

Dark surfaces absorb light. Bright surfaces reflect it.

Semi-gloss paint reflects more than flat paint, but it also shows up wall imperfections.

A white paint generally will reflect 80-90 percent of the light, pale pastels 70 percent. Mustard and medium brown will reflect about 35 percent, blue and green only 20-30 percent. So dark walls will double the requirement for light.

There is another kind of light we haven't talked about but which some customers will like. It is natural daylight. It comes from windows. But bathrooms often are in the building interior where there are no windows.

We often can create a window in an interior space with a skylight. The idea of a skylight is fascinating to many homeowners (Fig. 3.4).

Natural light is not as controllable as artificial light. It constantly changes. In the morning it has a lot of blue. In the afternoon it has a lot of red. It changes from winter, when daylight lasts only eight hours, to summer when a day can be 16 hours long. Any day might be clear and bright or it might be cloudy.

A skylight in a north-facing roof can provide a soft, gentle light. But in a south-facing roof it can cause glare. In a west-facing roof it can bring in a lot of heat, perhaps too much. In addition, if it opens (it then becomes a "roof window") it must be placed *at least* 24" (61cm) below the top of the vent stack and *at least* 60" (152cm) to the side of it.

If you put in a skylight it can perform double-duty by ventilating the bathroom if it can be opened and closed, preferably by a motor with remote control.

Because of the changes in daylight, it can be a good idea to install lighting in the skylight

Light and Color Are Interactive

A bathroom designer must be able to talk authoritatively to a client about color. Here are some of the basics.

Hue is the name of a color. *Value* is the lightness or darkness of a hue. *Intensity* is the saturation, or brightness or dullness, of a hue. Adding black to a color gives a *shade*. Adding white gives a *tint*. Adding gray gives a *tone*. Colors opposite each other on the color wheel are *complementary*. Colors next to each other are *analogous*.

Regular light (*white* light) carries all colors. Objects reflect color selectively. An apple is red because it absorbs all colors except red, which it reflects. Because of this there is another color wheel that shows *pigment* colors, slightly different.

Colors are of different wave lengths, so they focus differently in the eye. A red room seems to "advance" and a blue room seems to "retreat" because red focuses behind the retina and blue focuses in front of the retina.

We need color balance in a room because the eye strives for it. If we see two complementary colors in a room they add up to a neutral gray, so the eye is satisfied. The eye doesn't demand equal amounts of these colors. If a room is mostly blue, a single red towel or soap dish can provide the needed balance.

In a bathroom, the fewer hues used, the better, so it is better to keep door and window trim the same color as the walls. Color intensifies in a north room (if there is daylight) or a small room, so tints might be better except for accents. North light is "cold," so if there is a north window we should use colors from the warm side of the color wheel. Warm hues tend to be cheerful and tend to increase the apparent size of objects, but when used as wall colors they decrease the apparent size of the room itself.

To create a color scheme for your room, a simple formula is to select a dominant hue, then decide where it will go. Then use the color wheel to select complementary colors, then decide where they will go.

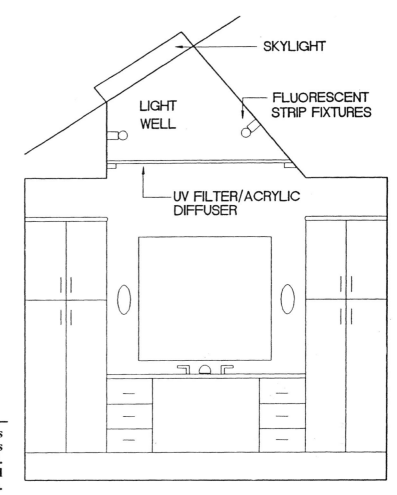

SKYLIGHT

LIGHT WELL

FLUORESCENT STRIP FIXTURES

UV FILTER/ACRYLIC DIFFUSER

Fig. 3.4. One side of the light well of this skylight is vertical, one side angled. Sides could be vertical or could be flared. Exterior-grade plywood is recommended for walls, painted flat white on inside.

Lighting/Design Terms You Should Know

Candela—Unit of measurement for foot candles. One candela equals 12.7 lumens.

Candle Power—Intensity of light from a source in a specific direction.

Footcandle—The illumination that falls on a surface one square foot in area and one foot from the candle.

Lumen—Measure of light output in all directions from the source.

Color Rendition Index—Or CRI, the measure of how accurately a light source shows an object's color.

Color Temperature—A measure of the coolness or warmth of a light source, expressed in degrees Kelvin. Low color temperatures emit warm or redder tones, less than 3500°Kelvin. Cool ranges between 3800° and 5000°K. For best color rendition, choose lamps with a color temperature between 3000° and 4000°K.

Uplight—a form of indirect lighting often concealed behind a crown molding, reflected from the ceiling.

Downlight—Light that shines straight down on the area it illuminates. It might be recessed, semi-recessed or surface-mounted. Recessed downlights are square or round canisters installed in soffit or attic space or floor joists.

Indirect Light—Light beamed toward a wall or ceiling so the room is illuminated by reflected light. It can be concealed in soffits or by valances.

Wall-Washing—Mounting light to illuminate the wall, but without shining into the room. This can be done with downlights, track lights or from a cornice. Lights are not aimed, and are put far enough from the wall (at least 24" (61 cm) so they don't show imperfections.

Wall-Grazing—Similar to wall-washing, but with lights close enough to the wall to show the texture. Good for brick wall surfaces or textured paint. The light source should be only inches from the wall, aimed to graze the surface.

shaft with an acrylic diffuser sheet at ceiling level. It would have to be an open diffuser to permit ventilation. If the light shaft goes through the attic, fluorescent strips on its two interior sides could provide lighting, caulked to prevent movement of moisture into the attic.

A bathroom skylight can pose one serious problem. The bathroom generates a lot of moisture, and when that moisture hits the cold glass of a skylight it will result in condensation. There could be a lot of dripping.

The solution is to install a skylight with a high energy efficiency rating. That means thermal panes, which are considerably heavier and more expensive.

Ventilation: Needed, but Ignored

To homeowners, ventilation is often a noisy evil that they know is probably necessary, but that they find easily resistible.

It is up to you, the bathroom designer, to convince them. Contractors in northern states who have been around bathroom remodeling over the years have seen the walls of ice after pulling off the interior wall covering of an uninsulated exterior wall of a bathroom.

Ice is not good for a wall. In southern states there seldom is ice, but there always is the moisture. Moisture is not good for a wall.

And all that moisture hangs around inside until it finds a way to work its way outside. It rots wood and peels paint and wreaks havoc on all of the interior furnishings, not only in the bathroom but in the whole house.

A family of three produces 20 lbs. (9kg) of water vapor in a day, which amounts to 2 1/2 gallons (9L) of water. Not all of it is produced in the bathroom, but a shower in this small space can push the relative humidity from normal level (40 per cent or less) to 99 per cent in less than 10 minutes.

The homeowner, who wants to spend the money on something else, will object to powered ventilation, pointing out that there is a window in the bathroom.

The CABO *One and Two Family Dwelling Code* specifies that bathrooms and toilet compartments have operable windows measuring a minimum of 3 sq. ft. (.3M²). Half of this space must be operable. A window is not required if a bathroom ventilating fan is used. That is not much of a window, and recent research indicates that a vent fan should be used even if there is a window. A vent fan will lower relative humidity to outside conditions within a half-hour after a 10-minute shower.

(CABO is the Council of American Building Officials. It is one of several code-making bodies, none of which is accepted universally.)

The American Society of Heating, Refrigerating and Air Conditioning Engineers (ASHRAE) has its own standard on Ventilation for Acceptable Indoor Air Quality, developed after the big push in the 1970s to insulate houses better for improvement of energy efficiency. That push resulted in homes being built so tightly that indoor air quality dropped to levels that were hazardous in many cases. Even the minimal emissions of formaldehyde from carpeting and furnishings became a problem for some who were hyper-sensitive.

ASHRAE decreed that a house must have at least 15 cubic feet per minute (cfm, .4M³) of fresh air per person. Bathrooms must have 50 cfm (1.4M³) of intermittent outside air, or 20 cfm (.6 M³) of fresh air if a fan operates continuously.

In planning bathroom ventilation we must be concerned with three factors:

1. The sound level, measured in sones. A vent fan that is perceived as too noisy won't be turned on, no matter how good it is. Ventilation units are rated for sones by the Home Ventilating Institute (HVI).

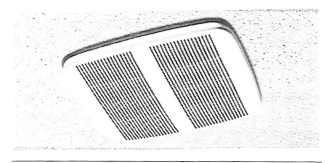

Fig. 3.5. Quiet Test fan from NuTone, above, is fan only. Below, NuTone's Heat-A-Ventlite combines fan, heat and light in a ceiling fixture.

Fig. 3.8. Broan's SensAire model combines ventilation and light, and has sensors that enable it to go on and off by detecting presence of either motion or extra humidity in the bathroom.

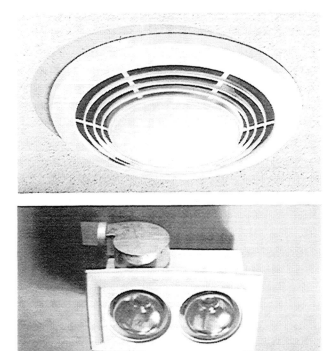

Fig. 3.6. NuTone's 2-bulb Heat-A-Vent combines venting and instant radiant heat.

2. The volume of air moved, in cfm. Most vent fans are rated for air movement by the HVI.

3. Length of and friction in ducts, which restrict air movement and cut efficiency. Each 10' (3M) of duct length will cut air movement by about 50 cfm. Each duct elbow is equivalent to adding 10' to its length.

Most fans in a small room will be noisy. One solution to this problem is a remote centrifugal (squirrel-cage) blower instead of a fan, moving it from the bathroom to the point of discharge to the outdoors, which might be in the attic or basement.

In tight, well-insulated houses in northern states, either the attic or basement might be subfreezing for long periods in winter. When this is true, moisture from the bathroom will condense and freeze in the duct, then drip back into the house when the ice melts. Some codes might require insulation on such ductwork for that reason, and ductwork might need a downward pitch. Whether this is required by code or not, our job is to serve the customer and therefore to recommend whatever measures are needed.

The drip problem might happen even when the vent is ducted directly through an outside wall in the bathroom. The dripping can be inside or there can be unsightly drip stains on the outside of the house. One possible answer to this is to install a small, unobtrusive drain pipe to take the water straight down to the ground. It might be possible to do this under the insulation or siding.

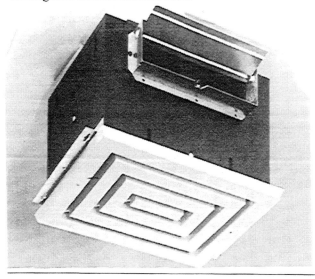

Fig. 3.7. Broan's 314 Lo-Sone is vent only, but will exhaust 140 cfm at only 1.5 sones.

The Home Ventilating Institute recommends eight air changes per hour for a bathroom. You can calculate how much fan power the bathroom will need by multiplying the square footage by a factor of 1.07 for a room with a standard 8' (244cm) ceiling. For example, for a room measuring 6' x 8' (183cm x 244cm), the formula would be:

6 x 8 x 1.07 = 51.36 cfm (1.5M³)

If the room has a different height, use the following formula:

Cubic feet of room (L x W x H) x 8 air changes per hour ÷60 = Required cfm rating. Thus, if the bathroom has a 10' (305cm) ceiling, the calculation would be:

6 x 8 x 10 = 480 cu. ft. (13.6M³)
480 x 8 = 3840, ÷ 60 = 64 cfm (2M³)

Modern tightly-built houses cannot exhaust all of that air without "make-up air" coming in. Without make-up air the fan would be unable to exhaust the air. It would be, in effect, spinning its wheels. This calls for an opening of 1/2" (1cm) minimum at the bottom of the door so new air can get into the bathroom, and a source for new air elsewhere in the house. A tight house should have an air-to-air exchanger that exhausts stale indoor air to the outdoors but recovers its temperature and transfers it to fresh incoming air. Air-to-air heat exchanger (or HRV—heat recovery ventilator) is a bulky name for an expensive product. If not operated at an outside wall it will require two sets of ducts in addition to existing ductwork. That could be difficult in retrofit.

A University of Minnesota study suggests that the forced air heating or cooling system should be turned on whenever a shower is taken in a "loose" house, plus the bathroom vent. It suggests the same for a tight house, but also a whole-house air-to-air heat exchanger set to operate continuously when the outside temperature is above 55° F (13°C). The HVI recommends a timer for the vent to keep it running for up to a half-hour after a shower.

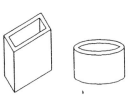

Duct usually is galvanized steel or aluminum in various sizes and shapes, and in flexible plastic. Popular round sizes are 3" (7.6 cm), 4" (10 cm), 6" (15 cm), 7" (18 cm) and 10" (25 cm); rectangular, 3 1/4" x 10" or 12" (8 cm x 25 or 30 cm).

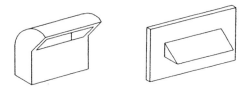

Roof cap or jack is an outside fitting for vertical duct. Pressure-activated damper opens when fan is operating, closes when it stops. Wall cap is an outside fitting for horizontal duct, in slanted shield or flush-mount versions.

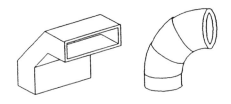

Elbows change direction of air.

Transition duct is for connecting round to rectangular duct, such as when duct must travel inside wall between studs.

Fig. 3.9. Ductwork and installation accessories include the following, except for one-piece plastic duct. These are fabricated on site.

Notes:

_____
_____
_____
_____
_____
_____
_____
_____
_____
_____
_____
_____
_____
_____
_____
_____
_____
_____
_____
_____
_____
_____
_____
_____
_____
_____
_____
_____
_____
_____
_____
_____
_____
_____
_____
_____
_____

The fan noise level in the bathroom should not be above three sones, less than two sones is preferable. Sones translate decibels of sound into how it affects the human ear. Ordinary conversation is four sones. A heavy truck is 64 sones. A jet plane landing is 256 sones. The pain threshold is 1024 sones. Many bathroom fans range up to 6.5 sones at top speed, but that is so noisy that many will not use it.

Note also that the sone rating can be affected by the way the fan is installed. It should be installed rock-solid with a layer of rubber between it and any house framing. And always check the manufacturer's installation instructions for tips on making it quieter.

We mentioned the problems of friction resistance and turns in ductwork. Smoother is better. Straight is better. For smoothness, the choice in duct usually will be galvanized steel or aluminum. But ductwork, round or flat, usually comes in flat pieces that must be fabricated on site, and the idea of flexible duct that need not be fabricated is very attractive.

The good news is that newer flexible duct is coated with plastic on the inside so it is very smooth and offers much less resistance than the corrugated material we might be familiar with. We buy the length we need, collapsed, then pull it out in the straight runs.

In cold attics, duct should be insulated with 4" (10cm) of material on all sides. But don't insulate a fan housing in this kind of space. It is hazardous and not allowed by electrical code. However, there are plastic "bubbles" available to fit over the housing, and insulation can be placed over the bubble. Also, be sure duct in a cold attic is pitched downward, like a plumbing drain pipe, so any condensation will drip outside and not back into the bathroom.

Warming up the Bathroom

When a homeowner gets out of a warm bed in the morning and goes to the bathroom, it is no time for cold floor tiles or cold air.

The same is true when stepping out of a shower. This is important to the bathroom designer who wants to sell a remodeling job.

Conventional house heating systems may not be adequate for the immediate warmth needed in a bathroom. These house systems normally use one or two thermostats to maintain an even temperature throughout the home, but in older houses the bathroom often does not have its own heat outlet from the system.

This situation calls for a quick secondary source of heat to raise the temperature right away. A good answer is either radiant heat, available easily from an infra-red heat lamp, or the somewhat slower action of an electric resistance heater (Figs. 3.5-3.8, 3.10, 3.11).

Electric resistance heaters use an electric heating element encased in metal. As the element heats due to resistance to the electrical current, the metal deflects the heat into the room. Electric heaters may be incorporated into a ventilation unit or may be installed separately as a wall or baseboard unit or recessed in the ceiling.

Some models incorporate heat, ventilation and light in an easily-installed ceiling fixture. They might require a separate circuit, but they definitely will require a triple wall switch so the three functions can be used independently. A minor problem is that this kind of heater must heat the air in the bathroom before it heats a body, and that takes a few minutes.

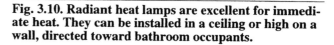

Fig. 3.10. Radiant heat lamps are excellent for immediate heat. They can be installed in a ceiling or high on a wall, directed toward bathroom occupants.

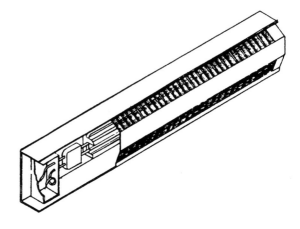

Fig. 3.11. Electric resistance baseboard heater has a heating element that works like the element in an electric range. Some models can be fitted into the kickspace of a vanity cabinet.

An infra-red heat lamp can be recessed in the ceiling or wall or might be surface-mounted in its own fixture. Infra-red is efficient in that it does not heat the air in the bathroom. Rather, its radiant heat warms any object it encounters, including the human body. It is immediate.

The bath specialist should have a working knowledge of the common residential central heating systems. These are:

1. Hydronic (hot water or steam), which utilizes a boiler as the heat source.

2. Forced hot air, from a furnace.

3. Radiant, from wiring in the floor, walls or ceiling, or from hot water pipes.

Hydronic heating systems use radiators or baseboard convectors to distribute heat throughout the house, although occasionally it is distributed by copper tubing embedded in a concrete slab foundation. Water is heated in a boiler or tank and distributed through risers or mains to the individual convectors. The hot water, at about 160° to 200° F (71-93°C), circulates through the convector, producing heat. A diverter inside the convector returns the cooled water back for reheating. This usually is considered the best, most comfortable kind of heating, It also is the most expensive.

You can get a similar radiant heat effect with electric wiring in a wall or floor. There are many new systems for this and, while it might sound scary to a homeowner, it is safe.

Hot air systems use ductwork to distribute heat. Air is heated in a furnace and blown mechanically through the ductwork which travels between floor joists and wall studs to feed heat to individual rooms. What the homeowner sees is an outlet covered by a grill. On a wall, the grill is called a register. On the floor or in the ceiling, it is called a diffuser.

The hot air system also has a cold air return. Cooled air circulates to the floor and the return ducts it back to the furnace for reheating. For this reason, the return is usually installed low on the wall or in the floor.

The ductwork in a forced hot air system can accommodate air conditioning. When used as a combined heating-cooling system, outlets should be high on the wall or in the ceiling. This height maximizes the cooling efficiency with little effect on heating efficiency.

A **heat pump,** which is not a different system but a source, like a boiler or furnace, can use hot air or hydronic distribution.

Heat pumps are combined heating and cooling units. They use electricity as a fuel and ductwork to distribute warm or cool air to the rooms.

Heat pumps extract heat from outside air or from ground or well water. (Even cold air and water have some heat.) When outdoor temperature is low, below 40°, an air-to-air heat pump's efficiency is reduced and supplemental electric resistance heaters might be required. If the heat pump gets its heat from a ground coil or from well water it is effective at much colder temperatures.

Resistance heaters may be in the form of baseboard units or strip heaters in the ductwork.

The heated air is blown into the room at 85° to 95° F (29-35°C). Although this temperature will warm the home, it will feel cool to the skin because it is cooler than body temperature. Placing the registers above head height will diminish this problem.

Heating systems can be revamped to fit your design. Electric, hydronic or forced air toe-space heaters can be added to existing systems by extending wiring, piping or ductwork. Consult with your local heating contractor to verify the feasibility of changes you propose. Usually a home heating system has ample capacity for this small added burden. But if it is a combination heating/cooling system, the cooling might be a problem. Cooling loads are more critical because they affect cycling on and off, and this can have an adverse effect on humidity.

But when it comes to heating contractors, you should be aware that there are differences. Generally, forced air heating is done by HVAC (heating, ventilating and air conditioning) contractors. These are the "sheet metal" people. If you want modifications of a hot water or steam system, this usually is done by plumbing contractors because it is a pipe-fitting or steam-fitting job.

Notes:

Fixtures and Fittings

New Materials Develop; Old Materials Improve

The three basic fixtures in a bathroom are the lavatory, tub/shower and toilet. But all of these are far different from when they were first known as the "bathroom group." The wood bowl of 100 years ago might now be replaced by granite or marble, or by a fancy plastic that might look like granite or marble, and might even be an integral part of the countertop. But the wood bowl itself can now show up as a very high-end lavatory, protected by sophisticated petro-chemical coatings that originated in an oil patch, and with matching tub and toilet tank.

Fittings also have metamorphosed. These, including faucets, shower heads and the like, have in many cases gone electronic. They now have electronic control panels, chips, sensors and touch-pads that regulate temperature, flow, and velocity and even can remember how you set it last time.

Your bathroom remodeling customer probably knows little of all this, so an educational process has to begin with basics. As a bathroom expert you will have to acquaint her and/or him with the materials, old and new, with the advanced technology, with code requirements, and also with U.S. legal restrictions on water flow to 2.5 gallons per minute (gpm) at the lav faucets and shower heads and to 1.6 gallons per flush (gpf) for the toilet. In some states these limits might be even more restrictive. These controls were new as of January 1, 1994, and manufacturers were allowed to exhaust their inventory of

the older, more wasteful fixtures. But as time goes on the limits might affect piping sizes.

Materials bath fixtures are made of are both old and new. They include the following:

Vitreous china—The typical material for toilets and urinals, also popular for lavatories and bidets. It is best for toilets and urinals because moisture absorption is almost nonexistent, less than one percent.

Porcelainized cast iron—Good for lavs, tubs, shower stalls and bidets. Because of its weight, tub sizes are limited to 72" x 42" (183 x 107 cm), and tubs are very difficult to maneuver up to and into an upstairs bathroom. To take out an old one, often all you can do is take a sledge hammer and knock it apart.

Enameled steel—or porcelain-on-steel. Steel is formed cold, enameled, then fired in an oven. Enameled steel tubs are more subject to chipping and denting, and hot water cools faster in a steel tub. But they are least expensive and comparatively light in weight.

Cultured marble, cultured onyx—Very popular for lavs and counters, usually with the lav an integral part of the counter. These are somewhat less durable because of their gelcoat surface, but usually last for many years. Tubs would be special order. Some look like granite, some like marble, and some are in solid colors, so you might prefer to call them "cast polymers." Cultured marble is opaque. Cultured onyx is translucent with richer, deeper coloring, and is more expensive.

Polyester and/or **acrylic solids**—These are generally called "solid surfaces." They include Avonite, Corian, Fountainhead, Gibraltar, Surell, Swanstone, and similar materials from regional fabricators or foreign sources. Some have integral lavs, and all come in a wide range of colors and patterns in 1/2" and 3/4" thicknesses. Thinner panels are available for wall coverings. Tubs of these solids would have to be fabricated on-site, but they are homogeneous—the same material and color all the way through—and can be worked (by experts) with wood-working tools.

Ceramic tile— Is sometimes used for lavs and tubs, but this is customized and done on site, so it is labor-intensive.

Wood—Beautiful exotic woods are used by some manufacturers for tubs, lavs, toilet seats and water closets (but not the toilet itself), with tough plastic finishes, combining one of the oldest materials with the newest. Environmental concerns limit the species available.

Stainless steel—This is sometimes used for lavs. Best is 18-gauge, which is thicker than 20-gauge. If you see a rating such as "18 and 8" it refers to 18% chrome content (for lasting finish) and 8% nickel content (to withstand corrosion). A brushed finish is easier for the homeowner to care for.

Acrylic/Fiberglass—These are confusing terms for tubs and shower stalls because they are used loosely. Fiberglass usually refers to a backing, acrylic to a surface. But sometimes a fixture is molded of fiberglass and surfaced with a gelcoat that was sprayed first into the mold. Some are molded of acrylic or ABS (acrilonitrile butadiene styrene), then sprayed with fiberglass for added support. Acrylic and ABS surfaces are more durable than gelcoat and have deeper color. These are used for big jetted tubs and are relatively light in weight. A sound-deadening under-coat is desirable, and any model selected should be checked for a sound bottom with bracing that rests on the floor.

New combinations by one manufacturer include an injection-molded process bonding a structural composite of sand, gravel and polymer on an acrylic shell, for tubs, sinks and shower bases, and new tubs with structural foam on a light-weight alloy with porcelain finish. (See Appendix B.)

Five kinds of lavatories

There are five kinds of lavs, categorized according to the way they are installed:

1. **Integral**
2. **Drop-in, or countertop**
3. **Wall-hung**
4. **Pedestal**
5. **Console**

Integral lavs are one piece with the counter in which they are molded. They are stock items, but can be ordered customized. The cast polymers can be ordered with extended tops to reach one or two side walls, but they must be ordered to fit because they are very difficult to cut in the field. Some of the solid surfaces can be ordered with extended counters that can be cut on-site to fit wall to wall, with a variety of choices for placement of one or more lavs.

Integral lav features include:

• **The counter provides space for toiletries.**

• **In conjunction with the vanity cabinet it hides plumbing and supports much weight.**

• **They avoid the expense of buying and installing a separate lav.**

• **Height to the bowl rim is determined by the vanity height. The old standard was 30 1/4" (77 cm). (Higher is recommended—Chap. 5.)**

• **Special bowl configurations are available in the cast polymers.**

• **A wide selection of colors and patterns is available in the cast polymers and solids.**

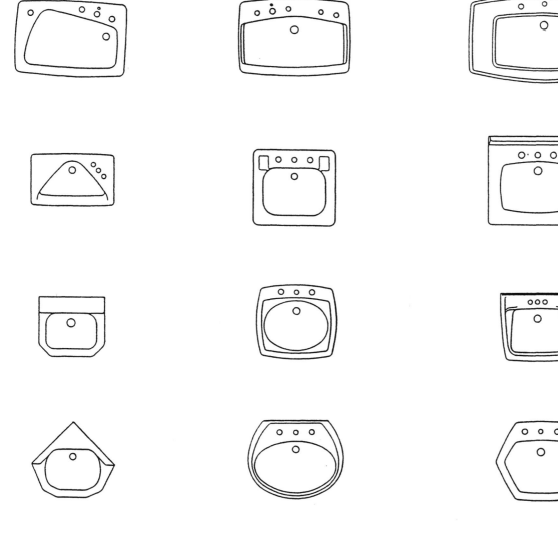

Fig. 4.1. Bathroom lavatories come in a variety of sizes and shapes. Faucet holes can be drilled in solid surface lavs, but are predrilled in others. It is necessary to check lav and faucet specs to be sure they will fit the holes before including some fancy faucets in the design.

- **Some cultured marbles are available with no-drip edges and coved backsplashes.**

- **Damages can be field-repaired in solids, but not in cast polymers.**

- **Easiest to clean of any lavs.**

- **Faucet hole spacing in cast polymers can be customized. Solids usually are not pre-drilled, so spacing can be decided on-site.**

Drop-in lavs must be fitted into a countertop cutout, either dropped in from above or under-mounted from below. Some newer models mount entirely above the countertop.

Self-rimming models have an integral rim of the same material. These often are vitreous china, but also popular are drop-in lavs of solid surface material in colors matching, harmonizing or contrasting with the solid surface or other type of counter. There is a broad selection of sizes, ranging from 21" x 13" (53 x 33cm) to 38" x 22" (97 x 56cm).

Rimmed models are least expensive and usually are porcelain on steel. They are dropped in and secured by a stainless steel sink rim with retaining clips underneath. Usual sizes vary from 17" x 14" (43 x 36cm) to 26" x 18" (66 x 46cm). The rims tend to collect soil, so these are not as easily kept clean as other types of lavs.

Rimless models are under-mounted and have rims although no rim is visible. They might be vitreous china, although some homeowners are attracted to a stainless steel bowl to add a new and different texture to the design. Some models are mounted under the counter with the counter overlapping the rim by a fraction of an inch.

A newer and more expensive technique is to under-mount a lav made of a solid surface material in a matching or harmonizing solid surface counter, smoothing the edges so the lav and countertop appear to be seamless and integral. Under-mounting is accomplished with retaining clips underneath.

Usual sizes are 17" x 14" (43 x 36cm) to 21 1/4" x 17 1/4" (54 x 44cm).

Faucets for all of these usually are 4" or 8" (10 or 20cm) on center. Sometimes they are off-set to the side or mounted on the deck.

Drop-in lav features include:

- **Normally used in conjunction with a vanity base to hide plumbing and support the weight of the counter.**

- **Counter provides space for toiletries.**

- **Will support more weight because of the vanity cabinet.**

- **Height of rim of bowl is determined by height of the vanity.**

- **Special bowl configurations are available to save space and facilitate use.**

- **Bowl can be anywhere in the top.**

Wall-hung lavs are fastened to the wall with a metal bracket and the fixture is cantilevered from the wall. This always requires addition of 2x4 or 2x6 backing between the studs in the wall to support the weight.

When replacing a wall-hung lav, the dimensions of the existing fixture must be compared with those of the new. Often the wall behind the old lav is unfinished, and if the new one is smaller it might necessitate refinishing the entire wall. No patching job will be good enough in an expertly remodeled bathroom.

Wall-hung lav features include:

- **Models are avaliable with high or low back-splash or flush deck.**

- **Special lavs for corner installation and for universal design are widely available.**

- **Space for toiletries is limited on many models. At least 4" of space around the bowl is desirable. If it isn't there, a shelf or other landing space must be provided nearby.**

- Load-bearing capacity is limited by the backing provided in the wall.

- Plumbing underneath is usually exposed, although some have a cover or "shroud."

- Sizes vary widely, but generally are from 13" wide x 13" deep (33cm) to 24" wide x 21" deep (61 x 53cm).

Pedestal lavs generally are identified with "period" design because the style dates back to the birth of the modern bathroom, and there are many models, both simple and very ornate, that fit in well with Early American, Provincial or Traditional styling. But there also are many modern versions with sleek, contemporary, even futuristic lines.

Pedestal lavs can present some installation difficulties not encountered with other lavs. For example, they come in two pieces, the bowl and the pedestal. Many come with brackets for attaching the bowl to the pedestal, but many do not. When they don't, the lav itself must be bolted to the wall.

In addition, the back of the pedestal is open. It might be open all the way. In other models it is solid up to 16" (41cm) above the finished floor and open above that. Some have a horizontal bar in back connecting the two sides of the pedestal.

Any of these configurations will affect the placement of the drain. Manufacturer specs must be checked carefully. Also, it is critical that the drain and supply lines be dimensionally balanced and aligned behind the pedestal, because in many models they can be visible. Rough-in must be centered perfectly on the pedestal.

Many pedestal lavs, like wall-hung models, have very little landing space around the rim. If the customer wants such a model, landing space must be provided either with a wall shelf behind the lav or with an adjacent countertop.

Pedestal lav features include:

- **They can make more of a design statement than other lavs.**

- Many sizes are available, from very small for a confined powder room to very large for such tasks as bathing a baby.

- Landing space is needed, either with a rim that is flat and at least 4" (10 cm) wide or an adjacent shelf or counter.

- Dimensions of rough-in are critical for both supply and waste lines.

- Any visible plumbing lines must be balanced and aligned.

- Shut-off valves are typically 22" (56cm) off the floor, but design of some pedestals limit shut-offs to about 16" (41cm) off the floor.

- Little flexibility in height, usually about 31" (79cm). A platform can be added at bottom to conform with recommendations in Bathroom Design Guidelines (Chap. 5).

- Can increase visual space in a small bathroom.

Console lavs usually consist of a counter with integral bowl, supported by two to four decorative legs. This creates the sense of space provided by a pedestal lav, but with space for toiletries. Cabinet storage must be designed elsewhere in the room.

Toilets: Gravity flow or pressurized

Toilets have gone low-consumption, restricted by law in the U.S. to no more than 1.6 gallons (6L) per flush (gpf) since Jan. 1, 1994. In some areas it is even less. Similar restrictions have been proposed in Canada.

This is the culmination of a trend. Twenty years ago all residential toilets used gravity flow for five or six gallons of water and a "water spot" of about 8" x 9" (20 x 23cm). Through the '80s many states became concerned about water supply and all felt the choke of growing population on their sewerage. Toilet manufacturers responded with 3.5-gpf (13L) models, and these quickly became standard.

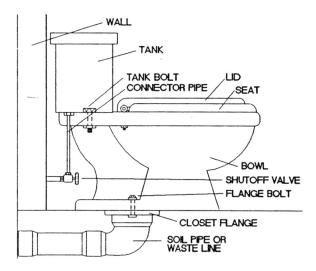

Fig. 4.2. Anatomy of a standard toilet. Rough-in for waste line is usually 12" (30cm) from wall, occasionally 10" (25cm) or 14" (36cm). Height of water supply line must be checked against toilet specs.

As the need for conservation grew, domestic manufacturers (and importers) moved to the 6-liter European standard, at first adapting existing models for lower water capacity, with taller tanks for more head and steeper bowl sides to increase gravity pull, and with smaller water spots of 4" to 5" (10-13cm).

Most of those modified models have now been replaced by toilets engineered for low consumption, either gravity-fed or pressurized, but the bathroom specialist should be aware that there still might be older, inefficient designs available that can require two or three flushes to remove solid waste.

In the last few years, many states and municipalities in the U.S. and Canada have encouraged use of low-consumption toilets with rebates for replacing older models. New York City, for example, offered $240 for replacing one toilet, $150 for replacing a second one. It is unlikely that the practice of giving rebates will spread now that low-consumption is the law, but it is worth

checking into. Without such incentives, the use of water-guzzling models can continue for years until retrofit. A rebate, plus savings in water and sewer fees, can greatly speed the payback period for a new toilet when a customer is undecided about keeping an old one.

There has been some question as to whether 1.6 gpf is sufficient to ensure the 40 feet (12M) of carry along the waste line required by American National Standards Institute (ANSI) standard A112.19.6. However, the industry consensus, backed by research, is that added water flow from showers and dishwashers is sufficient to meet the carry requirement.

This is not a problem with pressure-assisted toilets. These have a separate pressure capsule with a flushometer valve in the tank that fills with air when the flush valve is actuated, then refills partially with water until it reaches a point of equilibrium, which pressurizes the air left in the capsule. On the next flush, the air pressure pushes water into the trap expelling waste with more than gravity force, and that is enough to carry waste as much as 60 feet (18M) along the waste line. Flushing action is somewhat noisier, but refilling is usually quieter.

The water spot on gravity toilets now ranges up to 7" x 8" (18 x 20cm) or more. On pressurized models it is about 10" x 12" (25 x 30cm).

A different action is employed in Kohler's Trocadero line. It uses a .2-hp electric pump that plugs into a conventional electric source and has dual flush buttons for 1.6 or 1 gpf. Electricity cost is reported to be about $1 per year.

Historically, there have been six basic approaches to designing the flushing action in toilets. These have been modified in the newer low-consumption models.

• **Siphon vortex**—This has diagonal rim outlets which cause a swirling action. Rapid filling of the trap triggers siphoning of the bowl

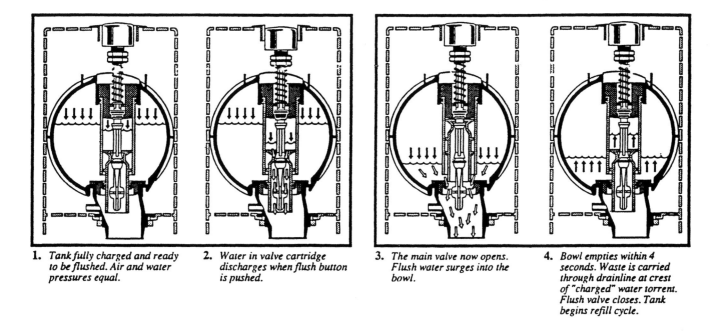

1. *Tank fully charged and ready to be flushed. Air and water pressures equal.*

2. *Water in valve cartridge discharges when flush button is pushed.*

3. *The main valve now opens. Flush water surges into the bowl.*

4. *Bowl empties within 4 seconds. Waste is carried through drainline at crest of "charged" water torrent. Flush valve closes. Tank begins refill cycle.*

Fig. 4.3. These four drawings demonstrate the theory of operation of a pressure-assisted toilet.

contents. Low-consumption action is similar, but it doesn't fit ANSI definitions for siphon vortex, so the name no longer applies until redefined.

• **Siphon action reverse trap**—This introduces water around the rim. It might or might not also have a jet outlet directed into the upward leg of the trap to enhance siphoning action.

• **Siphon wash**—Relies entirely on incoming rush of water from the rim with rapid filling of the trap, triggering siphoning of the bowl contents. Some low-consumption models also have a jet, which wasn't there before.

• **Siphon jet**—This type now comes only in pressurized models. It is similar in concept to the siphon action reverse trap, but is more efficient, with a jet to begin siphoning action instantly with no rise in the water level in the bowl before the contents are drawn out. Characteristically, it has a larger water spot.

• **Blowout**—These are tankless, found mostly in commercial applications, but will be found in many residences in older cities such as Chicago and New York. There are no low-con-

sumption models with this action. They use a flush valve and the water pressure of the supply line to exhaust the bowl. Some of these may be wall-hung.

• **Washdown**—An efficient action with the trap in front, but noisier than other models and with a smaller water spot. They are identifiable by a large protrusion in front and were in wide use in Canada, but not many are available now.

Of these five, three types might be pressurized: Siphon action reverse trap, siphon jet or blowout. Generally, standard pressurized models will cost the consumer about twice the price of standard gravity models.

In **construction**, toilets can be:

1. One-piece, sometimes referred to as "low profile" or "low boy."

2. Close-coupled, consisting of separate tank and bowl fastened together.

3. Two-piece, an old-fashioned style with very high tank near the ceiling, available now from a few manufacturers largely for use as a fashion statement.

(Up-to-date manufacturer literature and spec sheets should be checked before specifying any toilet, because most product lines are undergoing a period of possible change in dimensions, flushing action and possibly in water supply and DWV requirements.)

One-piece, low profile toilets are the only ones that have required a 1/2" (1cm) supply line. It must be placed low on the wall, a factor that can affect the designer's use of a tile baseboard. The toilet normally is placed less than 1" from the wall with the drain rough-in 12" (30cm) from the stud wall.

Close-coupled models also are roughed in less than 1" from the stud wall, but the drain rough-in might be 10", 12" or 14" (25, 30 or 36cm) from the wall. The supply line is 3/8" (93mm). Some of these are wall-hung, requiring special drainage fittings and extra-sturdy backing in the wall. Corner models are available for special design applications.

Two-piece models use a 3/8" (93mm) supply line and the drain is roughed in 10" or 12" (25 or 30cm) from the wall. The flush tank is secured to the wall with a metal hanger.

Tips from the Pros

Clients should be advised of certain characteristics of modern toilets.

Pressure-assisted toilets are noisier when flushed than older models.

In California surveys, where low-consumption models have been used and surveyed for the last few years, there were many complaints of "skid marks" in gravity-fed models, requiring frequent cleaning of the bowl.

Because of this, decorative toilet brushes hanging near the toilet were part of the design.

These problems may not continue as toilets are improved, but the bath specialist must be aware of them and know the products.

With imports increasing, designers should be aware of wide size differences available.

With imports and domestic models, toilet widths can vary from 14" to 24" (36-61cm).

These variations can be important when there are space problems in the bathroom.

Two types of bidets

The bidet is used by both men and women for cleansing the perineal area of the body. Like a lav, it has hot and cold water supply and a drain. But it has no seat. The user straddles the fixture, sitting on the rim facing the faucets, with body weight distributed on the thighs. The faucets might be on the fixture or on the wall.

There are two types of bidets. In one, water is directed to the area to be cleansed from a vertical stream or spray directed upward from the bottom of the bowl. In the other, water comes from an above-the-rim horizontal spout.

The user directs a vertical spray to the desired area simply by moving back and forth. Rim outlets can fill the bowl if desired. This type of spray requires individual hot and cold valves, a diverter valve, a pop-up drain control, the spray fitting and connections to the water supply. The specialist must specify deck-mount or wall-mount fittings. The vertical spray model can be filled above the spray fitting, which makes it possible for contaminated water to back up into the potable water system, which necessitates a vacuum breaker (Fig. 4.4).

An over-rim bidet is filled by a deck-mounted

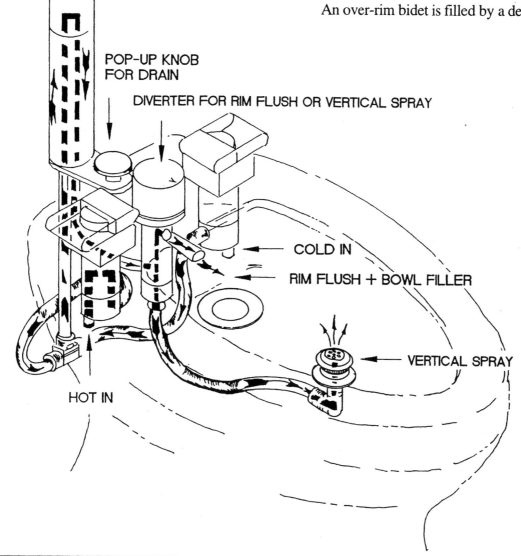

VACUUM BREAKER

POP-UP KNOB FOR DRAIN

DIVERTER FOR RIM FLUSH OR VERTICAL SPRAY

COLD IN

RIM FLUSH + BOWL FILLER

VERTICAL SPRAY

HOT IN

Fig. 4.4. Bidet with vertical spray needs a vacuum breaker behind to prevent contamination due to backflow. It allows air into piping system. Breaker must have proper fitting for bidet.

faucet, so there is no need for a vacuum breaker. It is generally less expensive to buy and install.

There is no fixed rough-in for the bidet, as it is more like a lavatory than it is like a toilet. But it must be matched in design, fittings and height, as much as possible, with the toilet, since it usually is installed adjacent to or across from the toilet. They often can be purchased as a matched pair. (The bidet feature also can be an add-on to a standard toilet.)

Bidet features include:

• **Drain rough-in varies usually from 11" to 16" (28-41cm) from the wall.**

• **Drain connections are 1 1/4"- 1 1/2" (3-4cm) with the trap under the floor.**

• **Water supply line is 3/8" (93mm).**

• **Some models have a rim flush.**

• **Ideal for elderly, as sitting is the safest position for cleaning the body.**

• **Can be used as a foot bath.**

• **Rim height is coordinated with toilet.**

Five types of bathtubs

Bathtubs now come in a wide variety of materials, shapes, sizes and features (Fig. 4.6).

If we categorize them by installation method, there are five broad types:

• **Recessed (or "skirted" or "apron"),** designed to fit into a recess with three sides hidden by walls and a finished front. This is most common. Some have removable apron panels (Fig. 4.5).

• **Corner,** usually with two angled unfinished sides and a finished front to be installed like a

recessed tub, but also available with three finished sides.

• **Free-standing,** to be installed in the middle of the room, or at least away from the wall. Some manufacturers now offer these in a claw-foot Victorian style. They also are available in a finely-finished wood. These are seldom recommended for showering, although some combination models are available with clear acrylic compartment showers at one end.

• **Platform,** with no finished panels, designed to drop into a platform for the "raised sunken tub" effect.

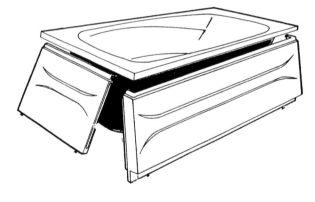

Fig. 4.5. Some bathtubs have removable apron panels.

• **Whirlpool,** designed specifically for the healthful hydromassage action of jetted water (Fig. 4.7), often oversized in many configurations (even heart-shaped), often designed for two or more persons to use simultaneously. **It should be noted, also, that any of the above tub types are available with whirlpool jets.** The difference is in the fact that they are not designed specifically for the action and this action is not their primary purpose. Any jetted tub must have an access panel for future servicing of the pump (Fig. 4.7).

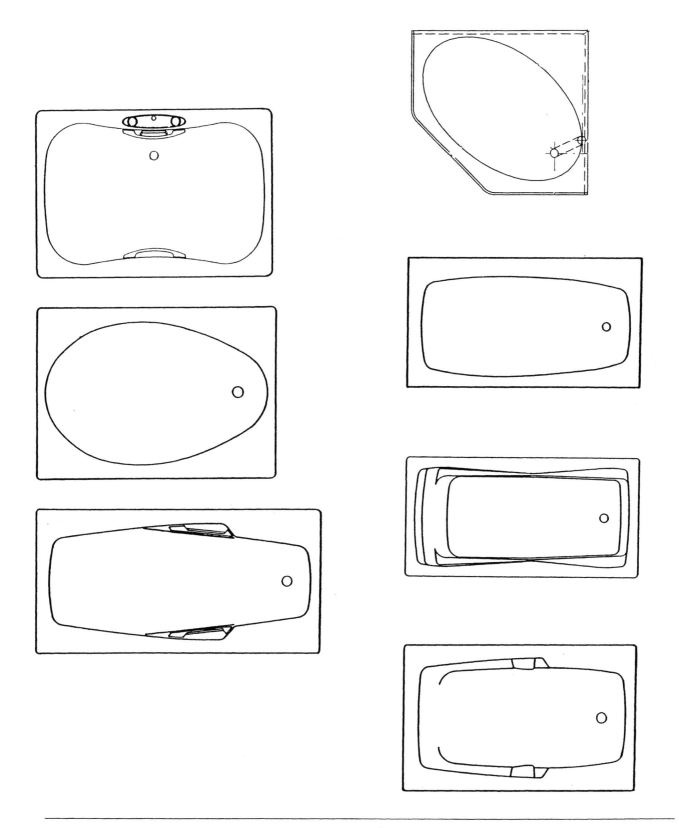

Fig. 4.6. Bathtubs are available in many sizes and shapes. Any of them can be jetted.

Bathtubs are available in enameled steel, cast iron, acrylic, fiberglass with acrylic or gelcoat surface, ABS, molded polymers (cultured marble) or wood. Cushioned surfaces also are available. Custom tubs are sometimes fabricated on-site of ceramic tile or of solid surface materials.

One of the most critical questions with any bathtub is whether it can be gotten into the house, up the stairs (if applicable) and into the bathroom. All openings must be measured, but it also is necessary to check every turn radius.

There also must be access to the shutoff valves in the water supply lines and the drain. If it is a recessed installation this might be done from a basement or crawl space, but it often is necessary to cut out an access panel in a closet or other wall behind the plumbing.

If the tub will be on an exterior wall you will have to install a 6-mil vapor barrier and insulation, and add an insulation blanket under the tub for a draft-free, warm bath.

The most common **recessed** bathtub size is 60" long by 30"-33" wide (152cm by 76-84cm), but some are available as short as 42" (107cm) and as long as 72" (183cm). They are available with the drain at either end. Some have grab bars built into the sides and available seats for universal-design bathtubs.

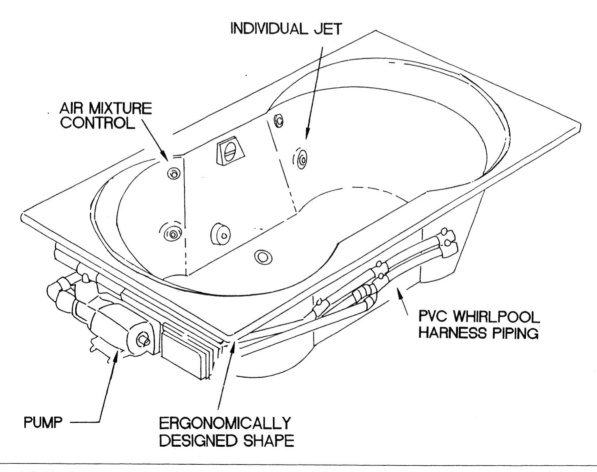

Fig. 4.7. Typical whirlpool bathtub system has several individual jets and an air mixture control. Pump usually is attached to the tub, but some models offer a remote pump.

Ideally, a bathroom will have a separate tub and shower. But in the real world, most recessed bathtubs have **combination showers.** This is accomplished with a simple diverter valve that directs the water to either the tub faucet spout or to the shower head.

In the simplest installations, hot and cold water supply pipes come up behind the wall where they connect to the faucet body, which also is behind the wall. The faucet body, which is all one piece, has an arm on either side that connects to the supply lines and three front openings into which the two faucet handles and spout are fitted. There is an opening on top for the shower supply pipe. Only the handles and spout protrude. The diverter valve usually is on the spout. Lifting, turning or pushing it diverts the water flow to the shower. The shower supply pipe extends upward from the faucet body, and a fitting emerges through the wall for the shower head.

Corner tubs usually require 4' (122cm) to 5' (152cm) along each wall of the corner, and extend 5' to 6' (183cm) from the corner into the room. However, in this age of easily-molded plastics, the front can be straight, bowed or sculpted and might be any dimension. They offer a space-efficient way to provide a luxurious whirlpool tub when wall space is limited.

Whirlpool tub installation

The growing popularity of **whirlpool** tubs, especially oversized models, raises another question that must concern the bathroom specialist: The **total weight factor.** The tub, plus water, plus body weight of the user can easily exceed the load capacity of the floor.

Most houses built in the U.S. in the last several decades were built to conform with the Minimum Property Standards (MPS) of the Federal Housing Administration (FHA). The MPS specify load-bearing capacity of 40 lbs. per square foot (18kg per 30cm²), but in sleeping areas this figure was reduced to 30 lbs. (14kg), which becomes more important if we are expanding a bathroom into a bedroom or closet.

Water weighs 8.33 lbs. per gallon (3.8kg per 3.8L). So if a tub 6' long by 3 1/2' wide (183cm x 107cm), weighing 150 lbs. (68kg) is filled with 100 gallons of water (379L) and the bather weighs 175 lbs. (79kg), the total weight is 1,158 lbs. (525kg).

Depending on wood species, 2"x10" floor joists (5 x 25cm), with standard installation, can hold 40-50 lbs. (18-23kg) per square foot. The tub occupies 21 sq. ft. (640cm²). The total weight divided by the square footage equals 55 lbs. per square foot, which is over the limit. This means you would have to either double the floor joists or build a platform to spread the tub's weight over a bigger area.

Some whirlpool systems have fewer jets with larger outlets, serviced by bigger water lines. The jets operate on a high-volume, low-pressure system that provides softly pulsating water.

Other systems have more jets with smaller outlets and smaller water lines, operating on a low-volume high-pressure system. The jets can be adjusted individually by the bather. These usually are quieter than those with larger jets.

Better systems inject the air into the water, providing a more effective massage. However, air at room temperature will cool the bath water, so the water will have to come in at a higher temperature.

Whirlpool pumps range in power from 1/2 HP to 1 1/2 HP. But more important than the horsepower is the jet system and the water flow pushed through the system. Generally this is five to seven gallons (19-27L) of water per minute. The pump nearly always is housed within the envelope of the tub, and access must be provided. Some manufacturers offer an alternative location for the pump, up to 5' (152cm) from the tub. In this case the pump might be concealed in a vanity cabinet or even an adjacent closet space. If you use a remote location, it must be on the same level as the base of the bathtub to assure complete draining and it must be no higher than the highest jet, which is 2" (5cm) below the water level, and no lower than the suction fitting.

The pump may be activated either by a timer switch installed on a wall, at least 60" (152cm) away to eliminate any danger of electrical accident, or by an air switch on the tub.

The air switch (in the tub) activates an electrical switch at the pump, and is more convenient and safer.

A more expensive "capitance" switch activates the whirlpool when it senses the electrical differences which occur when a person touches the control panel.

There are three ways to design a jetted whirlpool tub system, depending on the desires of the customer.

• **You can buy a complete, engineered integrated system. This will include the tub, the on/off activator, the water suction intake, all the jets and related trim, all the rigid, self-draining piping and the pump. Selection of sizes, features and configurations is almost limitless.**

• **You can design a totally customized bathtub fabricated on the jobsite of cultured marble, solid surface, ceramic tile or natural stone.**

• **You can buy a bathtub, then have it jetted by a local specialty source.**

The customized system gives you complete design flexibility, and some clients will want this. But you must have the expertise and the craftspeople necessary to do it and do it right. And you must assume complete responsibility.

The locally-jetted tub might be excellent if you have a stable, reputable firm to do the work.

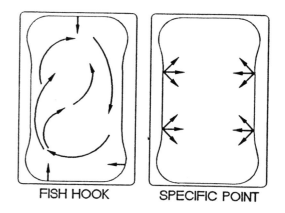

FISH HOOK   SPECIFIC POINT

Fig. 4.8. Whirlpool tubs have differing flow patterns. Common patterns are shown here, but they also can be customized. In some, jets are individually controlled.

But you must be responsible for the system and the workmanship. Sometimes even stable, reputable firms vanish and, as with the customized system, you must uphold the warranty.

The other option, the total system designed, engineered and fabricated by an established, reputable manufacturer, would seem to be the most trustworthy choice unless there are other factors to influence the decision.

Shower stall often needed

Showering is usually the cleansing method of choice for early morning, and most often it will be in a combination tub/shower. But, if space permits, a separate shower stall always is a better choice. It is safer than a tub shower because it almost entirely eliminates the danger of slipping and falling, and removing the shower from the tub opens more design options in tub placement and installation.

Shower stalls may be built on the jobsite with a shower receptor base and waterproof wall materials, or might be prefabricated in one piece or several pieces to be assembled on the jobsite.

In job-built showers, an important consideration is size. Building codes (which vary by locality, state and province) usually set a minimum of 1,024 square inches (6,606cm²), which translates to a 32" x 32" square (81 x 81 cm). That is

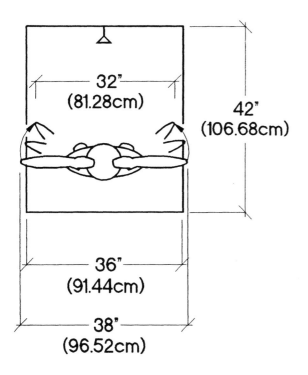

Fig. 4.9. A person of average size washing hair in a shower needs 38" (97 cm) of space to avoid bumping elbows against the sides of the shower stall. A larger person could need more.

not large enough to accommodate the flying elbows of an adult (Fig. 4.9) or to permit bending over to pick up a dropped bar of soap (Fig. 4.10).

(See Guideline 16, Chap. 5, on size.)

There also should be space in the shower stall for a small seat, for safety and convenience in washing the feet, shaving the legs, etc. (Fig. 4.11.) These are molded into the wall of many modern prefabricated shower stalls along with soap dishes, shelving and grab bars.

The height of the shower head off the floor also should be considered and related to the height of the users. It should be high enough to allow the user to shower without wetting the hair, but also to allow the user to lean forward easily to wet the hair. Typically, a plumber will rough-in the shower at 66" (168cm) off the floor. The shower spray usually begins 6" (15cm) below the rough-in dimension, and that is too low for convenient use. Recommended rough-in

height for the stub-out for an "average" male and female of 5'10" (178cm) and 5'4" (163cm), respectively, is 72" to 78" (183-198cm).

In a job-built shower stall, each corner of the receptor base should slope toward the drain by 1/4" per foot (63mm per 30cm). The drain usually is in the center of a square or round receptor, but might be in a corner of a rectangular one. The receptor usually is about 4 1/2" (11cm) high. The drain stub-out must be the proper height and at the right location for the receptor.

The walls of the job-built shower often are ceramic tile. Solid surface and cast polymer manufacturers make thinner sheets of the material, usually 1/4" or 3/8" (63-93mm) thick, for this use or for tub/shower surrounds.

Factory-made receptors, or pans, can be of masonry or stone (including marble or granite), ceramic tile, solid surface, fiberglass, acrylic or cast polymer. In any of these except stone or masonry, the entire shower structure can be made of the same material, even all in one piece (Fig. 4.13). If it is all one piece, of course, it raises the problem of maneuvering it into the house and into the bathroom.

Showers can have two showerheads for simultaneous use by two persons. But showers also can be purchased or custom-made on the job with multiple heads or sprays for individual use. These can provide a hydromassage action up and down the body in addition to the overhead shower spray and often a hand-held spray. These usually will have separate controls for each spray, or bank of sprays, and these controls are available with memory chips so they turn the water on at the same temperature as the last previous use.

When this is done each spray must be within the 2.5 gpm (9.5L) legal limit. Collectively, however, they add up to a lot more.

A common problem in these multiple spray installations is failure of the several heads to discharge water with the same pressure and at the

Notes:

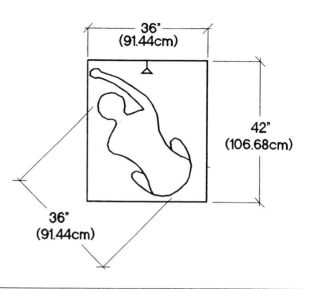

Fig. 4.10. Bending over to pick up an object from the shower floor requires at least 36" (91cm) of diagonal space, but that is cramped.

same temperature. Any straight manifold will have higher pressure at the first outlet and diminishing pressure at each ensuing outlet. To compensate for this, each bank of heads should have a manifold loop to equalize pressure at all of the heads and sprays on that side (Fig. 4.14).

This probably will call for a 3/4" (2cm) supply line and a 3/4" mixing valve. This will deliver 30 to 35 gallons per minute (114-132L) at 45 psi. To determine how many heads can be used on a supply line, divide the showerhead flow rate into the flow rating of the mixing valve fed by the supply line.

This must be specified by the bathroom specialist. A plumber who is not trained in this kind of work cannot necessarily be depended on to do it properly. A good course to follow here is to call on the services of a Decorative Plumbing & Hardware firm that specializes in these luxury showers.

(For specifics on tubs and showers, see Guidelines 16-22, and Guideline 26 and Clarifications, Chap. 5.)

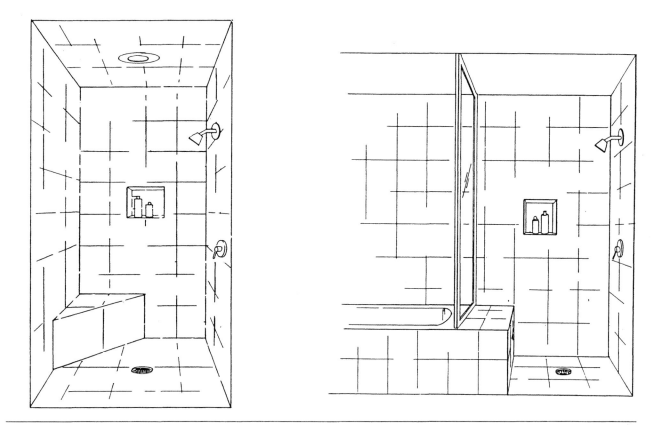

Fig. 4.11. There are many ways to design a bench or seat in a shower.

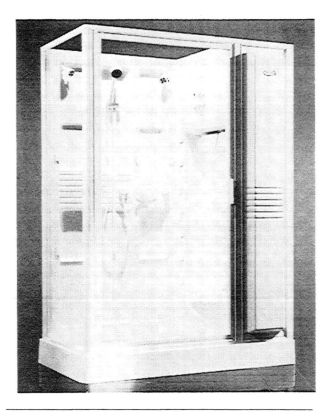

Fig. 4.12. Programmed shower system with multiple heads and sprays comes ready to install from the factory.

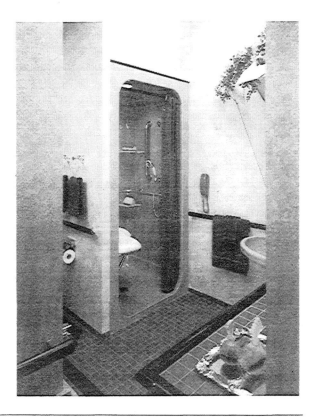

Fig. 4.13. Shower stall in one piece has minimal curve on shower floor, making it easier to use in universal design.

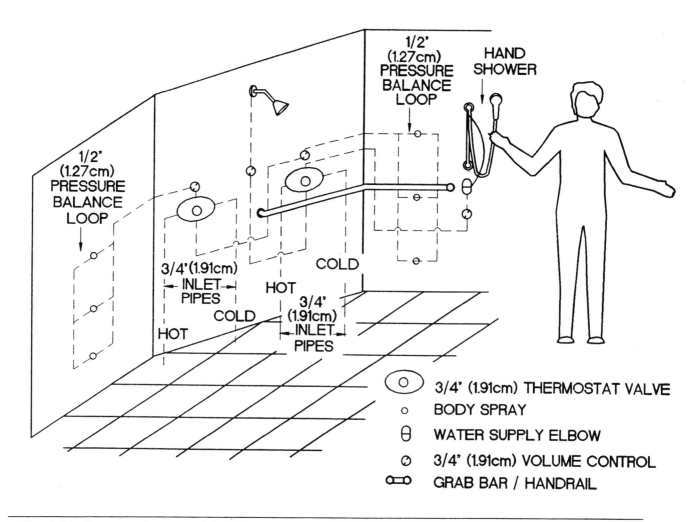

1/2'
(1.27cm)
PRESSURE
BALANCE
LOOP

1/2'
(1.27cm)
PRESSURE
BALANCE
LOOP

HAND
SHOWER

3/4'(1.91cm)
←INLET→
PIPES

HOT

COLD

COLD

HOT

3/4'
(1.91cm)
←INLET→
PIPES

HOT

	3/4' (1.91cm) THERMOSTAT VALVE
o	BODY SPRAY
θ	WATER SUPPLY ELBOW
⊘	3/4" (1.91cm) VOLUME CONTROL
⊙═⊙	GRAB BAR / HANDRAIL

Fig. 4.14. Custom shower with multiple shower heads and sprays needs a pressure-balancing loop to make sure all heads deliver same pressure and temperature. Left, center and right walls are shown.

Steam baths and saunas

A steam bath, once featured only in plush private clubs, now can be added easily and inexpensively to any bathroom. Steam generators for home use now are small enough to be fitted into any vanity cabinet or into a wall. From there they can feed steam into any tub or shower stall.

The steam generator is simply a heater with a water supply line and an outlet for the steam. The steam line usually is 1/2" (1cm) copper tubing, because copper can withstand the 190° heat of the steam in the line. The steam supply line should be installed with a downward pitch to drain condensation, entering a shower stall 6" to 12" (15-30cm) above the floor or 6" above the tub ledge. The steam line should not be more than 30' (9M) from the heater, but closer is preferable and more effective.

Other than addition of the steam generator, the only difference in the bathroom is the need to make it vapor-proof. That means a completely-enclosed glass door for the shower or vapor-proof glass doors for the tub. If the door does not reach the ceiling, build a bulkhead or enclose the space with a glass panel. The ceiling should be slanted downward away from the seat so condensation will not drip on the user.

The heater will take a 3/8" (93mm) supply line off the hot water line, and a separate 220V circuit with a 30-50-amp GFCI breaker.

The steam generator is sized for cubic footage of the enclosed space, but porosity of the wall surface will affect sizing. For example, for ceramic tile on cement board, add 20% to actual footage. For fiberglass, acrylic or cultured marble, decrease footage by 20%.

If you take all of the humidity (nearly 100%) out of a steam bath, you have a sauna, (humidity, 7% to 25%). Both cause sweating, but a sauna uses dry heat. In a steam bath, temperature from steam is 100°-115° F. (38°-46°C). In a sauna it varies from 175°-195° F (79°-91°C) for women to 190°-220° F (88°-104°C) for men. The usual bath, in hot steam or hot air, is about 20 minutes. And the next thing a person wants to do is take a shower.

But, while a steam bath logically belongs in a bathtub or shower stall, the sauna doesn't have to be in the bathroom. It is an insulated room, usually made of kiln-dried redwood. Redwood can withstand extreme temperature changes and acts as an insulator on walls, ceiling and floor. It diffuses heat, so its surfaces remain warm to the touch but don't get hot.

When saunas originated in Finland, the sauna bather created heat with red hot stones, then threw water on them to create steam, then went out and rolled in the snow. Time has modified the custom and the steam is gone, except for purists who sometimes like a bit of steam from water on hot coals in the final moments.

Complete, self-contained sauna kits are available from manufacturers to be fitted into a nearby closet, a basement or even a corner of a bedroom. Some are as small as 3' x 4' (91 x 122 cm), which is the minimum size for one person. For more users, allow 6 sq. ft. (183cm²) per person. For any size sauna, a 7' (213 cm) ceiling to prevent heat from rising into unused space, and a narrow door, less than 24" (61cm) wide, with no lock, are recommended.

Prefabricated units usually have an intake vent near the floor, an outlet for cross ventilation and soft lighting. A stove in the sauna may be electric or gas.

UL requirements include:

• **No electrical connections inside the sauna;**
• **A protective fence around the heater;**
• **Heaters must be UL listed.**
• **UL listed temperature controls, timers and safety shut-off.**

A Food & Drug Administration (FDA) requirement is that elderly persons or those with heart diseases and/or high blood pressure must consult a physician before using a sauna or steam bath.

Fittings control the flow

After all of the bathroom fixtures have been selected, the next step for the bathroom specialist and client is to select fittings that coordinate with the chosen colors, textures, surfaces and shapes.

The fittings might be called, collectively, the "brass" or the "faucets." And while many of them might have a base of brass, they might have a finish of brass, gold, ceramic, chrome, enamel, crystal, plastic, pewter or a colored epoxy. The surface might be polished, matte or antique.

If your client wants a gold finish—and it is increasingly popular—you should be able to discuss it. According to industry standards, plating to a thickness of less than 7 millionths of an inch is a "gold wash" or "gold flash," between 8 and 12 millionths is "gold plating," and from 13 to 50 millionths is "heavy gold plating."

All quality gold-plated fittings should be heavy gold plating. This is not easy to measure, so be sure the supplier is reputable and ask for data on the parts.

Fittings include the faucets and their handles and spouts, but they also include any other visible components that contribute to the movement and control of water. For example, they include pop-up drains; trip levers for the toilet; mixing valves for the shower which, in this era of low water consumption, should have thermostatic and/or pressure regulators; supplemental hand sprays or other added sprays in the shower; outlets and controls in the whirlpool tub, etc.

In coordinating fixtures, fittings and accessories, it sometimes is better to choose colors that harmonize or contrast rather than match. If, for example, a client wants an all-white bathroom, the whiteness of a ceramic faucet handle will not match the whiteness of a solid surface counter. The materials have inherent differences in light reflectance that will prevent a perfect match.

Matching the fittings to each other is easier. Many manufacturers of faucets offer whole families of fittings that match in color, style, finish and material.

Many differences in faucets

There are several different ways to categorize bathroom faucets.

• They can have one handle or two, or be controlled with electronics and no handle .

A single-handle control lifts to control water flow, then pushes from side to side for temperature control. Some shut off flow only in the center-down position. Others can be left at the temperature setting and pushed down to shut off the water. The factor to watch for here is a wide arc for temperature control. Humans are comfortable with water at 95°-105° F (35°-41°C). A handle is more satisfactory with a 120-degree arc from hottest to coldest, and with a 40-degree arc in that comfort zone. This control is lost when an electronic proximity sensor turns the water on as the user gets near, and for that reason these are popular in public restrooms but not in homes. The other electronic control is with touch pads. Different pads control temperature and flow. These mount flush in the counter or in the faucet.

When a faucet has two handles they might be 4" or 8" apart (10 or 20cm).

• They can be constructed to fit into one, two or three holes.

Single-hole faucets can have a single handle or two handles attached to the spout. These often are shipped with escutcheon plates to cover other holes that might be predrilled in a lav.

• They can have compression valving, with two handles and washers.

In these, water enters through a valve seat and is controlled by a rubber washer. When a handle is turned the stem turns, raising the washer out of the seat. There also is a primary seal to shut the water off and a secondary seal to prevent leaking. Hard turning can abuse and wear out the washers.

There are other types of compression valves with different actions, but all are subject to washer wear-out.

• They can be washerless, with a cartridge assembly inside.

Most washerless faucets do have neoprene rubber seals or O-rings. One two-handle model has plastic discs with holes, assembled as a cartridge to the valve stem. The discs rotate against rubber seats that are forced against the the disc by separate springs. Water flow is controlled by rotating holes in the disc to align with seats and a hole in the valve body.

Other somewhat similar types have either a plastic disc or sleeve that rotates against the seat within a self-contained cartridge. This cartridge can be replaced easily by a homeowner.

• They can operate with a rotating ball.

A hollow plastic, brass or stainless steel ball at the end of the stem rotates against soft rubber seats pushed upward by springs. The ball valve is held by a bonnet screwed on with an O-ring. Water is controlled by aligning holes in the ball against water inlets. These are inexpensive but can require frequent service.

• They can have ceramic discs in cartridges.

These are best when top quality. They have sheer action valving, in 1-handle or 2-handle versions. Two ceramic discs rotate against each other and allow water to pass through when holes are aligned. Discs are very hard, polished to almost perfect smoothness so there is no room for air or water to seep between the two discs. They are unaffected by water temperature or chemical action or debris in the line. These are more expensive, but lowest life-cycle cost.

Water for the bathtub

Bathtub faucets, or "fillers" as they are called on oversize tubs, are not subject to the flow restrictions imposed on lav faucets and showerheads. The objective here is to deliver water into the tub fast enough so the water does not cool before the bather gets in.

Usually a 3/4" line (2cm) serves a bathroom with three fixtures, and 1/2" lines then bring hot and cold water to 1/2" tub fittings. These restrict the flow to 9 gallons (34L) per minute. A larger tub needs a flow of 10-20 gallons (38-76L) per minute, and that requires 3/4" supply lines all the way, with 3/4" fittings. In these cases, it is necessary to specify 3/4" fittings, spout and valve.

Restricted-flow showerheads might be uncomfortable to the users, accustomed as many are to a full water flow. But more important than comfort is the scalding hazard. If the shower is on the same water supply line as the toilet (and it usually is) and someone flushes the toilet when another person is showering, it can starve the cold water line to the shower, leaving the hot water on at full force.

There are four general categories of valves that can guard against this hazard:

- **A pressure-balancing valve.**
- **A thermostatic valve.**
- **A combination pressure-balancing and thermostatic valve.**
- **A temperature-limiting valve.**

The **pressure-balancing** valve responds to a change in water pressure between the hot and cold water supplies. If the pressure diminishes

on one side it increases the flow from that side or reduces the flow from the other side (Fig. 4.15). This type of valve does not respond to a change in temperature.

The **thermostatic** valve adjusts the mix of hot and cold water in response to a change in temperature. The response is not immediate, so there might be a second or two when the user notices a temperature change while the valve adjusts, but it is relatively constant and the scalding hazard is eliminated.

The **combination** valve reacts to either or both, a pressure change or a temperature change.

The **temperature-limiting** valve has a high-temperature limit stop that is adjustable by the installer or by the user. This device is usually under the lever and escutcheon of a single-handle faucet, and requires only a screwdriver for access.

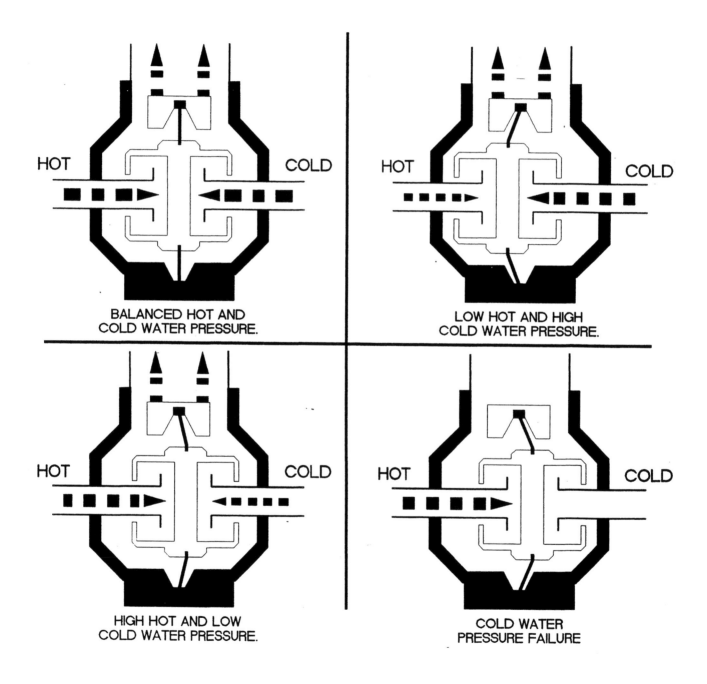

BALANCED HOT AND
COLD WATER PRESSURE.

LOW HOT AND HIGH
COLD WATER PRESSURE.

HOT COLD

HOT COLD

HOT COLD

HOT COLD

HIGH HOT AND LOW
COLD WATER PRESSURE.

COLD WATER
PRESSURE FAILURE

Fig. 4.15. Low water consumption showerheads increase risk of scalding when another fixture on the same line is turned on. Pressure control valves cut off the hot water when this happens.

Notes:

How to Design Bathrooms
The Principles, Elements, and 41 Guidelines

The concepts of planning, layout and design are difficult to separate. They all work together to achieve a final "look" in a room that is both functional and beautiful. Design is the factor that makes it beautiful.

There are three basic *principles* of design:
• **Balance** • **Rhythm** • **Emphasis**

There are six *elements* of design:
• **Line** • **Form**
• **Shape** • **Texture**
• **Space** • **Color**

The elements are the tools we use in pursuit of good design. The principles of design guide us in the use of those tools.

Lines are the simplest shapes we have to work with. They show movement and direction, and in doing so they can stretch or shrink space visually. Vertical lines carry the eye upward and make a space look higher (Fig. 5.1), but that impact is affected also by the width and spacing of the lines. Thin vertical lines spaced closely can visually widen a room rather than add height.

Horizontal lines are much more stable. They widen the area being viewed (Fig. 5.2). They feel calm and suggest rest and relaxation. A horizontal molding placed close to a ceiling can seem to lower that ceiling

Curved lines can help soften the bathroom

that is made up mostly of hard edges and hard textures. Diagonal lines are dramatic and can add movement to square forms that might otherwise be monotonous.

Shape is a combination or configuration of lines. Square shapes tend to be stagnant and un-interesting. Rectangular shapes, usually horizontal, are most common and easiest to work with. Diagonal shapes are the least stable, but are good for a feeling of movement. A triangular shape is most stable when its base is at the bottom.

Space is defined by the shapes and forms in the bathroom. Curved space stretches the area visually because it leads the eye continuously. As you add angled shapes to a room with four sides, it tends to become more and more circular.

Form is more than the physical shape of an object. It is the shape plus the apparent weight and ornamentation and its relationship to other objects nearby.

Weight refers to the physical size *as you view it,* which can be increased or diminished in any design. For example, a vanity with raised panel doors and moldings would contrast sharply with a stark, contemporary wall treatment around it, adding to its weight and, therefore, its apparent size. Similarly, a dark linen cabinet against a light wall would gain weight and look larger, but it would lose weight and look smaller against a dark wall.

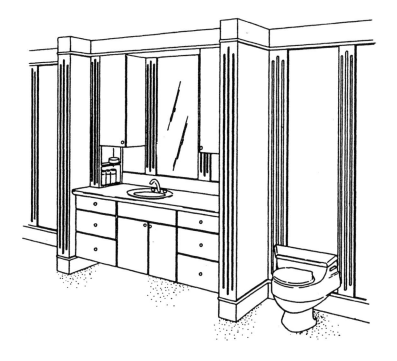

Fig. 5.1. Vertical lines impart a rigid feel and lead the eye upward, adding height.

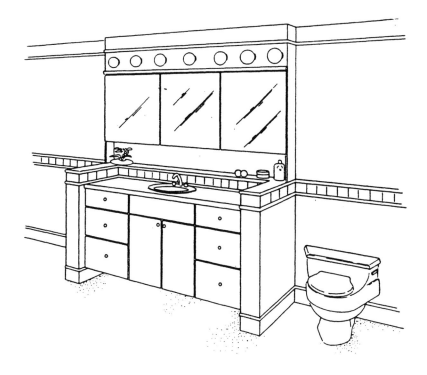

Fig. 5.2. Horizontal lines tend to be restful. They can help widen a space.

Texture can be actual or apparent. Actual texture is tactile. It can be felt as well as seen. Apparent texture can be seen, but not felt. For example, a piece of woven cane has tactile texture. You can feel it. But woven cane in a decorative laminate has apparent, or visual, texture. It can be seen, but not felt.

Many textures have pattern. Texture and pattern can be used to increase weight in an object. You can combine similar textures such as wood, brick and basket weaves, and add contrast with glass, tile or porcelain bath fixtures. A pattern that repeats a dominant shape or line will add unity.

As a general rule, casual environments work best with strongly-textured surfaces. Soft textures support delicate, feminine environments. Classic, traditional rooms need sharp edges and smooth surfaces. Contemporary rooms generally work well with both smooth surfaces and strong textures.

Color and the color wheel were introduced in the section on lighting in Chapter. It was necessary there, because color is light and light has color.

Of all the elements of design, color can have the most dramatic effect in any room. It can be advancing or receding, happy or sad, warm or cool.

• Warm colors (yellow, orange, red) are advancing. They make a room seem smaller or make an object in the room seem larger.

• Receding cool colors (blue, green, violet) make a room seem larger or make an object in the room seem smaller.

• Light colors decrease the weight of an object, which increases the spatial perception of the area.

• Dark colors increase weight of an object, decreasing spatial perception of the area.

Color harmony chart

ANALOGOUS

Analogous—Colors adjacent to one another on the color chart are used. One color dominates. They can vary in value and intensity. Overall scheme can be warm or cool.

ANALOGOUS WITH COMPLEMENTARY ACCENT

Analogous with complementary accent—Accents the analogous relationship with a color from opposite side of wheel, such as a hunter green accent on wall opposite almond cabinets and fixtures, rose floor and tub enclosure.

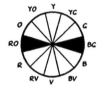
COMPLEMENTARY

Complementary—Features colors opposite one another. One is always warm, the other always cool. Maintains the natural value of the colors, such as almond (a lighter orange) and navy blue, which is darker.

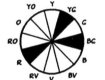
SPLIT COMPLEMENTARY

Split complementary—A color along with the colors on each side of its opposite, such as yellow plus blue-violet and red-violet.

DOUBLE SPLIT COMPLEMENTARY

Double split complementary—Two colors on either side of a color plus the two colors on either side of its complementary color. For example, red-orange and red-violet on either side of red, plus yellow-green and blue-green on either side of green.

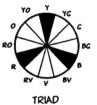
TRIAD

Triad—Uses three colors equidistant from each other. For example, the three primaries, yellow, blue and red may be used in intense colors for a happy theme; or the yellow may be toned to gold, the red shaded to claret and the blue to indigo to create an elegant, luxurious theme.

Fig. 5.3. Proper color selection starts with the customers. Using their choices, we can contrast colors by using these time-tested color schemes.

• The same color throughout an area can help camouflage structural problems.

• Use heavily textured surfaces to absorb light and dull the intensity of a color if you want to decrease the apparent size and add warmth to the object.

• Use smooth, shiny surfaces to reflect light and to intensify the color of an object. This will increase its apparent size.

Those elements are our tools, but we have to know how to combine and use them. The principles of design comprise an instruction sheet on how to do it.

Balance refers to equilibrium, one side balancing the other. There are three kinds of balance we'll work with in bathroom design.

• *Symmetrical* balance is formal and static. It occurs when two elements in the room are exactly the same. For example, a medicine cabinet centered with two matching lights on each side, or identical tall cabinets installed on either side of a lav area. In both cases, one side mirrors the other (Fig. 5.4).

• *Asymmetrical* balance is informal. It does not rely on objects equally sized or equally spaced. Equilibrium is achieved with dissimilar objects arranged to create a sense of balance, so the mind of the viewer perceives an imaginary fulcrum shifted off-center. For example, a lav may be placed off-center in a vanity top and balanced with towel bars and rings arranged informally, or round forms can offset square ones, or high shapes can balance low shapes (Fig. 5.5).

• *Radial* balance is far less common. It is achieved when lines or forms radiate from a central point. We often see it in arrangements of appetizers at a dining room table. In a bathroom we might accomplish it in a floor pattern, or in a master suite with a centrally-placed tub.

Continuity, or **Rhythm** refers to the way all of the objects or elements in a room relate to

Notes:

_____

_____

_____

_____

_____

_____

_____

_____

_____

_____

_____

_____

_____

each other. The room might have many elements that are well-designed, but if they don't have rhythm, if they don't have the glue of continuity, the room just doesn't make it.

Continuity might come from repeating a sequence, such as wallpaper patterns, floor patterns and color. It might come from alternating some patterns, shapes or colors. However you achieve it, it must be there to make the parts of the room look as though they go together instead of looking isolated and unrelated.

Repetition is a technique that can be used to establish continuity. It always will work, but it can be monotonous when the sequence used is too simple, such as when all of the elements are the same size and the same shape and/or the

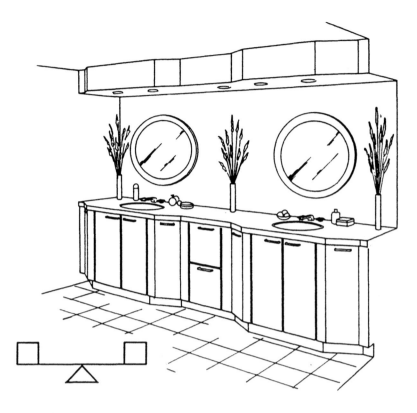

Fig. 5.4. A vanity wall balanced symmetrically

Fig. 5.5. A bathtub area balanced asymmetrically

same color. This is a 1, 1, 1, 1, etc., sequence. The eye moves from one element to the next, but it always is seeing the same design element (Fig. 5.6):

Fig. 5.6.

Alternation is a more interesting way to achieve rhythm. This technique uses alternating shapes or colors or patterns (or all of those) which adds variety. It can be depicted graphically as 1, 2, 1, 2, 1, 2 (Fig. 5.7):

Fig. 5.7.

Progression can produce more interest and vitality. It is change through small increments, which might be gradations of color, size or shape. It is a 1, 2, 3, 4, 5 pattern (Fig. 5.8):

Fig. 5.8.

Of course, continuity also can come from continuous lines which cause the eye to follow along in the same direction. Simple ways to use continuous lines include moldings, borders and chair rails.

Emphasis, the third principle of design, revolves around a center of interest, or a focal point that is emphasized in the design. The eye might stray from it, but it keeps returning continually to this dominant focal point.

While the focal point is the dominant element in the room, there are two other levels of dominance that support it. They are the subdominant and the subordinate. The subdominant layer is not as important as the dominant one, but features in it act as accents to the key element. The subordinate elements might include molding details and accessories, adding definition to the total design.

Generally, an area emphasis as well as a theme emphasis is established within the space.

You may wish to emphasize the vanity area because of its complexity and then allow the shower, bathtub and toilet to be subdominant by carrying through with the same materials used in the vanity area. Or you may select the bathing area as the highlight of the space.

You establish the focal point with emphasis, which might be area emphasis or theme emphasis. The emphasis might be in the overall arrangement of the various centers of the bathroom, which would be area emphasis, or it might be the natural focus of attention caused by color or materials or the dramatic shape of a product, which would be theme emphasis.

In any case, you do it with dramatic details and contrasts either in the area or in the theme (Fig. 5.9.)

You also can create emphasis by allowing the surface selection to dominate the space. A ceramic tile design might be featured on the floor, the tub/shower surround, a tub platform and vanity. You might do it with high-gloss decorative laminate or by use of glass blocks.

An important warning about emphasis is to avoid overdoing it. If you end up with both area emphasis and theme emphasis you get a room that is over-designed, and such a room is hard to view for any length of time.

So the way most good designers do it is by selecting one of the two alternatives: Either highlight one area in the room and allow everything to be subordinate to it, or select one product to highlight and keep all areas and other surfaces subordinate to it.

Fig. 5.9. Vanity area is emphasized as the focus in this bathroom design by Allmilmo.

Guidelines for Designing a

Bathroom

*41 new NKBA Guidelines to assist in planning
for function, comfort and safety*

For much too long the bathroom has been an inadequate space accommodated in the smallest area of the home for the least amount of money. In the past, bathroom planning standards were based on minimum requirements established by the Department of Housing and Urban Development (HUD) which focused solely on the space required for the basic fixtures, and little or no consideration was given to the anatomy of the user and his or her safe, comfortable movement in the space.

In the years ahead, successful bathroom designers will plan rooms that are designed around the people who will use them, rather than the fixtures that will be installed in them.

"The bathroom is no longer a room reserved for simple personal hygiene," says Annette M. DePaepe, CKD, CBD, ASID. "Today, people spend more time in the space. Some gather to enjoy the therapeutic pleasure of a hydromassage bath or a sauna. Others use the bathroom as a secluded spot away from hectic family and job responsibilities."

In keeping with the changing needs of the family and issues such as safety and universal accessibility, the NKBA has developed new planning guidelines for bathroom design which are based on the space required for the user(s) to function in the room comfortably and safely.

Following is a complete explanation of those new planning guidelines.

SECTION 1
Clear Floor Spaces and Door Openings

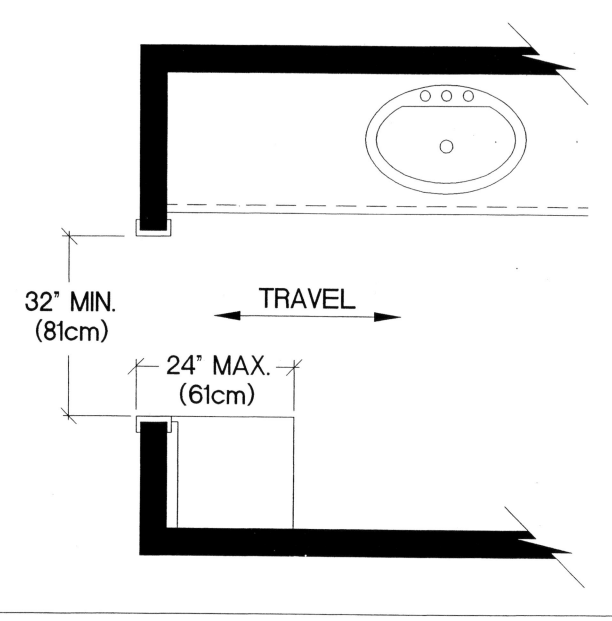

32" MIN.
(81cm)

TRAVEL

24" MAX.
(61cm)

Guideline 1a
The clear space at doorways should be at least 32" (81cm) wide and not more than 24" (61cm) deep in the direction of travel.

Guideline 1a Clarification While a designer should always try to meet this goal, physical constraints of a jobsite may require deviation from the guideline. Be aware that a lesser clearance may not allow for full use by all people.

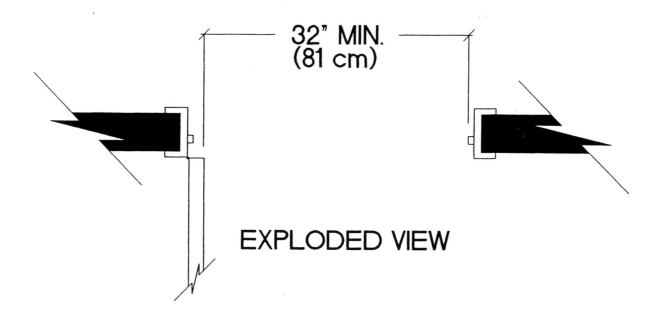

32" MIN.
(81 cm)

EXPLODED VIEW

Guideline 1b
The clear space at a doorway must be measured at the narrowest point.

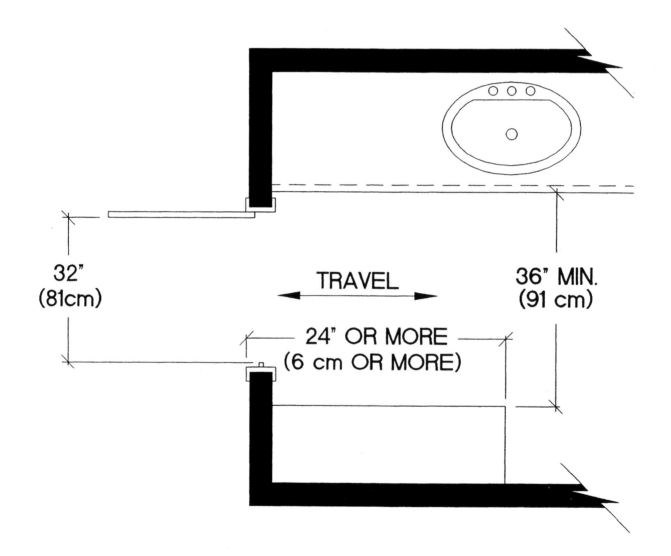

32"
(81cm)

TRAVEL

36" MIN.
(91 cm)

24" OR MORE
(6 cm OR MORE)

Guideline 1c

Walkways (passages between vertical objects greater than 24" (61cm) deep in the
direction of travel) should be a minimum of 36" (91cm) wide.

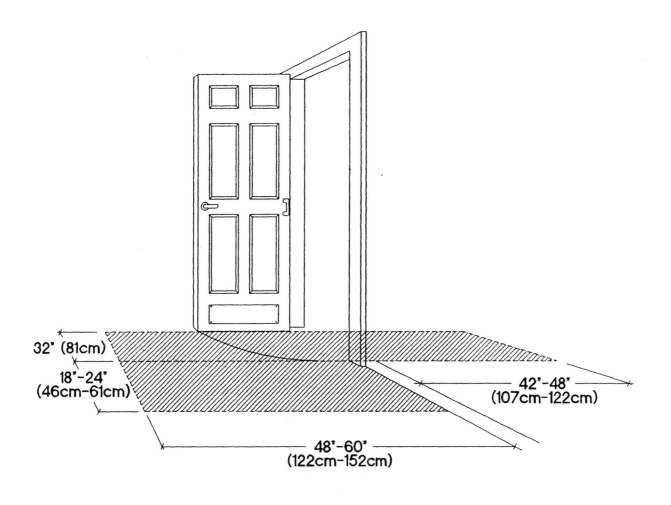

32" (81cm)

18"-24"
(46cm-61cm)

42"-48"
(107cm-122cm)

48"-60"
(122cm-152cm)

Guideline 2

A clear floor space at least the width of the door on the push side and a larger clear floor space on the pull side should be planned at doors for maneuvering to open, close and pass through the doorway. The exact amount needed will depend on the type of door and the approach.

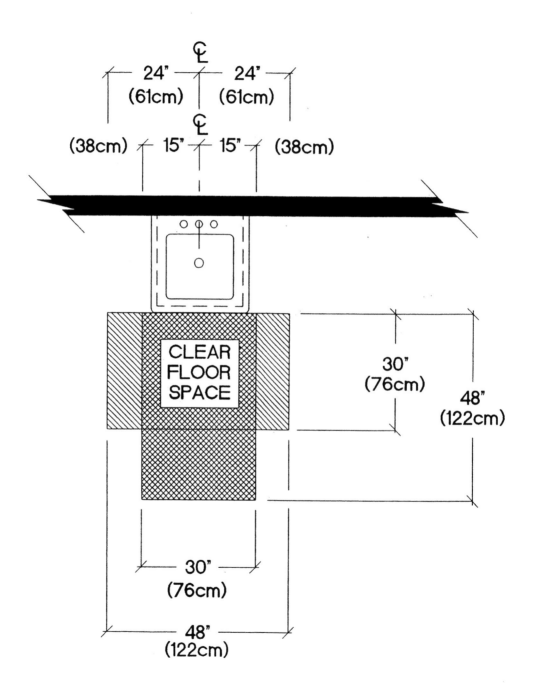

Guideline 3

A minimum clear floor space of 30" x 48" (76cm x 122cm) either parallel or perpendicular should be provided at the lavatory.

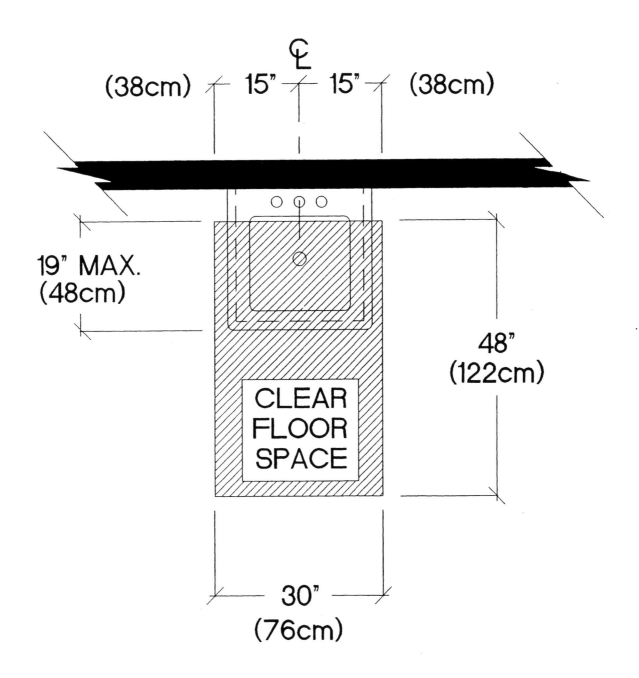

Guideline 3 Clarification Up to 19" (48cm) of the 48" (122cm) clear floor space dimension can extend under the lavatory when a knee space is provided.

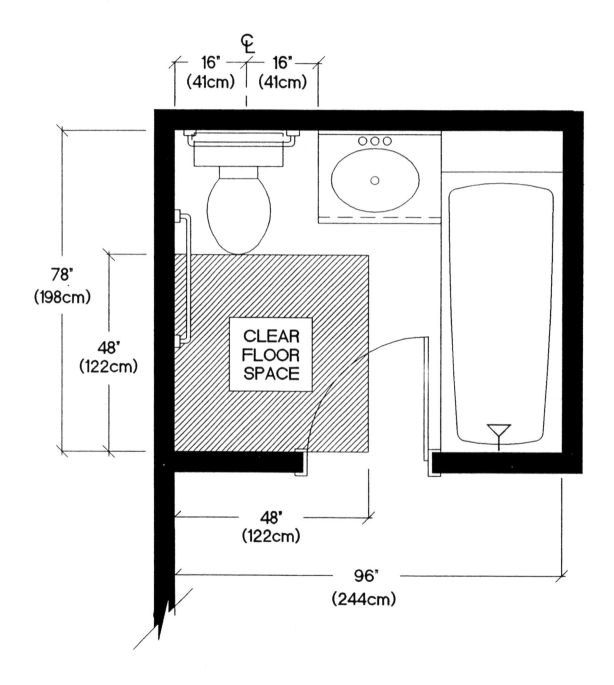

Guideline 4a

A minimum clear floor space of 48" x 48" (122cm x 122cm) should be provided in front of the toilet. A minimum of 16" (41cm) of that clear floor space must extend to each side of the centerline of the fixture.

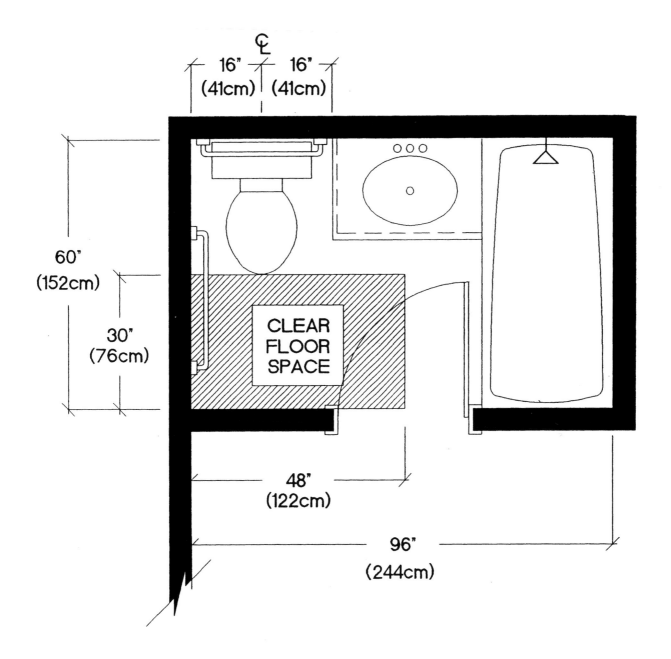

Guideline 4a Clarification While a designer should always try to meet this goal, physical constraints of a job site may require deviation from the guideline. If 48" x 48" (122cm x 122cm) clear floor space is unavailable, this space may be reduced to 30" x 48" (76cm x 122cm). This compromise may not allow for full use by all people.

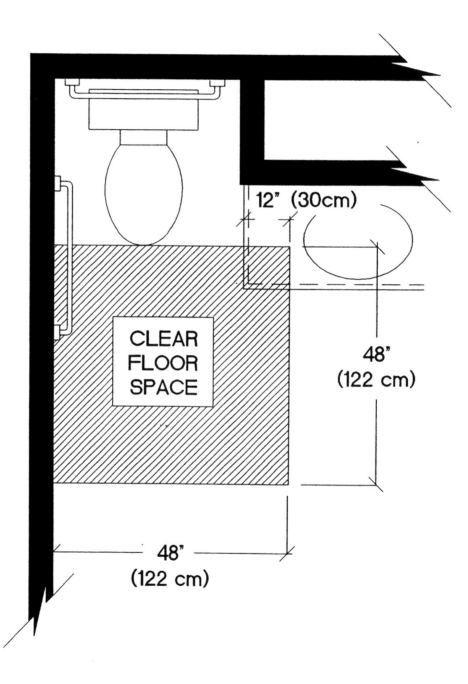

12" (30cm)

48"
(122 cm)

CLEAR
FLOOR
SPACE

48"
(122 cm)

Guideline 4b
Up to 12" (30cm) of the 48" x 48" (122cm x 122cm) clear floor space can extend
under the lavatory when total access to a knee space is provided.

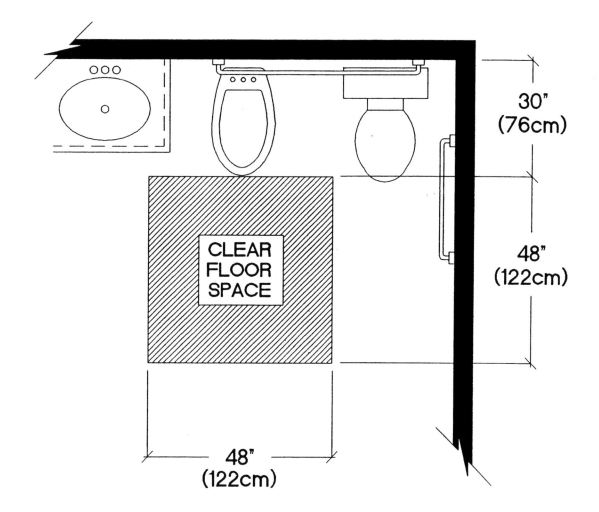

30"
(76cm)

48"
(122cm)

CLEAR
FLOOR
SPACE

48"
(122cm)

Guideline 5
A minimum clear floor space of 48" x 48" (122cm x 122cm) from the front of the bidet should be provided.

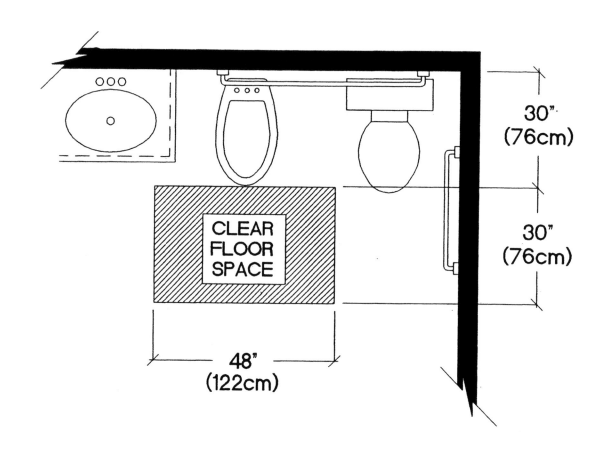

Guideline 5 Clarification 1 While a designer always should try to meet this goal, physical constraints of a job site may require deviation from the guideline. If 48" x 48" (122cm x 122cm) clear floor space is not available, this space may be reduced to 30" x 48" (76cm x 122cm). This compromise may not allow for full use by all people.

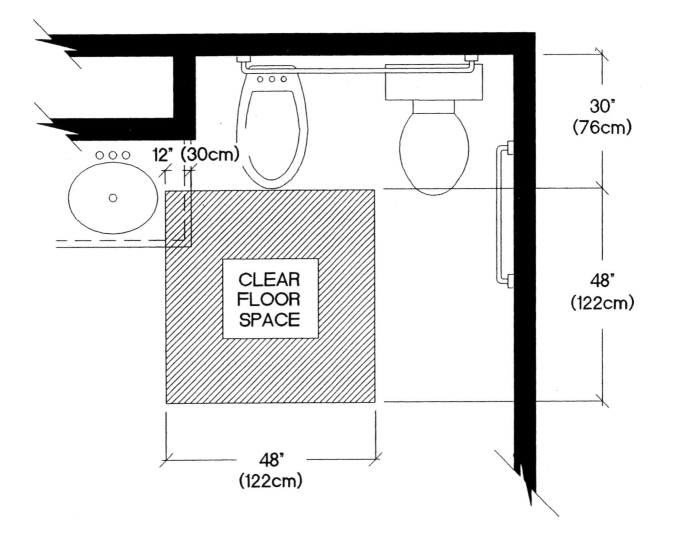

Guideline 5 Clarification 2 Up to 12" (30cm) of the 48" x 48" (122cm x 122cm) of the clear floor space can extend under the lavatory when total access to a knee space is provided.

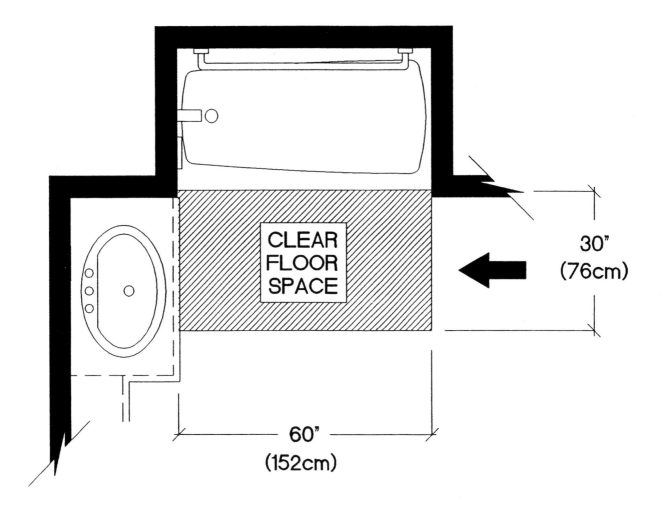

PARALLEL APPROACH

Guideline 6a

The minimum clear floor space at a bathtub is 60" (152cm) wide by 30" (76cm) deep for a parallel approach, even with the length of the tub.

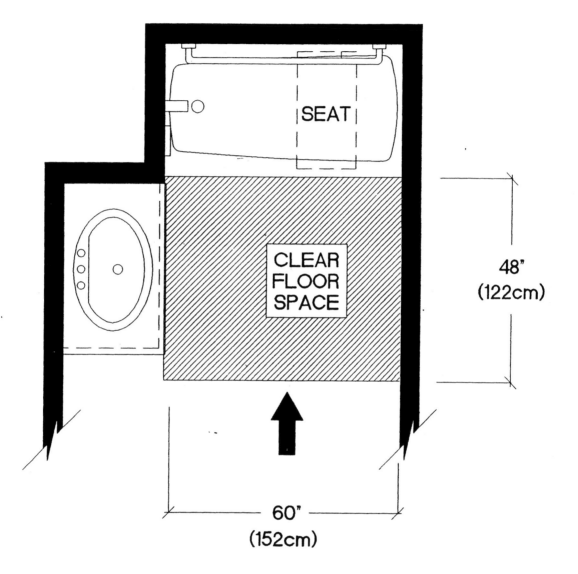

PERPENDICULAR APPROACH

Guideline 6b

The minimum clear floor space at a bathtub is 60" (152cm) wide x 48" (122cm) deep for a perpendicular approach.

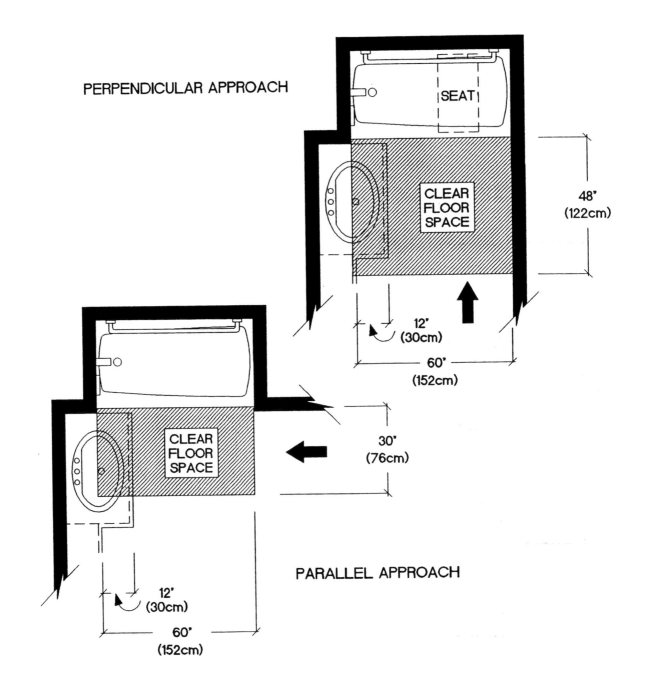

PERPENDICULAR APPROACH

SEAT

CLEAR FLOOR SPACE

48" (122cm)

12" (30cm)

60" (152cm)

CLEAR FLOOR SPACE

30" (76cm)

PARALLEL APPROACH

12" (30cm)

60" (152cm)

Guideline 6a, 6b Clarification 1 Up to 12" (30cm) of the 60" (152cm) clear floor space required for parallel or perpendicular approach can extend under the lavatory when total access to a kneespace is provided.

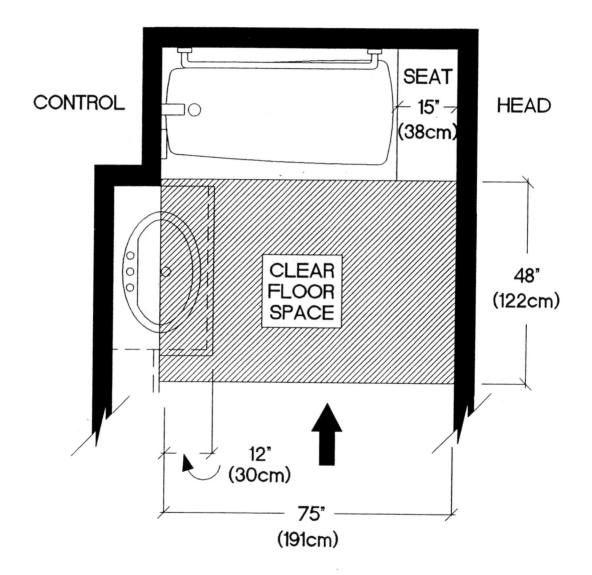

CONTROL

SEAT

HEAD

15"
(38cm)

CLEAR
FLOOR
SPACE

48"
(122cm)

12"
(30cm)

75"
(191cm)

Guideline 6a, 6b Clarification 2 If a built-in seat is planned, increase the width of the clear floor space by the depth of the seat, a minimum of 15" (38cm).

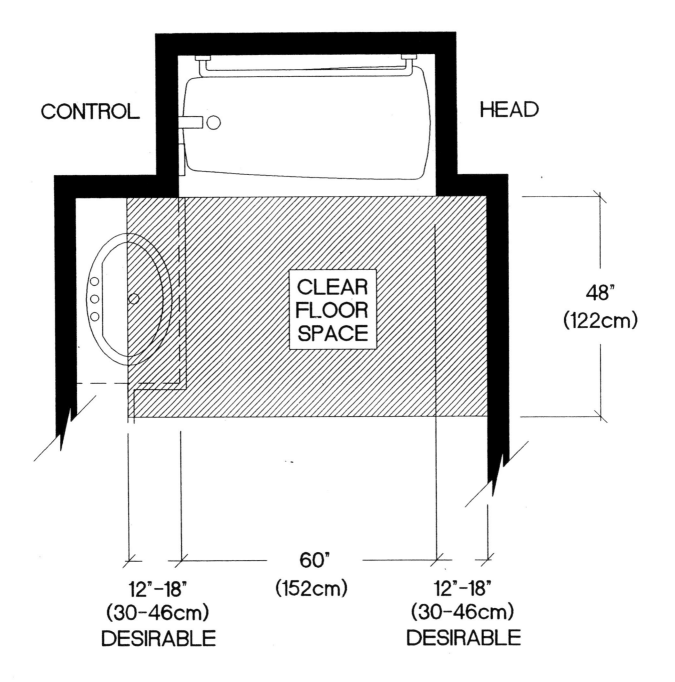

CONTROL

HEAD

CLEAR
FLOOR
SPACE

48"
(122cm)

12"-18"
(30-46cm)
DESIRABLE

60"
(152cm)

12"-18"
(30-46cm)
DESIRABLE

Guideline 6a, 6b Clarification 3 An additional 12"-18" (30cm-46cm) of clear floor space beyond the control wall is desirable to ease access to controls. The same 12"-18" (30cm-46cm) of clear floor space is desirable beyond the head of the tub for maneuvering mobility aids for transfer.

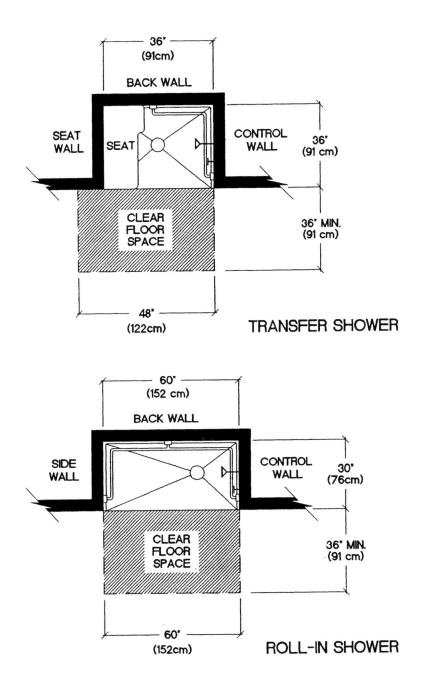

TRANSFER SHOWER

36" (91cm)
BACK WALL
SEAT WALL
SEAT
CONTROL WALL
36" (91 cm)
CLEAR FLOOR SPACE
36" MIN. (91 cm)
48" (122cm)

ROLL-IN SHOWER

60" (152 cm)
BACK WALL
SIDE WALL
CONTROL WALL
30" (76cm)
CLEAR FLOOR SPACE
36" MIN. (91 cm)
60" (152cm)

Guideline 7

The minimum clear floor space at showers less than 60" (152cm) wide should be 36" (91cm) deep x the width of the shower plus 12" (30cm). The 12" (30cm) should extend beyond the seat wall. At a shower that is 60" (152cm) wide or greater, clear floor space should be 36" (91cm) deep x the width of the shower.

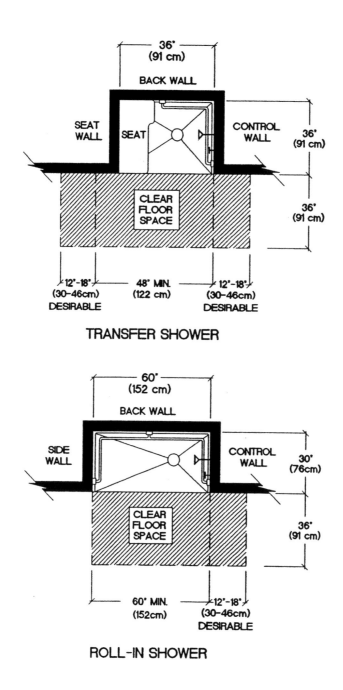

TRANSFER SHOWER

ROLL-IN SHOWER

Guideline 7 Clarification An additional 12"-18" (30cm-46cm) of clear floor space beyond the control wall is desirable to ease access to controls. The same 12"-18" (30cm-46cm) of clear floor space is desirable beyond the side wall opposite the control wall for maneuvering aids for transfer.

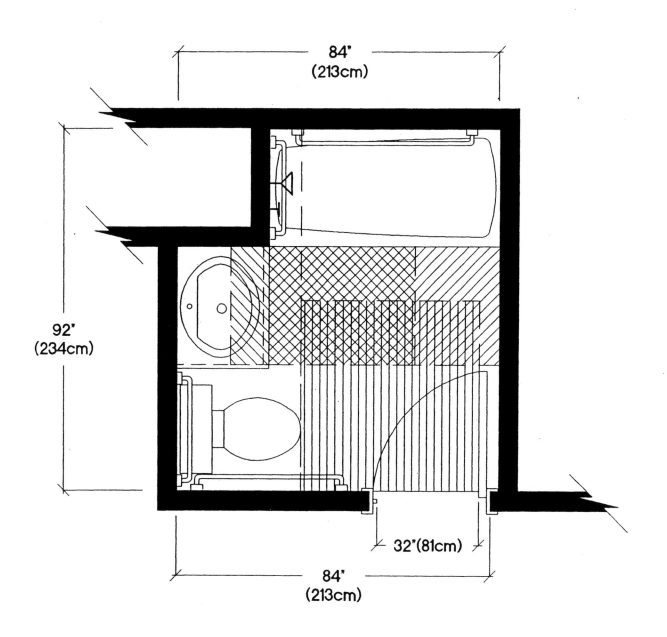

Guideline 8
Clear floor spaces required at each fixture may overlap.

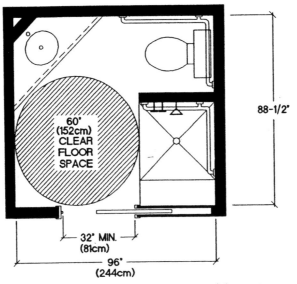

88-1/2"

60"
(152cm)
CLEAR
FLOOR
SPACE

32" MIN.
(81cm)

96"
(244cm)

MINIMUM 60" (152cm) DIAMETER FOR 360° TURNS

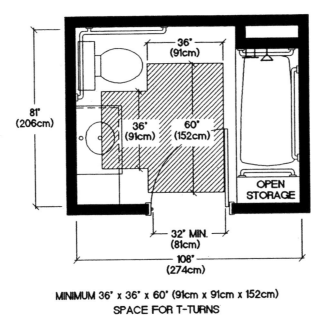

81"
(206cm)

36"
(91cm)

36"
(91cm)

60"
(152cm)

OPEN
STORAGE

32" MIN.
(81cm)

108"
(274cm)

MINIMUM 36" x 36" x 60" (91cm x 91cm x 152cm)
SPACE FOR T-TURNS

Guideline 9

Space for turning (mobility aids) 180° should be planned in the bathroom. A minimum diameter of 60" (152cm) for 360° turns and/or a minimum T-turn space of 36" (91cm) x 36" (91cm) x 60" (152cm).

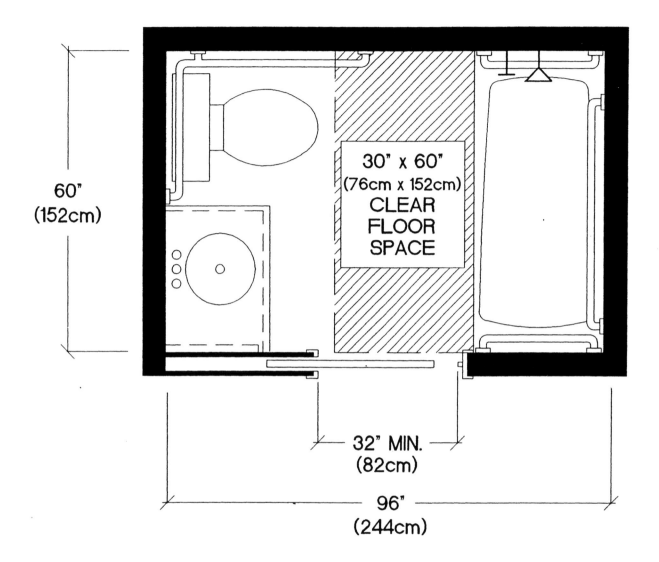

60"
(152cm)

30" x 60"
(76cm x 152cm)
CLEAR
FLOOR
SPACE

32" MIN.
(82cm)

96"
(244cm)

ALTERNATIVE TO TURNING SPACE
30" x 60" (76cm x 152cm) CLEAR FLOOR SPACE

Guideline 9 Clarification While a designer should always try to meet this goal, physical constraints of a job site may require deviation from the guideline. When space for a 360° diameter or T-turn is unavailable, a 30" x 60" (76cm x 152cm) clear floor space can be substituted but this compromise will not allow full access by all users.

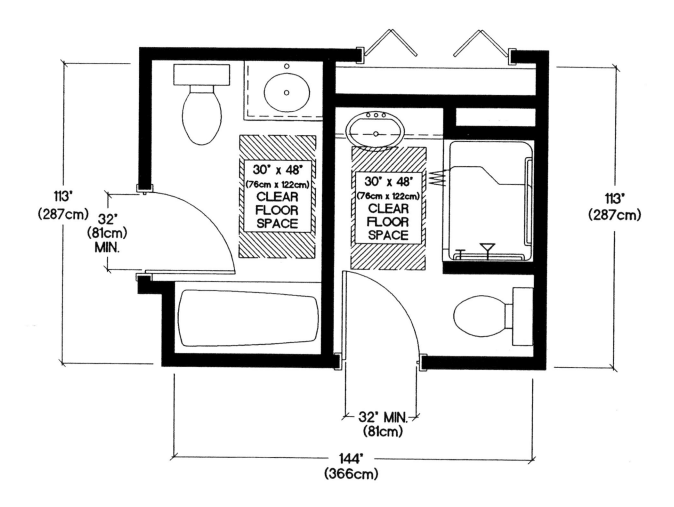

Guideline 10

A minimum clear floor space of 30" x 48" (76cm x 122cm) is *required* beyond the door swing in a bathroom.

SECTION 2
Lavatories

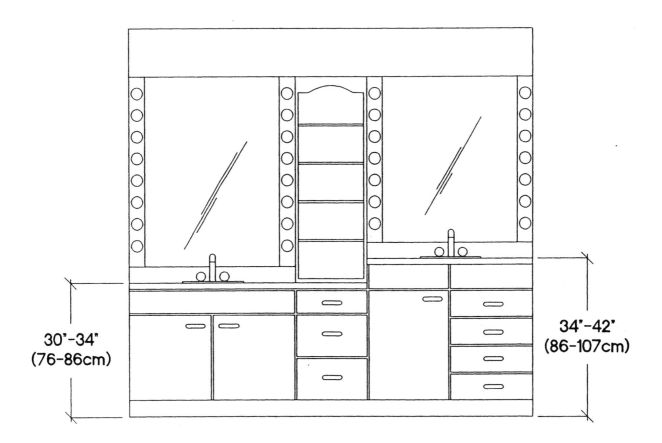

VARIED VANITY COUNTER HEIGHTS ARE DESIRABLE

30"-34"
(76-86cm)

34"-42"
(86-107cm)

Guideline 11
When more than one vanity is included, one may be 30"-34" (76cm -86cm) high and another 34"-42" (86cm-107cm) high. Vanity height should fit the user(s).

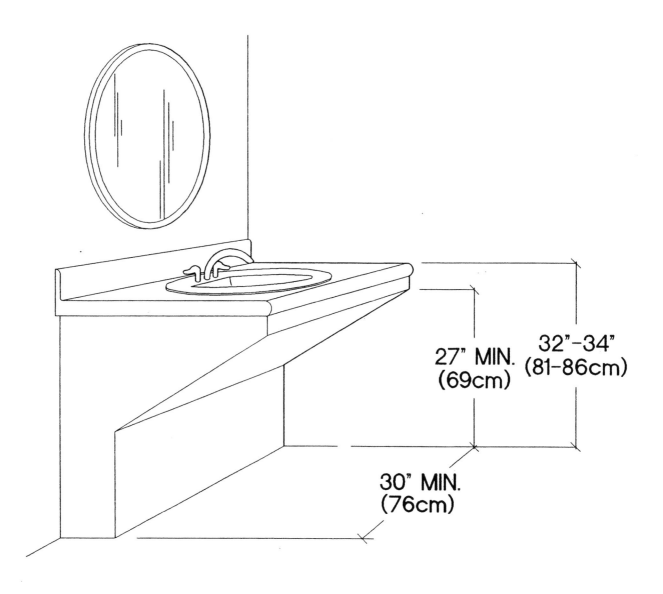

Guideline 12
Kneespace (which may be open or adaptable) should be provided at a lavatory.
The kneespace should be a minimum of 27" (69cm) above the floor at the front
edge, decreasing progressively as the depth increases, and the recommended width
is a minimum of 30" (76cm) wide.

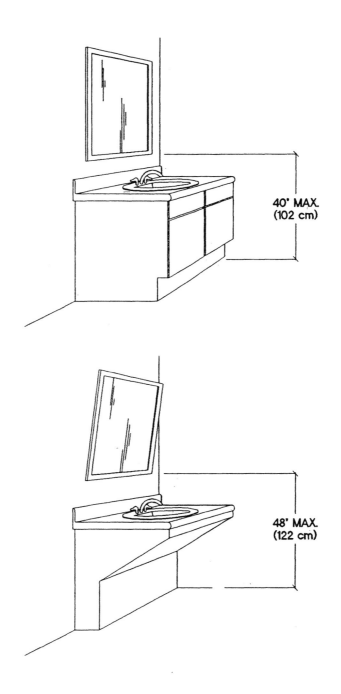

Guideline 13
The bottom edge of the mirror over the lavatory should be a maximum of 40" (102cm) above the floor or a maximum of 48" (122cm) above the floor if it is tilted.

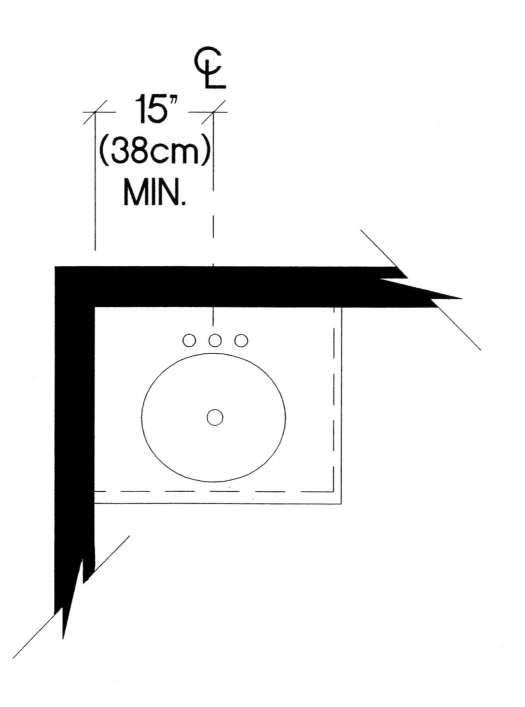

15"
(38cm)
MIN.

Guideline 14
Minimum clearance from the centerline of the lavatory to any side wall is 15" (38cm).

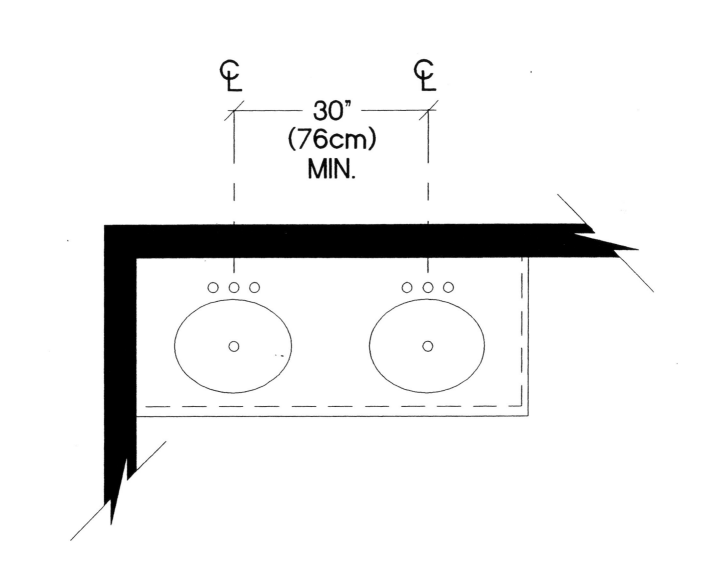

Guideline 15
The minimum clearance between two bowls in the lavatory center is 30" (76cm), centerline to centerline.

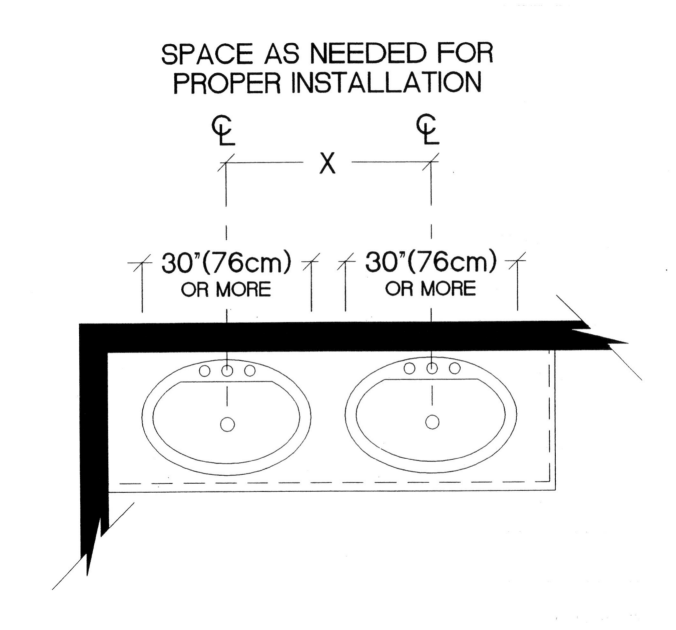

SPACE AS NEEDED FOR
PROPER INSTALLATION

X

30"(76cm)
OR MORE

30"(76cm)
OR MORE

Guideline 15 Clarification When using lavatories that are 30" (76cm) wide or greater, the minimum distance of 30" (76cm) between centerlines of the two bowls must be increased to allow proper installation of each lavatory.

SECTION 3
Showers and Bathtubs

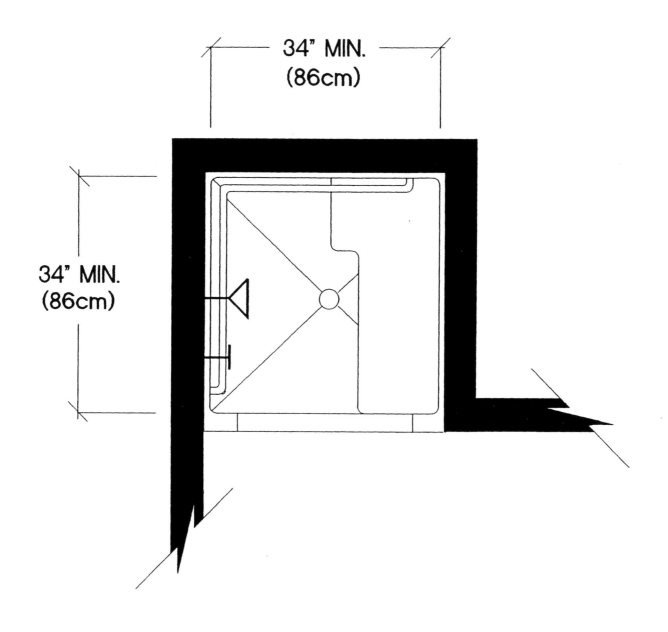

Guideline 16

In an enclosed shower, the minimum usable interior dimensions are 34" x 34" (86cm x 86cm). These dimensions are measured from wall to wall. Grab bars, controls, moving and folding seats do not diminish the measurement.

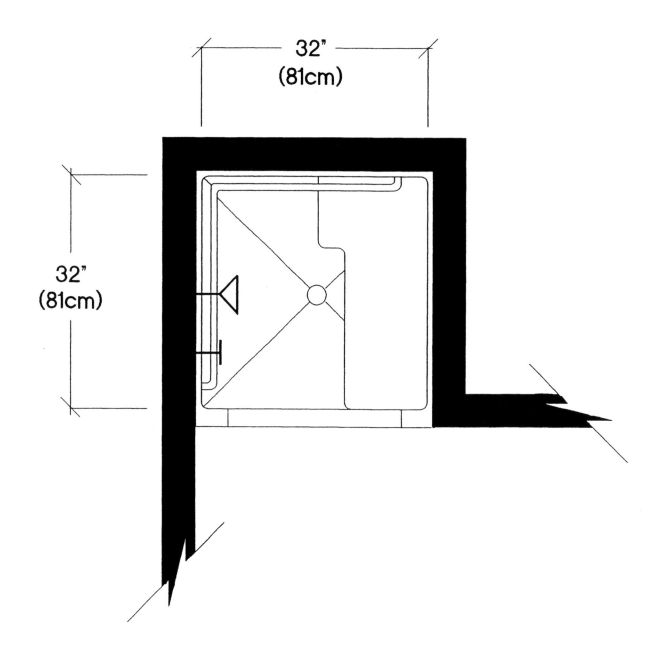

Guideline 16 Clarification While a designer should always try to meet this goal, physical constraints of a job site may require deviation from the guideline. If a 34" x 34" (86cm x 86cm) interior dimension is unavailable, these dimensions may be reduced to 32" x 32" (81cm x 81cm). Be aware that this compromise may not allow for full use by all people.

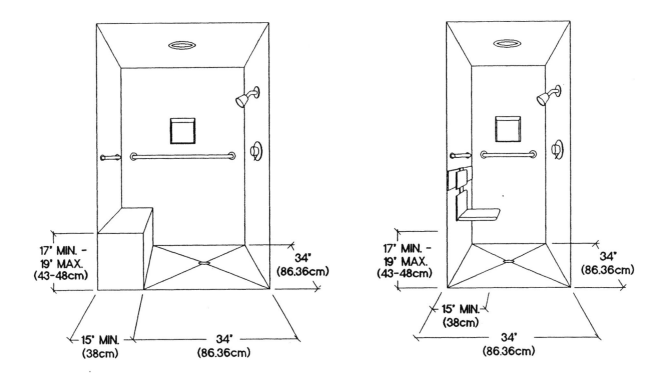

Guideline 17

Showers should include a bench or seat that is 17"-19" (43cm-48cm) above the floor and a minimum of 15" (38cm) deep.

Guideline 17 Clarification 1 Built-in permanent seats should not encroach upon the minimum 34" x 34" (86cm x 86cm) interior clear floor space of the shower.

Guideline 17 Clarification 2 Reinforced wall supports for future placement of hanging and folding seat hardware should be planned at the time of shower installation.

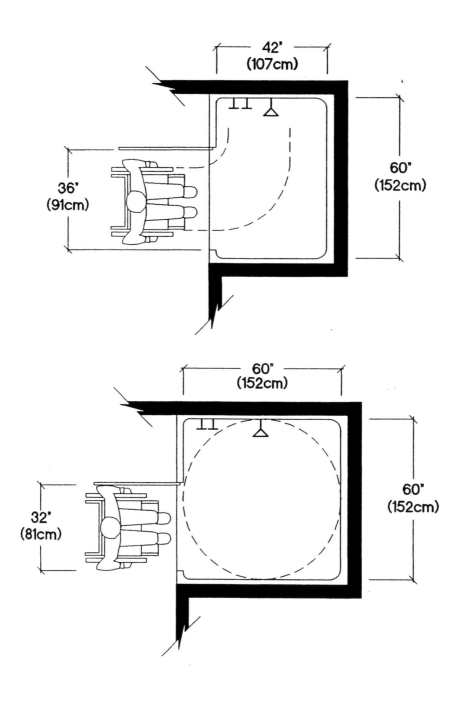

Guideline 18

The width of the door opening must take into consideration the interior space in the shower for entry and maneuvering. When the shower is 60" (152cm) deep, a person can enter straight into the shower and turn after entry, therefore 32" (81cm) is adequate. If the shower is 42" (107cm) deep, the entry must be increased to 36" (91cm) in order to allow for turning space.

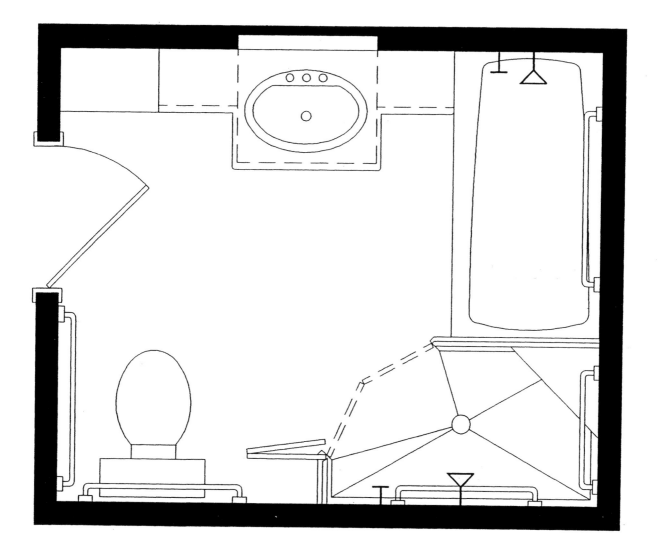

Guideline 19
Shower doors should open *into* the bathroom.

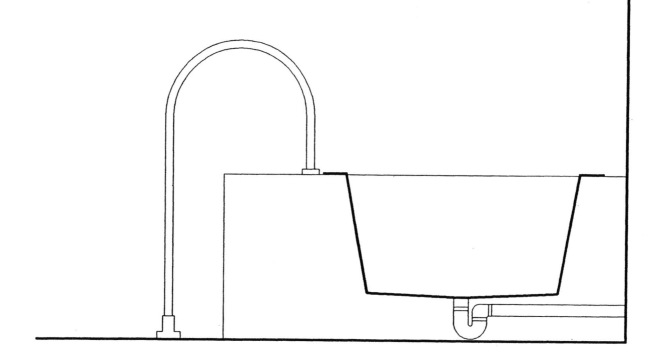

Guideline 20
Steps should *not* be planned at the tub or shower area. Safety rails should be installed to facilitate transfer to and from the fixture.

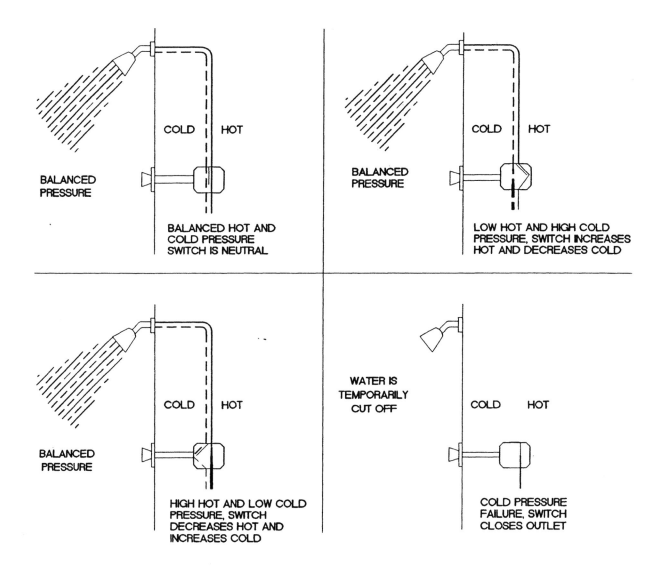

BALANCED PRESSURE

COLD | HOT

BALANCED HOT AND COLD PRESSURE SWITCH IS NEUTRAL

BALANCED PRESSURE

COLD | HOT

LOW HOT AND HIGH COLD PRESSURE, SWITCH INCREASES HOT AND DECREASES COLD

BALANCED PRESSURE

COLD | HOT

HIGH HOT AND LOW COLD PRESSURE, SWITCH DECREASES HOT AND INCREASES COLD

WATER IS TEMPORARILY CUT OFF

COLD   HOT

COLD PRESSURE FAILURE, SWITCH CLOSES OUTLET

Guideline 21
All showerheads should be equipped with pressure balance/temperature regulator or temperature limiting device.

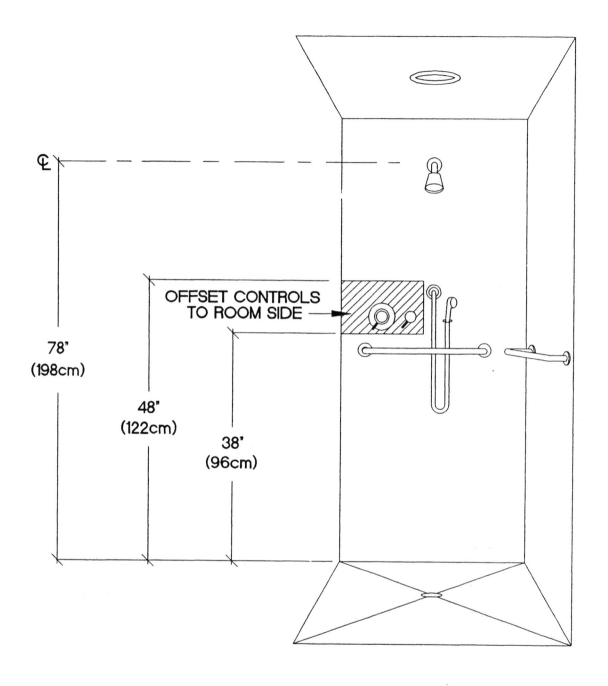

CL

78"
(198cm)

48"
(122cm)

38"
(96cm)

OFFSET CONTROLS
TO ROOM SIDE →

Guideline 22a
Shower controls should be accessible from inside and outside the fixture. Shower controls should be located between 38"-48" (96cm-122cm) above the floor (placed above the grab bar) and offset toward the room.

Guideline 22a Clarification A hand-held showerhead may be used in place of or in addition to a fixed showerhead. When mounted, a hand-held showerhead should be no higher than 48" (122cm) in its lowest position.

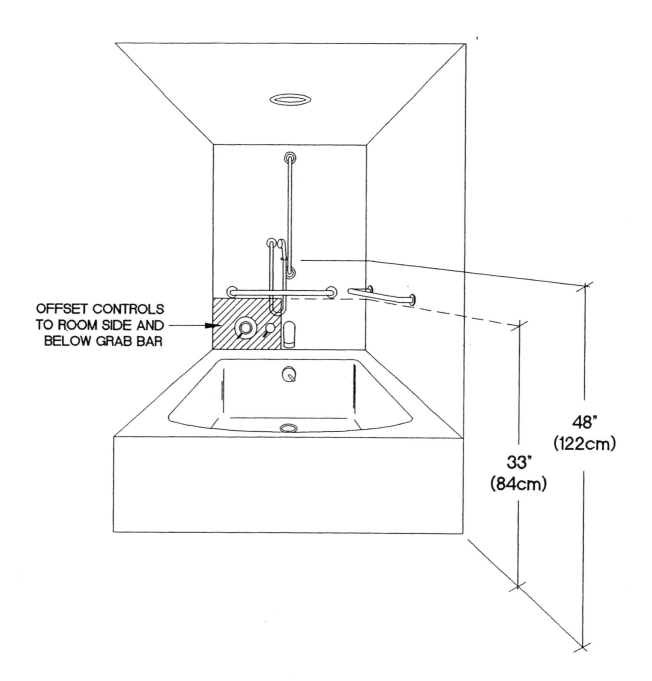

OFFSET CONTROLS
TO ROOM SIDE AND
BELOW GRAB BAR

48"
(122cm)

33"
(84cm)

Guideline 22b

Tub controls should be accessible from inside and outside the fixture. Tub controls should be located between the rim of the tub and 33" (84cm) above the floor, placed below the grab bar and offset toward the room.

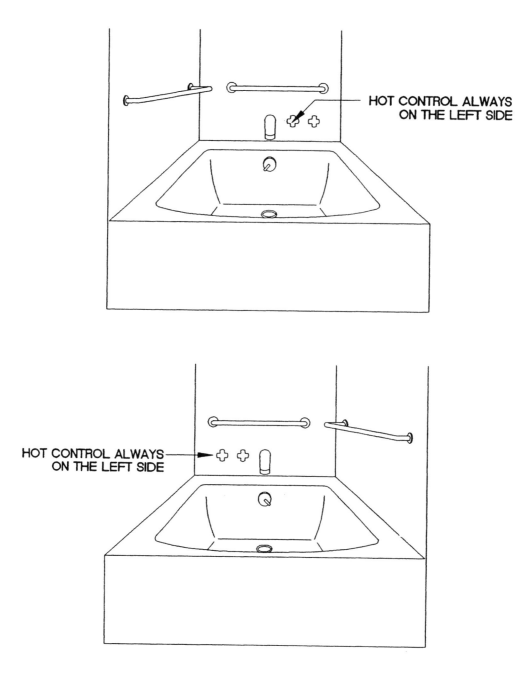

HOT CONTROL ALWAYS
ON THE LEFT SIDE

HOT CONTROL ALWAYS
ON THE LEFT SIDE

Guideline 22b Clarification If separate hot and cold controls are used in a bathtub (not permissible in a shower), for safe use the hot control is always on the left as viewed from inside the fixture.

SECTION 4
Toilets and Bidets

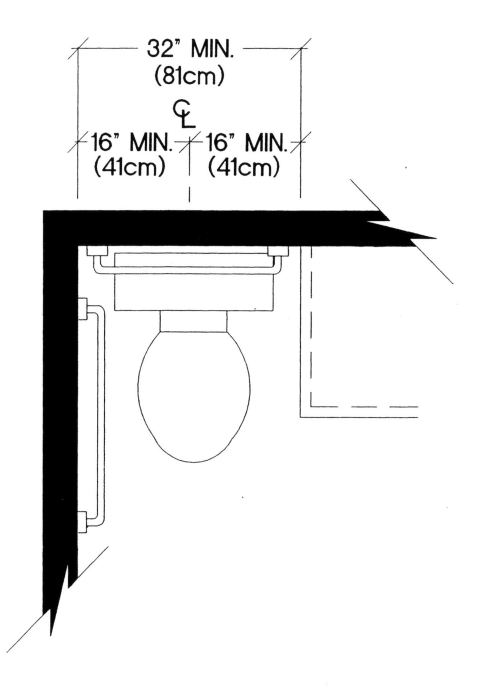

Guideline 23a
A minimum 16" (41cm) clearance should be allowed from the centerline of the toilet or bidet to any obstruction, fixture or equipment (except grab bars) on either side.

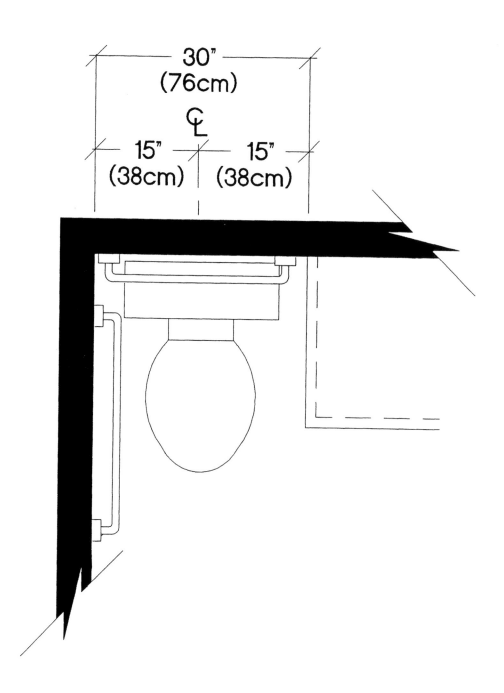

Guideline 23a Clarification While a designer should always try to meet this goal, physical constraints of a job site may require deviation from the guideline. If a 32" (81cm) clearance is unavailable, this space may be reduced to 30" (76cm). Be aware that this compromise may not allow for full use by all people.

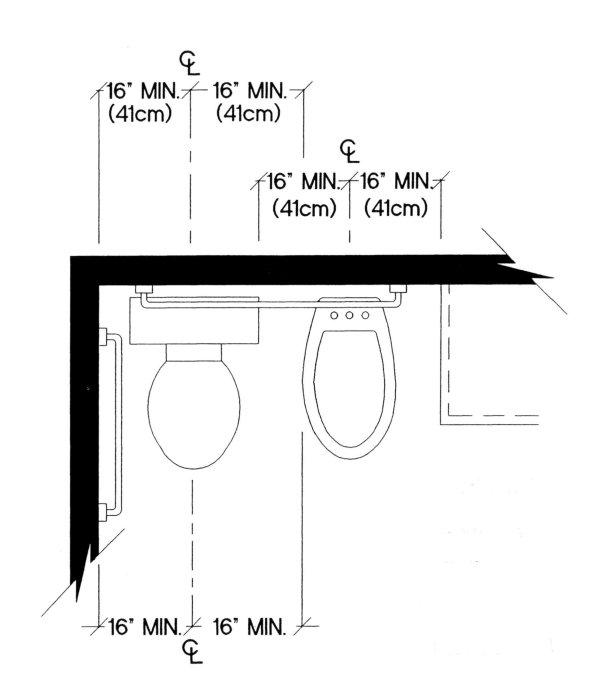

Guideline 23b
When the toilet and bidet are planned adjacent to one another, the 16" (41cm) minimum centerline clearance to all obstructions should be maintained.

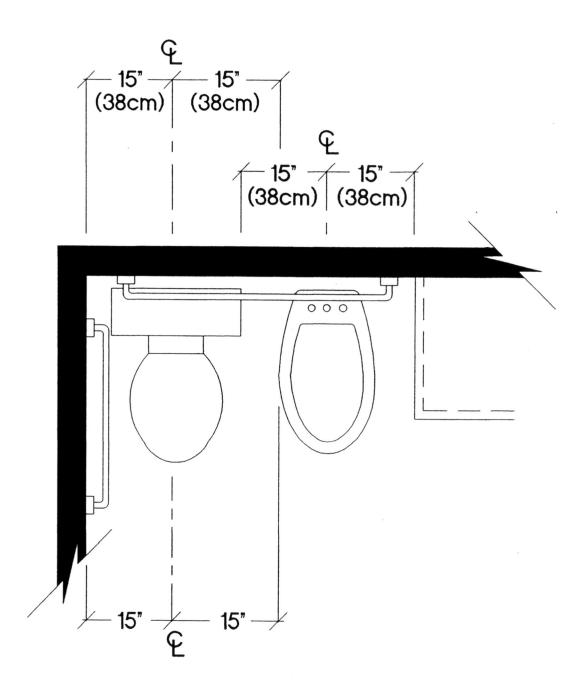

Guideline 23b Clarification While a designer should always try to meet this goal, physical constraints of a job site may require deviation from the guideline. If a 16" (41cm) centerline clearance to any obstruction is unavailable, this centerline clearance may be reduced to 15" (38cm). Be aware that this compromise may not allow for full use by all people.

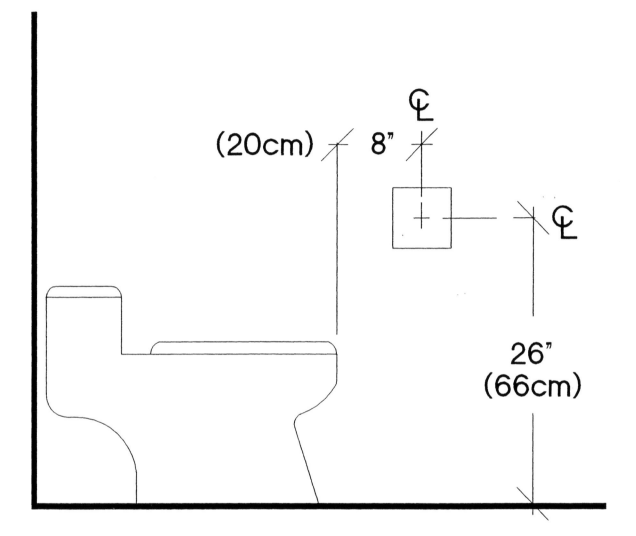

RECOMMENDED TOILET PAPER HOLDER LOCATION

Guideline 24

The toilet paper holder should be installed within reach of a person seated on the toilet. Ideal location is slightly in front of the edge of the toilet bowl, centered at 26" (66cm) above the floor.

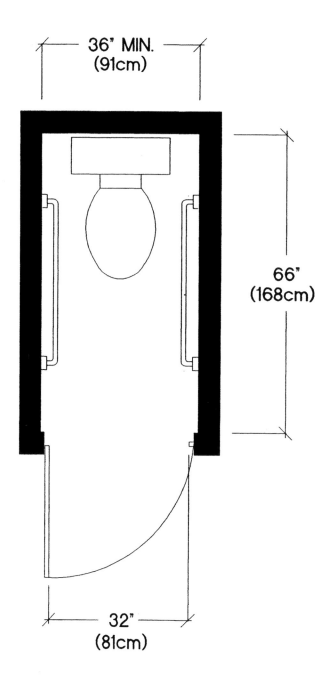

Guideline 25

Compartmental toilet areas should be a minimum 36" x 66" (91cm x 168cm) with a swing-out door or a pocket door.

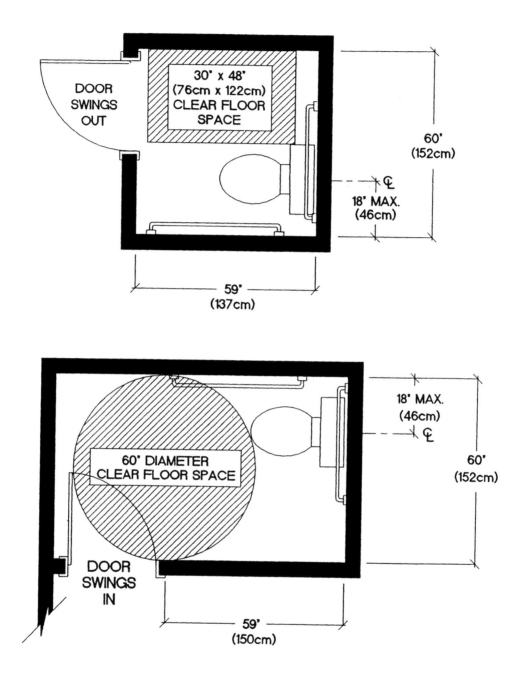

Guideline 25 Clarification The amount of space needed for a private toilet area will be affected by the mobility of the person using it.

SECTION 5
Grab Bars, Storage and Flooring

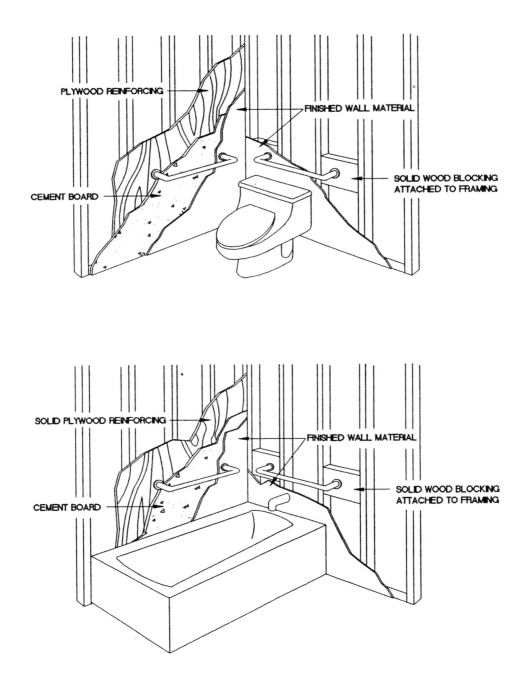

Guideline 26

Walls *should* be prepared (reinforced) to receive grab bars at the time of construction. Grab bars *should* also be installed in the bathtub, shower and toilet areas at the time of construction.

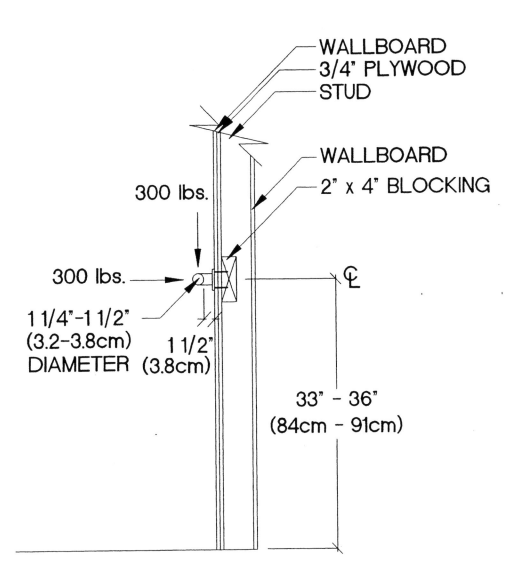

WALLBOARD
3/4" PLYWOOD
STUD

WALLBOARD
2" x 4" BLOCKING

300 lbs.

300 lbs.

1 1/4"-1 1/2"
(3.2-3.8cm)
DIAMETER

1 1/2"
(3.8cm)

₵

33" - 36"
(84cm - 91cm)

GRAB BAR SPECIFICATIONS

Guideline 26 Clarification 1 Reinforced areas must bear a static load of 300 lbs. (136kg). The use of cement board does not negate the need for blocking or plywood reinforcing.

Guideline 26 Clarification 2 Grab bars should be installed 33"-36" (84cm-91cm) above the floor, should be 1 1/4"-1 1/2" (3.2cm-3.8cm) diameter, extend 1 1/2" (3.8cm) from the wall, support a 300 lbs. (136kg) load, and they should have a slip-resistant surface. When shapes other than round are used for grab bars, the width of the largest point should not exceed 2" (5.1cm). Towel bars should not be substituted as grab bars.

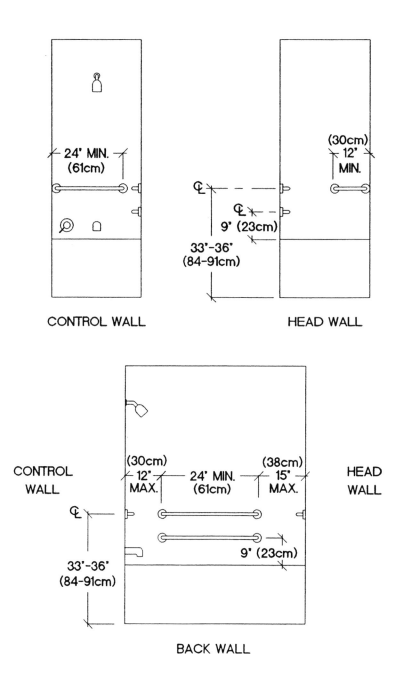

CONTROL WALL

HEAD WALL

BACK WALL

Guideline 26 Clarification 3 Grab bars in bathtub/shower areas should be at least 24" (61cm) wide on the control wall, at least 12" (30cm) wide on the head wall and at least 24" (61cm) wide on the back wall, beginning no more than 12" (30cm) from the control wall and no more than 15" (38cm) from the head wall. If a second grab bar is desired on the back wall, it should be located 9" (23cm) above the bathtub deck, the same width as the grab bar above it.

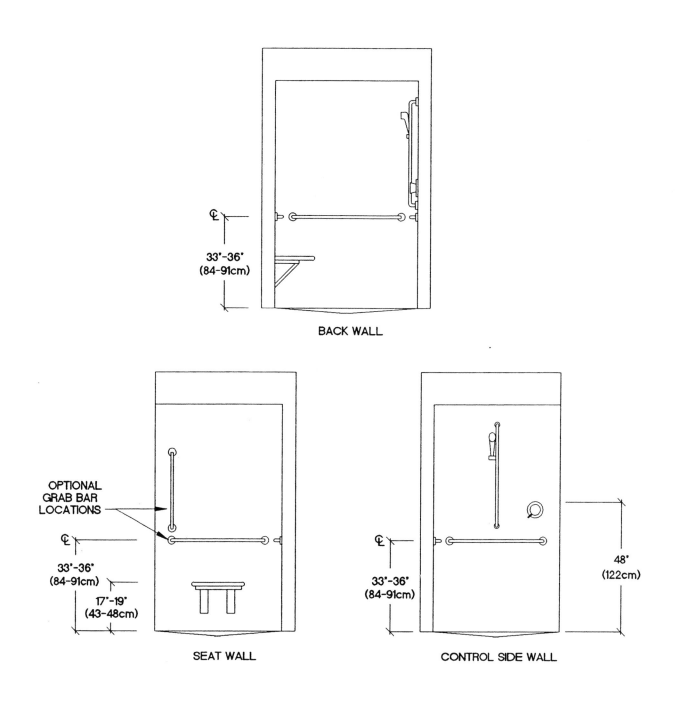

BACK WALL

OPTIONAL GRAB BAR LOCATIONS

33"-36"
(84-91cm)

17"-19"
(43-48cm)

SEAT WALL

33"-36"
(84-91cm)

48"
(122cm)

CONTROL SIDE WALL

Guideline 26 Clarification 4 Grab bars in shower stalls should be included on each surrounding wall (optional on wall where bench is located) and should be no more than 9" (23cm) shorter than the width of the wall to which they are attached.

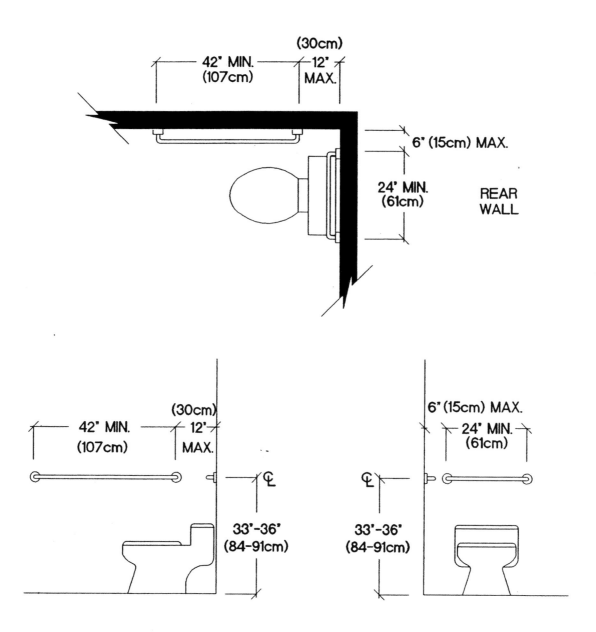

Guideline 26 Clarification 5a The first grab bar in the toilet area should be located on the side wall closest to the toilet, a maximum of 12" (30cm) from the rear wall. It should be at least 42" (107cm) wide. An optional secondary grab bar in the toilet area may be located on the rear wall, a maximum 6" (15cm) from the side wall. It should be at least 24" (61cm) wide.

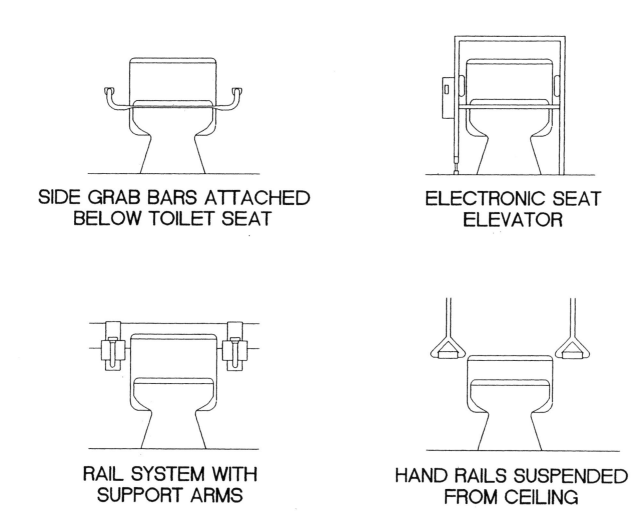

SIDE GRAB BARS ATTACHED
BELOW TOILET SEAT

ELECTRONIC SEAT
ELEVATOR

RAIL SYSTEM WITH
SUPPORT ARMS

HAND RAILS SUSPENDED
FROM CEILING

Guideline 26 Clarification 5b Alternatives for grab bars in the toilet area include, but are not limited to, side grab bars attached below the toilet seat, a rail system mounted to the back wall with perpendicular support arms at sides of the toilet seat, an electronic seat elevator or hand rails suspended from the ceiling.

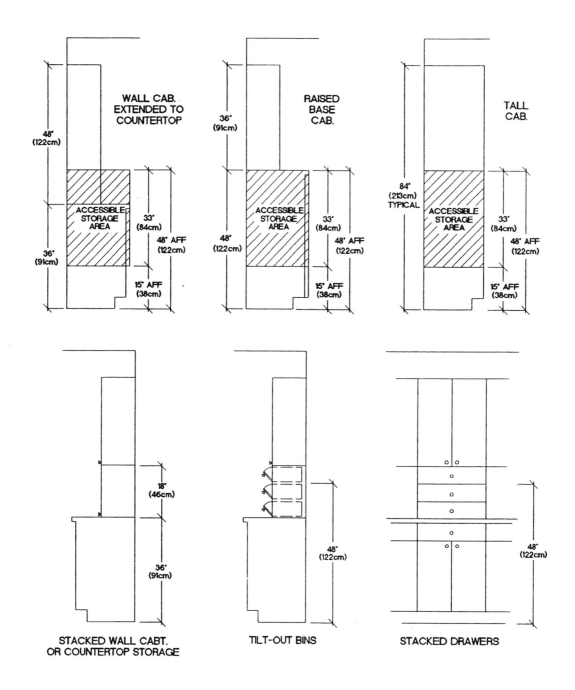

Guideline 27

Storage for toiletries, linens, grooming and general bathroom supplies should be provided within 15"-48" (38cm-122cm) above the floor.

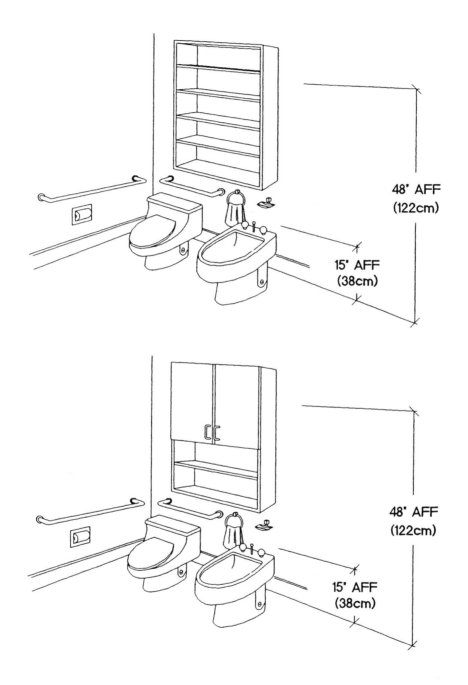

48" AFF
(122cm)

15" AFF
(38cm)

48" AFF
(122cm)

15" AFF
(38cm)

Guideline 28

Storage for soap, towels and other personal hygiene items should be installed within reach of a person seated on the bidet or toilet and within 15"-48" (38cm-122cm) above the floor. Storage areas should not interfere with the use of the fixture.

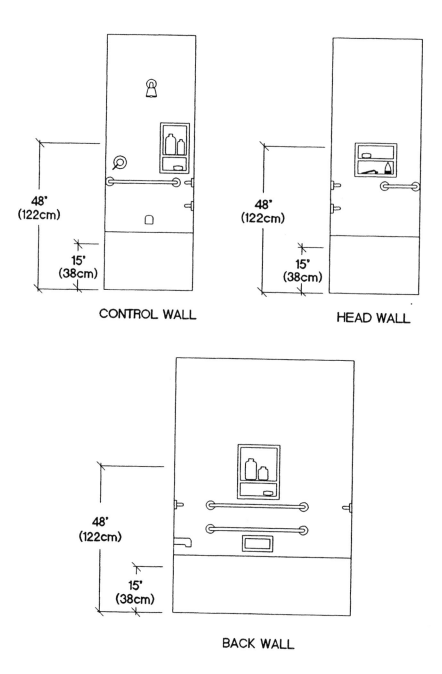

CONTROL WALL

HEAD WALL

BACK WALL

Guideline 29

In the tub/shower area, storage for soap and other personal hygiene items should be provided within 15"-48" (38cm-122cm) above the floor within the universal reach range.

Guideline 30
All flooring should be slip-resistant.

SECTION 6
Controls and Mechanical Systems

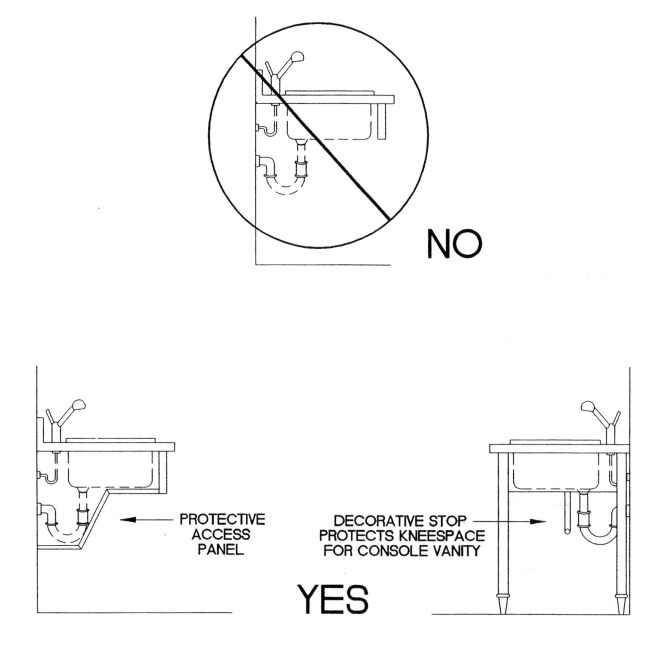

PROTECTIVE
ACCESS
PANEL

DECORATIVE STOP
PROTECTS KNEESPACE
FOR CONSOLE VANITY

NO

YES

Guideline 31

Exposed pipes and mechanicals should be covered by a protective panel or shroud. When using a console table, care must be taken to keep plumbing attractive and out of contact with a seated user.

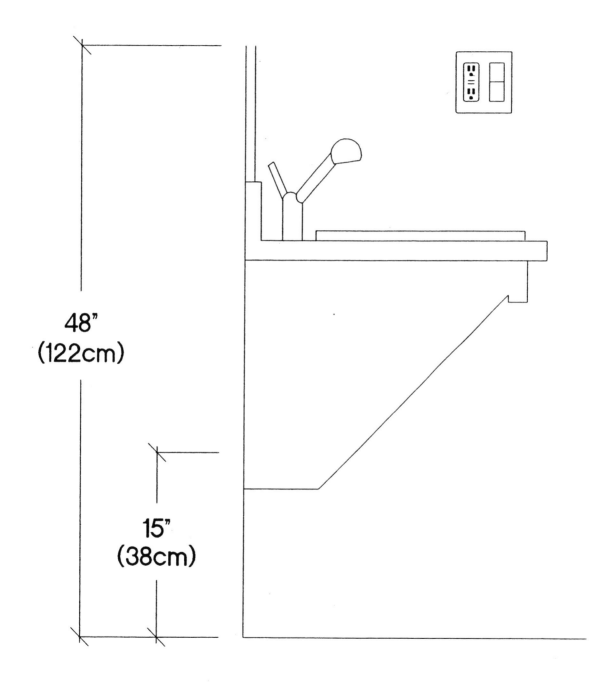

48"
(122cm)

15"
(38cm)

Guideline 32
Controls, dispensers, outlets and operating mechanisms should be 15"-48"
(38cm-122cm) above the floor and should be operable with a closed fist.

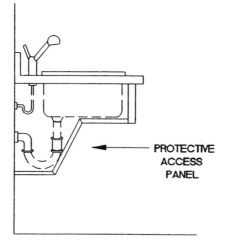

PROTECTIVE
ACCESS
PANEL

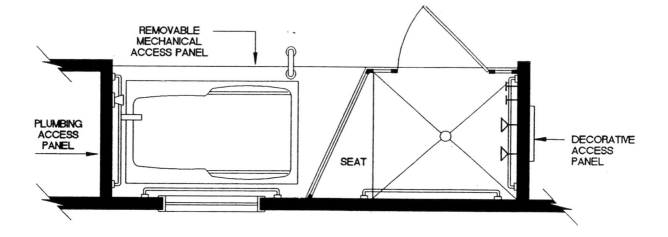

REMOVABLE
MECHANICAL
ACCESS PANEL

PLUMBING
ACCESS
PANEL

SEAT

DECORATIVE
ACCESS
PANEL

Guideline 33

All mechanical, electrical and plumbing systems should have access panels.

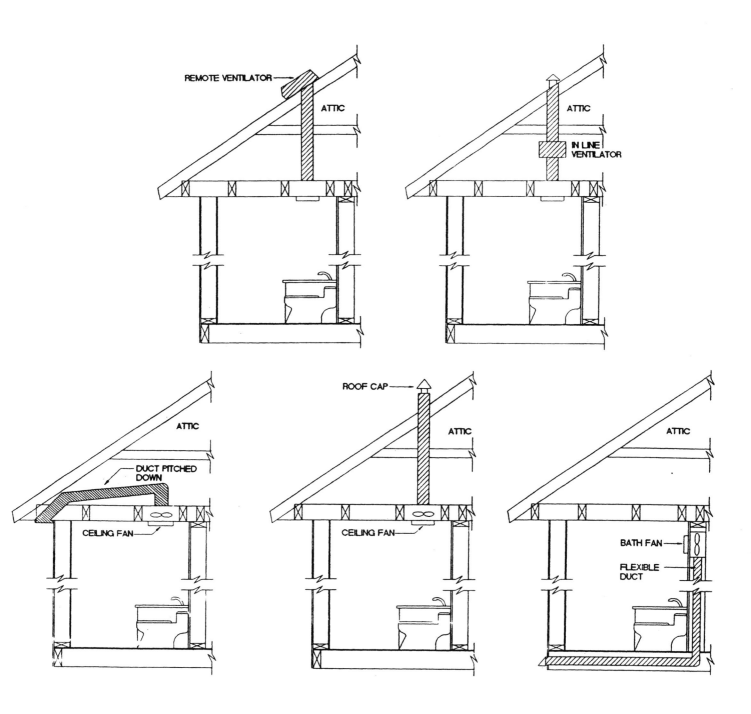

Guideline 34

Mechanical ventilation systems to the outside should be included in the plan to vent the entire room. The minimum size of the system can be calculated as follows:

$$\frac{\text{Cubic space (LxWxH) x 8 (changes of air per hour)}}{60 \text{ minutes}}$$
$$= \text{minimum cubic feet per minute (CFM)}$$

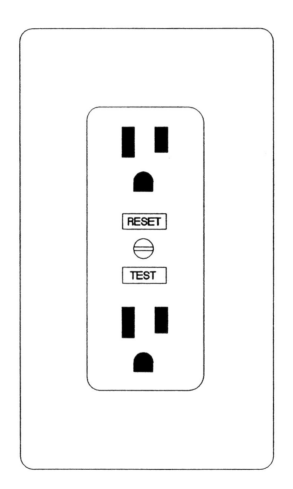

Guideline 35

Ground fault circuit interrupters must be specified on all receptacles, lights and switches in the bathroom. All light fixtures above the bathtub/shower units must be moisture-proof special-purpose fixtures.

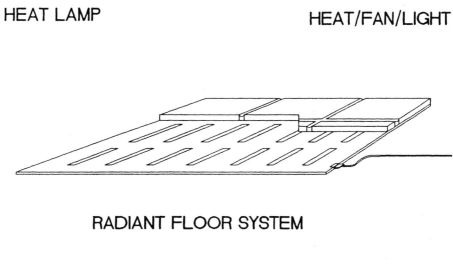

HEAT LAMP

HEAT/FAN/LIGHT

RADIANT FLOOR SYSTEM

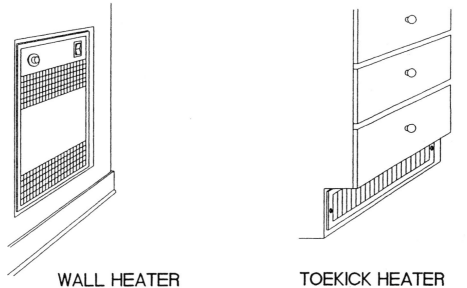

WALL HEATER

TOEKICK HEATER

Guideline 36

In addition to a primary heat source, auxiliary heating may be planned in the bathroom.

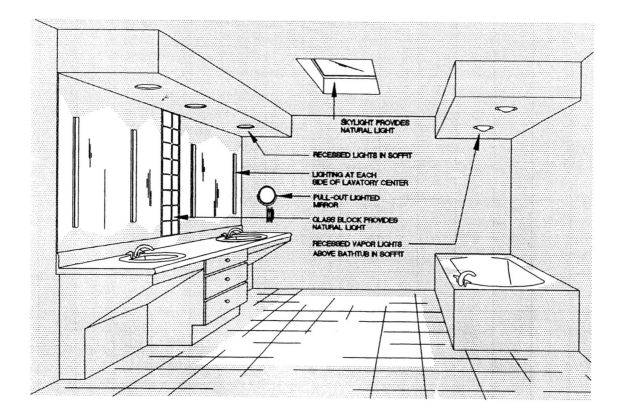

SKYLIGHT PROVIDES
NATURAL LIGHT

RECESSED LIGHTS IN SOFFIT

LIGHTING AT EACH
SIDE OF LAVATORY CENTER

PULL-OUT LIGHTED
MIRROR

GLASS BLOCK PROVIDES
NATURAL LIGHT

RECESSED VAPOR LIGHTS
ABOVE BATHTUB IN SOFFIT

Guideline 37

Every functional area in the bathroom should be well-illuminated by appropriate task lighting, night lights and/or general lighting. No lighting fixture, including hanging fixtures, should be within reach of a person seated or standing in the tub/ shower area.

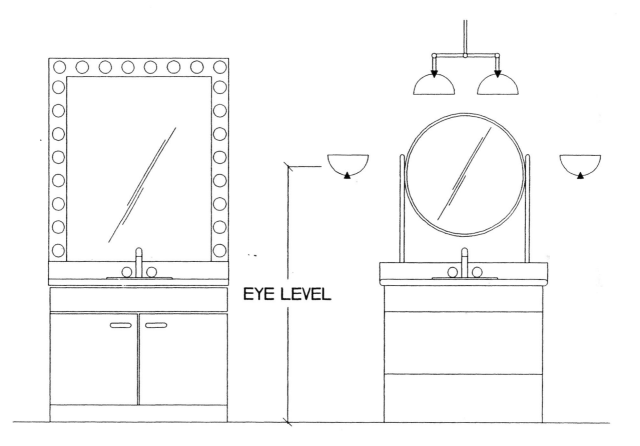

EYE LEVEL

Guideline 37 Clarification The vanity area should include both overhead and side lighting locations. Side lighting may be planned at eye level, which will be approximately 3" (7.6cm) below a user's overall height.

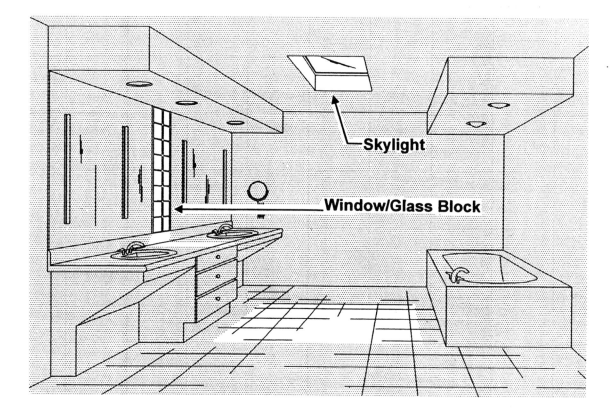

Skylight

Window/Glass Block

Guideline 38
When possible, bathroom lighting should include a window/skylight area equal to a minimum of 10% of the square footage of the bathroom.

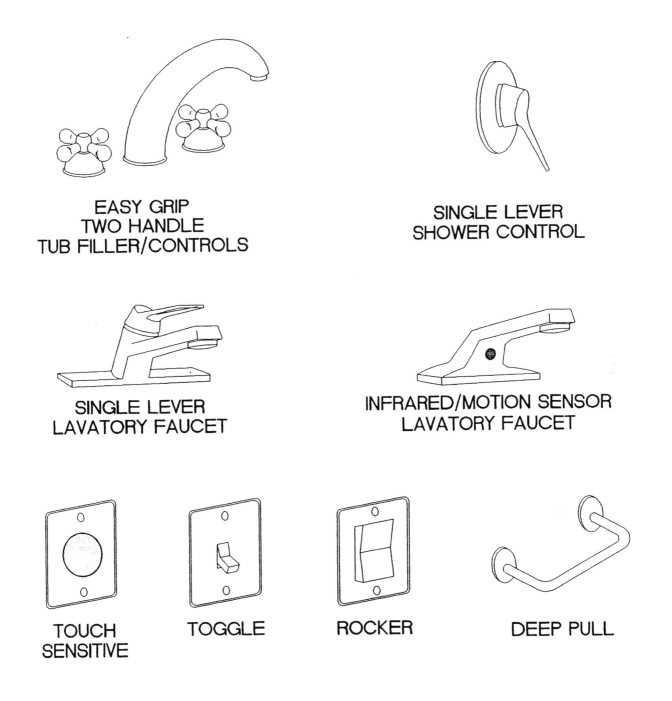

EASY GRIP
TWO HANDLE
TUB FILLER/CONTROLS

SINGLE LEVER
SHOWER CONTROL

SINGLE LEVER
LAVATORY FAUCET

INFRARED/MOTION SENSOR
LAVATORY FAUCET

TOUCH
SENSITIVE

TOGGLE

ROCKER

DEEP PULL

Guideline 39
Controls, handles and door/drawer pulls should be operable with one hand, require only a minimal amount of strength for operation, and should not require tight grasping, pinching or twisting of the wrist. (Includes handles, knobs/pulls on entry and exit doors, cabinets, drawers and plumbing fixtures, as well as light and thermostat controls/switches, intercoms, and other room controls.)

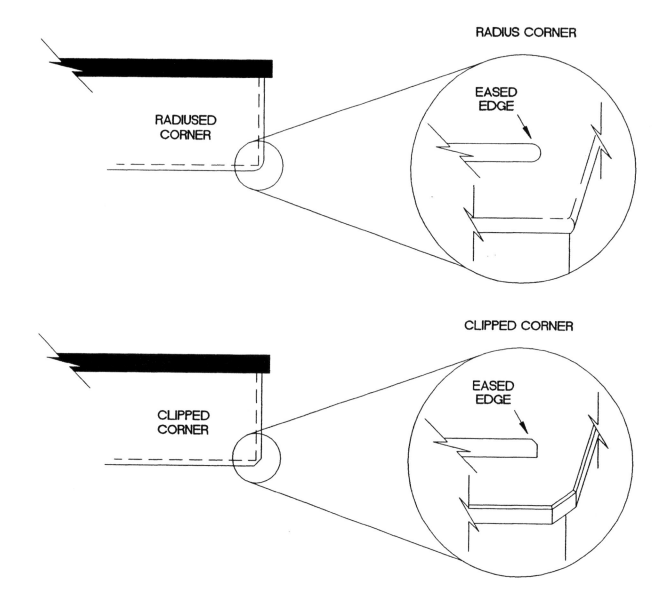

RADIUS CORNER

RADIUSED CORNER

EASED EDGE

CLIPPED CORNER

CLIPPED CORNER

EASED EDGE

Guideline 40

Use clipped or radius corners for open countertops. Countertop edges should be eased to eliminate sharp edges.

Guideline 41

Any glass used as a tub/shower enclosure, partition, or other glass application within 18" (46cm) of the floor should be one of three kinds of safety glazing: Laminated glass with a plastic interlayer, tempered glass or approved plastics such as those found in the model safety glazing code.

Notes:

How to Plan It and Lay It Out

Interview for Problems, then Create Solutions

There's no way to start laying out a bathroom without first doing the planning that has to go into it. And there's no way to start the planning without finding out what the customer wants, what the customer is able and willing to pay for, and the physical characteristics and limitations of the building and the space itself.

So it starts with the interview of the customer and inspection of the space.

Ideally, both of these will be done at the same time in the customer's home. Asking a customer to "bring in the measurements" is not always a good idea unless you go out and confirm them because the measurements can so easily be wrong, and the customer's measurements won't tell you where the water supply, waste lines or vents are located or what's behind the walls.

To facilitate the interview and help make sure it is complete, NKBA has a **"Bath Design Survey Form"** (copyrighted, for use by members only). Developed for a complete bathroom remodeling job, it has 13 pages.

If you are not a full-service bath design firm you might not use all of these pages.

NKBA members can modify them as

needed to fit their business. But following this kind of form is the only way to be sure of getting all of the information you might need.

The form covers:

1. General project information—Who, where, kind of work, appointments, directions, and any other professionals who might be involved (Fig. 6.1).

2. General client information—When the house was built, how long they have lived there, how they learned about your firm, desired time frame, budget range, who makes decisions (Fig. 6.2).

3. Specific bathroom questions—Type of bathroom, who uses it, when, grooming and other habits that apply, any physical limitations of family members (Fig. 6.3).

4. Design information—Styling, colors, design features of adjacent rooms, ideas they might have clipped (Fig. 6.4).

5. Storage checklist—Even the smallest room needs storage, and you must know what is important to them to customize properly (Fig. 6.5).

6. Project specs—Kind of cabinets they like, counter materials, surfaces, kinds of fixtures, ventilation, heat, accessories, exercise equipment (Figs. 6.6-6.10).

7. Construction details—House itself, location of bathroom, joist direction, walls, windows, piping, sewerage, vents, wiring (Fig. 6.11).

8. Existing dimensioning—Schematic drawings making it easy to fill in all pertinent measurements of existing fixtures and details (Figs. 6.12, 6.13).

At the jobsite: Inspect and measure

Before going through the form, let's consider our procedure for getting the information.

First, we must make the appointment to visit the home. These appointments often are at night when all interested parties will be at home. We know we want to inspect the house inside and outside, and the neighborhood generally.

In the summer, a night appointment will still be in daylight. But in winter it will be dark, and that might necessitate a pre-appointment walk-by while there is enough daylight to see.

Our look at the neighborhood can give us a little more feel for how affluent this customer is and how much money is reasonable for the investment they are about to make.

In looking at the house we want to see where the vent stacks are, because they have to be within specific distances from the fixtures. We want to note chimney locations, because inside the house their reason for being might be long gone but the chimney will remain in the wall where we might want to put supply or drain pipes. We want to note the wall construction and siding, because we may want to put a vent outlet through it. We want to look for any detail that might affect the job we will want to do.

Inside the house we will establish rapport and conduct the interview, following our NKBA form, until we reach the page on "Existing Construction Details." At this point we have all of the information we need from the homeowner and must start inspecting the bathroom space and the inside of the house.

First, go to the basement and/or attic.

• **Note where the water supply pipes are.**

• **Note where the drains are.**

• **Are there rooms above and below the bathroom?**

• **What is the condition of the walls and floors?**

• **What direction do the floor and ceiling joists run?**

• **What kind of windows and doors does the house have, and can they be moved?**

• **Where is the wiring, and what is its condition?**

• **Where do the ducts run, and will they affect any proposed work on the bathroom walls?**

• **Can you get equipment (such as a new bathtub) to and into the bathroom?**

All of this must be entered on the survey form. **Then you get to one of the most important jobs you will do: Measuring the space.**

Don't accept the homeowner's assurance that "I have already measured it." You must do it yourself. You have to concentrate, without any distraction, so invite the client to look at literature while you measure.

Add a sheet of graph paper to your survey form on which you can sketch the room. It is not enough just to have the figures. You need a picture of it.

Notes:

You will need a carpenter's square and a good rule. Most designers prefer a carpenter's folding rule to a steel tape, because the tape is flexible and can sag in the middle. Also, with a steel tape you must add the length of the case to some measurements, and it is easy to forget.

Measure at a height of 30" to 36" (76-91 cm) above the floor.

Where there is a window or door, measure to the framing, measure the framing, and measure the door or window. If there is an offset, measure to it and then measure the amount of offset. When you complete one wall, add up all the elements and then make an overall wall-to-wall measurement. Make sure your total of elements is equal to the overall measurement.

Use the square to make sure every corner is truly square. Usually it won't be.

Use the 3-4-5 rule to see how much it is out of square. To do this, measure 3' (91 cm) along one wall and make a mark. Measure 4' (122 cm) along the adjacent wall and make a mark. The distance between marks (the hypotenuse of a right triangle) should be precisely 5' (152 cm).

If it is more than that, the wall goes out. If it is less, the wall comes in. If you have a countertop that goes wall to wall it will have to fit the lesser measurement, unless you can shave the wall.

But still, you must allow at least a quarter-inch (.6 cm) of clearance, because there is no way you can install a counter if it fits precisely. If access is limited, it may be necessary to bring the counter in and fabricate or assemble it in the room.

Now let's go through the survey form, starting on page 140.

BATH DESIGN SURVEY FORM

Name: _____

Residence Address: _____

_____

Jobsite Address: _____

_____

Phone: _____

Work: _____

Work: _____

Date: _____

Designer: _____

Appointment:

Scheduled: _____

Call When Ready: _____

Times Available: _____

Directions: _____

Allied Professionals:

Name: _____

Firm: _____

Address: _____

Phone: _____

Fig. 6.1. Cover sheet must include addresses of residence and jobsite—they might differ. It should include phone numbers where any involved parties can be reached, and appointment scheduling to remind you. Also, there might be a builder or a designer involved, or some other professional, and you should know about this from the start.

General Client Information

1. How long have you lived at, or how much time do you spend at the jobsite residence?_____

2. When was the house built?_____ How old is the present bathroom? _____

3. How did you learn about our firm?_____

4. When would you like to start the project?_____

5. When would you like the project to be completed?_____
_____

6. Has anyone assisted you in preparing a design for the bathroom? _____
_____

7. Do you plan on retaining an interior designer or architect to assist in the bathroom planning?_____
_____

8. Do you have a specific builder/contractor or other subcontractor/specialist with whom you would like to work? _____
_____

9. What portion of the project, if any, will be your responsibility?_____
_____

10. What budget range have you established for your bathroom project?_____

11. How long do you intend to own the jobsite residence?_____

12. What are your plans regarding this home? _____
    a. Is it a long or short-term investment?_____
    b. Is return on investment a primary concern? _____
    c. Do you plan on renting the jobsite residence in the future? _____

13. What family members will share in the final decision-making process?_____
_____

14. Would you like our firm to assist you in securing project financing? _____ Yes _____ No

15. What do you dislike most about your present bathroom? _____
_____
_____

16. What do you like about your present bathroom? _____
_____
_____

1

BMF7

Fig. 6.2. General client information must include construction information. It also should include where they heard about your firm, a time frame and a rough idea of their budget.

Specific Bathroom Questions

1. Is this a master _____ , children _____ , or guest _____ bath project?

2. How many bathrooms are in the home?_____
   _____

3. Who will use the bathroom?_____

4. What is the primary time of day that the bathroom is used? _____

5. On an average, how long does each user stay in the bathroom?_____
   _____

6. How many family members will use the bathroom at one time?_____

7. Have you considered privacy zoning to allow several users to occupy the space at one time? _____

8. Do you prefer separate showering and bathing areas?_____

9. Would you like to consider either a tub or shower that will accommodate more than one person?_____

10. Do you prefer that the water closet and/or bidet be separated from the other fixtures, and placed in its own compartment? _____

11. What activities will take place in the bathroom?

Applying Make-up/	Dressing _____	Reading/Lounging_____	Water Relax
Hair Care _____	Exercising _____	Showering _____	1. Sauna _____
Bathing _____	Laundering _____	Su____	2. Steam _____
			3. Whirlpool _____

12. What appliances do you plan on using in the bathroom?

Bar Sink _____	Curling ____	Microwa__	Towel Warmer:
Blowdryer:	Electric ____	__dio _____	Hydronic _____
Hand-Held ____	Toothbrush ____	__igerat__	Electric _____
Wallmount ____	Hot Plate ____	__vision _____	
Coffeemaker ____	Hot Rollers ____	Other _____	

13. Other: _____

14. Family Member Characteristics:

Name	Age	Handed (left or right)	Height	Physical Limitations

BMF7

Fig. 6.3. Now you know about the building and the family. It is time for specific bathroom questions that will tell you about who will use the bathroom and their activities there.

Design Information

1. What type of feeling would you like your new bathroom space to have?

   Sleek/Contemporary _____ Welcoming/Country _____ Traditional _____

   Strictly Functional _____ An Adult Retreat Feeling _____ Other _____

2. What colors are you considering for your new bathroom? _____

3. What colors do you like _____ and dislike_____ ?

4. What are color preferences of other family members?_____

5. How important is it to you that the bathroom flow to adjacent spaces, from a design similarity standpoint?_____

   _____

6. Can the bathroom make its own individual design statement? _____

7. Have you made a sketch or collected pictures of ideas for your new bathroom? _____

8. Design Notes:

   _____

   _____

   _____

   _____

   _____

   _____

   _____

   _____

   _____

   _____

   _____

   _____

Fig. 6.4. The fixtures you specify will insure that the bathroom functions well, but you need design information to make sure it also looks right to the customer and that the customer will be proud of it. Make all the notes you need here.

Storage Checklist

1. Clothing Closets   Yes_____ No_____   Shelf Length: His_____ Hers _____
   Double Pole _____ Single Pole _____

2. Laundry Facilities   Yes_____ No_____   Equipment Size _____

3. Plant Area, Sunning Space   Yes_____ No_____   Size _____

4. Medicine Storage   Yes_____ No_____   Shelf Length _____

5. Bath Linen Storage   Yes_____ No_____   Shelf Length _____

6. Bathroom Paper Product Storage   Yes_____ No_____   Shelf Length _____

7. Shoe Polishing Paraphernalia Storage   Yes_____ No_____   Shelf Length _____

8. Cleaning Supply Storage   Yes_____ No_____   Shelf Length _____

9. Hair Grooming Equipment Storage   Yes_____ No_____   For Whom _____
   What type or equipment _____
   _____
   _____ Shelf Length _____

10. Hand and Foot Grooming Storage   Yes_____ No_____   For Whom _____
    What type of equipment _____
    _____
    _____ Shelf Length _____

11. Personal Hygiene Equipment Storage   Yes_____ No_____   For Whom _____

12. Make-up and Shaving Equipment Storage   Yes_____ No_____   For Whom _____
    What type of equipment _____
    _____

13. Personal Pampering Item Storage   Yes_____ No_____   For Whom _____
    What type of equipment _____
    _____
    _____ Shelf Length _____

14. Other_____
    _____
    _____
    _____
    _____
    _____
    _____
    _____
    _____

BMF7

Fig. 6.5. The storage checklist is important whether you are working with a small space or a large one. Whatever the space available, you will have to provide places to put things both for momentary use and for the long run.

Project Specifications

Category	Source					Description
	Furn By		Install By			
	Use Exist	BS	O/OA	BS	O/OA	Check Appropriate Space(s)
Cabinetry						_____ Wood Species _____ Decorative Lam. _____ Steel _____ Other Accessories _____
Countertops						_____ Wood _____ Decorative Lam. _____ Marble _____ Cultured Marble _____ Granite _____ Solid Surface _____ Tile _____ Size _____ Grout _____ Countertop Ext. over Water Closet Backsplash: Height _____ Edge Treatment _____ End Splash Sides _____
Fascia/Soffit						_____ Open _____ Flush _____ Extended _____ Recessed _____ Wallpaper _____ Paint _____ Wood _____ Lighted _____ Gallery Rail Other _____
Bath Fixtures Fittings & Finishes Water Closet						_____ 1 Piece _____ 2 Piece _____ Wall Hung _____ High Flush Tank _____ Elongated _____ Round _____ Handicapped Color _____ Trip Lever Finish _____ Stop & Supply Finish _____
Bidet						_____ Vert. Spray _____ Horiz. Spray Color _____ Faucet Finish _____ Vacuum Breaker _____
Tub						_____ Cast Iron _____ Steel _____ Fiberglass _____ Acrylic _____ Ceramic Tile _____ Whirlpool _____ Cult. Marble _____ Skirted _____ Platform _____ Platform w/steps _____ Left Drain _____ Right Drain _____ Other Color _____ Whirlpool Access _____ Waste & Overflow Finish _____ Fitting Type _____ Finish _____ Fitting Location _____

KEY   BS = Bathroom Specialist   O = Owner   OA = Owner's Agent

BMF7

Fig. 6.6. Project specs are provided for by category. This must be complete especially if others in your firm do the drawings or purchasing. Everything must be listed, so this part of the survey has five pages.

Category	Source					Description
		Furn By		Install By		
	Use Exist	BS	O/OA	BS	O/OA	Check Appropriate Space(s)
Bath Fixtures (Continued) Shower						_____ 1 Piece _____ Multiple Piece Shower Wall Material _____ Shower Floor Material _____ Shower Valve #1 Type _____ Shower Valve #2 Type _____ Shower Head #1 Type _____ Shower Head #2 Type _____ Body Sprays _____ Hand-Held Showers _____ Diverter _____ Shower Drain _____ Finish _____ Grooming Recess _____ Size _____ Bench _____ Size _____ Other _____
Lavatory						_____ Pedestal/ _____ Wall-Hung Trap Cover _____ Rimmed _____ Self-Rimmed _____ Under-Counter _____ Integral _____ 4" Centers _____ 8" Centers _____ Single Hole No. of Bowls _____ Size _____ Adjacent to one another? _____ Separate from one another? _____ Both in bathroom? _____ One located outside of bathroom? _____ Color _____ Fitting Type _____ Finish _____ Drilling Spread _____
Ventilation						_____ Fan _____ Fan, Light (Combo) _____ Fan, Light, Heat (Combo) _____ Switch _____ Timer CFM Capacity _____ Duct Work Space _____
Heat Lamp						_____ Switch _____ Timer Placement _____
Enclosures (Steam Door/s, Shower Doors, Drapes, Etc.)						_____ Tub _____ Shower _____ Steam Finish _____ Size _____ Type _____ Material _____ Curtain Rod Finish _____ Size _____ Curtain(s) Color _____ Size _____
Light Fixtures						_____ Incandescent _____ Fluorescent _____ Vapor Proof _____ Halogen

BMF7

Fig. 6.7. Project Specifications (cont.)

Category	Source					Description
	Use Exist	Furn. By		Install By		Check appropriate space(s)
		BS	O/OA	BS	O/OA	
Accessories Glass Shelves Medicine Cabinet, Mirror						_____ Surface Mt. _____ Recessed Size _____ Color _____ Mirror Size _____ Shelf Size _____ Edge Treatment _____
Towel Bars						Finish _____ Size _____ No. _____
Towel Rings						Finish _____ Size _____ No. _____
Robe Hooks						Finish _____ Size _____ No. _____
Tub Soap Dish						_____ Surface Mt. _____ Recessed Finish _____ Placement _____
Shower Soap Dish						_____ Surface Mt. _____ Recessed Finish _____ Placement _____
Bidet Soap Dish						_____ Surface Mt. _____ Recessed Finish _____ Placement _____
Lavatory Soap Dish						_____ Surface Mt. _____ Recessed Finish _____ Placement _____
Tub/Shower Grab Bars						Finish _____ Placement _____
Paper Holder						_____ Surface Mt. _____ Recessed Finish _____ Placement _____
Magazine Rack						_____ Surface Mt. _____ Recessed Finish _____ Placement _____
Soap/Lotion Dispenser						Finish _____ Placement _____
Tumbler						Finish _____ Placement _____
Tissue Holder						Finish _____ Placement _____
Scale						Finish _____ Placement _____
Toothbrush Holder						Finish _____ Placement _____
Hamper						Finish _____ Placement _____
Windows and Doors Windows						Casing: _____ Match Existing _____ Finish _____ Replace All _____ Finish _____ Size _____ Profile Size _____ Finish _____ _____ Slider _____ Bow _____ Casement _____ Bay _____ Double-Hung _____ Support _____ Skylight _____ Roof Other _____ Exterior Wall Patch _____ Sink Vent Relocation _____ Pass-Thru Surfacing _____ New Window Sizes: _____ #1 _____ Screen _____ #2 _____ Screen _____ #3 _____ Screen _____ #4 _____ Screen _____

BMF7

Fig. 6.8. Project Specifications (cont.)

Category	Source					Description
	Furn By		Install By			
	Use Exist	BS	O/OA	BS	O/OA	Check Appropriate Space(s)
Doors						Casing _____ Match Existing _____ Finish _____ Replace All _____ Finish _____ Size _____ Profile New Doors: _____ Solid Core Size _____ _____ Hinge _____ Screen _____ _____ Steel Size _____ _____ Hinge _____ Screen _____ _____ Hollow Core Size _____ Hinge _____ _____ Bifold Size _____ Hinge _____ _____ Pocket Size _____ Hinge _____ _____ Accordian Size _____ Hinge _____ Other _____ Ext. Wall/Floor Patch _____ Hardware: Finish _____ _____ Passage _____ Knob _____ Privacy _____ Lever
Flooring						_____ Carpet _____ Vinyl _____ Marble _____ Wood _____ Tile _____ Size _____ Grout _____ Other _____ _____ Underlayment _____ Sub Floor _____ Water Damage _____ Baseboards _____ Threshholds _____
Decorative Surfaces Wall Covering						Wall Material _____ Ceiling Material _____ Tub Walls & Ceiling _____ Shower Walls & Ceiling _____ Water Damage _____
Window Treatment						_____ Horiz. Blind _____ Vert. Blind _____ Woven Wood _____ Draperies _____ Shade _____ Roman Shade _____ Shutters _____ Greenhouse _____ Other _____
Sauna						Capacity _____ Interior _____ Style _____ Heater _____ Timer Location _____ Wall Material _____ Floor Material _____
Steam Bath						_____ Tub _____ Shower Steam Generator Location _____ Timer Location _____ Wall Material _____ Floor Material _____

BMF7

Fig. 6.9. Project Specifications (cont.)

Category	Source					Description
		Furn By		Install By		
	Use Exist	BS	O/OA	BS	O/OA	Check Appropriate Space(s)
Exercise Equipment						Types
Construction Electrical						
Plumbing						
General Carpentry Demolition						
Trash Removal						
Structural Changes						
Installation						
Other						

Miscellaneous Information _____

_____

_____

_____

_____

_____

BMF7

Fig. 6.10. Project Specifications (cont.)

Existing Construction Details

Construction:

    Construction of House: ☐ Single Story ☐ Multi Story   Style of house _____

    Room above or below bathroom: _____

    Condition and covering of walls: _____

                     floors: _____

                  ceilings: _____

              soffit/fascia: _____

    Squareness of corners _____ Parallel walls to within 3/4" _____

    Construction of Floor: ☐ Slab ☐ Frame

    Direction of floor joist: ☐ Parallel to longest wall ☐ Perpendicular to longest wall   Joist Height _____

    Exterior: ☐ Brick ☐ Aluminum ☐ Stucco ☐ Wood ☐ Other

    Interior: ☐ Drywall ☐ Lath & Plaster ☐ Wood ☐ Stone/Brick

    Windows can be changed: ☐ Yes ☐ No

    Windows: ☐ Sliders ☐ Double-Hung ☐ Skylights ☐ Casement ☐ Greenhouse

    Doors can be relocated: ☐ Yes ☐ No

    Location of walls can be changed: ☐ Yes ☐ No   Direction of load bearing partition _____

    Sewage System: ☐ City Service ☐ Septic System ☐ Other

    Type of roof material _____ of roof

    Household heating/cooling system _____ home _____

Access:

    Can equipment fit into room? _____

        Basement _____ Crawl Space _____ Attic _____

    Material Storage _____ Trash Collection Area _____

Plumbing:

    Location of existing vent stack _____ Type of trap_____

Electrical:

    GFCI existing: ☐ Yes ☐ No

    New wiring access: ☐ Hard ☐ Average ☐ Easy

    Existing electrical service capacity _____ The following # of 120V circuits available: _____

    The following # of 240V circuits available: _____

    Can the location of the fixtures be changed?

    Water Closet ☐ Yes ☐ No   Bidet ☐ Yes ☐ No

    Lavatory #1 ☐ Yes ☐ No   Lavatory #2 ☐ Yes ☐ No

    Bathtub ☐ Yes ☐ No   Shower ☐ Yes ☐ No

Miscellaneous Information: _____

_____

_____

BMF7

Fig. 6.11. You must know details of existing construction, piping, wiring, whether you have rooms or crawl space above and below, and what you can change or relocate.

Existing Wall Elevation Dimensioning

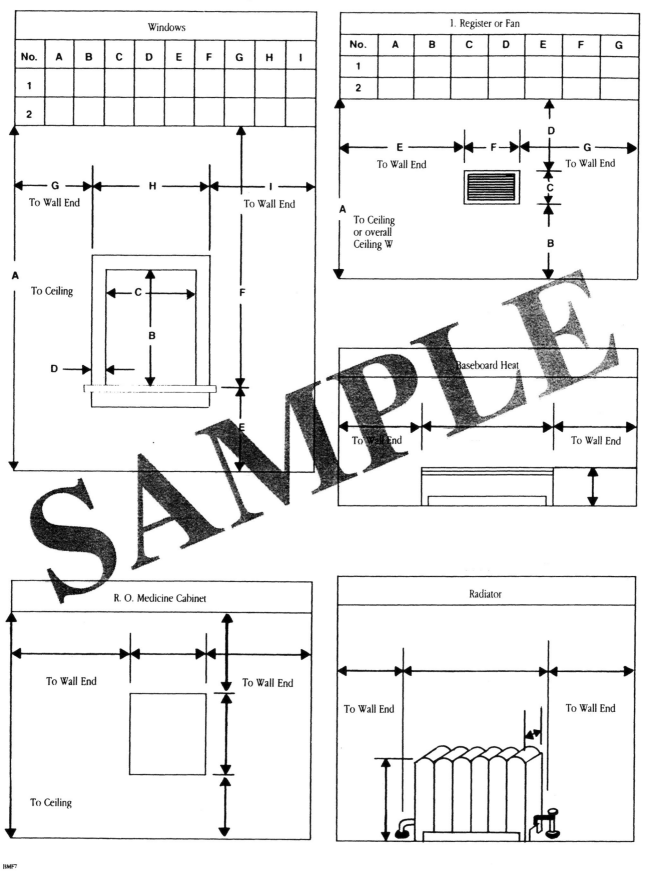

Windows

No.	A	B	C	D	E	F	G	H	I
1									
2									

1. Register or Fan

No.	A	B	C	D	E	F	G
1							
2							

Baseboard Heat

R. O. Medicine Cabinet

Radiator

BMF7

Fig. 6.12. Measurements of existing walls, windows and other elements can be recorded easily on this page without the need to draw a sketch.

Existing Fixture Dimensioning

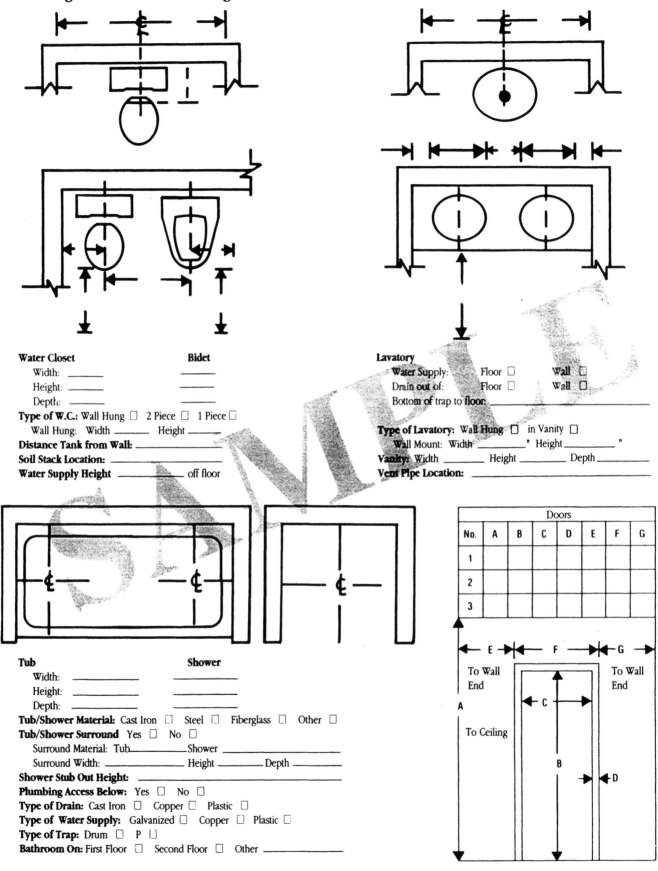

Water Closet   **Bidet**

     Width: _____   _____

     Height: _____   _____

     Depth: _____   _____

Type of W.C.: Wall Hung ☐   2 Piece ☐   1 Piece ☐

     Wall Hung: Width _____ Height _____

Distance Tank from Wall: _____

Soil Stack Location: _____

Water Supply Height _____ off floor

Lavatory

     Water Supply: Floor ☐   **Wall** ☐

     Drain out of: Floor ☐   Wall ☐

     Bottom of trap to floor: _____

Type of Lavatory: Wall Hung ☐   in Vanity ☐

     Wall Mount: Width _____" Height _____"

Vanity: Width _____ Height _____ Depth _____

Vent Pipe Location: _____

Tub   **Shower**

     Width: _____   _____

     Height: _____   _____

     Depth: _____

Tub/Shower Material: Cast Iron ☐   Steel ☐   Fiberglass ☐   Other ☐

Tub/Shower Surround   Yes ☐   No ☐

     Surround Material: Tub _____ Shower _____

     Surround Width: _____ Height _____ Depth _____

Shower Stub Out Height: _____

Plumbing Access Below: Yes ☐   No ☐

Type of Drain: Cast Iron ☐   Copper ☐   Plastic ☐

Type of Water Supply: Galvanized ☐   Copper ☐   Plastic ☐

Type of Trap: Drum ☐   P ☐

Bathroom On: First Floor ☐   Second Floor ☐   Other _____

Doors							
No.	A	B	C	D	E	F	G
1							
2							
3							

BMF7

Fig. 6.13. It is necessary also to note sizes and placement of all existing fixtures.

Using the survey data

Once you have all the information you need written in the survey form, you can plan the bathroom in your office.

You plan it to meet five human needs: Sanitation, utility, grooming, comfort and aesthetics.

• **Sanitation**—This need is fulfilled by the bathroom fixtures. (Figs. 6.6-6.8).

• **Utility**—This need can be satisfied by providing the right kinds of storage at the best possible places for the space available. Space is needed for towels, medicines, toiletries, electrical appliances, grooming aids, personal hygiene items, cosmetics, cleaning supplies and freestanding accessories. (Figs. 6.3, 6.5.)

When planning small bathrooms, divide the customer's storage needs into primary and secondary zones. Determine which items can be stored in the bathroom and which ones can be stored in adjacent or nearby areas. It might be possible to borrow space from adjacent bedrooms or small closets (Fig. 6.14).

Note particularly the need for counter or shelf space when the customer chooses a pedestal or wall-hung lav that has no space around the sides of the bowl. At the very least, a shelf will be needed on the wall behind the lav. This could be part of the medicine cabinet.

• **Grooming**—This refers to such activities as shaving, application of cosmetics, and combing or styling the hair. They require adequate mirrors, electrical outlets and lighting (Fig. 6.3).

Questions to be addressed are:

1. What type of lighting, fluorescent or incandescent?

2. How much lighting, and where?

3. Is a separate make-up area advisable?

Fig. 6.14. Proper storage space must be provided in the bathroom or nearby. Often creative use of cabinetry can keep most items in the bathroom. These mirrored cabinets are stackable. (Robern photo)

• **Comfort**—This has many facets. It concerns the individual's preferences and habits, such as soaking, reading or relaxing.

An important factor in overall comfort also is *safety* for the individual and for other members of the family.

At least 25% of all accidents and 3% of all fatalities that occur in the home happen in the bathroom. Other statistics add to the warning. According to the National Safety Council, the National Safe Kids Campaign and the National Center of Health Statistics, more than 200,000 persons are injured each year in the bathroom with 400 of these injuries resulting in death.

Most common cause of these injuries is slips and falls, but each year 5,000 children are scalded in the bathtub.

Consider also that 7 million Americans are over 55 years of age and 500 turn 65 every day. Of these, more than half are physically challenged in some way.

Potential bathroom hazards, in addition to slipping and scalding, include electrical shock, broken glass, poisoning and door-swinging.

1–Slipping. Usually occurs in the tub. Many slips can be prevented by specifying non-slip surfaces in the tub. These surfaces are integral and cost very little extra. Tubs without non-slip surfaces should have rubber or plastic mats with suction cups to grip the surface.

To further reduce the risk, grab bars are essential in all bathtubs and shower stalls. Grab bars should be 1 1/4" to 1 1/2" (3.2cm-3.8cm) in diameter, and 1 1/2" from the wall for knuckle clearance. The bars must be strong enough and mounted firmly enough to support a 300 lb. (136kg) static load. A strong backing material can be provided by nailing a section of 2 x 4 between the studs to which the grab bar will be anchored, or by nailing a sheet of 3/4" exterior-grade plywood over the studs.

A grab bar should be installed horizontally, 33" to 36" (84-91cm) above the tub floor. In addition, there should be either a horizontal bar in the center of the wall with the water controls or a vertical bar of the same length near the place of entry to the shower or tub. Horizontal bars are more desirable than vertical ones.

(For more details on grab bars, see Guideline 26 and Clarifications, Chap. 5.)

Use of a shower seat and hand-held shower can help prevent slipping. These have been used for many years in universal design but ignored in normal home use. It is precarious to balance on one foot while washing the other.

Bathroom floors also can be slippery, especially where the bather exits the tub and especially if large tiles rather than mosaics are used as a floor surface. Mosaics are so small that several grout lines provide traction. Even so, non-slip mats are advisable.

2–Electrical shock. The conjunction of electricity and water presents the greatest hazard in the bathroom. For this reason the National Electrical Code requires that any room with high humidity, water and electricity must have Ground Fault Circuit Interrupters (GFCIs). *(See Chap. 2.)*

3–Scalding. This can result when water temperature exceeds 115°F (46C). Danger temperature is lower for infants. Most domestic water heaters are set within three ranges: High, 180°+F (82°C); medium, 140°-160°F (60°-71°C); or low, 120°-140°F (49°-60°C). Each temperature range varies according to the water heater, its distance from the faucet and the appliances being served. A setting of 115°F is usually not hot enough for most homes.

Faucets with thermostatic or pressure balancing (Fig. 6.15) are recommended to maintain safe water temperature in the lav and shower. This becomes even more critical with low-flow valving, when a toilet flush on the same line could starve the cold water line. Some faucets have a special stop that must be pressed to permit the temperature to go above 100° (38°C).

4—Broken glass. This can cause severe injury in case of a slip or fall. All glass enclosures should be made of tempered glass that complies with ANSI Standard 297.1 and Architectural Glazing Standard 16CFK1201. Tempered glass tends to crumble into peanut-like pieces rather than sharp shards. Shatter-proof plastic works equally well.

5—Poisoning. This can be a problem in all homes, not just those with small children. Drugs and prescriptions often are kept in medicine cabinets for years. Labels can become smeared or otherwise unreadable, or simply come off. So for protection against poisoning, advise clients:

- Discard old prescriptions.

- Keep medicine cabinets secured from small children.

- Keep the telephone number of the local Poison Control Center readily available.

6—Door swings. Most bathroom doors swing inward to avoid blocking hall traffic. But if someone slipped and was propped unconscious against the door, it could be very difficult to get in to help. Or if a vanity drawer next to a door that swings in were left open, access would be impossible.

An entry door that swings outward could be safer, and also could provide additional wall and floor space in the bathroom. However, this could pose a hazard to someone walking in the hall who could bump into the opening door. All of this must be discussed with the customer so an informed decision can be made.

An in-swinging door should open against a blank wall or a tub area. Pocket doors can avoid

Fig. 6.15. Safest valve for the shower will balance both pressure and temperature. This also has built-in volume control. (Grohe Photo)

the in-swing problem, but they require a hollow wall to slide into, and one of these would necessitate reframing. Pocket doors can have handles that are difficult to operate, and they might not close tightly enough for privacy. In addition, they might not allow enough make-up air for good ventilation.

Builders commonly install smaller doors for bathroom access than those for surrounding

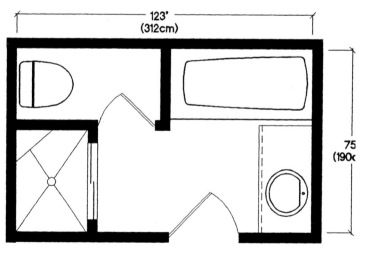

Fig. 6.16. Here is one way to zone an average family bath. Toilet is compartmentalized, could conceivably take another entry door on top wall.

rooms. Bathroom doorways should never be less than 32" (81cm) wide, and this is the minimum width specified in NKBA's Bathroom Design Guidelines *(Chap. 5, Section 1)*. For an accessible design, the door should be 36" (91cm) wide.

• **Aesthetics**—This refers to how the room appears to the eye, and to achieve the right effect is a complex procedure. It is a combination of all parts making up the whole, and it demands knowledge and use of the elements and principles of design. *(See Chap. 5.)*

Planning the space for the client

The bathroom plan can vary as the clients vary, but basically the bathroom plan can be approached from one of five directions:

1. The family bathroom.
2. The adult master suite.
3. The powder room.
4. The children's bathroom.
5. The accessible or universal bathroom.

The **family bathroom** might be divided into zones, when space allows. The tub/shower and toilet might be one space with a single or double lav in a second area. A combination heat/light/vent unit should be included in the tub/shower/toilet area. Include bath towel bars within the compartment. To expand the area visually, a window or skylight is a good addition. When space is small, a shower curtain or clear glass or plastic door is better than frosted glass. Provide storage for extra toilet paper, bathing, grooming and reading material.

Another common arrangement places the toilet in its own compartment. A small hand-washing lav might also go in the cubicle. A second entry door from the hallway would keep the toilet available to family members when other parts of the room are in use. This small area would need natural or powered ventilation.

To ease possible morning congestion, consider adding a small grooming station in a bed-

room or utility room. It would be least expensive if it could go on a bathroom wet wall that backs up to a bedroom. Add a vanity and mirrored medicine cabinet. In a utility room, add a medicine cabinet on a wall over the sink.

A family bath may require some special provisions for children or for a family member for whom universal design is appropriate. We'll cover them in this chapter, but remember that special provisions might be desirable for any of your clients. Maladies such as arthritis or ailing joints often afflict the young as well as the old.

A **master suite** bathroom nearly always is designed as a total adult environment in conjunction with the master bedroom (Fig. 6.17).

It is relatively easy to plan into a new home, but space for it usually has to be created in an existing structure. That often calls for moving and reframing walls.

In an older home a bedroom might become available after the children have grown and gone, and this can be ideal for designing a master suite incorporating the master bedroom and a luxurious bath. Even a physical fitness space and a sauna might be included if that is desired.

But more often the challenge will be to convert an existing bedroom with its private bath or an adjacent family bathroom into a master suite.

If a family bathroom is to be used, it could require adding a replacement facility elsewhere in the house. Obviously, this becomes a very involved project at this point, and it is important for the bathroom specialist to know why the client wants this kind of superbath. Some will want it as an adult retreat to be shared with someone, but others will want total privacy. And some will want it only because they can afford it, the "monument to me" syndrome. In such cases the specialist must probe for private desires because the grandest monument could be totally unsatisfactory from a functional viewpoint.

In devising a plan for a master suite that

must be squeezed into existing space, think first of total floor space available and how it can be adapted. The first step usually will be to plan how existing closet space can be incorporated, and then how it can be replaced.

For example, a walk-in closet in the bedroom and adjacent to the bathroom can be sacrificed to gain its floor space. It becomes part of the bathroom space, and then its storage space can be replaced with a cabinet wall system covering an opposite wall. The wall system could move that wall inward as little as 24" (61cm), but if it is a 20' (610cm) wall it would add 320 cubic feet (9M³) of storage space, possibly more than the walk-in closet it replaced. In effect, the "walk-in" space would be in the bedroom instead of in the closet.

The job then becomes a matter of tearing out the wall between the bathroom and closet to consolidate the space, planning a new bathroom, rerouting the plumbing and wiring as needed, planning a wide opening to integrate the bedroom and the new bath into a master suite, and redesigning the total space to make it attractive as well as functional.

In tearing out any wall or portion of a wall it is important to maintain structural integrity. Installation of double headers probably would be necessary wherever studs are cut, and it might be necessary to reinforce floor joists if an oversized tub will be installed (see Chap. 2).

The **powder room,** or half-bath, usually includes only a toilet and lav, plus vanity cabinet and mirrored medicine cabinet (Fig. 6.18). It excludes tub and shower. In one-bathroom homes or two-bathroom homes where both baths are upstairs with the bedrooms, a powder room adds convenience for guests and the home's occupants on the first floor. It always is a small room, and one of the challenges for the bath specialist is in finding a space for it in a home where it has not been provided. Common locations are stair

wells, closets and utility rooms, but it is not uncommon to bump out a wall from the kitchen to create new space for it.

As a last resort, and although it violates the Guidelines for Bathroom Design, a powder room can be accommodated quite well in a space as small as 33" x 72" (84 x 183cm) with a 24" (61cm) out-swinging door, unless special consideration is needed for an accessible design. (Fig. 6.18 shows powder room arrangements with in-swinging doors, but they can cramp the turn-around space. It also might be a good place for a pocket door. Let the client know the options.)

Since a powder room often serves largely as a guest bathroom it is advisable, if possible, to screen the entry from view. It would be ungracious for the homeowner to ask a guest to enter this room through a door in the living or dining room. The guest would rather go upstairs.

While the first challenge is to find or create space for a powder room, an equal challenge is to design it for visual impact. This may be the only such facility the guest will see in a home, so special attention should be given to colors, textures, materials and surfaces.

This small room will need good venting and good sound control. In a 1992 California survey of low-flow toilets (which now are mandatory across the U.S.) consumers reported dissatisfaction with higher noise levels. The bath specialist should explain this to the homeowner to justify the price of a better, quieter fixture.

The vent fan also should be insulated as much as possible. Since powder rooms do not have the high humidity that comes with bathing or showering, vent units that don't exhaust direct through a wall often are ducted for discharge into the attic.

A **children's bathroom** is not something you'll get a lot of calls for. Children grow up too quickly and a bathroom designed specifically for a child would have to be redone in a few years.

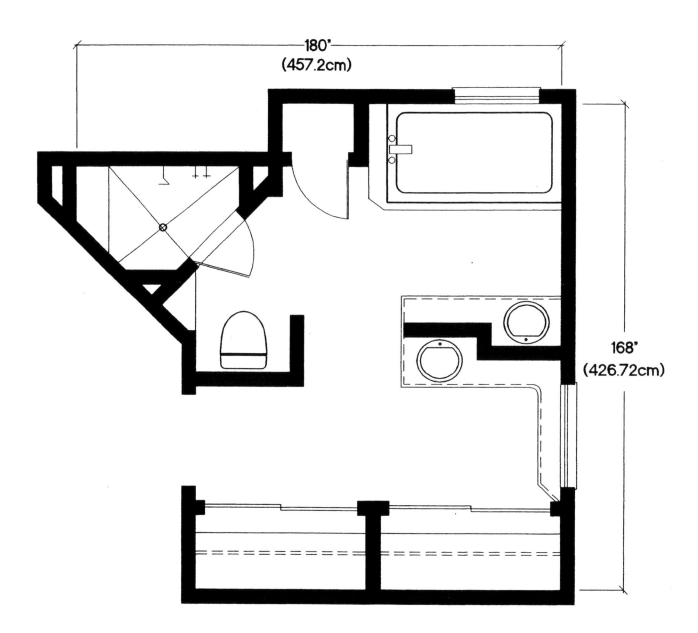

Fig. 6.17. This master suite is partially open to the bedroom (not shown, to left). It includes two sliding-door closets at bottom, and a grooming area that can be used without actually going into the bathroom.

The bathroom specialist would do better to design a family bathroom that is adaptable and adjustable to the growing child. The specialist also should be aware that many of the features of a child's bathroom are similar to those of an accessible bath.

• This means it should have surfaces that can withstand spilling, splashing, spotting, dripping, bumping, chipping, breaking and scratching, and if any of these things happen the surfaces should be easily repairable and cleanable.

• It should have a stall shower rather than a tub shower, to guard against falls. It would be a good idea to install a shower head that slides up and down on a pole so it can be adjusted for a child's height and then readjusted for an adult's. Specify a single handle valve with pressure balance and temperature control.

• A pull-up step or stool can be installed in the vanity cabinet, under the lav, to bring a child up to lav height and then be removed when no longer needed. At least one of these is available that mounts on the vanity door but has four feet that rest solidly on the floor when in use.

• One lav made for an accessible bathroom would be excellent for a child's use in an adult bathroom. It has flexible plumbing, and moves up and down and side to side at the touch of a lever (Fig. 6.19). But check local codes that might prohibit lavs with this kind of movement.

• Medicine cabinet doors, of course, should be lockable, even if they seem to be out of a child's reach.

• A child's toiletries and grooming aids can be stored within reach in a vanity cabinet drawer or in a basket shelf inside a vanity door. They also could go in a tilt-out tray in the vanity base such as is used in a kitchen sink base.

• Towel bars placed low for a child's use would have to be replaced and the walls repaired in later years. This might be avoided by using a portable towel tree to provide for the child temporarily.

• Specify door locks that can be opened from the outside in case of emergency.

Notes:

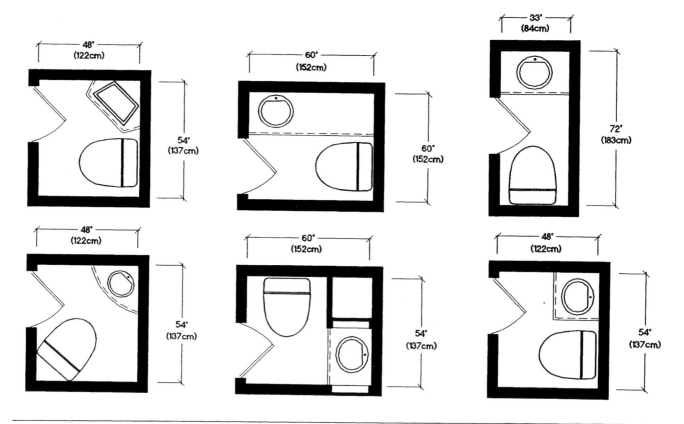

Fig. 6.18. Powder rooms usually have two fixtures in very limited space, plus vanity and medicine cabinets. Homeowners might prefer a door that swings outward, so the options should be explained to them.

Fig. 6.19. American Standard Pressalit lav, made for an accessible bathroom, can be one choice for a family bath used also by a child. It moves up and down and side to side at the touch of a lever.

An **accessible** bathroom increases the usability of the room to more types of people.

These people might be young or old and there might be varying degrees of disability. But the biggest challenge is to design for a person confined to a wheelchair. Design factors include:

• **Space occupied** by the wheelchair
• Its **maneuverability**
• **Access** to the fixtures used.

Dimensions of a typical wheelchair are:
Length—43" (109cm). Add 5" (13cm) when occupied.
Width—24.5" (62cm), plus 5" for elbows.
Seat height—19.5" (50cm).
Seat depth—16" (41cm).
Arm height—29.5" (75cm).
Overall height—36" (91cm).
Reach while sitting:
Vertical—54"-78" (137-198cm).
Horizontal—28.5"-33" (72-84cm)
Diagonal—48" (122cm).

These figures are only for preliminary planning. Actual dimensions of the wheelchair and its occupant will be needed for the final design. You also will have to modify the dimensions according to the person's arm strength, grasping strength and flexibility.

It also is important to remember that transfer methods must be planned to move the person in and out of the wheelchair. There must be no floor-level changes, because wheelchairs can't step up or down, and you have to allow space for the arm and foot rests.

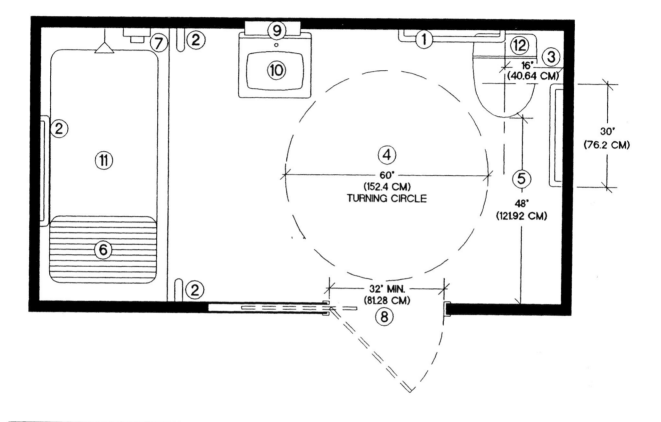

Fig. 6.20. Following are some basics for a universally accessible bathroom. For more, see NKBA's Universal Bathroom Planning book.

1. Two grab bars starting from the toilet c/l, behind and in front, each 30" long (76cm).
2. Two grab bars in tub area, horizontal and vertical.
3. Minimum clearance from c/l of toilet to wall, 16" (46cm).
4. 60" (152cm) diameter circle of unobstructed space needed for full turn-around.
5. 48" (122cm) minimum clearance required in front of toilet.
6. Tub seat 19" high (48cm) and at least 15" (38cm) deep.
7. Temperature/pressure-balanced tub and shower control 30" high (76cm).

8. Out-swing door or pocket door, minimum 32" (81cm), but anything more than that is desirable.
9. Maximum of 40" (102cm) from floor to bottoms of all mirrors and medicine cabinets. A mirror angled down preferred.
10. Minimum clearance of 29" (74cm) from floor to bottom of lav. Insulate or recess all pipes to prevent burns. If a vanity is used, allow 30"-wide (76cm) opening at lav.
11. Preferred tub height is 19.5" (50cm).
12. Preferred height of toilet is 18" (46cm), with grab bars centered on seat.

Laying it out—the subtraction method

Most routine bathroom projects appear to be easy to lay out because they consist only of a basic bathroom group in limited space. But if they appear easy, it is mostly because you have a bank of experience to draw on, experience in laying out bathrooms or kitchens.

But, whether you realize it or not, you do use a systematic approach even though many of the steps are in your subconscious mind. The system you use, in more formal language, is called *the subtraction method.*

A time comes when you are working with a larger space and a much larger budget and the task is to lay out a *total environment.* Instead of a tub/shower your client will want a tub and a separate shower stall, perhaps a whirlpool tub or two shower heads, perhaps two lavs where two persons can groom together or groom isolated from each other, perhaps a bidet along with the toilet, perhaps steam, perhaps a sauna, exercise equipment, a skylight.

At this point the facts and figures you kept in your head won't be enough. You will have to work with the room and its dimensions, the clearances and the traffic patterns, the storage capacity and where to put it. Now the subtraction method will give you a way to systematize your thinking and your layout.

In the following example we won't go through the creative process and all the options you would consider in an actual project. We'll show how it is done so you will be able to apply it to the options you will have on a job.

1. Draw an outline of the space, noting what must stay as is (Fig. 6.21).

2. Make a set of templates of the activity centers that the client wants, to the same scale as the room, and mark their measurements (Fig. 6.22). You can move these around in the space and test them for clearances, walkways and aesthetic balance.

(For all recommended clearances, see Guidelines for Bathroom Design, Chap.5).

3. Select the priority area. This will be the toilet and bidet because of the importance of clearances around them and because you have

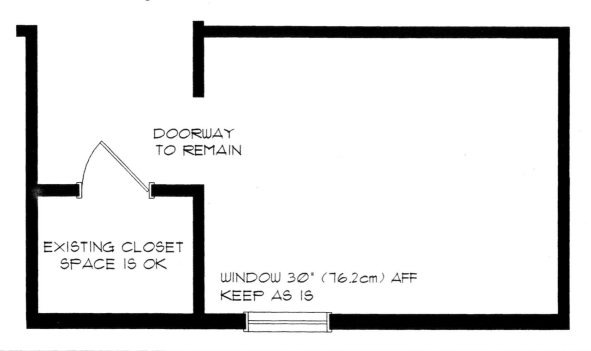

DOORWAY
TO REMAIN

EXISTING CLOSET
SPACE IS OK

WINDOW 30" (76.2cm) AFF
KEEP AS IS

Fig. 6.21. Step 1 is to draw an outline of the space, to scale, and mark what must or can stay as is. In this example we assume complete freedom with placement of the wiring and plumbing.

flexibility in cabinets to place next to them.

4. Decide, and subtract to check fit. The client wants two lavs, roughly together, but you have to decide on one, two or three vanity cabinets and consider the aesthetics of the doors. Here you decide on spreading the lavs to leave 15" (38cm) clearance space at either end, with two matching lav cabinets with a drawer bank between them. To get the cabinet sizes, take the full wall width, 144" (366cm), subtract the toilet and bidet and their clearances, 66" (168cm), and that leaves 78" (198cm) for the three cabinets. Allowing for 15" (38cm) clearance on the far side of each lav, this means you can have two 30" (76cm) vanities with a drawer cabinet of 18" (46cm) (Fig. 6.23).

5. Draw the solution.

Remember to draw a dashed line to indicate cabinet depth and a solid line for the counter overhang (Fig. 6.24).

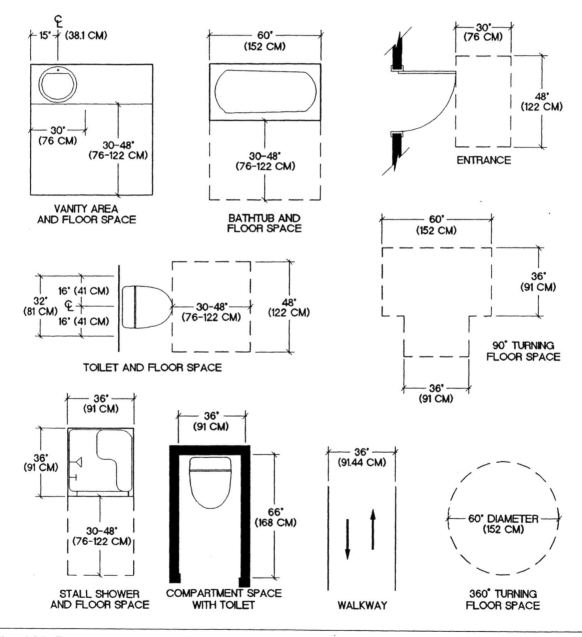

Fig. 6.22. Draw templates of the centers of activity, including the products the client wants, including their necessary clearance space. You then can move the templates around the floorplan to check various ideas you might have.

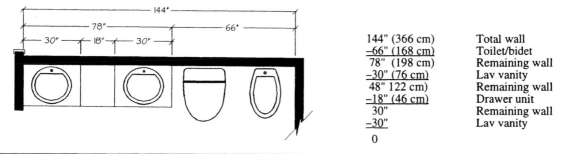

144" (366 cm)	Total wall
−66" (168 cm)	Toilet/bidet
78" (198 cm)	Remaining wall
−30" (76 cm)	Lav vanity
48" 122 cm)	Remaining wall
−18" (46 cm)	Drawer unit
30"	Remaining wall
−30"	Lav vanity
0	

Fig. 6.23. This shows the subtraction process graphically. Extend it around room for other walls.

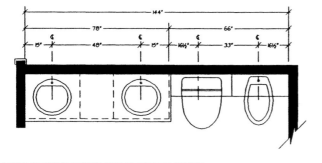

Fig. 6.24. Draw the solution

Metric Note:

All metric equivalents are of imperial sizes as manufactured in the U.S. This does not conform with customary metric cabinet size increments. These figures, however, show the recommended procedure.

You can continue this method around the room for placement of other units. But remember, you are laying out for a *total environment* and you are a professional designer, so you also have to consider *vertical* placements and the way everything lines up and balances.

So, to continue with this same wall you continue with the subtraction method.

Visualize it, and sketch it the way you think it should be. Here you visualize a band of narrow cabinets above the toilet/bidet area, and a tall unit extending above the drawer base in the

Fig. 6.25. Visualize the wall as you would like to approach it from a design standpoint. Then make a rough sketch to establish vertical relationships, then make final drawing.

Gallery of Ideas

Suggested master bathroom arrangements

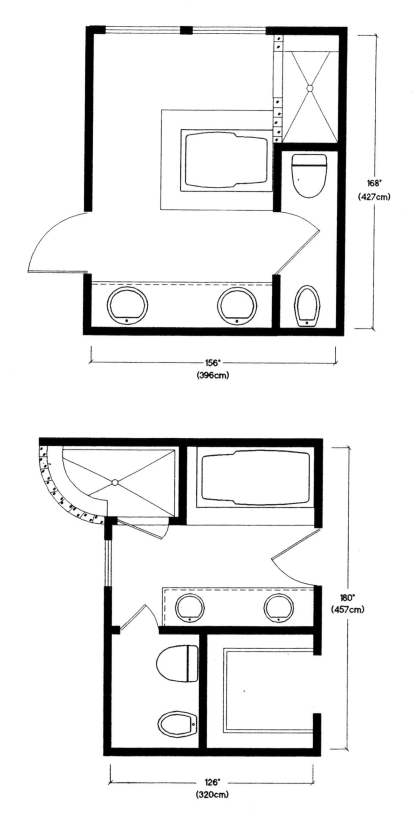

lav area. You go for vertical symmetry in the spacing of towels over the fixtures (Fig. 6.25). (We omit metric numbers here because the numbers themselves are unimportant. It's the procedure that counts.)

What the subtraction tells you here is that the height of your band of wall cabinets will be 15". You get it by subtracting all of the other elements first, including towels and spaces.

You follow this system for every detail, including the size and placement of the lavs and the mirrored medicine cabinets above and the size of the tambour and upper door in the center wall cabinet.

The subtraction method eliminates all of the guesstimating. It tells you precisely where to put what to get the effect you want.

Gallery of Ideas
Suggested master bathroom arrangements

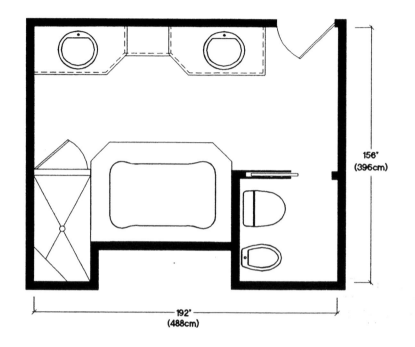

156"
(396cm)

192"
(488cm)

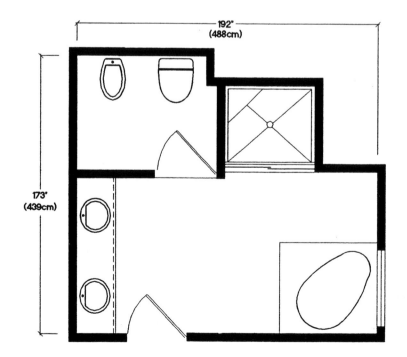

192"
(488cm)

173"
(439cm)

Gallery of Ideas
Suggested master bathroom arrangements

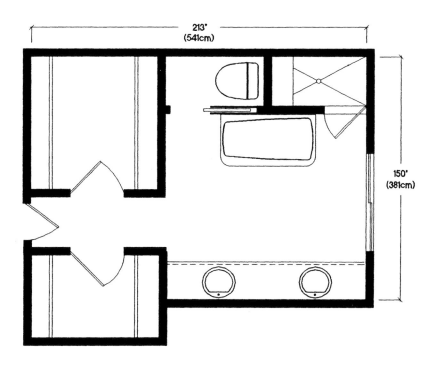

213"
(541cm)

150"
(381cm)

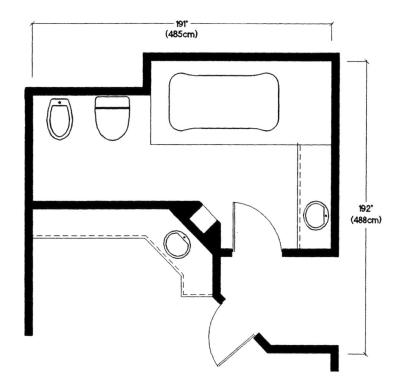

191"
(485cm)

192"
(488cm)

Gallery of Ideas

Sketch a rough floorplan of your own home, or that of a friend. Then sketch an area showing how you would expand a bathroom into a master suite.
(Scale: 1/2"=1'.

Gallery of Ideas

Sketch a rough floorplan of your home, or that of a friend. Then sketch an area showing how and where you would add a second bathroom.
(Scale: 1/2"=1'.'

Gallery of Ideas

Sketch a rough floorplan of your home or the home of a friend. Then in another sketch, show where you would add a half-bath.
(Scale: 1/2"=1'.

Notes:

Accessories: The Final Touch
They Should Add to the Design as well as the Function

The range of accessory items for a modern bathroom is wide, and it gets wider each day as innovative designers and manufacturers develop new ways to make life more convenient.

All of these are important to the bathroom designer. There is a tendency to think of some accessories (such as towels, for example) as minor because they are available at many other outlets, but the bathroom designer has many sources of supply that are unknown to the average consumer. The designer, for example, can get towels designed to match the bathroom tile. For another example, towel bars and soap dishes are available everywhere, but the designer knows these are available to match lav and tub fittings, medicine cabinets, shelves, even lights.

Also, the designer is concerned not only with the layout of fixtures but also with vertical relationships such as how high the towel bars are installed and how low the towels hang. Everything, large and small, becomes part of the overall design impression. Everything is important, from every-day functional accessories to convenience items.

Some accessories are necessities. Others are added conveniences. Their role varies from bathroom to bathroom. In a typical small bathroom a triple-mirrored medicine cabinet might be classi-

Fig. 7.1. Electric towel warmers can plug in or be hardwired, built-in or free-standing, come in several finishes. They have timers for automatic turn-on and off. They also may have hydronic heat. (Epánel photo)

fied as a basic need. But in a master suite with ample mirrors and storage it could be little more than another design element.

Medicine cabinets

This is a utilitarian name for a cabinet that might be small and inexpensive with a mirrored door or quite large and beautifully designed with two or three mirrored doors. Some models have lighting and convenience electrical outlets, small drawers, and locking doors for securing medicines that could be harmful to children.

Medicine cabinets can be recessed into the wall or surface-mounted. Standard cabinets are sized to be recessed between the wall studs of a typical framing system in a North American house which features studs spaced 16" (41cm) on center. Standard studs are 2" x 4" (5 x 10cm) nominal size, but actual size after machining is 1 1/2" x 3 1/2" (4 x 9cm). Actual space between studs is 14 1/2" (37cm). The standard cabinet is sized to fit these dimensions precisely, with a door oversized by about 1/2" on three sides fitting almost flush against the wall.

Wider recessed cabinets are double that width plus the 3 1/2" of the middle stud that must be cut out. When a stud is cut in this manner and it is not a load-bearing wall, the hole is framed with a 2x4 header and sill laid flat. Rough-in sizes are supplied by the manufacturer.

Before cutting into a wall the bath specialist should determine that there is no ductwork, plumbing, wiring or other obstruction where the cabinet is to be installed.

Surface-mounted medicine cabinets might be any width. The only restriction on depth is that they not protrude so far from the wall that they interfere with a person using the lav. Common depths range from 4" (10cm) minimum to 7" (18cm) for fancier models with drawers. Check this against the heights of users. A deeper cabinet can annoy a person with a tall upper body who bends over the lav farther. The back edge of the lav's rim should be no closer to the wall than the front edge of the cabinet above. If the desired cabinet is too deep it may be necessary to install the lav a little farther from the wall.

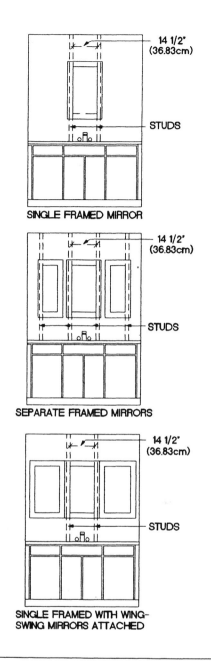

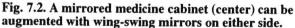

Fig. 7.2. A mirrored medicine cabinet (center) can be augmented with wing-swing mirrors on either side.

Position on the wall also must be related to the size of users. If one family member is tall and another is short, a taller cabinet may have to be mounted lower to accommodate both.

Keep in mind also that some manufacturers make medicine cabinets so they can be arranged in various design configurations. Some can be combined side-by-side, and others are stackable vertically. (See Fig. 7.3 and Appendix C.) Conceivably, these can be designed into a floor-to-ceiling wall system around the lavatory.

Medicine cabinets are available with hinged or sliding doors. Remember that sliding doors always block at least half of the opening, and make sure that a hinged door does not collide with towel bars or other wall-mounted accessories installed at right angles to the cabinet.

Mirrors: Functional and decorative

The mirrors on the medicine cabinet often are the only ones in existing small bathrooms. A remodeled bathroom should have more than that. Mirrors are essential for grooming and dressing, but they also expand the visual perception of space and add life and movement to any room.

Plate glass is recommended for bathroom or other home mirrors in either 3/16" or 1/4" thickness (47 or 63mm).

The problem in a small bathroom is in finding a place to put them. One place that is always available is the inside of the entry door. It also might be possible to mount two tall, narrow mirrors on either side of the toilet or the vanity, or two stacked mirrored medicine cabinets on either side of the vanity cabinet (Fig. 7.3). Foot-square mirror tiles also can be used this way. Heated mirrors are available that minimize fogging.

Other accessories

Built-in accessories all relate to the utilitarian, storage and sanitary needs of the family. Glass holders and soap holders serve utilitarian needs. Towel bars, rings or trees provide a type of storage. Toilet bowl brushes and their holders fulfill sanitary requirements. All of these also are designed to save space. If these accessories were not provided at the point of first use they would use up space in vanity cabinets, medicine cabinets and closets.

Fig. 7.3. One way to get mirrors in a small bathroom is with mirrored medicine cabinets. Two stackable units are on either side, a large one in the center. This is all glass, but the stacked units could also go on either side of a vanity cabinet. (Robern photo)

Fig. 7.4. Wall-mounted hair dryer can be a useful bathroom accessory. It is direct-wired. (Broan photo)

The most common built-in accessories, which may be flush-mounted or recessed, are:

- Towel bars, rings, hooks, trees.
- Soap holders.
- Toilet paper dispensers.
- Toothbrush and glass holders.
- Grab bars—Straight, L or U shaped.
- Scales.
- Toilet brush holders.
- Robe hooks.
- Make-up mirrors.
- Tub trays—Hanging, on poles, corner.
- Waste baskets.
- Magazine racks.
- Shelves.
- Razor blade dispensers.
- Tissue dispensers.
- Towel warmers.

Soap dish placement must be within conve-nient reach. In a tub/shower area, two soap dishes are needed. One, for bathers, should be 24" (61cm) above the floor and 30" (76cm) from the "head" end of the tub; the other, for showerers, 54" (127cm) above the floor and 15" to 21" (53cm) from the plumbing wall. Towel bars or a towel ring should be placed about mid-way between the floor and ceiling, and one should be no more than 6" (15cm) from the en-trance to the tub or shower. Towels must be within easy reach of the lav.

Stacked towel bars should allow space for grasping and replacing the hanging towels. Al-low 6"-8" (15-20cm) for washcloths, 8"-10" (20-25cm) for fingertip towels, 14"-16" (36-41cm) for hand towels and 22"-24" (56-61cm) for bath towels.

Notes:

The Process of Selling Bathrooms
For a Full-Service Firm, It Takes Three Sales Calls

There are various ways to sell bathrooms and bathroom products, depending on the type of business doing the selling.

The types of businesses were outlined briefly in Chapter 1.

Full-service firms sell design, the products included in the design, and either install or supervise installation.

Some firms (who might be individuals) sell design only.

Others sell products only. There are other variations.

But before we get into the issue of how bathrooms are sold we should consider the question of who buys bathrooms? It affects the sales process. Our customers include:

• **Homeowners** who want a good **family** bathroom to replace an old one in existing space, or who want to add a bathroom or half-bath. This can be a good, solid sale, open to creativity and possibly to some extension of the space in an existing bathroom.

• **Homeowners** who want a **luxury** bathroom either separate or as part of a master suite. These require thorough planning and careful job management. Because these customers are

spending a lot, they might expect more than is in the contract. It can be easy to lose profit on the big jobs.

• **Homeowners** who want **cosmetic** updating or remodeling to add value to a home they want to sell soon. These sometimes will be low budget and low profit, and possibly will involve a lot of do-it-yourself work. For these prospects it is important to offer good value for the money. That can result in a good sale. But these prospects also might be shopping only for the lowest price, so we also must be careful not to waste time on jobs that cost profit.

• **Landlords** who must update in one or more houses or apartments. This can be good business, but some landlords who do not actually use these bathrooms might not be concerned with quality of products or workmanship, and profit margins might be too low. We must be sure we want these kinds of jobs before investing a lot of time in them.

• **Builders** or **architects** who need bathrooms for either custom or spec homes. In custom homes we sometimes can sell them on the idea of allotting the space and letting us deal directly with the customer, sometimes with a separate contract. Sometimes, as with kitchens, they will give the homebuyer an allowance for the bathroom and let us work on a separate contract. Builders will be price-oriented, but they also will look for good value for the money. They often must be educated to good value, because they might not be fully up-to-date on the newest bathroom products and materials. However, once you establish a relationship and you both know you can trust each other, it can become easy to continue for years.

Independent architects and architectural firms who do bathrooms will be design-oriented. In some cases they might establish a bathroom profit center and be a full-service bathroom supplier, or they might design bathrooms for builders and/or homeowners.

• **Do-it-yourselfers** might be any of the above. Some work this way to save money, but some will do it because they like it and are good at it, and they might want to reward themselves with the best products. Some might need and want good planning and be willing to pay for it, in which case they would simply be taking the labor problem off our hands. Whoever we are and however we sell, it will pay us to pay attention to this category and find out what they are capable of, realistically, and what they really want and need.

We all can be sure of one thing. *From any customer contact we will get referrals,* good or bad.

• **Commercial users.** There are many commercial users of bathroom products. But there also is a whole new class of customers who can be considered commercial—the millions of Americans who have become victims of "downsizing" or of intolerable commuting problems.

They now work at home in a home office, or will start doing so soon. If they are still connected to a business and doing a full-day's work at home instead of at an office, it is quite likely that they need a new half-bath in their new home office. And if they need that, they also might need cabinetry, counters and a well-planned work space, or other things you sell. Sure, they can buy a desk. But commercial desks are sized

for downtown offices, not for the restricted space they might have in the home. It's a new market worth looking into.

How we sell our bathrooms

Selling a bathroom, be it new or remodeled, is essentially the same as selling a kitchen.

• For a full-service **bathroom specialist** working out of a showroom and selling products as well as design, it has to be a three-step process. This includes:

1. **An initial consultation in the showroom.**

2. **A meeting in the home for an interview, inspection of the site, and measuring the space (see Chapter 6).**

3. **Presentation of the plans and closing the sale in the showroom.**

• For an **independent designer** working from an office it can be a two-step or three-step process. This includes:

1. **An initial consultation, which might be at the office or in the home, or in the office of a builder or architect. If it is in the home it might be possible to do the site inspection and measuring on this call, but it is more likely that another visit will be necessary for these essential steps.**

2. **Inspection and measuring.**

3. **Presentation of the plans and closing the sale. When working with a homeowner this should be done in the designer's office where there is no concern about rescission clauses. (In the U.S. federal law allows a customer three days to rescind any contract that has been signed in the home.) With a builder or architect the signing might be in either office, but usually it will be in theirs.**

For either of these, the bathroom specialist

or the designer, there might have to be more contacts with the customer for revisions of the plans. That's part of the job. But it is controllable, to some extent, by how well and how thoroughly the initial interview was conducted. **Experience teaches us to leave no question unanswered at that time.**

• For a **home center** or other over-the-counter outlet, it becomes quite a different matter. Although they are price-oriented, the modern chains now feature very high-end as well as low-end products, and many have designers on the floor with the products.

But there are some notable differences between these multi-branch retailers and other bathroom design firms:

1. They have a lot more capitalization.

2. They do more advertising and promotion.

3. They have much more foot traffic.

4. They have more sophisticated accounting. This means they know their costs better, and this means their selling price may be as high as or higher than the independent specialist's, all other things being equal.

5. They also have bookkeepers looking over their shoulders. If the bathroom display space doesn't pay, it's out.

There is evidence that in some cases the "contract" departments are more profitable than the over-the-counter departments.

Increasingly, the modern chains of the '90s want certified specialists on the staff. Increasingly they encourage key personnel to become certified and they are willing to help them do so.

Historically, the industry has found that increased bath/kitchen advertising and promotion by any stores or chains increase business for all bath/kitchen businesses in an area. This activity gets more consumers conscious of remodeling,

gets them thinking, makes them want to look into it. Some will opt to shop the big advertiser. Others will opt for the smaller independent.

But in either case, these are only prospects. The sales job is still to be done.

Other ways to sell

We have been dealing mostly with the contract sales process. Most full-service specialists sell on contract. They are not set up to handle cash in the store and tend to avoid it.

But many do set up for it and enjoy brisk sales, as the home centers do. They do this with retail bath accessories, hardware, fancy faucets, anything that's related, even softgoods. This provides three advantages:

• **It brings in traffic, thus gaining added exposure for the bathroom displays.**

• **It provides day-to-day cash flow.**

• **It can be quite profitable in itself.**

However, except for home centers, for success in these over-the-counter sales the merchandise must be different and *distinctive*. That usually means high-end, because there is no way to win a price battle on *routine* merchandise with discount stores.

Bath/kitchen full-service contractors also can do well with occasional "warehouse" or "sidewalk" sales. They can stock up with extra vanity stock, for example, and then use these sales to move out damaged inventory, old displays or ordering mistakes.

Sales of this kind can be stimulated greatly by adding impulse items to advertise and sell at cost and that are not in the usual product mix. An example could be tempered glass counter savers for the kitchen or bathroom.

Sales of this kind gain excellent exposure

for the bathroom displays, move out unwanted inventory and raise cash.

Estimating as a sales tool

On the one hand we have "bring in your bathroom measurements and get a free estimate." And that's all right for sale of a product or a replacement bathroom group.

On the other hand we have the full-service bathroom specialist or anyone else who sells on contract. To them, this kind of estimate is either meaningless or a shortcut to disaster. To them, *accurate* estimating is essential for protecting profit. If the estimate is too high it loses sales. If it is too low it loses money.

A customer's request for a written estimate represents a glitch in the sales process. That doesn't mean it is bad, but it may mean the customer wants to shop around. That doesn't mean the sale is lost, but to protect the sale and your investment of time and talent it does mean:

- **You must have done a sound selling job to this point.**

- **You must not have given away your ideas any more than necessary to your selling job. Any responsible business person will not hesitate to put figures in writing, but keep the plans.**

- **You should make this point come as early as possible in the process. The earlier it comes, the less time you will have wasted in case the prospect decides to buy elsewhere.**

This means that in qualifying your prospect you should try to determine, subtly, whether this prospect is going to want a written estimate. If the answer is yes, your estimate must be accurate.

Accurate estimates depend on three major controls:

1. An up-to-date **estimating book.**
2. A thorough **estimating form.**
3. A constant **markup percentage.**

The **estimating book** should contain up-to-date prices for all of your products and services, materials and labor.

To develop it, first you must sit down with all of your subcontractors and work out as many flat-rate prices as possible. You want a price, but you also want a time estimate because it will affect how you schedule the trades.

For example (and these figures will vary wildly by locale) the plumbing contractor might give you a flat fee of $550 for disconnect and connect of a three-piece bathroom group, and $200 for any single fixture, including reuse of existing wastes, vents, drains, traps and water lines. It could provide that shut-off valves be included at no added charge. The plumbing contractor might specify that it will take two hours for disconnect and four hours for connecting the fixtures.

You must be specific. A two-piece toilet connect might be different from a one-piece connect. Connection of a pressurized model with an electrical feed might be different.

Continue this with all plumbing and electrical products, tile setting and any other trades. **Always avoid time-and-material pricing** by the subs. Agree that you will call each other if **any** problems or questions arise.

The estimating book also must include up-to-date prices for materials and labor. These prices are readily available from suppliers, and they **must be kept current.**

When the estimating book is complete you should have 90-95% accuracy. The 5-10% possible errors will be due to lost time from travel time, unloading, clean-up, maintaining customer good will, etc. These are unpredictable, and it is smart to include a contingency factor for them.

A thorough estimating form also provides the accounting department with all job costs. For this to be effective, each job must be analyzed immediately after completion, verifying all product, labor and material costs and comparing them with the estimate. Any differences must be checked back to the source. If there is an error in the estimating book, subs should be called to verify their billing, and any changes should be entered in the estimating book immediately.

As an example of what can happen, assume your estimating book has 120V electrical connections at $35 each, and there is an average of five connections per bathroom, totaling $175. The electrical contractor has a price increase and neglects to inform you that each connection now will cost you $45. If you do 50 jobs per year, your loss on this alone is $2,500.

A **constant markup rate** is necessary to assure a fair profit, and businesses run on profit. Break-even figures are not good enough.

Your constant markup rate will be a fixed gross profit percentage you must make on all jobs. This will vary by firm, depending on overhead. A large business with several trucks, designers, installers and expediters will need a larger gross profit than a small shop. A leading expert in the estimating field has suggested that 33% gross profit should be the *minimum* for a remodeling firm. But if you have a showroom and displays, this percentage will increase.

You will have to consult with your accountant to determine an estimated rate at which you can work for a year, the minimum gross profit you need to break even, and the gross profit you need to make the desired net profit.

The only feasible way to maintain consistency of markup is to multiply your total job costs by a constant percentage. For example, assume total estimated cost on a remodeling job is $4,500 (including overhead). You want to earn 33% gross profit. The constant markup figure for 33% gross profit is 50%.

Your cost ($4,500)
plus 50% markup ($2,250)
= your selling price ($6,750).

Another simple way to calculate selling price is to put a 1 in front of the markup figure, 50%, making the constant 1.50. Multiply the cost ($4,500) times 1.50 and you arrive at the same selling price, $6,750.

But you must determine your own constant markup percentage, based on your own overhead costs and job costs. In bathroom and kitchen remodeling, most full-service firms have found they must mark up more than 60% and earn a gross profit margin of more than 40% to make a profit. The following table relates markup to gross profit margin.

COSTS	MARKUP	PRICE	GROSS PROFIT
$3000	100% ($3000)	$6000	50%
$3000	75% ($2250)	$5250	42.8%
$3000	67% ($2010)	$5010	40%
$3000	50% ($1500)	$4500	33%
$3000	43% ($1290)	$4290	30%

Many serious shoppers may ask for an estimate and say they want only a "ballpark" figure. But this figure probably will be matched against the figures of other competitors, and there are big differences among ballparks.

That's why the professional designer/firm should show estimating is serious business by using a business-like form such as that developed by NKBA (Figs. 8.1-8.8). This form does not mean that specs can't be changed in the design procedure, but it does mean that the specialist can assure the customer the job won't come in at 15% or 20% over the estimated figure, and because it is complete it will be believable. And it will enable the specialist to warn the customer to make sure any other "ballpark" estimates are based on the same elements.

NKBA
The Finest Professionals in the Kitchen & Bath Industry
National Kitchen & Bath Association℠

STANDARD ESTIMATE FOR BATHROOM DESIGN AND INSTALLATION

Name: _____

Home Address: _____

City: _____ State _____ Phone (Home) _____

(Office) _____

(Office) _____

(Jobsite) _____

Jobsite Address _____

By

Hereafter called "Bathroom Specialist."

Bathroom Specialist will supply and deliver only such equipment and material as described in these specifications. Labor connected with this bathroom installation will be supplied by the Bathroom Specialist only as herein specified.

Any equipment, material and labor designated here as "Owner's responsibility" must be furnished and completed by the Owner, or the Owner's Agent in accordance with the work schedule established by the Bathroom Specialist.

Equipment, material and labor not included in these specifications can be supplied by the Bathroom Specialist at an additional cost for which authorization must be given in writing by the Owner, or the Owner's Agent.

All dimensions and cabinet designations shown on the floor plan, which are part of these specifications, are subject to adjustments dictated by job conditions.

All surfaces of walls, ceilings, windows and woodwork, except those of factory-made equipment, will be left unpainted or unfinished unless otherwise specified.

If specifications call for re-use of existing equipment, no responsibility on the part of the Bathroom Specialist for appearance, functioning or service shall be implied.

For factory-made equipment, the manufacturer's specifications for quality, design, dimensions, function and installation shall in any case take precedence over any others.

(over)

Fig. 8.1. The NKBA estimate form cover sheet spells out some conditions for the project.

Est.	Actual				
		Cabinetry (as per approved drawing)			
		Manufacturer			
		Cabinet Exterior ☐ Wood ☐ Steel ☐ Decorative Laminate ☐ Other			
		Cabinet Exterior Finish Cabinet Interior Material Finish			
		Door Style Hardware			
Subtotal		Special Cabinet Notes			
Tax					
Labor					
Total		Furnished By ☐ Bathroom Specialist ☐ Owner ☐ Owner's Agent			
Differential		Installation By ☐ Bathroom Specialist ☐ Owner ☐ Owner's Agent			
		Countertops (as per approved drawing)			
		Manufacturer Material			
		Design Details Deck Thickness _____ Color _____ Edging Thickness _____ Color _____			
Subtotal		Backsplash Thickness _____ Height _____ Color _____ End Splash Thickness _____ Height _____ Color _____			
Tax		Special Countertop Notes			
Labor					
Total		Furnished By ☐ Bathroom Specialist ☐ Owner ☐ Owner's Agent			
Differential		Installation By ☐ Bathroom Specialist ☐ Owner ☐ Owner's Agent			
		Fascia & Soffit (as per approved drawing)			
		Construction ☐ Flush ☐ Extended ☐ Recessed ☐ N/A (Open)			
Subtotal		Finish Material			
Tax		Special Fascia/Soffit Notes			
Labor					
Total		Furnished By ☐ Bathroom Specialist ☐ Owner ☐ Owner's Agent			
Differential		Installation By ☐ Bathroom Specialist ☐ Owner ☐ Owner's Agent			

Lighting System

Description	Qty.	Model Number	Finish	Lamp Req.	Furnished By B.S.	Furnished By O/OA	Installed By B.S.	Installed By O/OA

Est./Actual column: Subtotal, Tax, Labor, Total, Differential

Special Lighting System Notes

KEY

B.S. = Bathroom Specialist   O = Owner   OA = Owner's Agent

BMF11

Fig. 8.2. The form includes peripheral items and specifies who will supply them.

Bath Fixtures, Fittings and Finishes

Est.	Actual

Item	Brand Name	Model	Finish	Furnished By		Installed By		Hook Up By	
				B.S.	O/OA	B.S.	O/OA	B.S.	O/OA
Water Closet									
Seat									
Fittings									
Stop and Supply									
Miscellaneous									
Bidet									
Fittings									
Stop and Supply									
Miscellaneous									
Urinal									
Fittings									
Stop and Supply									
Miscellaneous									
Bathtub									
Fittings									
Waste and Overflow									
Stop and Supply									
Enclosure									
Wall Surround									
Drapery Rod									
Bathtub Drapery									
Miscellaneous									
Whirlpool System									
Fittings									
Miscellaneous									
Shower									
Fittings									
Drain									
Showerhead 1									
Showerhead 2									
Stop and Supply									
Enclosure									
Wall Surround									
Shower Floor									
Drapery Rod									
Shower Drapery									
Miscellaneous									

Subtotal
Tax
Labor
Total
Differential

BMF11

Fig. 8.3. Fixtures, fittings and finishes include all possible products that might go into the bath.

Bath Fixtures, Fittings and Finishes (Continued)

Est.	Actual	Item	Brand Name	Model	Finish	Furnished By		Installed By		Hook Up By	
						B.S.	O/OA	B.S.	O/OA	B.S.	O/OA
		Lavatory 1									
		Fittings									
		Drilling Spread									
		Stop and Supply									
		Pedestal Trap Cover									
		Miscellaneous									
		Lavatory 2									
		Fittings									
		Drilling Spread									
		Stop and Supply									
		Pedestal Trap Cover									
		Miscellaneous									
		Steam Bath									
		Steam Enclosure									
		Steam Generator									
		Timer									
		Miscellaneous									
		Sauna									
		Interior									
		Heater									
		Timer									
		Miscellaneous									
		Spa/Hot Tub									
		Fittings									
		Timer									
		Heater									
		Cover									
		Skimmer									
		Miscellaneous									
		Exercise Equipment									
		Miscellaneous									
Subtotal											
Tax											
Labor											
Total											
Differential											

BMF11

Fig. 8.4. Some items, possibly such as steam and sauna, might be ruled out quickly and simply be crossed out, saving time.

Accessories (as per approved drawing)

Est.	Actual	Item	Brand Name	Model	Size	Finish	Furnished By		Installed By		Hook Up By	
							B.S.	O/OA	B.S.	O/OA	B.S.	O/OA
		Mirror										
		Medicine Cabinet										
		Glass Shelves										
		Towel Bar(s)										
		Hydronic/Electric										
		Towel Ring(s)										
		Robe Hook(s)										
		Tub Soap Dish(es)										
		Shower Soap Dish(es)										
		Bidet Soap Dish										
		Lavatory Soap Dish(es)										
		Grab Bars										
		Paper Holder										
		Magazine Rack										
		Soap/Lotion Dispenser										
		Tumbler										
		Tissue Holder										
		Scale										
		Toothbrush Holder										
Subtotal		Hamper										
Tax		Other										
Labor												
Total												
Differential												

Closet Specifications

Est.	Actual	Item	Brand Name	Model	Size	Finish	Furnished By		Installed By		Hook Up By	
							B.S.	O/OA	B.S.	O/OA	B.S.	O/OA
		Poles										
		Shelf(ves)										
		Drawers										
		Shoe Racks										
		Belt/Tie/Scarf Rack(s)										
		Safe										
		Ironing Board										
		Miscellaneous										
Subtotal		Other Storage										
Tax												
Labor												
Total												
Differential												

Fig. 8.5. Accessories prove to the customer that you are thinking of everything.

Windows and Doors

Est.	Actual	Item	Brand Name	Model	Finish	Hardware	Furnished By		Installed By	
							K.S.	O/OA	K.S.	O/OA
Subtotal										
Tax		Special Window and Door Notes:								
Labor										
Total										
Differential										

Flooring

Est.	Actual		Furnished By		Installed By	
			K.S.	O/OA	K.S.	O/OA
		Removal of Existing Floor Covering				
		Preparation of Floor For New Surface				
		Installation of Subfloor/Underlayment				
		New Floor covering Material Description:				
		Manufacturer Pattern Name				
		Pattern Number Pattern Repeat				
		Floor Covering Installation				
		Baseboard Material				
		Transition Treatment				
		Remove and Repair Water Damaged Area				
Subtotal		Special Flooring Notes:				
Tax						
Labor						
Total						
Differential						

SAMPLE

Decorative Surfaces (wall, ceiling, window materials)

Removal Work: Wall _____ Ceiling _____ Window ——— Preparation Work: Wall _____ Ceiling _____ Window _____

Est.	Actual	Description	Brand Name	Model	Finish	Material Quantity	Furnished By		Installed By	
							K.S.	O/OA	K.S.	O/OA
Subtotal										
Tax		Special Decorative Surface Notes:								
Labor										
Total										
Differential										

BMF10

Fig. 8.6. Such items as windows, doors and flooring are usually not included in a "ballpark" figure.

Est.	Actual	**Electrical Work** (except as described above in specific equipment sections)	Furnished By		Installed By	
			B.S.	O/OA	B.S.	O/OA
		Heating System Alteration				
		New Service Panel				
		Code Update				
		Details				
Subtotal						
Tax						
Labor						
Total						
Differential						

Est.	Actual	**Plumbing** (except as described above in specific equipment sections)	Furnished By		Installed By	
			B.S.	O/OA	B.S.	O/OA
		Heating System Alterations				
		New Rough-in Requirements				
		Modifications to Existing Lines				
		Details				
Subtotal						
Tax						
Labor						
Total						
Differential						

Est.	Actual	**General Carpentry** (except as described above in specific equipment sections)	Furnished By		Installed By	
			B.S.	O/OA	B.S.	O/OA
		Demolition Work				
		Existing Fixture and Equipment Removal				
		Trash Removal				
		Reconstruction Work (Except as Previously Stated)				
		Windows				
		Doors				
		Interior Walls				
		Exterior Walls				
		Details				
Subtotal						
Tax						
Labor						
Total						
Differential						

Fig. 8.7. Electrical work, plumbing and carpentry are important to the pricing.

Est.	Actual	Miscellaneous Work		Responsibility	
				B.S.	O/OA
		Trash Removal			
		Jobsite/Room Cleanup			
		Building Permit(s)			
		Structural Engineering/Architectural Fees			
		Inspection Fees			
		Jobsite Delivery			
		Other			
Subtotal					
Tax					
Labor					
Total					
Differential					

TOTALS

I have read these specifications and approve:

Accepted: _____

Accepted: _____

Date: _____

Authorized Company Representative

By: _____

By: _____

Date: _____

BMFll

Fig. 8.8. Trash removal and cleanup are important parts of any estimate.

Notes:

102 Ideas to Help You Sell More Bathrooms

(Adapted from a feature in Kitchen & Bath Business magazine by Patrick J. Galvin.)

Selling more bathrooms is basically simple. We have to get more leads, follow up on them, qualify the prospects and close the sales. And back in the office we have to manage the business to assure good service and reasonable profit. Here are 102 ideas to take with you. But don't stop at these. Use them as thought-starters, and dream up another 102 of your own.

1 SELL A HOLIDAY BATH
What better holiday or birthday gift than a remodeled bathroom or new half-bath? If time is too short for installation, give customers a gift-wrapped color perspective for the tree.

2 SELL ONE FOR SPRING
Miss no opportunity. Spring means house-cleaning and "out with the old" is a good selling approach for a new bathroom in the spring season.

3 BATH WITH EVERY KITCHEN
Make this a standard sales approach for all salespeople: To try to sell a bathroom with every kitchen sale. They will sell some, but even where they don't it will provide you with something for future follow-up.

4 CREATE YOUR ACCESSORIES
You don't want to sell softgoods items that are available cheap at other stores. Pick a great tile, perhaps imported, and have accessories made to match it, such as toilet seat, tank cover, towels, soap dishes, etc. It will give you an exclusive high-end package for bigger-ticket sales.

5 ADD A TELEPHONE
A phone in a hotel bathroom thrills all, although we seldom use it there. But we do at home, and it is easy to wire a telephone jack into any bathroom. Show it in your displays.

6 SELL SPACE PLANNING
It's your forte. More than anything else, you are a professional space planner. Establish this from the first contact and, throughout, make it clear that this is what you are doing. It's what customers lose if they go elsewhere.

7 SELL CUSTOMIZING
Like space planning, customers can get true customizing only from you, not from the general remodeler or others who don't have your expertise. So design in some custom touches, such as shaped or sculpted counter edges and matching backsplash, and be sure to tell the customer about them.

8 SELL IT IN SECTIONS
If the customer can't afford the complete job right now, sell it anyway but on a 2-year or 3-year plan. Schedule it all out, do what is needed most first, but keep it livable. Give them a color perspective for the wall so they don't lose track of what they're aiming at.

9 SELL THE BENEFITS
The high-end products you want to sell are just products, like any others, until you explain the benefits to a customer in understandable terms. Specialists who do it have proven that customers want better products, but the benefits must be detailed.

10 SHOW ALTERNATE PLANS
It works well for upgrading builders. It can work with homeowners also. Show the super bath plan first. If they turn white at the price you can steer them to the alternate. But if they turn green with envy or desire, color them sold.

11 SELL WITH PERSPECTIVES
Many try to avoid perspective drawings in bathroom jobs, but in such cramped space they can be more important than in kitchens because visualization is more difficult. Where talk and floorplans might not sell, perspectives can.

12 DESIGN IN RADIO AND TV
Many customers want these in the bathroom, but when they do it themselves at home it adds danger. In your displays show these features, designed-in and built-in. TV is best recessed in a wall between studs, possibly with the box in an adjacent closet. Comply with codes and keep it safe for them.

13 HELP THE D-I-Y'ers
Do-it-yourselfers aren't going to disappear, so give them help and let them know you *can* help them. You still will sell your space planning and customizing, and possibly some high-end merchandise also, and this is where the profit is anyway.

14 HIRE A REAL ARTIST
Bathroom jobs are labor-intensive, and they also are cost-intensive. It is difficult for a buyer to see where that $14,000 is going. Good artwork can do more than anything else to show them they are getting their money's worth, and help a sale that might otherwise get away.

15 SELL IN NEARBY TOWNS
Country folks often go to the city to buy, but you can get a jump on the competition by outfitting a trailer or mobile home with a good display, scheduling it in nearby towns, and then advertising the hours and locations.

16 SOLVE A PROBLEM
As with kitchens, solving a problem is the most effective way to sell a bathroom remodeling job. But homeowners often live with problems so long that they get used to them and fail to recognize them. Quiz the prospects long enough to coax some complaints out of them, then identify the problems for them and show how your redesign can solve them.

17 PUT AN "OUTLET" NEXT DOOR
Many good prospects never overcome their fear of an expensive-looking showroom. So rent a store next door. Put a sign across the front that reads "OUTLET" and nothing more. Stock it with vanities, cabinets, and a "used and bruised" department for trade-ins or old displays. Have an open door to your real showroom and many will overcome their fear and wander in.

18 MAKE A LENDABLE SCRAPBOOK
Clip ideas from magazines and newspapers. Add your literature and pictures of your installations and displays. Paste them all in a scrap book and use as a sales tool. Let any good prospect take it home over night and return it the next morning.

19 AFTER IT'S IN, SEND AN ORCHID
Any woman who receives an orchid corsage on Saturday will wear it to church or brunch Sunday. Send one the Saturday after installation and her friends will hear about it.

20 PAY PROFIT BILL FIRST
In costing out labor, materials, overhead, write down "Profit" in black and white. Give it a specific figure and pay this bill first, to your own company. It will help prevent your doing foolish things later with other figures.

21 UTILIZE ALL DEALER AIDS
Manufacturers often offer good literature in envelope sizes that gather dust in dealer store rooms. Note all the small stuffers you get with bills from department stores and gasoline companies. Similar stuffers can be effective for you as direct mail, and, at worst, they can't hurt.

22 MOVE INTO MULTIPLES

There are developments in your town, each with hundreds of homes and only four or five different bathroom floorplans. Get those floorplans, all minimal because they were spec projects, and design great bathrooms for them. Then advertise, or go door-to-door, showing both before and after artwork. In your own office you can design an A plan (complete job) and lesser B and C plans, and get new jobs with low sales cost. This can be a very productive activity for a slow period.

23 FOLLOW HOME TRANSFERS

Purchase of an existing home is a signal for a probable need for remodeling, and usually the bathroom and kitchen come first. Have a mailing prepared for these, and follow up a week after with a phone call.

24 FOLLOW JOB TRANSFERS

A job transfer also is a signal for a new family moving into an existing home. Make a congratulatory call to the person moving out and ask about disposition of the house. The transferee might want to fix it up for sale, or might tip you off to new ownership. Invite feedback from every person in your firm on these transfers.

25 GET HELP FROM HELP

You have, say, six persons in your firm, and you work with four subs and know five or six of each of their people, and each of these 25 or 30 people knows 20 others. Make up an incentive plan to get your non-sales help working for you. Set up a six-month contest for all of them, not to sell but to get leads.

26 SELL A BATHROOM LAUNDRY

Few homeowners realize how convenient a bathroom laundry can be, which makes it a good selling possibility. The plumbing is there and it is a point of last use for dirty clothing. Draw some small-space designs, taking advantage of the various side-by-side and over-under conformations, and advertise the benefits.

27 SELL IMPULSE ITEMS

You might prefer to avoid cash business, but it can improve cash flow. Impulse items can include extra fancy vanity or medicine cabinets, mirrors, tops, accessories. If they are in displays just mark them for separate sale, but be sure to have some in stock so you don't rob displays.

28 GO AFTER APARTMENTS

Apartment bathrooms get remodeled, on the average, every 14 years. Usually this is just replacement business. But it is worth a try with some creative selling for a big upgrading job on a lot of units in one sale.

29 CREATE NEW SPACE

Only you, the professional space planner, realize how easily you can move into a closet or borrow space from another room for more bathroom space. Or, more often, you can reframe a door to get an added six inches along a wall that will permit a cabinet run. This creation of new space can sell bathroom jobs.

30 CLOSE WITH "WHICH-HUNT"

At the close, don't invite a "no" answer. Ask *which* plan the customer wants, *which* fixture, *which* material, *which* week to start the job. Think positive.

31 MAKE AN OPTIONS LIST

At the close, have a list of needed things in the plan, but also have an options list. Then if the price is a stumbling block to closing, you can go through the options and discuss them one by one, explaining why they are in the plan and defending them, but clearing the way for moving the price down into acceptable range.

32 SELL A DESIGN PACKAGE

Many prospects insist on buying some things from their own sources. But it cost you $70 or more for this lead, so don't lose them easily. Make up design packages in which you do the design and space-planning job with some materials (the A package), another with consultation but no materials (the B package), or with just planning and drawings.

33 SELL A BEDROOM LAV
Customers seldom think of a vanity cabinet, lav and fancy medicine cabinet in the bedroom. That's what makes it a great idea. Add it to the bathroom sale, or sell it to save a job that might be getting away.

34 SELL STRUCTURAL LIGHTING
Lighting fixtures are fine, but you have to buy them. Structural lighting–soffit, bracket, cornice, valance–can be much more dramatic and effective, and be more profitable because you design it and make it yourself with ordinary building materials..

Advertising and Promotion for More and Better Leads

35 AIM ADVERTISING FOR LEADS
Except for special sales, the aim of all bathroom advertising always should be for more leads. So don't try to sell a bathroom in an ad. Just try to get prospects in and onto lead cards. Ads don't sell bathrooms. Salespeople sell bathrooms.

36 TELL THEM THEIR NEEDS
In many cases, prospects don't realize they really need a bathroom remodeling. They have gotten used to getting by. So, in advertising and promotion, tell them what they need and why. Tell them about energy saving and water conservation, ask if there have been recent family changes, etc.

37 TRY TO CREATE DESIRE
Since prospects don't even know their bathroom needs, they do not have desire for a change in their bathrooms. So create ads that stimulate desire, stressing new comfort, convenience, aesthetics, pride.

38 FOCUS ON THE NEWEST
Advertise the newest available products, especially if they have been publicized in consumer magazines. Invite people in to see the new wonders of the bathroom world, in your showroom.

39 FIGHT FLIGHT TO FRANCE
Try being specific. You are selling against foreign vacations and other similar uses of "disposable" money, so compare them in terms of value for the money, depreciation, forgettability, long-term satisfaction, investment potential.

40 PROMOTE BATH SEMINARS
Advertise seminars for architects, for designers, for the public, or even for the home economics classes in local schools. Stage them in the showroom, but don't hesitate to go to a group if you are invited. Talk about opportunities for finding more space in small bathrooms, and make sure your remarks get into the local papers.

41 ADVERTISE A COMPLETE JOB
In any area, many people think they must deal with several trades for a new bathroom. In advertising, tell them you do it all, from design to installation, and there is no one else to deal with.

42 BE A CLUB SPEAKER
Every local group needs a program, be it Lions, Rotary, church, PTA, women or men. Offer your services with demonstrations of new materials, new products and bathroom design ideas. If you feel you can't do this well, designate a good speaker in your firm.

43 TRY A BIRTHDAY PARTY
It might be for your firm, for your showroom, for your affiliation with a supplier, or even for city hall. The Quaker Maid dealers of New Jersey did this and it gave them something great to advertise and promote. It can be good for spring, for fall, or both.

44 PUT BATH IN KITCHEN ADS
If you have gone into bathroom remodeling from the kitchen business, as so many dealers have, add a line or two in every kitchen ad to tell the public you also are the bathroom headquarters in your area. This applies also, of course, for general remodelers, independent designers and others.

45 GO INTO OTHER WINDOWS

Specialty and department stores often are on the lookout for fresh ideas for their display windows. Approach them with a few suggested perspective drawings of bathroom displays as themes for a window and you might get a month of free promotion.

46 TRY FOR A BANK DISPLAY

Banks everywhere are scrambling for second mortgage loans for home remodeling, and a major or minor bathroom remodeling job might easily require the kind of money that will interest them. Again, make up a few perspectives of model bathroom displays in different sizes, and give it a try.

47 TRACK ALL LEADS

Leads are the lifeblood of your business, but they must tell you where they came from so you can measure the effectiveness of your advertising media. Track them all, keep records, and check them frequently.

48 CANVASS WITH STAY-AT-HOMES

You can mail to the neighborhood when a job is going in, but another effective way to get more leads is to pay area housewives, househusbands or whoever is staying at home to knock on doors. They will have time periods between the comings and goings of the children, they need the extra money and the freedom to choose their own time to work. Pay them by the hour to make calls and fill in lead cards, but not for sales pitches. For sales, follow up with real salespeople.

49 CALL OLD CUSTOMERS

You probably have many, many customers who bought your services in years past. They know you and your work. Contact them, by mail or by phone, to let them know what's new in bathroom products, and ask them to come in see for themselves.

50 DISPLAY IN BATH BOUTIQUES

Bath boutiques (primarily softgoods) can be found everywhere. Make a deal with them to display their wares in your displays if they will let you put in a fancy bathroom display in their place. Work with them for more leads.

51 MONITOR AD EFFECTIVENESS

Ads that don't work represent money thrown away, a cost factor that must be added to your pricing. Discard the ones that don't work, and do it right now. And don't confuse contributions (ads in such media as the Boy Scout yearbook) with advertising.

52 ADVERTISE HELPFUL TIPS

This is a self-help era, and readers of your advertising want to know a lot about a lot of things. It might be how to fix a dent in a cabinet door, how to adjust hinges, how to clean a marble top, how to repair a countertop, etc. Ads of this type get high readership. But always invite readers to the showroom for more information. Remember, you are after leads.

53 ADVERTISE ON VEHICLES

All of your vehicles have space that you have paid for. Use it. Perhaps you can put kitchens on one side and baths on the other, or other services on both sides and baths on the back. But use this ad space for bathrooms as well as your other products or services.

54 JAZZ UP JOBSITE SIGNS

A company name and logo are better than nothing, but try for more. Try for a come-on message, such as "Another Home Made Happier by a Jones Bathroom. See More at Jones Baths and Kitchens," etc.

55 CO-OP WITH OTHERS

There are other bathroom firms in your area who would like TV ads, but find them too expensive. Talk with them. A few of you can get together for occasional TV or for an occasional full page in the paper that you couldn't afford otherwise. You don't step on each other's toes if you are on opposite sides of town.

Use Showroom Imaginatively with Displays that Stimulate

56 SHOW COMPLETE BATHROOMS Products alone sell only products, and shoppers might as well go to where they can get the lowest price. Vignettes are better, but they tend to invite price comparisons. Complete bathroom displays are more likely to sell complete bathroom jobs, so show them complete.

57 SHOW GLAMOR PRODUCTS A whirlpool bath with water churning packs a more potent punch than a catalog picture. So do the real things, the real marble and the real gold, the fancy crystal mirrors and the real steam bath. Sure, it takes money, but it also makes sales.

58 ADD DISPLAY FLAIR Your displays should show your design ability. Add all the accessories that might be found in that bathroom in the home, and do it with an eye to colors and textures. Remember, your displays sell you.

59 SHOW INTERESTING IDEAS What puts you ahead of others is your ideas, your way of working with available products. For example, show a dropped vanity top for a child, with a lowered medicine cabinet, so the upper one can be locked. Instead of a six-foot tub, show a five-foot tub with planter and grow lights at the end. Put at least one great idea in every display.

60 REPEAT OPEN HOUSES Many firms have open houses when they change their displays—every year or two or three. A showroom is much too important and too expensive and valuable for such infrequent exposure. Plan at least two a year, and keep your mind open to more when the occasion warrants. An exciting new product is reason enough, or a bathday party, or any holiday.

61 TAKE ALL TO THE MALL Perhaps you do it with kitchen or other services, but do it separately with bathrooms. Malls in all areas are where it's happening, and they rent space for "shows" in their public areas. Try it with bathrooms only, excluding your other services or products. Combined, it might be too much for such a busy, fleeting audience and you could end up with confused lead cards.

62 RETIRE THE OUTMODED Your showroom is the showcase for all of your genius, so don't keep out-of-date products or ideas in it just because they are paid for. Keep it entirely fresh and current, or it loses sales value.

63 STOCK ALL CABINETS Nobody can appreciate some of the innovative medicine cabinets, especially foreign ones, unless you put things in all of those interesting spaces. And this applies to bath systems and anything beyond the ordinary. Do a complete job in displays for maximum sellability.

64 SHOW RELATED CONCEPTS In some space in the showroom, show some of the other activities that can go in or with the bathroom. This includes such things as a health spa, exercise machines, a sauna, etc.

65 HAVE A HALL OF FAME Your Hall of Fame can be color photos of beautiful bathrooms, preferably ones you did yourself but, if necessary, get photos from suppliers. Cover an entire wall with these, with names and addresses where possible, as silent testimonials and to suggest ideas to prospects.

66 LIST SATISFIED CUSTOMERS After a few years you should have hundreds of names. One known dealer has thousands. He lists name, address, phone number, duplicates them and leaves them in several bound books around the showroom for browsers to look at—a powerful sales tool.

67 USE A/V STATIONS
Several audio/visual systems are available that use slides or film strips, with and without narrative. They deliver good sales messages, unattended, through the hours when you have them turned on. People who wouldn't hear the same thing from a salesperson will listen avidly to these robots and get your message.

68 BE JUDICIOUS WITH MASS
Mass displays are good where emphasis is on products, such as home centers or high-end decorative plumbing and hardware stores. But in a full-service bathroom remodeling showroom they invite only price comparison and shopping. So make sure your displays fit the kind of business you want to do.

69 PITCH EMPTY NESTERS
What do empty nesters have? Vacated rooms. If there is space for it, put in a display to suggest moving the bathroom to a bigger room for more comfort and convenience.

70 CHANGE DISPLAYS OFTEN
You can't replace entire displays often because it would be too expensive. But you can change them in other ways. You can replace fixtures with different colors, change acessories, reposition some displays, so repeat visitors won't be tempted to think they've already seen everything and walk out. Next time you design displays, plan and build them for some of these occasional changes.

71 LIGHT THEM DRAMATICALLY
Use lighting for drama. Choose bold fixtures. Don't think of whether customers will buy the lighting. Think of whether it will attract the attention of customers. That's the important thing in a showroom. Get prospects' attention, and then you can sell them what they'll buy.

72 USE THEME DISPLAYS
You've done this, or seen it, with kitchen displays—the Country Kitchen, or Swiss, or French, etc. Plan themes for bathrooms also for more appeal and design cohesion.

73 ADD A "PRIVATE" AREA
Behind a locked door marked "Private" in the showroom, show your really super items, the very expensive ones such as a deluxe spa, lavs with real gold faucets, etc. Allude to it only to good prospects so they'll ask to look, and then let the ego appeal help you sell the ultra high end.

74 SHOWCASE THE RESTROOMS
Since every showroom must have a restroom available, make it spectacular. Make it one of your best displays. When anyone goes in there, that person has time to admire and to think in total privacy. That time can work for you and perhaps lead to a sale.

75 GIVE VIGNETTES A THEME
Vignettes often are used to show added door styles or tops. Make each vignette do more than that. Dig up a theme idea for each one, such as a home office, or a beer cellar, or a barbecue area, etc.

76 SHARE WITH A PLUMBER
If some other firm, such as a plumbing contractor, has the bathroom remodeling business sewed up in your area through fixture sales, offer to join your planning and design expertise with his or her sales, share showroom displays and sales so you both profit.

77 GIVE A SHOWROOM MAP
Pictures and the printed word can be effective in a showroom. Make a map of displays, with pictures or drawings, explaining features, and give it to the browser. It can free personnel from preliminaries for more productive work and, at the same time, give prospects time to sell themselves.

78 SHOW LOCAL SOLUTIONS
If your area has many bathroom radiators or chimney protrusions, show solutions to these problems in your displays. Some older neighborhoods have balloon construction rather than platform, so room corners might not be defined well. Show what you can do with problems here.

79 QUALITY ABOVE QUANTITY

We're concerned with bathroom displays here, but keep it in perspective. If you have been designing and selling kitchens for years, that will continue to be the main part of your business. So aim for quality, not quantity, in the bathroom displays, and concentrate on getting the most out of every square foot.

Effective Management Will Help You Sell More and Protect Profit

80 PAY SUBS IMMEDIATELY

Fast pay is your ticket to much better service from you subcontractors, and more control with fewer headaches. The results of fast pay will be much more valuable than the discount for EOM plus 30.

81 KEEP SUBS OFF BILL

Until the final contract, keep subcontractor bills separate. They can kill the sale. If you can, let subs bill separately. But if you general the job, include sub bills in your price because you deserve a markup on subcontracts.

82 DON'T QUIBBLE WITH SUBS

Let them know if there is a problem, and settle it. But pay them and don't waste time and patience on minor problems. Quibbling leads only to poorer service.

83 NOR WITH CUSTOMERS

Don't quibble with good customers, either. Remember, any satisfied customer is worth at least two more jobs and possibly a lot more. Check the cost of the problem first, then decide whether you want to pay the price for arguing with the customer.

84 INCLUDE A BATH SURVEY

In every survey for a kitchen job or other service you sell, include as many facts as you can for a potential bathroom job. Depending on each circumstance, you can include the pitch with the kitchen or postpone it until later. But at least you will have a lead card for a bath job.

85 HAVE ANSWERS ON MONEY

Most customers make their own deals on financing before they sign. But there are those who have no idea what to do. Check with all lending institutions in your area and know their policies, and be prepared also to advise on life insurance loans in your state.

86 PUT PROFIT FIRST

There are jobs not worth doing. There are products not worth handling. All have a direct effect on profitability, and lack of profit can put you out of business. Take only jobs that you can do right—and profitably!

87 UPGRADE YOUR BUILDERS

Never have builders been better candidates for upgrading. House prices are high, they look a lot the same on the outside, and need something inside to justify the prices. Bathrooms and kitchens can be the beneficiaries. Have open houses for builders and their architects, encourage them to consult with you before their houses are blueprinted, and show them how moving a door or window can save enough to pay for a better bathroom.

88 SEND CLERKS TO SCHOOL

Clerks, drivers, and anyone else in your firm who deals with customers should know something about planning, design and installation. Send them to available schools along with sales personnel. Many good salespeople got their start this way.

89 MAKE CHANGES FAST

If you are new in bathrooms, you will deal with new suppliers and new products. Sometimes the synergy just isn't there. If changes are called for, make them right away. Delays will only cost more in the long run.

90 STRESS CABINET SALES

Cabinets always have been our main profit sources, so always think of cabinets in any bathroom. Look for ways to move the tub and the lav to make space for a cabinet wall system.

91 KNOW THE PRODUCTS

Product knowledge, for all of your people, is as important in the bathroom business as it is in the kitchen business. They must know about what you sell and what your competitors sell, or the customer will lose confidence fast.

92 REDUCE IT AND CLEAR IT

When you make mistakes in your purchases, and everybody does, don't put all that stuff in the back room. Storage costs you money. Reduce it to cost and clear it out immediately. You even can make it a good promotional event worth advertising.

93 BUY FROM DISTRIBUTORS

As with kitchens, in buying bathroom merchandise your best friend is your independent distributor. Direct deals tie up capital and you might be buying a dozen mistakes. A good distributor provides services you need, and when you give him loyalty you get loyalty in return.

94 QUALIFY LEADS EARLY

Most wasted sales time is lost on browsers who never were prospects. Develop a system to find out if the browser can and might buy, or won't. And a system that works in Waco won't work in Westchester, so develop your own.

95 MEASURE IT ALL TWICE

You can plug a lot of profit leaks if you double-check all measurements before ordering. Bathrooms are even more critical than kitchens. And this includes making sure you can get items up the stairs and through the doors.

96 TRY FOR FLAT PRICES

If you pay subs by the hour you pay for coffee breaks and gab fests. Try for flat rates per job or per operation, or, at worst, per day.

97 BE A CONSUMER HERO

Most cities and many communities have expert panels to mediate disputes between home improvement contractors and homeowners. But such panels have few experts. Volunteer. Be the expert, and a hero.

98 ASK SUPPLIER HELP

If bathrooms are new to you, you might need help on buying, stocking, financial management. Your custom manufacturer, rep and distributor have a vested interest in your success and can give you a lot of help. Don't wait until the boat is sinking. Get advice in advance, and consult with them on how to build sales for a sound business.

99 CHECK YOUR ESTIMATES

Most dealers fall into systems in their estimating. It is important to recap all jobs and check real figures against estimates quarterly. Estimate bases can change rapidly, and if you let them go for two quarters you can lose a lot of money, and the more business you do the more you can lose.

100 DEAL LEADS SELECTIVELY

Any remodeling salesperson should be able to sell a bathroom job, but it is a fact that some resist it, some love it, and sales performance is variable from person to person. Find out which of your people do well with bathrooms, and try to match the salesperson's personality with that of the prospect before you deal out the leads.

101 ESTABLISH PRO IDENTITY

Have you been to an NKBA school? To other schools? Have you been Rotary president, United Fund chairman? Anything–put up the shingles where they show. Remember, you are selling against others who are less qualified, against fly-by-nighters. These pieces of paper help establish you as a pro and a permanent member of the community. That helps you sell.

102 MEAN BUSINESS!

The first rule of success is "you gotta believe!" Enthusiasm is contagious. The bathroom business is a great business, a challenging business, a business of helping people with their problems, and no business is more satisfying or more fun. Generate enthusiasm in all your employees (you can't generate if you don't have it yourself) and that will transmit to customers.

Notes

Contemporary Sales Techniques

Answer Questions with More Questions

(Based on material by Cameron Snyder, CKD)

Now that we know how bathrooms are supposed to be sold it's time to address the sales techniques that can result in a successful sale to a satisfied customer with a reasonable profit for your firm and an endless string of referrals.

When we talk about a reasonable profit we are not talking only about the owner of the firm we work for. We are talking about you and me, because all of us, whether we own the place or work for salary or commission, are really operating our own business. Our earnings, our welfare, our happiness and our success all depend on how we do it. And the earnings and success of the firm that employs us also depend on how we run our own businesses.

What we all should realize early in this game is that structures exist that enable all of us to do the job right within a reasonable amount of time. We only have to follow established procedures that have been proven in the field, but *follow them with commitment and enthusiasm.*

Selling starts at first contact

The structures that help you organize the job all the way through completion start with your first contact with the customer, who at this time is only a prospect. We would like this first contact to be in the showroom, but frequently it is a telephone call, and it might present an immediate problem that we have to deal with. That's fine,

because a problem gives us an opportunity right from the start to show who we are and how we work. For example, the caller speaks:

"Hi. My name is John Smith and I've been thinking about redoing the main bathroom in our house. I saw in the yellow pages that you folks remodel bathrooms, so how about coming out here and taking a look?"

This kind of proposal is not infrequent, and it gives you several options. You can answer:

"Sure. I can get out there tomorrow and look at it. Where do you live?"

It should be obvious that this is not a good answer. You said you would visit without knowing where the caller lives, which might be in another town miles away. And you committed to the time and expense of the trip without any attempt at qualifying the caller, with no idea of whether this is a good prospect or no prospect at all. Alternatively, you could have answered:

"Sorry, Mr. Smith, but we don't work that way. You have to come into the showroom first so we can talk it over and we can show you what we have. Come in when you have a chance, and we'll discuss it."

This is too negative, and instead of inviting

his business you are telling him what to do. And you haven't even attempted to make a showroom appointment. Think of how you, yourself, would react. Probably you would go immediately back to the yellow pages to look for someone else to call. What you really want to do is *invite* this caller to come to the showroom, and *convince* him it is the best course of action. Here's one way:

"That's great. I appreciate you calling us at Designer Baths. My name is Larry. Do you mind if I get a little information from you first—like, how do you spell your name, Mr. Smith?"

"That's OK. It's S-m-i-t-h."

"Fine, Mr. Smith, and where do you live?"

"We're at 614 Shadwell Dr."

"Oh, yes, that's a nice area. We've done several kitchens and bathrooms out there. And your phone number?"

"606-0606."

"Have you ever been to our showroom?"

"No. I just decided it's time to do something, so I looked in the book and picked up the phone."

"Well, you called the right place, Mr. Smith, and I'd love to come out and look. But my experience always has been that it is far better if you come in here first, where you can see the many ideas we show in our displays, and the new materials and fantastic new products, not to mention all the services we offer. If it's OK with you, let's set up an appointment when you can come in and we can talk here."

"OK, I guess we could do that."

"Fine. When would be a good time? How about Thursday at 4?"

"No, not Thursday. But I'm free today. How about 4 this afternoon?"

"I can make that. Will your wife be involved in this project?

"You bet. Why do you think I made this call? She'll be there with me."

"Fine. Again, my name is Larry, and I'll see you both this afternoon at 4."

Here, Larry has gotten a grip on an apparently good prospect. He has gotten a start on qualifying him, knows where he lives, knows both he and his wife are interested in a bathroom and that the wife is apparently the driving force, has steered the first meeting to the showroom, and has shown, in both words and attitude, that he is proud of his firm and what it can do.

This is much better than throwing away the telephone call. But it is only a start.

Now let's follow a typical prospect and a typical designer/salesperson through the procedure, step by step, when the first meeting is in the showroom. As we do, remember we are discussing *typical* acts in *typical* situations. There always will be atypical prospects or situations. When such cases arise remember that, as a professional with a full-service professional firm, these might be prospects that you do not want as customers and that your company can't serve properly and profitably. For all practical purposes, however, from this point on in this chapter we are dealing with professional selling practices that apply, to some extent, to any sales situation.

Remember also that you have a goal if you are a designer/salesperson, and that is to complete the sale with three customer contacts: (1) a showroom visit, (2) a visit to the home for interview and measuring, and (3) a visit to the showroom for your presentation, the close and the contract signing. *Even in sales that do not involve a full redesign, if your firm will be responsible for the project it would be unwise to skip the home inspection.*

The Technique of Asking Questions to Guide the Sales Process

Asking questions is a way to get information we need. But to the skilled salesperson with the right technique it has several purposes:

A. To obtain information
B. To control the sale
C. To answer objections
D. To appear more professional
E. To prepare for the close
F. _____
G. _____

There are two kinds of questions.

A. *Open-ended* questions invite discussion. Use them when you want the customer to talk. For example:

"Tell me, what is it about your present bathroom that you don't like?"

"What are the most important things you will consider when choosing your new bathroom?"

"If you could describe the perfect bathroom for your family, what words would you use?"

B. *Closed-ended* questions cut off discussion by demanding a one-word answer, such as:

"Do you prefer a cultured marble counter with lavatory, or a solid surface, or a decorative laminate?"

"If I can design a bathroom that fulfills all of your requirements within your budget, will you be prepared to place an order at our next meeting?"

Use a closed-ended question when you can't get a customer to answer an open-ended question, or to get minor agreement, or to close.

"Mr. Smith, would you prefer we start installation the first week in April, or the second week?"

"If you were to choose between the granite counter or the solid surface, which would you choose?"

People buy emotionally, but they justify their purchase logically. **"The Rule of Three"** breaks down the logical barrier and gets the customer to reveal emotions. This means it takes three or more questions and rephrasing them to get to the emotional level. Example:

Customer: **"Is that vanity solid wood?"**
Designer: **"Are you interested in solid wood?"**
Customer: **"Yes."**
Designer: **"Can you tell me why solid wood is so important to you?"**
Customer: **"Yes. I had a vanity before that was made of flakeboard, and it warped."**
Designer: **"Let me explain the construction of our vanity cabinets and why they won't warp."**

Answer a question with a question.

Example: Your customers inquire about the lead time and possible delivery on a product. Normal response would be to give a specific answer, such as "six to eight weeks." If they do not need the product for 12 weeks, your answer would give them four more weeks to make a decision and perhaps shop around a little bit more.

A better response would be to ask them another question:

"When will you be ready for the product?"
"In 12 weeks."
"That is just about right. We should finalize the plan now and get it all ordered so we can keep that 12-week delivery constraint."

Another example:

Customer: **"Can I get a stainless steel sink with this solid surface counter?"**
Designer: **"Would you like a stainless steel sink with that counter?"**
Customer: **"I don't know. I was just curious. Actually, I think I'd prefer the counter and sink all in one piece. But my aunt said stainless steel is better."**

The designer now can explain the differences. A yes or no answer might have wasted time and boxed the designer into a corner.

It won't always work out with just three contacts. At times you will have to redo the plans and make a second presentation. But if you remember the goal and focus on it you will be prepared at that first presentation with your best plan and with alternate plans in mind so you will be able to make fast changes and get the contract signed with one presentation. This one factor can make the difference between 8-hour days and 12-hour days.

Step 1. The meeting.

You see them peering in through the showroom window, a man and woman. You see them pointing with a lot of smiles and "yes" nods, then they open the door and come in.

(Start observing them at the earliest moment. So far this looks good, all positive from the nods to the smiles.)

You let them walk around, looking, feeling the finishes. They are animated and interested, particularly in a triple vanity cabinet with two drawer banks, sculptured top and under-mounted lav. When you see them starting to slow down, you approach:

"Good afternoon. I'm George Marsh. I designed that bath display you were looking at. I designed the vanity cabinet for two persons so each could have a separate set of drawers, so it does take quite a lot of space. Is your bathroom large enough for this kind of arrangement?

That, in essence, is how a showroom should be used. It should show a variety of ideas as well as merchandise. It should have clean, neat displays that stimulate the desires of the prospects who see them, and it should show that you know how to solve bathroom design problems.

That means, obviously, that you should not have taken a fixture or accessory out of a display

to fill an order. A vanity counter without a lav would indicate to the prospects that you sell holes in countertops. Your cabinets should be filled with bath towels, wash cloths and the other things that go in a bathroom, not with literature and the receptionist's purse.

You don't know who these people are yet. But you started off well with a cheerful greeting, you introduced yourself and you fed them a question about something you saw they were interested in. Give them a few seconds. If they volunteer their names it is another positive sign. If they are coy about volunteering, ask them. In this case the woman volunteers:

"Hi. I'm Shirley Smith and this is my husband, Bill. We were just driving by and saw your place. This is nice, with the big cabinets and with the shower separate from the tub, but I'm afraid it might be too big for our house."

Step 2. Qualifying the prospect.

Qualifying is a procedure for finding facts without offending. You want to know:

• That the prospect lives in your trading area;

• That the prospect is genuinely interested in buying products that you represent;

• That the prospect can afford to buy;

• That *Now* is the time the prospect wants to buy (critical for clients building a new home);

• That one or more of the people visiting with you will make the buying decision.

• That you can sell to this prospect and complete the project profitably.

(For business planning reasons, you will also

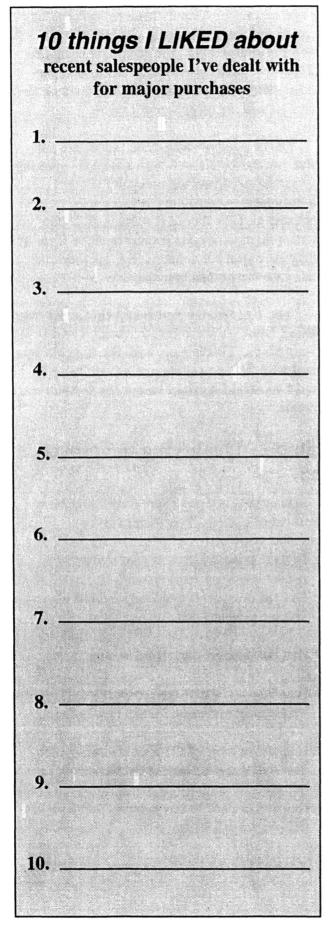

10 things I LIKED about
recent salespeople I've dealt with
for major purchases

1. _____

2. _____

3. _____

4. _____

5. _____

6. _____

7. _____

8. _____

9. _____

10. _____

want to ask how they learned about your firm: Referral? Location? Promotion? Advertisement?)

How do you find out these things? You ask, but tactfully.

1. "What part of town do you live in?" There can be no problem with that question, and you find out quickly if they are local or from far away. Also, it gives you an opportunity to name customers you have served in their area.

2. "Are you planning a new home, or are you thinking of remodeling?" This is a good ice-breaker question and it will give you timing insights. For example, if they are dreaming about a bathroom for a new home on the drawing board for next year, you can't serve them today as well as you can serve a couple with a new home under construction right now. But take care to be diplomatic. Even if their house is a year away *your selling job has already started.* Be helpful. Tell them they will get information on new bathroom equipment from you over the next year while they are completing their planning (and kitchen equipment also, if you also sell kitchens). Get their address and stay in touch. But, meanwhile, get on to the other prospects who need a bathroom right now.

3. "Are you interested in a bathroom?" Too bland. How about **"Are you having some problems with the bathroom you have now?"** That's a leading question, and any emotion in their response can tip you off to how much they need it or how soon.

Now is the time to start matching the prospect's needs and wants with the products you represent. Structure your showroom presentation around this specific client information. For example, don't spend 20 minutes telling the prospect about the wonderful custom vanities you have (which take 16 weeks to get) when the prospects just told you they are remodeling their bathroom to be ready for a wedding reception that will be held at home next month. Some firms do develop a set "tour" through the showroom from which they rarely deviate, but many successful selling pros do well tailoring their tour to the clients' specific interests. In our fast-paced world, most clients feel special when they receive special, customized services and attention. And they buy from salespeople who make them feel special.

4. "Have you decided on a figure yet for your bathroom investment?" Some prospects will have definite ideas about what they will spend or how much a bathroom ought to cost. But usually they will be fishing for answers just as you will. They may ask **"How much does this display bathroom cost?"** Tell them, but point out how the price is affected by the cabinet line, the fixtures, the counters, floor and wall materials and the unique design features. Prices change, of course, but you can tell them honestly that **"in one recent price list, you could buy a toilet for $152 or another model of the same brand for $1,385, or another brand for $102 or for $1,041. I saw one listed at $3,850."** Or they may ask how much the "average" bathroom costs. Without sounding hostile or condescending, answer them with a question: **"There really isn't any average, just as with cars or houses. How much are you willing to invest?"**

You can judge their affordability quotient somewhat by the neighborhood they live in, by the car they drive, by what they say about their home, by what they do for a living and how many incomes they have, by their attitude about expensive products in the showroom. (But beware. If they drive a luxury car it might mean their money is committed and they *can't* afford a new bathroom rather than that they can.)

5. "How soon would you like to have your new bathroom?" That's one way to find out if they want to buy now. However, they did come into the showroom now, showing basic interest. For prospects planning a remodeling project, this is a time when your own enthusiasm and creativity can shift the buying decision from later to now.

Trade magazines have researched how long

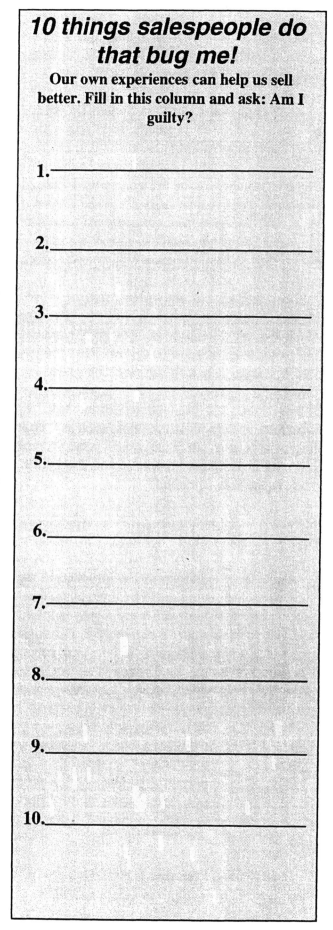

10 things salespeople do that bug me!

Our own experiences can help us sell better. Fill in this column and ask: Am I guilty?

1.

2.

3.

4.

5.

6.

7.

8.

9.

10.

families live in a house before remodeling it. There seem to be two clear trends: Either they remodel immediately after purchasing, or they wait until they have lived in it 14-17 years.

6. Do you want to sell to them? Do you have the right products and the right prices for this particular prospect? Can you do the entire job in a way that will be satisfactory to them? Some customers can be difficult to work with. Be aware, but don't be hasty about quitting on them. Always give your customer the benefit of the doubt and never decide to abandon a prospect until you first discuss it with your manager.

During this initial showroom visit, the most important thing for you to do is to stimulate conversation, because the more they say the more they will reveal about themselves. But "conversation" means *they talk, not you.* They talk. You listen. Questions they can answer with a yes or no tend to close a conversation. Ask questions that open conversation, such as **"what do you like most (or least) about your present bathroom"** or **"how long have you lived with your present bathroom?"**

Step 3. Sell yourself, your firm.

At this first meeting with the prospects in the showroom it is important to let them know that you are creative, innovative and totally helpful, and that your company is *dependable, thorough and the best in the business.* If your company has been in business for 30 years, that fact is important to the prospect because there has to be a reason. If your company has been in business for three years, talk of the growth that proves good work and be prepared to offer referrals.

That is not important to people who are out to buy a pound of nails. It can make all the difference when they are going to spend $10,000 for a new bathroom.

If you can get the prospect excited about your talent and your firm's dependability, that prospect can't wait to spend the money.

Step 4. Sell the Appointment.

When everything looks favorable, you want to make an appointment to get into the home to survey these prospects and measure the space.

This is important. If they will make the appointment the job is 90% sold. All you have to do then is be careful not to unsell it. These prospects now become clients.

They know very well that when they commit to an appointment they are almost committing to buying, so they tend to resist even when they really want to buy. Nobody is in a hurry to spend thousands of dollars. You have to sell them

• **on the benefits of doing it right now,**

• **on not depriving themselves needlessly of something they are going to buy anyway,**

• **on getting started before the manufacturers raise prices,**

• **on having their new bathroom before the holidays or before their next party,**

• **on doing it before your busy season,**

• **or any other reasons you can think of.**

When the appointment has been set, tell the clients what to expect. Tell them you will ask a lot of questions and the design will be tailored according to their answers so the new bathroom will be personalized specifically for them, so it will be important that both spouses be present. Advise them to meet with all members of the household and to list their needs, their desires and their bathroom problems, and to rate their relative importance before you arrive.

In the real world, one person alone may meet with you in the survey appointment. If this is the case, be sure all pertinent information gets passed

What are you selling? A remodeling project or a design fee?

Wherever bathroom/kitchen specialists gather, the question of design fees comes up. Whether you call it that or a retainer, it requires certain specific sales techniques.

First, the sales focus is different. When selling a project your emphasis is on products, service, guarantees and total cost of the project.

These are important and need to be discussed in your first meeting, but any in-depth talk on these issues should be saved for a later meeting after the plan has been developed.

If you are selling a retainer you need to talk in terms of design expertise, professionalism, rules of design, and the like. You are selling an abstract concept rather than a physical product. Your goal is to convince the customer that it is in their best interest to work with you in planning their space and they need not continue talking to other dealers. Lift them out of the market!

Face it. There are dozens of places our customers can go and have their projects designed free. If you ask for a retainer, the customer will conclude naturally that you will be more expensive. You should address that concern early in your conversation.

For example, your customer tells you they have gotten several free estimates, so why should they give you a retainer? I answer this with a question (never forget the value of questions):

"Mrs. Customer, let me ask you, if I may, which designer do you think will pay more attention to detail and your individual needs, as well as your budget, and invest the necessary amount of time and expertise into your project, the person who does dozens of quick plans for everyone or the designer who is retained to do so for just a few qualified projects a month?"

The answer to this question is obvious, as the customer will start thinking not only about your expertise but also about the level of commitment. The question really is, Mrs. Customer, which individual would you prefer to work with?

As salespeople, we would always try to close as many sales as there are customers who walk into our showroom. But as designers we do have a choice regarding the type of client we want to work with. We must decide if we would rather spend several hours of our time with those customers who want to explore all the design possibilities for their space or be someone who is only selling products at the lowest price.

If the customer just wants a free design and estimate, then perhaps this is not a customer we want. But if they still hesitate, here is another approach:

"Mrs. Customer, I understand your concern about retaining my services without knowing if I can create the right design for you. But let me remind you, my goal is *not* to charge you a design fee but *to do your project.* If I just did designs for a fee, I would not need this beautiful but expensive showroom. I'd just need a studio. Since the retainer will be credited towards the cost of your bathroom, my design and the time we will spend together will really be free, and its only implication is a mutual commitment from both of us. Now, will you make this investment and schedule our next meeting in your home so we can analyze the space and carefully survey your needs?"

This conversation is simplified, but the goal is to focus on what the customer is really buying. If they had been presented with the right plan within their budget, they would not have come to us looking for another one.

The customer really is buying your time and expertise to design the perfect environment for their family. Product, at this point, is secondary. Your mission is to fulfill their dreams by designing not what can be sold quickly, but what can be bought with complete satisfaction.

—Cameron Snyder, CKD

to any decision-makers (husband, wife, mother-in-law, whoever is paying for the bathroom) in the family. Otherwise you might face unexpected objections in your office presentation.

Step 5. Interviewing, Measuring.

There is no way to overstate the importance of the interview in the home. It is critical to identifying design challenges and problems and to creating design solutions. You cannot go back to the office and develop the right design for this particular client without having all of the questions and answers at your fingertips. It can shake their confidence in you if you have to call them to ask additional questions, and without that confidence you will have trouble getting the contract signed.

That is why NKBA developed the Bathroom Design Survey Form (See Chapter 6). It is lengthy and detailed because it has to be. By using it, you will be selling your company, its reliability and standing in the community, and your own expertise and professionalism. You have to focus on it every minute, with every word, because you want to close this sale at the next meeting and you can unsell the whole job in seconds.

To reassure the homeowners that they have selected the right person and the right firm, show up on the right day and be on time. Missed appointments and unexplained tardiness are the most common complaints consumers have about design and building professionals. Set an odd time to meet with the client, such as 9:10 a.m.

As you drive up, notice the neighborhood and the specific house you will visit. If need be, be a little early and stop down the street where you can review your showroom tour notes and get into a frame of mind that can focus totally on the client you are about to meet with.

During the survey appointment you must accomplish the following to continue the selling process successfully:

1. Reassure the prospects that they have selected the right person and the right firm to handle their project;

2. Identify the prospects' priorities for the project (their "hot button").

3. Establish budget parameters for the project.

4. Complete the product match-up and define the project specification and "who does what."

5. Continue to increase the perceived value of the new bathroom in the prospects' mind.

If you can accomplish these five things and measure the room accurately, you will have a very high closing rate and a very healthy referral business to fuel future successes. At the end, the clients will have absolutely no reason NOT to sign the contract.

Step 6: Presenting the Plan.

Back in the office you now have a wealth of information on these customers, gained from the survey, the visit to the home and extensive conversations with them. You can now design the perfect bathroom for their needs and their budget. But you still must prepare a presentation that will make them **want** to sign a "sales agreement" (that sounds friendlier than "contract") where you will close the sale.

The only potential problem here is that Mr. and Mrs. Smith still do not know how much they will pay for their new bathroom. You have bracketed it pretty well and they know the range, but there still are the variables of product choice and price. You have options here.

Many professionals believe the best way is to design the perfect bathroom for this couple. Some even prepare a sample board with swatches of materials they will use. If this is your course of action, you know this is right for them, so be prepared to present it with enthusiasm.

Other pros believe in holding the price lower, so they show a plan they consider workable, affordable and reasonable.

Whatever way you choose, it is important to have contingency plans. If you show the best, be prepared with options in products and materials to lower the price if necessary. If you prepare a plan that is more affordable, be prepared to show better choices to upgrade the sale. The key words here are "be prepared," because you DO want to close this sale with this presentation today, and you know by now that they are ready to buy.

Step 7. Closing the Sale.

In any sales presentation, when you are ready to close the sale the customers will have some objections. Don't let them throw you. Objections nearly always are simply a way of asking for more information or clarification. So be prepared to deal with them. There are several ways to do this.

1. Anticipate them. There always are questions in our industry, and our experience familiarizes us with many of them. For example, the use of particleboard in vanity doors is one; noisy flushes in low-consumption toilets is another. Answer such objections in earlier discussions.

2. Agree with them. A sales pro agrees with a client's objection, then continues with an alternative view for the client to consider. For example, "This toilet seems a lot more expensive than the ones I see advertised." Agree, but then explain the life-cycle cost. For example, the pressurized toilet you recommend will almost eliminate double-flushing and save a lot of water, so in the 20 years of its life it will be much less expensive.

3. Postpone them. Tell them you are coming

to that point a little later, then be sure you do. But if they ask again before you come to it, stop and answer or they will think you are evading it.

4. Question them. Remember the rule of 3: *If you ask three questions, you'll get down to what the real question is.* If the clients say they are going elsewhere because the top and lav are $1,000 cheaper you might think it is a price problem. Questions might reveal that they are pricing a cast polymer against your solid surface, and you then can offer them a choice–one or the other.

5. Offset them. Many times an objection really is relatively minor, but just happens to be something that bothers the client. Talk about the long-term value, the lifetime satisfaction they are buying, and make it big enough so the objection shows up as a minor point compared with the product quality and the super design.

6. Use logic where appropriate. Appeal to **emotion** where appropriate. Refer to **facts** or **a higher authority** where needed, such as research, or authoritative recommendations.

7. Capitalize on them. For example, if "it is just too much to spend on a house in my neighborhood and, besides, we'll probably want to sell the house in a few years," you can appeal to their sense of pride in having the best bathroom in the neighborhood.

Besides, you can point out, a "few years" can be a long time in which they can either put up with the old or enjoy the bathroom they have chosen, and if and when they do decide to sell, real estate figures show the bathroom often will pay for itself when it really is a great one.

Whatever the questions, there always are answers or ways to deal with them. It is important, however, to know what any objection really is. To deal with them:

1. Acknowledge the objection.

2. Elicit the exact scope of the objection.

Here are some "real world" objections and possible responses.

"This project costs too much."

A. "I can see why you might think that at first glance, Mr. and Mrs. Customer. Our company had a choice. We could either design the project to do as little as possible so we could sell it as cheaply as possible, or we could design this project to do as much as possible so, in the long run, your cost would be substantially lower.

"When we made the decision to build the best possible project with the best possible products for you, we actually placed ourselves in your shoes. We tried to determine what we would want if we were in your position. That's the reason we unhesitatingly recommend this project so highly and know you would want what is the best value for you."

B. "I don't think there is any question about the price being high, but when you add the benefits of quality, subtract the disappointments of cheapness, multiply the pleasure of buying a high-quality product and divide the cost over a period of time, the arithmetic comes out in your favor."

When the client believes you are charging too much, it is important to explain your costs to the client. People can understand charging 10-15% overhead if they know the exact things you are paying for–social security taxes, liability insurance, workman's compensation, rent. When explaining these costs, it is sometimes helpful to compare it to costs the client has–their social security payment, their car insurance, etc.

"We're waiting for the bank to approve the loan."

A. Before the presentation of the contract, explain to the customers clearly that you expect a certain percentage on signing of the contract. Ask your customers if they have secured financing. If they haven't, get the process started as soon as possible.

Also, arrange with your bank to get quick turnaround on clients that need financing approval.

B. If you do get to the contract signing and their bank still has not approved their loan, go ahead and get the contract signed with the contingency that if the bank doesn't okay their financing (which you are sure they will, appealing to their ego) you will cancel the sale. If your company doesn't offer financing now, you may wish to investigate this powerful sales tool. See NKBA's book *"Leveraging Design, Finance and the Kitchen and Bath Specialist."*

"I like the competitor's product better."

You should have built up enthusiasm for your product during your showroom presentation. You should show the unique characteristics of your product and services that they cannot get anywhere else. If you get to the final presentation and this is still a concern, use the Rule of Three to find out the true meaning of their objection, then answer it.

"Before we go ahead, we really want our interior decorator to help with color selection."

"I understand. Thank you for bringing that up. (Here you are acknowledging the objection.) You will be pleased to know that we can still go ahead and get your bathroom ordered today. All of the colors you are interested in are in the same price range."

"The lavatory being so far from the end of the counter doesn't make sense. It wastes space."

"I appreciate what you are saying, Mr. and Mrs. Client. Research (evidence) has established that the minimum space needed beside the lav, from its center to the end of the counter, is 15 inches (fact). The National Kitchen & Bath Association (professional organization) views this as necessary for your comfort and convenience."

"We really want to place the order with you, but unless we can get Autumn Haze (a stain color) on maple we will have to take our project

somewhere else."

"I understand that having Autumn Haze on maple is a concern to you. As you know, Autumn Haze only comes on oak and pine (rule). But if I can get the factory (bigger rule) to apply Autumn Haze on maple, will you go ahead with the order today?"

"We are really concerned about spending too much money on this project."

A. "Doesn't your family deserve the best possible bathroom?" (This appeals to love of family. On hearing this, the customers start thinking to themselves "yeah, my family does deserve the best.")

B. "You know, your present bathroom is so inefficient that this was a major concern to you and your spouse when you came in. This new bathroom will really save you a lot of time by solving the problem of traffic and congestion in the mornings, and it will save cleanup time, so you can spend more quality time together. And in the long run, it will save a lot of money by cutting your use of water and energy." (This appeals to love and concern for the family, plus long-term savings to override concern for the remodeling cost.)

"We would really like to wait until after the holidays to start this project."

"I understand that, Mr. and Mrs. Client. However, if you go ahead and place your order today, we won't start your project until after the holidays. By placing your order now we also can guarantee this price against any increases by the factories in the future." (Urgency.)

"No, I just don't want counters with plastic granite. I love real granite."

(In this case we want to find out just how much they love granite. We want to **measure the depth** of the objection. In the planning stage we have checked comparative prices of other mate-

rials, so we are prepared to answer.)

"We planned and priced this with a beautiful granite pattern in decorative laminate. But if you want real granite, of course we can do that. Changing the counters to real granite would add approximately $1,740 to the price of your project."

Their response might be: "Oh, it will cost that much? We do like granite, but at this price I just don't know."

Now we have discovered that the real depth of their objection is not very strong. They might hate decorative laminate, but they don't hate it $1,740 worth.

On the other hand, they might tell you to go ahead with the real granite. In this case, you can be sure it was a true and strong objection.

"We want to think it over."

"Fine. Let's think it over together, right here where we have all the plans and facts. Just what is it that we want to think over? Just what is it that is of concern to you?"

Push for an answer. Find out precisely what this objection is so you can handle it.

If it is price you know where you can make substitutions, but defend what you have done and what it costs because this is right for them. It is based on their budget figure, so convince them it is worth it.

If it is a quality question, use the Rule of 3 to pin it down specifically. Quality questions can be answered and backed up with facts.

If it is a layout problem, remember you have worked together to develop this layout and it is based on their family and their needs. Ask more questions to find out specifically what the objection is. Perhaps you simply haven't explained it sufficiently.

Listen to what they are saying. And don't feel you have to bury objections in graves 10 feet deep. Answer, and get back quickly to their wants and their needs and how you can supply these.

When it all comes down to the signature on the dotted line, professional salespeople have several techniques that can help.

For one, they just assume that it is a go. Their every action is confident, positive, and they never use the word "if." Instead, they always say "when." This same positive attitude will seep into the customer and overcome their indecision.

Or a salesperson might hasten the decision by referring to outside events, such as the coming holidays, starting dates, lead time, or the ever-present possibility of price increases.

There also is the minor concession technique. If only one objection seems to stand in the way, the concession is "all right, I'll do this for you, so (pick up the pen and hand it to her) let's get going on this project."

Maybe it really is price. Maybe your analysis of their ability to pay is inaccurate. And maybe it isn't. In either event, you may have to scale down the price. Be ready for it. Have your own breakdown in mind so you can scale down the fixture models, change the surfacing without changing the appearance dramatically, change the countertop material or take other measures to meet any new and unexpected challenge, whatever it might be.

But never do that until you are forced to. The only thing worse than overestimating a client's ability to pay is underestimating it.

To sum it all up, it is up to you.

The sale will be made when the customers trust you to solve their problems for a price they perceive to be equal to or less than what the solution is worth.

Notes:

_____
_____
_____
_____
_____
_____
_____
_____
_____
_____
_____
_____
_____
_____

Appendices Contents

Notes:

Appendix A:
Reading Plans and Blueprints

Appendix A—Reading Plans & Blueprints

Any new construction requires a set of working plans that accurately represents all aspects of the project. The bathroom designer might or might not encounter these plans in a remodeling project, but they certainly will be part of any new building project and the designer will have to understand and interpret them.

Collectively, these plans are called "blueprints." The name dates back to a common method of reproducing working drawings with a photographic contact print and then fixing them in a solution of ammonia and water. The exposed parts of the paper turned a dark blue, and the coating on the unexposed portions was washed away, leaving a white linework image of the original. In the 1960s, a dry ammonia process was developed that used ammonia vapors to treat the exposed print paper. Diazo prints could be processed with a desktop-sized printing machine that made it possible for small firms and individuals to make their own prints. The blueprinting process is seldom used now, but the name lingers for a set of working drawings.

A set of working drawings should be organized according to the sequence of work and the major disciplines involved. This will include:

Title Sheet Site Drawing—vicinity map, legends, abbreviations.

Architectural—plans, elevations, sections, details, schedules.

Structural—plans, details, schedules, notes.

HVAC—plans, schedules, notes.

Plumbing—plans, fixture schedules, riser diagrams, notes.

Electrical—plans, panel diagrams, fixture schedules, notes.

Landscape—plans, paving details, plant material schedules, details.

While that is the complete package, there will be variations according to locality and according to the habits of individual architectural firms.

In Fig. A.1, note that each drawing has a different scale beneath the identification of the view. The front elevation, for example, has a scale of 1/4" to 1'. The rear view is drawn to a different scale, as are the two end views. This saves space on the pages of the plans, and it is acceptable as long as the scale is noted. Figs. A.2 and A.3 both are drawn to 1/4" scale so readers of the plans can see detail.

Those familiar with measuring interior spaces will see a difference here.

At the top of Fig. A.2, note the 21' 4" measurement from the left end of the house to the laundry room inside is from the *outside* of the exterior wall to the *center of the interior wall* of the laundry room.

Note also the "2030" designation of the laundry room window. This interprets as a window that is 2' 0" x 3' 0".

In studying this drawing, we can see that the left wall of the laundry room is a 6" wall, while all of the other interior walls are standard stud walls. This is because the thicker one is a wet wall, or a wall that contains the plumbing stacks.

In Fig. A.3 we see that the 6" wall continues up through the second story where it also serves the upstairs bathroom.

Looking again at Fig. A.2, we see a broken line extending outward from the laundry room. This is to tell us there is a structure above. Looking at Fig. A.3, we see that this is, in fact, the dressing room/bathroom that is cantilevered out from the house structure. Fig. A.2 shows the 2 x 10" joists extending outward to support the structure above.

There is no quick way to read plans such as these, but they can tell us all we have to know in creating or remodeling a bathroom. When we have to know the weight the floor can carry, we can check structure below all the way to placement, size and composition of the footings. We can check the roof to see if a skylight is possible, and how big it might be. But the drawings require close study.

In reading plans, the first thing is to check the scale. Then, regardless of the number of drawings we have, it is essential that we do our own measuring (Fig. A.4). Drawings can have inaccurate figures, and many times plans can change in mid-construction.

We must check for any overhead truss system, and check the kind of floor in the bathroom area. Check all entrances for size, and clearance around them for moving bath fixtures and materials in. Check for possible ventilation paths and the distances involved. Check the plumbing water supplies and drains and locate them on your own drawing.

And check drawings against each other. For example, a designer looking at Fig. A.3 might be tempted to plan a window into the right wall of the dining room. But in checking it against Fig. A.2, we find there is a fireplace below. Although it doesn't show in Fig. A.3, there must be a chimney in that wall.

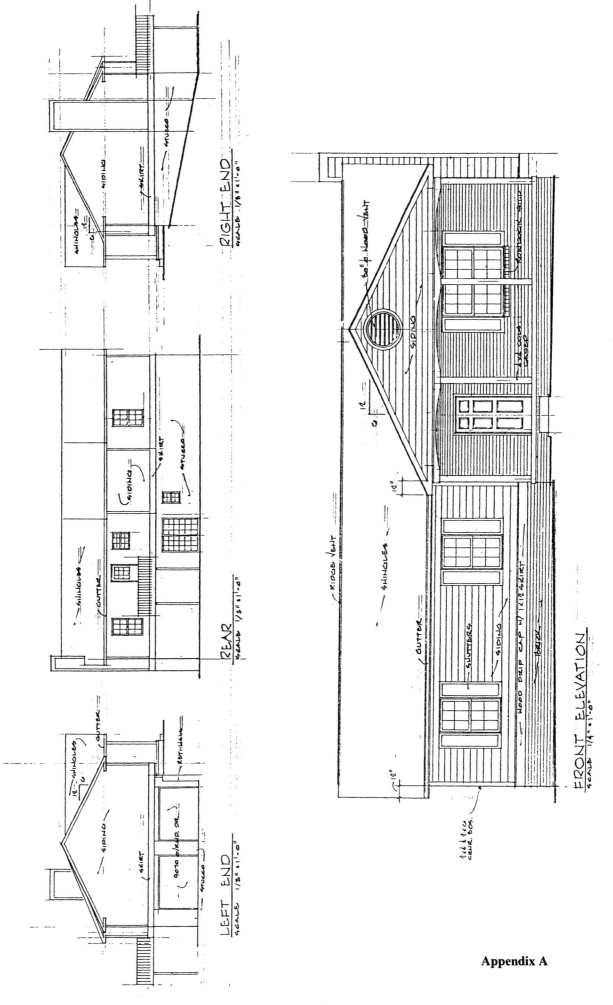

Fig. A.1. Architectural elevations will give the bathroom designer a general idea of the house and its orientation.

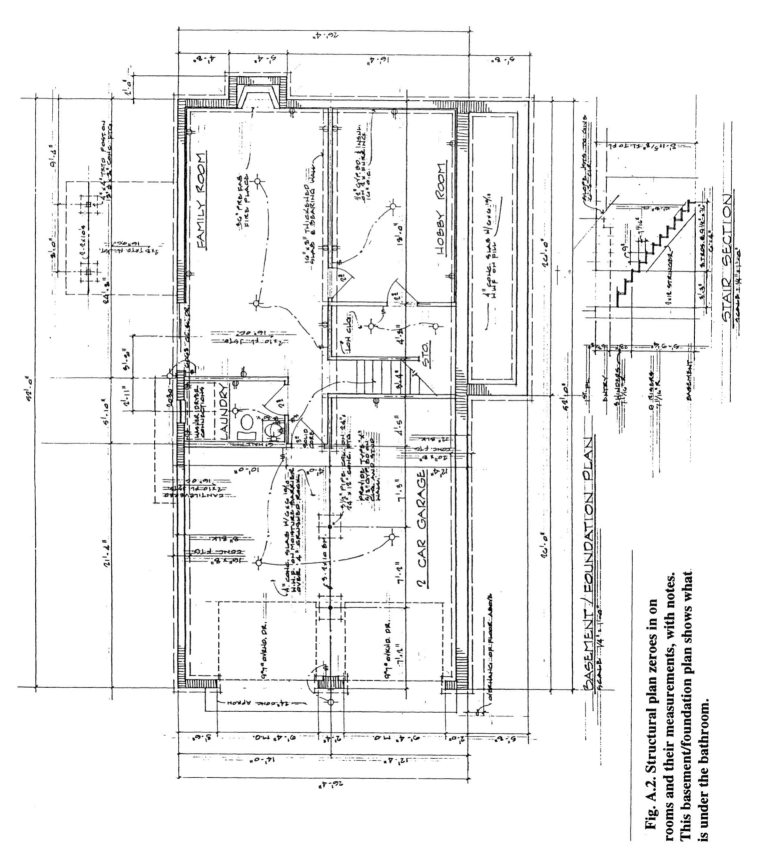

Fig. A.2. Structural plan zeroes in on rooms and their measurements, with notes. This basement/foundation plan shows what is under the bathroom.

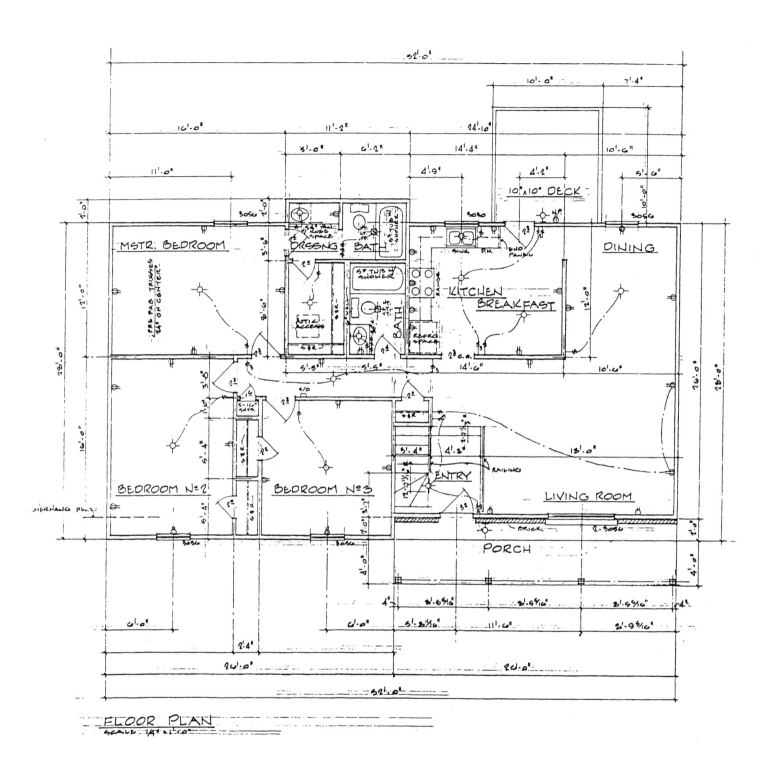

Fig. A.3. Floorplan shows a "house" bathroom and the second bathroom opening to the master bedroom, with dressing room.

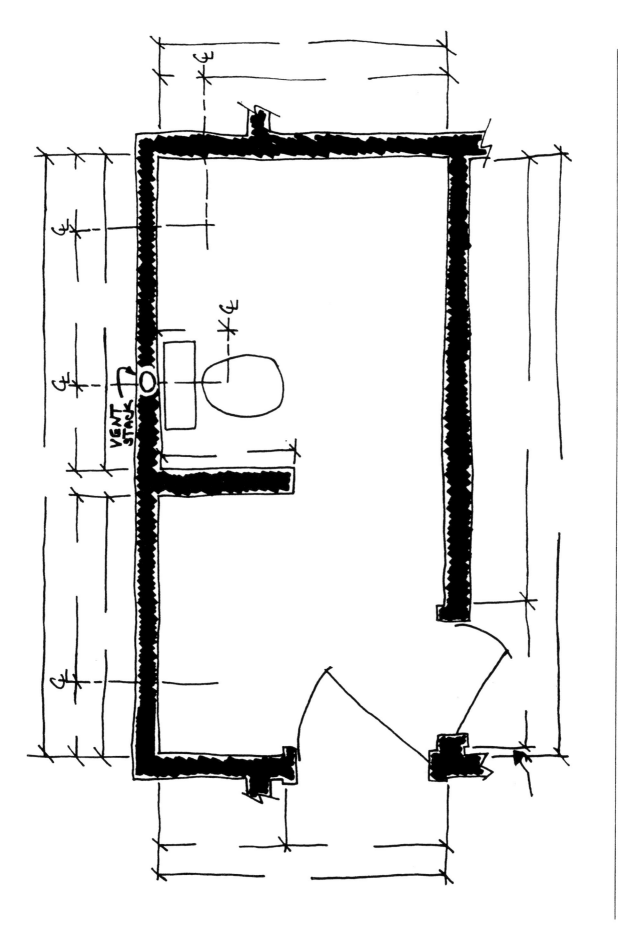

Fig. A.4. Regardless of what the plans and blueprints say, all measurements in the bathroom must be checked and either verified or corrected. Note all room dimensions and drain lines.

Appendix B:
Surfacing Materials

Appendix B—Surfacing Materials

Several materials are available for bathroom counter and wall surfaces in addition to wallpaper or paint. These include:

1. **Cast polymers, such as cultured marble and onyx.**
2. **Solid surface materials, such as Avonite, Corian, Fountainhead, Gibraltar, Surell, Swanstone and others from regional or foreign sources.**
3. Ceramic tile.
4. **High-pressure (HP) decorative laminates.**
5. **Low-pressure (LP) melamine laminated board.**
6. **Specialty laminates, such as Formica's Nuvel (a laminate with performance characteristics of solid surface materials); Nevamar's Vitricor (a high-gloss acrylic laminate), or Surflex-MR (a high-gloss polymer laminate that comes in sheets or rolls).**
7. **Wood.**
8. **Glass blocks, or plastic blocks simulating glass.**
9. **Paint and wallpaper.**
10. **Natural stone, such as granite and marble.**

HP decorative laminates are among the most popular of these materials for countertops, and also are widely used for tub and shower surrounds. They are very durable, easy to clean, and come in hundreds of colors and patterns. Another advantage is that they have been around for so long that every worker knows how to handle and install them.

The material comes in a maximum sheet size of 5' x 12' (152 x 366 cm). In some areas you can buy sheets in widths of 30" and 36" (76 and 91 cm), and in lengths of 72" and 120" (183 and 305 cm), sized for convenience in making kitchen countertops and backsplashes. Matching edgebanding usually is 1 5/8" (4 cm) x 144" (366 cm) and can be cold-formed to a 3" (76 mm) outside radius or a 1" (25 mm) inside radius.

There are three grades of the sheet material. Standard is 1/16" (1.6 mm) thick, always recommended for countertops in the kitchen; vertical, which is 1/32" (.8 mm) thick, for cabinets and other vertical applications, but considered adequate for bathroom counters; and a postforming grade which can be formed on a postforming machine to 5/8" (15.88 mm) outside radius or 1/8" (3 mm) inside radius at 325° F (163°C).

When a top is self-edged, the top surface overlays the edge and is routed to a slight bevel, exposing a dark band. This can be avoided with "color-through" laminates which show the same color all the way through when routed, or a pattern of layered colors if ordered that way. This is more expensive than standard laminate.

Postformed counters in the bathroom usually have a rolled front edge and a backsplash. However, curved fronts are impossible with formed counters because the laminate is incapable of a compound curve, so for shaped fronts it will be necessary to specify a "square-edge" top, which might be "self-edged" with a strip of the same material as the top surface or might have a wood or other edge.

Cast polymers such as cultured marble, cultured onyx and granite also rate high in popularity for bathroom counters and, in thinner sheets, for walls. They got their start several decades ago as bases for pen holders and still are going though the process of change. They are beautiful, they offer a wide range of colors, they are low in cost, and a big advantage is the fact that they usually come with an integral lav. Thus they offer further savings by eliminating the need to buy and install a separate lav.

New universal resins, lightweight fillers and nonporous polyesters are now available to create a homogeneous material that does not need a gelcoat surface and will be workable and repairable, such as the solid surfaces. These materials make it possible for smaller cultured marble manufacturers anywhere to go into the solid surface business, which is why you might find solid surfaces under any brand name.

Despite all these improvements, the gelcoat surface might still be best for bathroom applications. Gelcoat variety is unlimited, it is very durable and it possibly is most resistant to stains.

Gelcoat surfaces are standard on cultured marble and cultured onyx, but not on the newer cultured granite which often is available from cultured marble manufacturers. The granite is a higher-density material and can be worked.

Cultured marble has a calcium carbonate filler which is opaque. Cultured onyx has a different filler which might be alumina trihydrate or a frit (a mixture of alkalies, or glass). The filler has a refractive index similar to the polyester binder resin, which makes it translucent.

The translucency of cultured onyx can be a problem. For example, a thin 3/8" (9.5 mm) sheet on a wall or backsplash, put up with a structural adhesive, can show the dabs or beads of adhesive through the onyx. Even white adhesive will show through, so it often is best to support sheets by the edges, such as with molding.

Solid surfaces all come with a matte finish, but all can be polished to a high gloss. Butted panels can be seamed so imperceptibly that you will have to look very hard to find a seam. All come in 1/4" (6.3 mm) thickness for walls as well as 1/2" and 3/4" (1 and 2 cm) thicknesses for counters. For counters you can rout curved fronts or create stylish, colorful edges and designs with supplementary tubes of the same material. Many designers specify wood edges, fitted into a groove in the top and glued.

While all of the solid surfaces are quite similar, all are made differently. Here is a rundown on the major national brands, alphabetically.

Avonite is a blend of polyester alloys and fillers. It is unique in that it, in effect, is made twice. After the minerals and resins are mixed and cured, the material is crushed and poured again into more liquid polyester resin, molded and cured again. From this material you can get panels that look like glass or wood or marble. It is made in 36" x 121" panels (91 x 307cm) or custom sizes. Thicknesses of 1/8" or 3/8" (3 or 9.5mm) can be special-ordered. It can be postformed. There are at least 19 colors, including granite.

Installation is with silicone adhesive on thin cross slats over the substrate. This allows for expansion. Contact adhesive cannot be used. It could crack the panel because the adhesive would not give with thermal expansion of the panel. The firm insists that the material be installed by certified installers only.

Corian, by DuPont, was the first solid surface, coming into general use in 1971. One big difference is that its filler is 100% acrylic, combined with solid minerals, crushed alloys or ceramics.

Corian comes in several sizes and combinations for kitchens and bathrooms, with or without integral lavs or with separate Corian lavs of different colors. One common combination for bathrooms is a slab 22" wide (56cm) with a piece 8" wide (20cm) for a backsplash. Standard lengths can be anywhere from 85" (216cm) to 145" (368cm). Wall material is 1/4" thick (6.3mm), 30" wide (76cm) and up to 80" (203cm) long. Installation is with silicone sealant around the perimeter, but only by people who have been to DuPont's installation school.

Fountainhead, by Nevamar, combines acrylic and polyester resins with alumina trihydrate as a filler. It comes in panels and separate lavs, in several colors for either the panels or lavs. Wall panel thickness is 1/4" (6.3mm) and panel sizes are 30" and 36" wide (76 and 91cm) in lengths of 98", 121" and 145" (249, 307 and 368cm).

Installation is with silicone adhesive around the perimeter and along cross slats.

There is a 10-year warranty, as with Avonite and Corian.

Gibraltar, by Wilsonart International, is unique in that it is a solid surface precisely color-matched to a whole family of Wilsonart decorative laminates. This gives a new measure of freedom to designers. For remodelers who do their own fabricating, it also eliminates the·problem and expense of off-fall, because left-over pieces of either material can be saved for other jobs requiring the same colors.

Gibraltar comes in sheets 30" or 36" wide (76 or 91 cm), by 8' or 12' lengths (244 or 366 cm). Thicknesses are 1/2", 3/4" and 1" (12.7, 19 and 25.4 mm). It has some unique certifications. For example, it has a National Sanitary Foundation rating for food contact, and it is UL labeled with a Class A fire rating.

Fig. B.1. Typical of materials developed specifically for high-humidity applications is this melamine-surfaced shower surround, made in sheets to simulate ceramic tile. This is Lionite. Georgia-Pacific photo.

Wilsonart Solid Surface Veneer reduces the cost of solid surfacing by an estimated 40%. It is a new product 1/8" thick, made by Aristech Acrylic in four solid colors and eight stone patterns. It takes a conventional substrate.

Surell, by Formica, is a densified polyester resin compound with added fillers. For walls it comes in 1/4" thickness (6.3mm), and panels are 30" or 36" wide (76 and 91cm) and 60" to 144" long (152 to 366cm). It also comes in vanity tops with integral or separate lavs.

Adhesives come in bulk and must be mixed for each job. As with others, expansion of the material could be a problem if fixed to a substrate, so support and perimeter gluing only is recommended.

Different materials include *Americast* and *Idealcast,* both by American Standard. Americast is based on a metal alloy, with a porcelain finish, injection molded on the reverse side with a structural foam. It is much lighter in weight than cast iron. Idealcast is injection molded, bonding a structural composite onto a vacuum-formed acrylic shell. Tubs and shower bases have a much more solid feel.

Other solid surfaces in national or regional distribution include *Swanstone,* by Swan Corp.; *Prism,* by Lippert Corp., and *DurAllure,* by VT Industries. They have similar

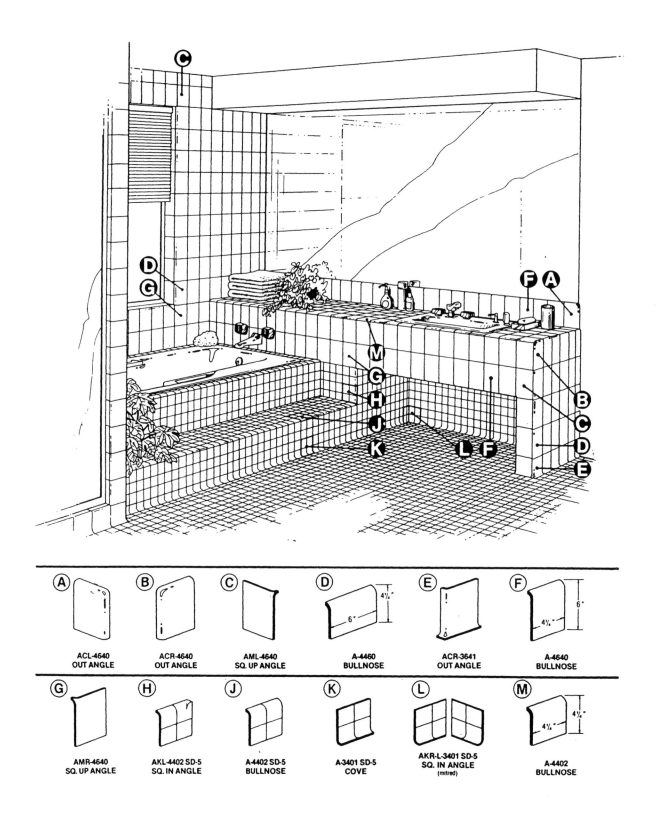

Fig. B.2. In selecting ceramic tile, you must specify the sizes, types and shapes of the tiles desired. It is important to select tile that has the wide range of trim pieces needed for corners, radiuses, coves, etc. American Olean artwork.

properties to other solid surfaces and come in similar sizes.

Floor and wall tiles in varying sizes also are available from at least two manufacturers.

Ceramic tile is available in a wide variety of types, sizes and colors, and for bathrooms some now come in pre-grouted sheets for easier installation. It can be installed with an adhesive on plywood, with an adhesive over an old laminate top, with conventional mortar on a wood base, or with a dryset morter on a cementaceous base.

It is important to select a tile line that has the wide range of trim pieces needed (Fig. B.2). In any application that involves more than a countertop or a floor, it is a good idea to make a perspective drawing before ordering so the right number and type of trim pieces can be determined.

To specify a proper tile in a bathroom you also must be aware of its porosity. Tiles are composed of clays, shales, porcelain or baked dirt which are pressed or extruded into shapes and then fired in a kiln, baked in an oven and then cured. All of these are variables that affect porosity.

"Glazed" tiles are sprayed with a coating of glass-forming minerals and coloring pigment before firing. Some end up with a shiny luster. Some can be slippery when wet. "Ceramic mosaics" are distinguished by their size. Each tile does not exceed 6 square inches in size (6 x 6cm). When these are made from natural clay and porcelain the color extends through the tile rather than just as a glaze. Their porosity is low.

Mosaics are recommended for bathroom floors because their small size provides more traction for bare feet and there is less danger of slipping.

Glazed wall tiles usually are either 4 1/4" or 6" square (11 or 16cm) and 1/4" to 5/8" thick (6.3 to 15.8mm). These are generally popular for counters, but are not as scratch-resistant as other types. Pavers might be glazed or un-glazed, with irregular edges, and are acceptable for counters or floors. They might be 4" x 6" or 4" x 8" (10 by 15 or 20cm) or up to 12" x 12" (30cm), and 3/8" to 5/8" thick (9.5-15.8mm). These are somewhat porous and can absorb stains, and there are not many trim pieces.

Another popular tile for counters or walls is monocottura. It started as an Italian import, but now is made by U.S. firms. The word refers to its being baked in the kiln once, together with the glazing material, making it stronger and very resistant to abrasion.

In any ceramic tile installation, grout is a fact of life and it should be discussed with the client. There are four broad categories of grout:

1. Epoxy grouts come in several colors and have superior strength and chemical resistance. They are more expensive than other types.

2. Silicone rubber grouts are white and advisable where elasticity and moisture resistance are required. They are good for bathroom walls, floors and vanity tops.

3. Dry-set grouts are non-sanded and come in white and colors. They are suited for joints not exceeding 1/8" (3mm) in width.

4. Sanded grouts come in white and colors and are used for grout joints up to 3/8" (9.5mm). The sand is added to ensure strength for the wider joint. These are most often used for floors and ceramic mosaics.

LP melamine laminated board is available under several brand names and is excellent for many bathroom applications. This is a "short cycle" laminate, with melamine applied to the substrate with heat, but not in finished sheets that are manufactured with high pressure and heat as is the case with HP decorative laminate. Melamine-laminated board is very durable for any use in the bathroom. It is not recommended as a replacement for HP laminate in hard-use areas such as kitchen countertops, but bathroom counters seldom get that kind of hard wear.

Melamine laminated board was introduced in the U.S. and Canada in the '70s by Formica as Melamine Component Panel (MCP). Current examples, quite different from each other, are Domtar and Georgia-Pacific Lionite (Fig. B.1). A Nevamar product, "LamMates," offers MCP panels that match the firm's HP laminates.

Domtar fuses melamine-impregnated sheets to particleboard or medium density fiberboard in a variety of textures and colors. Panel sizes are 4' x 8' (122 x 244cm), 5' x 6' (152 x 183cm), 5' x 8' (152 x 244cm) and 5' x 9' (152 x 284cm). Thickness are from 1/4" to 1 1/2" (6.35 mm to 4 cm). The quarter-inch thickness is in 4' x 8' panels only, and all are made to order.

Georgia-Pacific bakes the melamine material onto hardboard for its Lionite tileboard, which comes in 4' x 8' panels. There is a variety of styles and colors. Tileboard is a low-cost alternative to ceramic tile in such applications as tub/shower surrounds.

Specialty laminates include some unique products.

Nuvel is a high-density mineral-filled polymer made of Valox, a General Electric sheet product distributed worldwide by Formica. It is .09 thick (2.3mm) and has the performance characteristics of a solid surface material, but it can be fabricated with standard HP laminate machinery, including postformers, and applied to typical substrates such as particleboard or medium-density fiberboard. It is flexible enough to be bent cold to a tight radius. It is available in several sizes up to 60" wide (152cm) and in any specified length.

Like solid surfaces, it is homogeneous and workable with woodworking tools. Impact resistance is said to be sufficient to withstand dropping of heavy pots or other objects. Seaming can be almost undetectable.

Fabrication, however, is somewhat more difficult with Nuvel than with standard laminates because it requires both a contact adhesive and a seaming compound. Seaming compound comes in double-cylinder cartridges, and uses a special applicator gun that combines the two viscous liquids in the proper proportions.

Contact adhesive must be spread on both the Nuvel and the substrate, leaving a clear area for seaming compound that is spread on the substrate. When Nuvel sheets are laid down, there must be enough seaming compound to squeeze up between the sheets when the second sheet is slid into position against the first sheet. This means, of course, that there can be no contact between the adhesive on the Nuvel and the substrate until the material is precisely in place. This is not easy, since the seaming compound sets up in less than 10 minutes. Joints must be clamped together for an hour.

Vitricor, by Nevamar, is an HP laminate with ultra high gloss, differing from other glossy laminates in that it has an acrylic surface and is 3/16" thick (4.76 mm), which gives the colors a deeper, richer appearance. This makes it look very similar to hand-lacquered finishes or to high-gloss polyesters.

The material comes in a full range of colors, including metallics, and is fabricated in the same way as other HP laminates.

Surflex-MR is a different kind of laminate, by Surface Imagery. It is a hard, high-gloss, color-through flexible polymer, 1/32" thick (.8mm), about the same as a vertical-surface high-pressure laminate, cold-formable to a 3" (7.6cm) radius with no special tools. It is available in 4' x 8' sheets (122 x 244cm) or in 450' rolls (137M) in 69 colors and patterns. It is suitable for tub/shower surrounds and other walls, backsplashes and cabinets, but is not recommended for the hard usage of a kitchen countertop. It is applied with a contact adhesive and handled like a regular laminate, but is more flexible.

Wood surfaces are common in bathroom window and door framing and vanity cabinets. These usually are well protected with paint, polyurethane or other finishes. In larger bathrooms, especially master suites, wood may be used on walls. This often is in the form of prefinished paneling which might be floor-to-ceiling or wainscot height. Some designers make effective use of cabinet doors as a wall surface. Some manufacturers offer fine wood furniture with typical furniture finishes for bathrooms.

The designer should remember that water will interact with any material, especially wood, so if wood is used the room should be very well ventilated to keep humidity low. In a humid room, if wood (with a "wood-look" finish) is not redwood or cedar it will weather and become discolored, eventually warping or rotting. Even multiple layers of spar varnish or polyurethane will break down and become cloudy.

Common wood paneling is hardboard or plywood with a painted or coated textured surface, 1/4" thick (6.3mm), and is available in 4' x 8' sheets (122 x 244cm). Solid wood veneered panels also are available in various species, generally from 3/8" to 3/4" thick (9.3mm-2cm). Hardwoods are more expensive than softwoods, and prices increase with increasing thickness. These are available unfinished or prefinished with a stain or other special finish.

Because of close joinery at the seams, wood panels need a flat surface. Uneven walls can be built out with furring. Horizontal paneling that runs perpendicular to studs will not need horizontal furring strips, but most vertical paneling, especially paneling that is random width, and 4'x8' sheets will require horizontal supports underneath. If the existing wall is even and flat and the paneling can be attached with mastic, it may not require furring.

If you are not certain whether moisture is seeping through an existing wall, apply a polyethylene vapor barrier before furring out. It can be applied to a plaster or concrete block wall with dabs of mastic.

Common hardboard panels are butted. Better wood panels might have tongue-and-groove, shiplap, V-groove or contemporary joints. Shiplap and V-groove are variations of tongue-and-groove, and contemporary joining has a lip on one panel that fits over a lip on the other.

Any wood board or paneling should be stored in the house for a few days before installation, with "stickers" between boards for air circulation, so it can adjust to the prevailing moisture level.

Glass blocks for walls or half-walls are popular with many bathroom designers because they are attractive and can be used to afford a measure of privacy without blocking light. They are hollow, translucent, and come in a variety of shapes, sizes, colors and textures.

When glass blocks are specified, it is essential that they be installed by a skilled mason. The blocks are heavy, non-porous, and slippery and difficult to align in installation.

Easier alternatives include plastic blocks made of acrylic or similar polymers. Visually they are essentially the same, but they are lighter and easier to install because they have guides that lock in alignment automatically. To add to the appearance of real glass, some manufacturers offer sealants that look like a mortar joint when installation is completed.

Paint is a part of practically every bathroom project. Modern paints combine pigments, for color; resins, which are binders to form a tough coat; plasticizers, which keep paint elastic after it dries, and solvents, which make the mixture thin enough to be spread with a brush, roller or spray.

The two major types of finishing paint are latex and alkyd. Latex is quick-drying and odor-free, and easy to clean up. But it's solvent is water, so it is used less in humid areas. Alkyds have replaced oil-based paints in most instances. They are more durable and can be used on any surface except bare drywall where they will raise a nap on the drywall's paper covering. Also, some areas have legislation controlling volatile organic compound (VOC) emissions, and oil-based paints produce more emissions than latex.

However, both oil-based and latex paints have changed a lot in recent years, largely as a result of VOC regulations. Both are better than they were only a year ago, and water-based paints (latex) now use acrylics that make them as effective as oil-based in most applications. The only measure of quality, really, is price. Use the best.

An important point to remember is that, like wallpapering, painting is primarily cosmetic; it is not intended to correct underlying structural defects. This means the surface to be painted must be prepared. It must be scraped free of any existing paint that is loose or that was applied excessively. Surface irregularities must be filled and sanded. Raw surfaces must be primed with a coating that is compatible with the final coat, in accord with information printed on the paint can.

Plaster surfaces must be cured thoroughly before painting. Latex can be applied as soon as plaster is dry to the touch, but to be sure of lasting results it is best to wait three to four weeks. The alkali in plaster can remain "hot" for up to three months, so if you are using an alkyd paint you *must* wait that long unless you prime the surface with an alkali reducer before applying a regular primer. When fully cured, plaster takes on a slight sheen.

Drywall can accept either latex or alkyd paint a day after any repairs with joint compound, preceded by a primer.

Vinyl wallcoverings may take paint well, but walls covered with paper or cloth may not. If painting over paper, look first for bubbles or loose spots, repaste them and let them dry. Sand down all seams and spackle any depressions. Unsanded seams will be very obvious after painting.

"Wallpaper" is an old name for many materials that include vinyl, fabric, flocks, foil, cork, rice paper, bamboo, burlap, hemp and wood veneer, backed with paper or cloth. More properly it would be called "wallcovering."

Vinyl is usually the most practical choice in rooms where there is a lot of traffic or a lot of moisture. That includes the bathroom on both counts. Most types of vinyl are washable. Cloth-backed vinyls are also strippable. Heavier vinyls can hide minor cracks and irregularities in the wall.

Before hanging any wallcovering on drywall or plaster, either must be sealed. An oil-base primer-sealer is excellent for either papering or painting. Don't use a *latex* primer-sealer beneath wallcoverings, because the latex coat can pull free from the wall if the wallcovering is too heavy. The sealing function used to be accomplished with a glutinous material called *size,* or *sizing.* Now, most modern pastes are presized to improve adherence, but the sealing

step is still needed to permit later removal of the covering without damaging the surface underneath.

Most wallpapers are 18" or 27" wide (46 or 69cm). Foils, flocks and prepasted coverings come in these sizes also. Heavier vinyls are also available in widths of 54" (137cm) and lengths up to 30 yards (27.4M). Single rolls cover 30 sq. ft. (2.79M²). Double and triple rolls are longer, in continuous strips, to help cut wastage. A waste factor is built into the coverage figure. For example, a roll that nominally covers 30 sq. ft. actually has 36 sq. ft. (3.34M²) of material.

Natural stone is increasingly popular for counters, floors, shelves and walls in upscale bathrooms. Forms of stone in common use are granite, marble and flagstone. They are not workable in the field, so all fabrication is done by the supplier. Another rock product, terrazzo, used mostly for floors, is a mixture of marble chips and cement.

Granite is naturally beautiful and durable. It comes from all over the world, but in different colors. Blacks come from India and Africa. Violets come from Saudi Arabia, blues from Norway and South America, and browns such as Dakota Mahogany come from South Dakota.

It is nonporous, so it is difficult to stain on a countertop. It is one of the hardest stones, but a lot of veining indicates weakness and that governs how much unsupported overhang you can have. An overhang of 12" (30cm) would be maximum for granite 1 1/4" (3cm) thick, but if it is 3/4" (19mm) thick any overhang should be supported. It can crack like glass if the support is not perfectly level. Lavatory cutouts are fragile, so a fabricator often will make them in parts, with a slab on either side and a connecting piece along the front and back. These parts are usually joined with silicon sealant, which always remains visible.

When specifying color in granite, include shade, clarity and "movement." Slabs will vary because of mineral content and veining. You can specify a highly polished finish, a rough-textured thermal finish, or a honed finish which has a matte surface good for bathroom floors.

Marble, like granite, comes from all over the world, but much of it is sent to Italy for cutting and preliminary polishing. While it can be used on most bathroom surfaces, it is not recommended for hard-use worktops because it stains and scratches easily. Spills must be cleaned up immediately with soap and warm water, and it needs buffing and polishing. An acidic or alcoholic spill will burn the finish. It needs a penetrating sealer that also is oil-repellant. Marble is slippery when wet, but it can do well on a bathroom floor, with good maintenance, if the finish has been etched, honed or pummeled.

The Marble Institute of America rates marble quality on an A-B-C-D scale, from the most sound to the most fragile. As in granite, veining represents weak areas. Italian fabricators often put fiberglass backing on weak marble. Grays tend to be more porous. Greens tend to be stronger because they have higher iron content. Whites can have iron, but it can rust and turn yellow. Blacks and other darker colors tend to be softer, so they scratch more easily. Further, there is little consistency to the color. You have to see the entire slab to know what color the marble is. Generally, the more decorative marbles are the most fragile.

As with granite, marble cutouts are possible but they also can be made in pieces. A cutout never should be closer than 3" to the edge. Any overhangs are dangerous. Minor overhangs can be supported by a plywood substrate, but an overhang of more than 18" should be supported by corbels or angled brackets.

Marble tiles are available 6" and 12" square (15 and 30cm) and 1/2" (12.7mm) thick. They are installed by a tile setter, following specs developed by the Ceramic Tile Institute.

Synthetic marbles are available. These use marble chips cast in molds with a polyester resin. The synthetics are more durable, more consistent and less expensive than natural marble.

Flagstone usually is either bluestone or slate that has been "flagged," used mostly for floors. Flagging is a process in which the stone is split into thin slabs suitable for paving.

Bluestone is a rough sandstone paver, available in buff, blue, green or gray. Slate is smooth and gray. They are heavy and break easily. Thicker pieces are stronger, but the weight must be calculated and related to the framing. Both absorb heat and can become uncomfortably hot if the floor is exposed to direct sunlight. This means, however, that they can be good heat sinks in a solar room.

Vinyl sheet and **vinyl tiles** are easy to install and to maintain on bathroom floors. It can simulate marble, ceramic tile, slate, wood or other materials, but geometrics and muted patterns are popular.

Inlaid sheets have the pattern going all the way through the wear layer. Rotogravure sheets have the pattern printed on the sheet. Either is covered with a clear polyurethane or vinyl wear layer. A vinyl wear layer is thicker, but it loses its gloss sooner. Some are cushioned for comfort, but cushioning invites dents from heavy dropped objects. Cushioned rotogravure rolls are available in 6', 9', 12' and 15' widths (183, 284, 366 and 457cm).

Solid or composition vinyl tiles are usually 12" (30cm) square. Composition tiles have a wear layer on top. Solid tiles don't.

For any vinyl floorcovering, the subfloor must be sound and dry. If required, exterior grade plywood can be laid over the existing subfloor. But never use particleboard, because most particleboards interact poorly with mastic and they can absorb water. Old resilient flooring can be used as the substrate if well attached and if it is free of finishing materials, including wax.

Notes:

Appendix C:
Bathroom Cabinetry & Doors

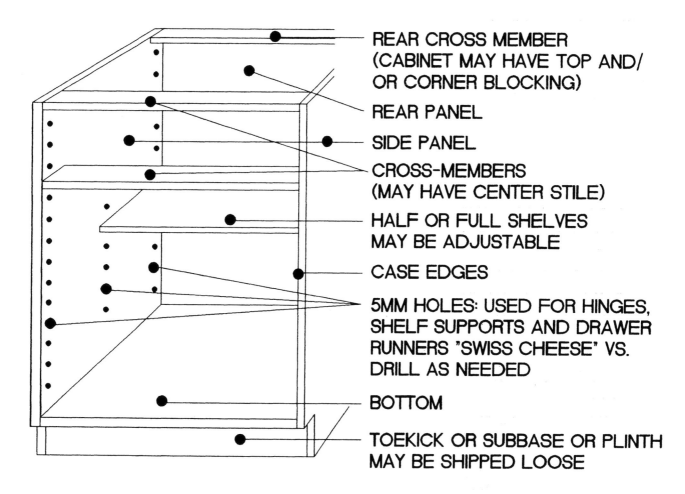

REAR CROSS MEMBER
(CABINET MAY HAVE TOP AND/
OR CORNER BLOCKING)

REAR PANEL

SIDE PANEL

CROSS-MEMBERS
(MAY HAVE CENTER STILE)

HALF OR FULL SHELVES
MAY BE ADJUSTABLE

CASE EDGES

5MM HOLES: USED FOR HINGES,
SHELF SUPPORTS AND DRAWER
RUNNERS "SWISS CHEESE" VS.
DRILL AS NEEDED

BOTTOM

TOEKICK OR SUBBASE OR PLINTH
MAY BE SHIPPED LOOSE

FRAMELESS CABINET CONSTRUCTION

Fig. C.1. Frameless cabinet construction might or might not be based on the 32 mm metric system developed in Europe. In this system, all needed holes are predrilled in flat stock, making assembly simple and easy.

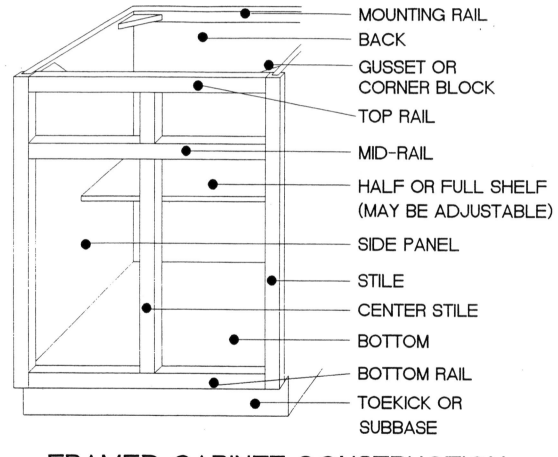

MOUNTING RAIL

BACK

GUSSET OR
CORNER BLOCK

TOP RAIL

MID-RAIL

HALF OR FULL SHELF
(MAY BE ADJUSTABLE)

SIDE PANEL

STILE

CENTER STILE

BOTTOM

BOTTOM RAIL

TOEKICK OR
SUBBASE

FRAMED CABINET CONSTRUCTION

Fig. C.2. Framed cabinet construction is the traditional American way. Cabinets have a face frame made of horizontal rails and vertical stiles. There might be other frame members at back corners and around top and bottom.

Cabinet Description		Nomenclature

VANITY CABINETS

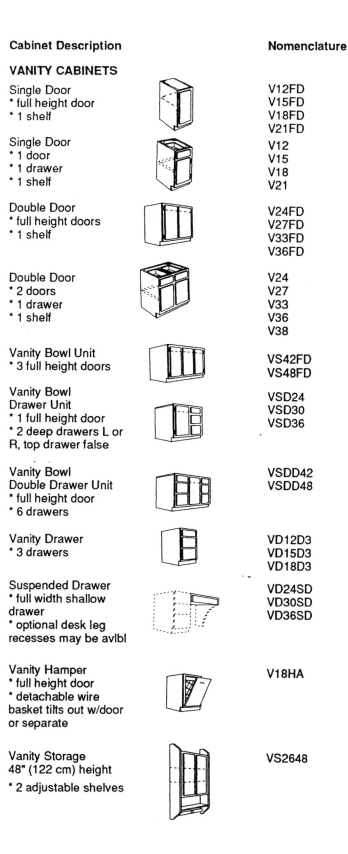

Single Door
* full height door
* 1 shelf

V12FD
V15FD
V18FD
V21FD

Single Door
* 1 door
* 1 drawer
* 1 shelf

V12
V15
V18
V21

Double Door
* full height doors
* 1 shelf

V24FD
V27FD
V33FD
V36FD

Double Door
* 2 doors
* 1 drawer
* 1 shelf

V24
V27
V33
V36
V38

Vanity Bowl Unit
* 3 full height doors

VS42FD
VS48FD

Vanity Bowl
Drawer Unit
* 1 full height door
* 2 deep drawers L or
R, top drawer false

VSD24
VSD30
VSD36

Vanity Bowl
Double Drawer Unit
* full height door
* 6 drawers

VSDD42
VSDD48

Vanity Drawer
* 3 drawers

VD12D3
VD15D3
VD18D3

Suspended Drawer
* full width shallow
drawer
* optional desk leg
recesses may be avlbl

VD24SD
VD30SD
VD36SD

Vanity Hamper
* full height door
* detachable wire
basket tilts out w/door
or separate

V18HA

Vanity Storage
48" (122 cm) height
* 2 adjustable shelves

VS2648

Fig. C.3. Typical vanity styles and sizes by a stock cabinet manufacturer.   Courtesy Merillat Industries

Doors set the style

In a kitchen, where most of the wall surfaces are covered by cabinets, we are accustomed to establishing style with cabinet doors and drawer fronts. They dominate by sheer mass.

It can be done to some extent in a bathroom, although there will be far less mass. Many average-size bathrooms have only one vanity cabinet with two doors and perhaps two or three drawer fronts. In a small room that can be enough to make a style statement. The designer can augment it, possibly with wall coverings or decorations and a shower curtain.

Common door styles include:

Slab—A flat, square-edge panel. This uncluttered look is good for contemporary styling.

Raised panel—A door made with two horizontal rails and two vertical stiles, all grooved to accept a center panel. The four edges of the panel are machined down to fit into the grooves.

   A. When the raised panel is square, the style is Square Raised Panel. It is suitable for contemporary styling.

   B. When the top rail and panel are curved, it becomes a Curved Raised Panel.

Recessed panel—Similar to a raised panel, but the center panel is flat.

Cathedral—Any of the above, with a cathedral arch at the top. Suitable for any style except contemporary.

Board-and-Batten—A door made of vertical boards with chamfered edges, held together by two horizontal battens on the back side. When the boards are horizontal, it is called a ladder door. This usually is identified with American, country or western styling. Sometimes grooves are routed on a slab door to simulate board-and-batten.

J-Channel—This is a slab door with a continuous wood or metal pull across the bottom, used especially in contemporary styling.

These are the basic styles, but they can be adapted in many ways. For example, a recessed panel might be frosted, leaded or mullioned glass. Curved doors with arcs at the corners might be provincial doors, and these might be French provincial, a relatively simple pattern, or the more ornate Italian provincial. The designer will have to select door styles consistent with the specific style desired, then follow through with appropriate accessories, colors and patterns.

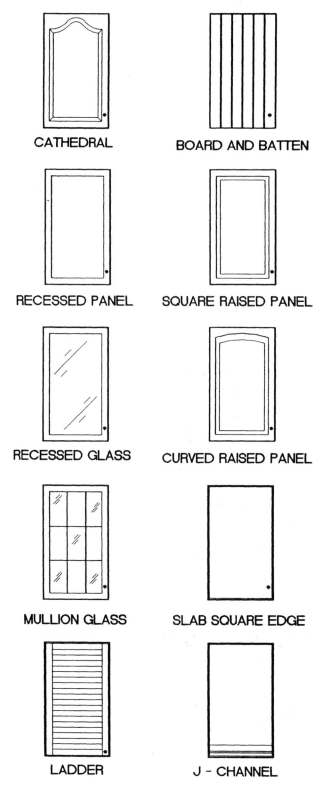

CATHEDRAL   BOARD AND BATTEN

RECESSED PANEL   SQUARE RAISED PANEL

RECESSED GLASS   CURVED RAISED PANEL

MULLION GLASS   SLAB SQUARE EDGE

LADDER   J - CHANNEL

Fig. C.4. Typical cabinet door styles.

Appendix D:
Decorative Plumbing & Hardware

Appendix D—Decorative Plumbing & Hardware

Decorative plumbing and hardware, as a category, bring artistry to what normally are practical fixtures, fittings and accessories in the bathroom.

That artistry might be in materials, form or color, or any combination of the three.

The category is generally considered upscale and much of it is foreign-sourced, but increasing numbers of these products are being designed and produced domestically in the U.S. and Canada by both main-line and specialty manufacturers.

Characteristic of the category is the "family" of products in which everything within a product line matches (Fig. D.1). This will include, for example, lav faucet handles, pop-up drain handle, lights, towel bars, glass holder, toothbrush holder, mirror and more, and in some cases even the lav itself.

This family of products might be expanded to include also the bidet, tub and shower fittings and accessories and even bathroom furniture.

Decorative plumbing and hardware dealers work from showrooms where they show lots of products, sometimes in vignette settings. Their customers are builders, architects and designers, for whom they commonly supply decorative materials for the entire house, and homeowners.

They generally do not provide artwork and avoid being competitive with their customers. But, when needed, they provide plumbing drawings and technical aid because some multiple shower installations are complex. They know the flow rates of their many products, but it also is necessary that they know water flow rates and pressures in the house where the products will go.

Members of NKBA can locate these suppliers by phoning the National Kitchen & Bath Association member services number, 1 (800) 948-7108, to obtain a listing of NKBA's Decorative Plumbing & Hardware Council.

Fig. D.1. Every item—lavatory, faucet, mirror frame, lights, towel bars, shelf brackets, everything—follows the point motif in this "Edition Point" line. The point tips can be red, turquoise, white, black, yellow, chrome or Durabrass. This is characteristic of the luxury plumbing and accessories available from Decorative Plumbing & Hardware sources. The collection also includes a bidet and a tub/shower, and their fittings. (Dornbracht photo.)

NKBA, 687 Willow Grove St., Hackettstown NJ 07840. Phone: (908) 852-0033. Fax: (908) 852-1695.

Appendix E:
NKBA Business Management Forms

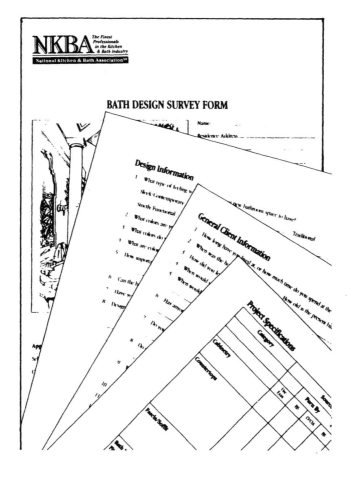

Appendix E—NKBA Business Management Forms System

The **Business Management Forms System** is comprised of forms to assist in operating a successful kitchen and bathroom business. Those pertinent to the bathroom business are:

Lead System

The four forms comprising the NKBA Lead System will provide:

1. A record of prospects
2. Information for the sales consultant
3. Information on the lead source
4. A record of processing activity
5. Statistical data for comparisons.

The **Registration Card** (right) is to be used at home shows, traveling displays, group consumer meetings, or any other situation where more time can't be spent with a prospect. It can be used to set appointments for future visits.

The **Lead Record** (below) should be filled out in duplicate with the person conducting the showroom visit with the prospect. On completion, it should be turned in to the office for further processing.

The **Lead Register** should be maintained by the office where it is reviewed weekly for further action and to determine effective processing of leads.

The **Lead Analysis** should be maintained monthly to compare sales consultant activities. It can be a tool in determining need for additional sales training and to measure results.

NKBA REGISTRATION CARD

Name _____

Address _____

City _____ Home Phone _____

Work Phone _____

☐ Just Browsing   ☐ Planning to Build a New House

☐ Planning to Remodel: ☐ Please have Your
☐ Our Kitchen   ☐ Our Bathroom   Consultant Call on Me

Best Time to Contact Me _____

LEAD RECORD

SAMPLE

Date _____ Time _____ No. _____

Inquiry Received _____

Inquiry Assigned To: _____

Name _____ Address _____

Residence Phone _____ City _____

Job Address: _____ City _____

Lead Source:	⬚ Yellow Pages	⬚ Newspaper	⬚ Radio	⬚ TV	⬚ Walk-in
	⬚ Open House	⬚ Factory Lead	⬚ Home show		⬚ Direct Mail
	⬚ Referral	⬚ Name:			Other _____

Remodel:	⬚ Kitchen	⬚ Bath	⬚ Addition	Other _____
	⬚ New Construction	Work To Be Performed By _____		

Work required:
- ⬚ Cabinets _____
- ⬚ Counter Tops _____
- ⬚ Appliances _____
- ⬚ Floor Covering
- ⬚ Painting

- ⬚ Plumbing
- ⬚ Electrical
- ⬚ Lighting
- ⬚ Wall Covering
- ⬚ Other

Design Fee $ _____ Design Fee Contract Signed: ⬚ Yes ⬚ No

Showroom Visit	Home Visit	Plans Comp.	Presentation	Results	

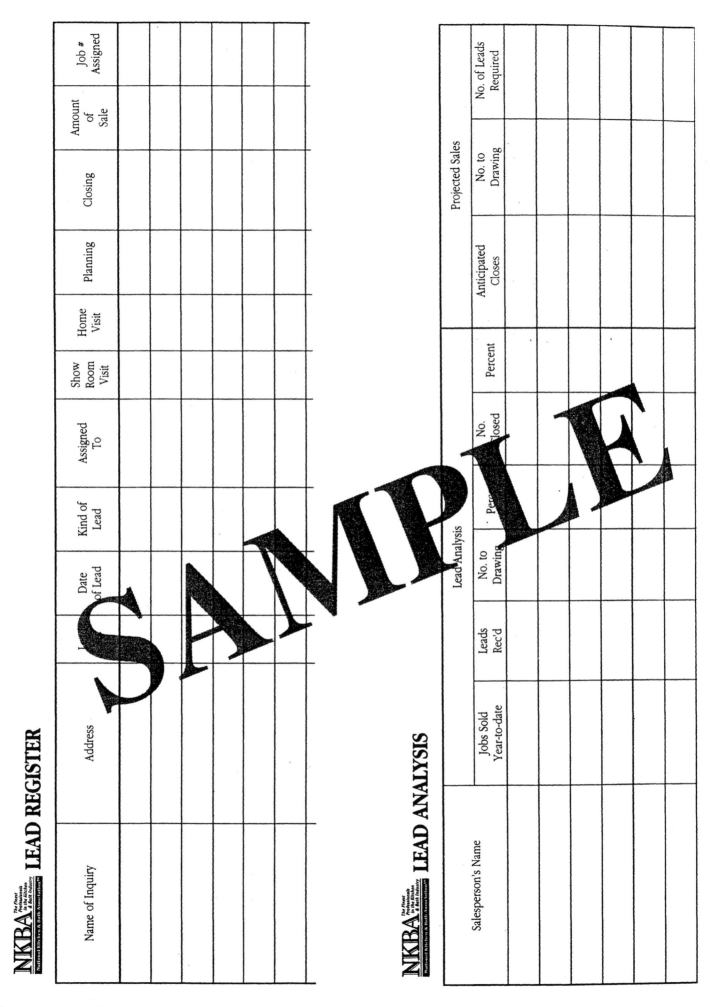

NKBA LEAD REGISTER

Name of Inquiry	Address	Date of Lead	Kind of Lead	Assigned To	Show Room Visit	Home Visit	Planning	Closing	Amount of Sale	Job # Assigned

NKBA LEAD ANALYSIS

Salesperson's Name	Jobs Sold Year-to-date	Leads Rec'd	Lead Analysis			Projected Sales		
			No. to Drawing	Percent	No. Closed	Percent	Anticipated Closes	No. to Drawing	No. of Leads Required

Price Quotation

Two Price Quotation forms are identical except for a "cost" column on one (shown). They provide:
1. a document to record price quotations and cost figures on projects other than installed remodeling jobs.
2. the client with a written price quotation and dated price protection;
3. a system to prevent discrepancies between quotations made at different times by different people.

They should be completed in duplicate, one for the client and one to be filed. All quotations for material only should by made only from the Price Quotation forms.

PRICE QUOTATION

NKBA
The Finest Professionals in the Kitchen & Bath Industry
National Kitchen & Bath Association℠

For:

Client _____

Address _____

_____

Date _____

Based on   Client's Plans ☐   Designers Plans ☐

Cost	We are pleased to quote the following:

Sub-total _____

Tax _____

Delivery _____

GRAND TOTAL _____

*Quote valid for _____ days.

_____
Kitchen/Bath Specialist

Note: *Prices are based on costs and conditions existing on date of quotation.

© 1991 NKBA   BMFSA-8/91-3M-DML

Specifications form—Pages 242-249.

This provides a standard form for all personnel. It has ample room for a detailed description of the products or details, and is a deterrent to overlooking any part of the project. Its format is similar to the estimate form.

The Contract—Pages 250-252.

This is the legally binding agreement that clearly defines what products and services will be supplied by the bathroom specialist.

The National Kitchen & Bath Assn. publishes this contract. All legal documents should be reviewed and approved by the firm's legal counsel before implementation.

STANDARD SPECIFICATIONS FOR BATHROOM DESIGN AND INSTALLATION

Name: _____

Home Address: _____

City: _____ State _____ Phone (Home) _____

(Office) _____

(Office) _____

(Jobsite) _____

Jobsite Address _____

By

Hereafter called "Bathroom Specialist."

Bathroom Specialist will supply and deliver only such equipment and material as described in these specifications. Labor connected with this bathroom installation will be supplied by the Bathroom Specialist only as herein specified.

Any equipment, material and labor designated here as "Owner's responsibility" must be furnished and completed by the Owner, or the Owner's Agent in accordance with the work schedule established by the Bathroom Specialist.

Equipment, material and labor not included in these specifications can be supplied by the Bathroom Specialist at an additional cost for which authorization must be given in writing by the Owner, or the Owner's Agent.

All dimensions and cabinet designations shown on the floor plan, which are part of these specifications, are subject to adjustments dictated by job conditions.

All surfaces of walls, ceilings, windows and woodwork, except those of factory-made equipment, will be left unpainted or unfinished unless otherwise specified.

If specifications call for re-use of existing equipment, no responsibility on the part of the Bathroom Specialist for appearance, functioning or service shall be implied.

For factory-made equipment, the manufacturer's specifications for quality, design, dimensions, function and installation shall in any case take precedence over any others.

(over)

Cabinetry (as per approved drawing)

Manufacturer

Cabinet Exterior	☐ Wood	☐ Steel	☐ Decorative Laminate	☐ Other

Cabinet Exterior Finish   Cabinet Interior Material   Finish

Door Style   Hardware

Special Cabinet Notes

Furnished By	☐ Bathroom Specialist	☐ Owner	☐ Owner's Agent
Installation By	☐ Bathroom Specialist	☐ Owner	☐ Owner's Agent

Countertops (as per approved drawing)

Manufacturer   Material

Design Details Deck Thickness _____ Color _____   Edging Thickness _____ Color _____

Backsplash Thickness _____ Height _____ Color _____   End Splash Thickness _____ Height _____ Color _____

Special Countertop Notes

Furnished By	☐ Bathroom Specialist	☐ Owner	☐ Owner's Agent
Installation By	☐ Bathroom Specialist	☐ Owner	☐ Owner's Agent

Fascia & Soffit (as per approved drawing)

Construction	☐ Flush	☐ Extended	☐ Recessed	☐ NA (Open)

Finish Material

Special Fascia/Soffit Notes

Furnished By	☐ Bathroom Specialist	☐ Owner	☐ Owner's Agent
Installation By	☐ Bathroom Specialist	☐ Owner	☐ Owner's Agent

Lighting System

Description	Qty.	Model Number	Finish	Lamp Req.	Furnished By		Installed By	
					B.S.	O/OA	B.S.	O/OA

Special Lighting System Notes

KEY

B.S. = Bathroom Specialist   O = Owner   OA = Owner's Agent

BMF13

Bath Fixtures, Fittings and Finishes

Item	Brand Name	Model	Finish	Furnished By		Installed By		Hook Up By	
				B.S.	O/OA	B.S.	O/OA	B.S.	O/OA
Water Closet									
Seat									
Fittings									
Stop and Supply									
Miscellaneous									
Bidet									
Fittings									
Stop and Supply									
Miscellaneous									
Urinal									
Fittings									
Stop and Supply									
Miscellaneous									
Bathtub									
Fittings									
Waste and Overflow									
Stop and Supply									
Enclosure									
Wall Surround									
Drapery Rod									
Bathtub Drapery									
Miscellaneous									
Whirlpool System									
Fittings									
Miscellaneous									
Shower									
Fittings									
Drain									
Showerhead 1									
Showerhead 2									
Stop and Supply									
Enclosure									
Wall Surround									
Shower Floor									
Drapery Rod									
Shower Drapery									
Miscellaneous									

BMF13

Bath Fixtures, Fittings and Finishes *(Continued)*

Item	Brand Name	Model	Finish	Furnished By		Installed By		Hook Up By	
				B.S.	O/OA	B.S.	O/OA	B.S.	O/OA
Lavatory 1									
Fittings									
Drilling Spread									
Stop and Supply									
Pedestal Trap Cover									
Miscellaneous									
Lavatory 2									
Fittings									
Drilling Spread									
Stop and Supply									
Pedestal Trap Cover									
Miscellaneous									
Steam Bath									
Steam Enclosure									
Steam Generator									
Timer									
Miscellaneous									
Sauna									
Interior									
Heater									
Timer									
Miscellaneous									
Spa/Hot Tub									
Fittings									
Timer									
Heater									
Miscellaneous									
Exercise Equipment									
Miscellaneous									

SBMF13

Accessories (as per approved drawing)

Item	Brand Name	Model	Size	Finish	Furnished By		Installed By		Hook Up By	
					B.S.	O/OA	B.S.	O/OA	B.S.	O/OA
Mirror										
Medicine Cabinet										
Glass Shelves										
Towel Bar(s)										
Hydronic/Electric										
Towel Ring(s)										
Robe Hook(s)										
Tub Soap Dish(es)										
Shower Soap Dish(es)										
Bidet Soap Dish										
Lavatory Soap Dish(es)										
Grab Bars										
Paper Holder										
Magazine Rack										
Soap/Lotion Dispenser										
Tumbler										
Tissue Holder										
Scale										
Toothbrush Holder										
Hamper										
Other										

Closet Specifications

Item	Brand Name	Model	Size	Finish	Furnished By		Installed By		Hook Up By	
					B.S.	O/OA	B.S.	O/OA	B.S.	O/OA
Poles										
Shelf(ve)										
Drawers										
Shoe Racks										
Belt/Tie/Scarf Rack(s)										
Safe										
Ironing Board										
Miscellaneous										
Other Storage										

Windows and Doors

Item	Brand Name	Model	Finish	Hardware	Furnished By B.S.	Furnished By O/OA	Installed By B.S.	Installed By O/OA

Special Window and Door Notes:

Flooring

	Furnished By B.S.	Furnished By O/OA	Installed By B.S.	Installed By O/OA
Removal of Existing Floor Covering				
Preparation of Floor for New Surface				
Installation of Subfloor/Underlayment				
New Floor Covering Material Description:				
Manufacturer Pattern Name				
Pattern Number Pattern Repeat				
Floor Covering Installation				
Baseboard Material				
Transition Treatment				
Remove and Repair Water Damaged Area				
Remove and Reset Usable Closet				
Special Flooring Notes:				

Decorative Surfaces (wall, ceiling, window materials)

Removal Work: Wall _____ Ceiling _____ Window ——— Preparation Work: Wall _____ Ceiling _____ Window _____

Description	Brand Name	Model	Finish	Material Quantity	Furnished By B.S.	Furnished By O/OA	Installed By B.S.	Installed By O/OA

Special Decorative Surface Notes:

SBMF15

Appendix E   247

Electrical Work (except as described above in specific equipment sections)

	Furnished By		Installed By	
	B.S.	O/OA	B.S.	O/OA
Heating System Alteration				
New Service Panel				
Code Update				
Details				

Plumbing (except as described above in specific equipment sections)

	Furnished By		Installed By	
	B.S.	O/OA	B.S.	O/OA
Heating System Alterations				
New Rough-in Requirements				
Modifications to Existing Lines				
Details				

General Carpentry (except as described above in specific equipment sections)

	Furnished By		Installed By	
	B.S.	O/OA	B.S.	O/OA
Demolition Work				
Existing Fixture and Equipment Removal				
Trash Removal				
Reconstruction Work (Except as Previously Stated)				
Windows				
Doors				
Interior Walls				
Exterior Walls				
Details				

BMF15

Miscellaneous Work

| | Responsibility | |
	B.S.	O/OA
Trash Removal		
Jobsite/Room Cleanup		
Building Permit(s)		
Structural Engineering/Architectural Fees		
Inspection Fees		
Jobsite Delivery		
Other		

I have read these specifications and approve:

Accepted: _____

Accepted: _____

Date: _____

Authorized Company Representative

By: _____

By: _____

Date: _____

STANDARD FORM OF AGREEMENT
FOR DESIGN AND INSTALLATION

Approved by the

National Kitchen & Bath Association

Between ....Purchaser

Home Address ....

City .... State .... Zip ....

Phone Number ....

Delivery Address ....

And Seller

1. The Seller agrees to furnish the materials and services set forth in the drawings (numbered.............................
and dated ....) and specifications annexed hereto.
The Purchaser agrees to make payment therefore in accordance with the schedule of payment.

Contract Price .... $ ....

Sales Tax (if applicable) .... $ ....

.... $ ....

Total Purchase Price .... $ ....

Schedule of Payment:

Upon signing of this agreement .... $ ....

Upon delivery of cabinets from manufacturer .... $ ....

Upon delivery of .... $ ....

Upon substantial installation of .... $ ....

This contract includes the terms and provisions as set forth herein. Please read and sign where indicated.

2. The standard form of warranty shall apply to the service and equipment furnished (except where other warranties of purchased products apply). The warranty shall become effective when signed by the Seller and delivered to the Purchaser. The warranty is for one year materials and labor.

3. The delivery date, when given, shall be deemed approximate and performance is subject to delays caused by strikes, fires, acts of God or other reasons not under the control of the Seller, as well as the availability of the product at the time of delivery.

4. The Purchaser agrees to accept delivery of the product or products when ready. The risk of loss, as to damage or destruction, shall be upon the Purchaser upon the delivery and receipt of the product.

5. The Purchaser understands that the products described are specially designed and custom built and that the Seller takes immediate steps upon execution of this Agreement to design, order and construct those items set forth herein; therefore, this Agreement is not subject to cancellation by the Purchaser for any reason.

6. No installation, plumbing, electrical, flooring, decorating or other construction work is to be provided unless specifically set forth herein. In the event the Seller is to perform the installation, it is understood that the price agreed upon herein does not include possible expense entailed in coping with hidden or unknown contingencies found at the job site. In the event such contingencies arise and the Seller is required to furnish labor or material or otherwise perform work not provided for or contemplated by the Seller, the actual costs plus (   ) thereof will be paid for by the Purchaser. Contingencies include but are not limited to: inability to reuse existing water, vent and waste pipes; air shafts, ducts, grilles, louvres and registers; the relocation of concealed pipes, wires, wiring or conduits, the presence of which cannot be determined until the work has started; or imperfections, rotting or decay in the structure or parts thereof necessitating replacement.

7. Title to the item sold pursuant to this Agreement shall not pass to the Purchaser until the full price as set forth in the Agreement is paid to the Seller.

8. Delays in payment shall be subject to interest charges of (   )% per annum, and in no event higher than the interest rate provided by law. If the Seller is required to engage the services of a collection agency or an attorney, the Purchaser agrees to reimburse the Seller for any reasonable amounts expended in order to collect the unpaid balance.

9. If any provision of this Agreement is declared invalid by any tribunal, the remaining provisions of the Agreement shall not be affected thereby.

10. This Agreement sets forth the entire transaction between the parties; any and all prior Agreements, warranties or representations made by either party are superseded by this Agreement. All changes in this Agreement shall be made by a separate document and executed with the same formalities. No agent of the Seller, unless authorized in writing by the Seller, has any authority to waive, alter, or enlarge this contract, or to make any new or substituted or different contracts, representations, or warranties.

11. The Seller retains the right upon breach of this Agreement by the Purchaser to sell those items in the Seller's possession. In effecting any resale on breach of this Agreement by the Purchaser, the Seller shall be deemed to act in the capacity of agent for the Purchaser. The purchaser shall be liable for any net deficiency on resale.

12. The Seller agrees that it will perform this contract in conformity with customary industry practices. The Purchaser agrees that any claim for adjustment shall not be reason or cause for failure to make payment of the purchase price in full. Any unresolved controversy or claim arising from or under this contract shall be settled by arbitration and judgment upon the award rendered may be entered in any court of competent jurisdiction. The arbitration shall be held under the rules of the American Arbitration Association.

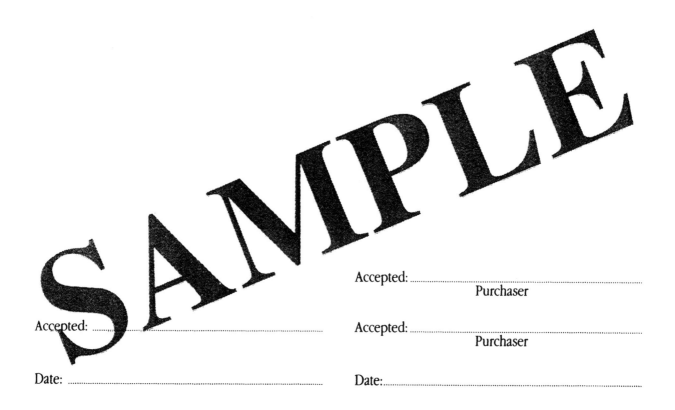

Accepted: ....
Purchaser

Accepted: ....

Accepted: ....
Purchaser

Date: ....

Date: ....

Job Progress—Page 254.

This form will provide an easy review of the job and the status of each section, and a ready instrument for scheduling of the job as it progresses. It should be attached to the inside cover of the job folder for easy access. The expeditor or person responsible for ordering labor, product and/or material should complete this form as the information is received or scheduled, generally on a daily basis.

Change Order System—Page 255.

This system includes two similar forms, one with an added column for cost (shown).

The forms provide a legal agreement authorizing and acknowledging any changes made in the contract, plans and/or specifications, and cost accounting information for the changes.

The forms should be completed whenever the client requests changes in the contract specifications and/or plans of the project. The changes should be explicit and costed in order to indicate any credit or additional charges for the changes. All parties signing the original contract for the project are required to sign the change order.

Completion Report and Follow-up System—Page 255-259.

This system includes a Completion Report, an NKBA Limited Warranty form, a follow-up letter and a Client Evaluation form.

The entire system should be designated as the sales consultant's responsibility, and he/she should visit the jobsite on the final day of completion. That individual should inspect the job, take care of minor adjustments or complaints, present the Warranty, have the Completion Report signed by the client and present the final bill. The signed copy of the Completion Report should be placed in the job folder.

The Client Evaluation form should be left with the client to be completed and mailed to your office. When it is received, it should be reviewed by the manager or owner, initialed, and placed in the job folder. Any names, prospects or recommendations should be handled as leads and assigned to the sales consultant who handled the job.

NKBA *The Finest Professionals in the kitchen & Bath Industry* JOB PROGRESS
National Kitchen & Bath Association℠

Name _____ Date Signed _____

Street _____ City/State _____ Zip _____

Home Phone _____ Business Phone _____ Permit # _____

Item	Supplier	PO# and Date Ordered	Due Scheduled	Received Measured	Delivered Installed	Notes
1. Cabinets						
2. Counter Top						
Deck						
Backsplash						
3. Flooring						
4. Decorating						
Material						
Painter						
Paperhanger						
Other						
5. Lighting						
6. Equipment						
Appliances & Fixtures						
7. Plumbing				Rough-in Insp.	Top-out Insp.	Finish Insp.
8. Electrical				Rough-in Insp.	Finish Insp.	
9. Construction & Alteration				Job Insp.	Tear-out	Construction Insp.
				Patch	Set	Trim
10. Inspection						
11. Trash						
12. Extras						

© 1991 NKBA   BMF16-12/91-2M-AD

CHANGE IN PLANS AND SPECIFICATIONS

NKBA
The Finest Professionals in the Kitchen & Bath Industry
National Kitchen & Bath Association

Client: _____ Date: _____

Street: _____ Job #: _____

City: _____ Change Order #: _____

Job Address: _____

I hereby authorize _____ to make the following change from the work originally set forth in the plans and specifications.

Description	Charge	Cost

Additional ☐ charge ☐ credit for above work is $ _____

Payment will be made as follows _____

Authorized signature _____ client

Authorized signature _____ Date _____

NKBA
The Finest Professionals in the Kitchen & Bath Industry
National Kitchen & Bath Association

COMPLETION REPORT

Client _____ Date _____

Street _____ Home Phone _____

City/State _____ Zip _____ Work Phone _____

This certifies that all labor and materials specified in the plans and specifications dated _____ , have been inspected and accepted as complete and satisfactory.

Client _____

Date _____

NKBA *The Finest Professionals in the Kitchen & Bath Industry*
National Kitchen & Bath Association℠

CUSTOMER COMPLAINT FORM

Customer's Name: _____ Home Phone: _____ Work Phone: _____

Address: _____ City/State: _____ Zip: _____

Date of Complaint: _____ Date Installed: _____ Job #: _____

Nature of Complaint: (be specific): _____
_____
_____
_____
_____
_____
_____
_____

Complaint Received By: _____

Corrective Action Taken: _____
_____
_____
_____
_____

Corrective Action Taken By: _____ Date: _____
Complaint Co_____ Date: _____
Requirements: _____
_____
_____
_____
_____

Completion Noted By: _____

Verified With Customer By: _____ Date: _____

Remarks: _____
_____
_____
_____
_____

SAMPLE

NKBA *The Finest Professionals in the Kitchen & Bath Industry*

National Kitchen & Bath Association[SM]

LIMITED WARRANTY

for the materials installed
in the home of

_____

At _____

_____

Commencement Date _____

Warrantor _____

Address _____

Phone No. _____

Signed _____

Title _____

Form Approved by the

**National Kitchen &
Bath Association**

NKBA *The Finest Professionals in the Kitchen & Bath Industry*

National Kitchen & Bath Association℠

The firm (warrantor), whose name, address and phone number appears on the face of this document, warrants and presents to the party in the space designated the following:

Materials covered by this warranty, supplied and installed by the firm, or under its direction and supervision shall be guaranteed for a period of one (1) year from the date given against defects in workmanship and material.

Installation performed by the firm, persons in its direct employ or subcontractors employed specifically by the firm warranted to be of good workmanlike quality in accordance with customary industry practices.

All articles supplied by the firm but manufactured by others shall not be covered by the warranty other than to the extent of the warranty given by such manufacturer or his distributor from whom the firm obtained the product.

In the event of defects in workmanship and material and the failure of products supplied by the firm to conform with the agreement or warranty, the firm will repair or replace said product or material provided that the defect or malfunction was not due to accidents, alterations by the customer, misuse, abuse or neglect. The firm shall not be responsible for shipment and installation costs as the result of repairing or replacing the item.

In order to obtain performance of any warranty obligation the customer shall immediately contact the firm in writing and cooperate fully in supplying the necessary information, as well as access to the premises, relative to the defect or malfunction.

The item purchased under this agreement shall be used exclusively by the customer and by no other person, and therefore there shall be no third party beneficiary to any of the warranties, express or implied, contained in this agreement.

The implied warranties of fitness and merchantability are to coincide with the duration of this warranty and not extend beyond that date. Some states do not allow limitations on how long an implied warranty lasts, so the above limitation may not apply to you.

The firm shall not be liable for consequential damages or loss caused by the malfunction of equipment not specifically installed by its own employees or subcontractors in it employ. Some states do not allow the exclusion or limitation of incidental or consequential damages, so the above limitation or exclusion may not apply to you.

This warranty gives you specific legal rights, and you may also have other rights which vary from state to state.

The firm warrants the materials identified on the cover of this warranty to be designed and engineered in accordance with the standards advocated and set forth by customary industry practices.

Completion Report

Client _____ Date _____

Street _____ Home Phone _____

City _____ State _____ Zip _____ Work Phone _____

This certifies that all labor and materials specifiec in the plans and specifications dated _____ , have been inspected and accepted as complete and satisfactory.

Client _____

(Please type on your letterhead)

Dear

Thank you for allowing us to serve you!

If we have failed to live up to your expectations, we hope that you will tell us why so that we can please you in the future.

We are constantly seeking ways and means to improve the quality of our service. Any deficiencies which your comments might reflect will be corrected immediately.

Please answer the following questions and mail in the envelope provided:

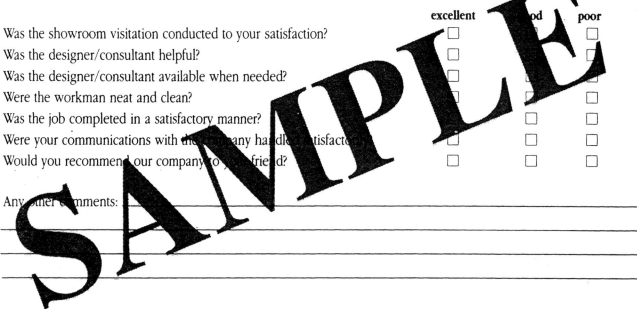

	excellent	good	poor
Was the showroom visitation conducted to your satisfaction?	☐	☐	☐
Was the designer/consultant helpful?	☐	☐	☐
Was the designer/consultant available when needed?	☐	☐	☐
Were the workman neat and clean?	☐	☐	☐
Was the job completed in a satisfactory manner?	☐	☐	☐
Were your communications with the company handled satisfactorily?	☐	☐	☐
Would you recommend our company to your friend?	☐	☐	☐

Any other comments: _____

_____

_____

_____

If any of your friends or acquaintances are interested in any of our products or services, may we use your name as a reference? (Please list the name and address of the interested person.)

_____

_____

_____

Thank you very much for the above information. We sincerely hope that we can be of service to you again in the future.

Notes:

Installation Management Forms

(First page only shown of multi-page forms)

Subcontractor Agreement

A 2-page form for use when any phases of installation are subcontracted. Not shown, a Contract Installer agreement, for use when entire job is contracted out, same as the Subcontractor agreement except for nomenclature.

Pre-Start Checklist for Bathroom Installation

A 2-page checklist for installer on status of all fixtures and materials.

Pre-Close-In Punchlist

A 2-page form to check satisfactory completion of all mechanical work after mechanical and electrical inspections are completed.

Final Inspection Punchlist

A 3-page universal form for use in either bathroom or kitchen.

Quality Control Punchlist

This one-page forms lists items to be completed before final payment.

Time Card

Form lists hours per day and week, includes payroll deductions.

Industry Response Feedback Form

This describes any problem, provides communication form between industry levels and lists possible solutions.

Jobsite Communication Form

Provides a medium for communication on the jobsite.

NKBA
The Finest Professionals in the Kitchen & Bath Industry
National Kitchen & Bath Association℠

SUBCONTRACTOR AGREEMENT

Job Phone		Date
Job Name		
Job Address		
Job No.		Designer

SUBCONTRACTOR to furnish, at SUBCONTRACTOR's own cost and expense, all labor and/or materials necessary for the completion of the job at premises set forth above, according to plan and the following terms and specifications:

_____

_____

_____

_____

_____

_____

_____

The start date for this agreement is _____ and all work shall be completed not later than _____.

The following items are attached to this contract for the purpose of describing the work of this agreement:
▢ Addendum   ▢ Plan   ▢ Specifications   ▢ Schedule   ▢ Fixture/Equipment Cut Sheets   ▢ Other: _____

SUBCONTRACTOR to furnish and install the above complete in accordance with specifications above for the sum of:

_____ Dollars ($_____)

Payment in full to SUBCONTRACTOR to be due upon final completion and acceptance of work and receipt of invoice, unless otherwise noted here:

_____

ACCEPTANCE BY CONTRACTOR	ACCEPTANCE BY SUBCONTRACTOR
The foregoing terms, specifications, and the conditions listed on the reverse side of this AGREEMENT are satisfactory and the same are hereby accepted and agreed upon.	The SUBCONTRACTOR, upon signing this AGREEMENT, represents that he or she has examined the existing conditions at the job premises, that the foregoing terms and specifications and the conditions listed on the reverse side of this AGREEMENT are satisfactory and the same are hereby accepted and agreed upon.
Company _____ Authorized Signature _____	Company _____ Authorized Signature _____

 **PRE-START CHECKLIST FOR BATHROOM INSTALLATION**

Name: _____ Phone (Home): _____

Home Address: _____ (Office): _____

City: _____ State: _____ (Job Site): _____

Job Site Address: _____

Rec'd in Local Stock	Material/Equipment Items	Date Ordered	Estimated Delivery
☐	Cabinets		
☐	Toilet		
☐	Bidet		
☐	Bathtub		
☐	Whirlpool System		
☐	Shower		
☐	Lavatory 1		
☐	Lavatory 2		
☐	Steam Bath		
☐	Sauna		
☐	Spa/Hot Tub		
☐	Lavatory Faucet(s)		
☐	Bath/Shower Fittings		
☐	Windows		
☐	Doors		
☐	Flooring		
☐	HVAC Vents and Accessories		
☐	Framing Lumber		
☐	Gypsum Wallboard and Accessories		
☐	Lighting Fixtures		
☐	Wall Finishes (Ceramic Tile, etc.)		
☐	Medicine Cabinet(s)		

PRE-CLOSE-IN PUNCHLIST

Job Name: _____

Job Address: _____

This punchlist to be completed after mechanical and electrical inspections are complete.

ELECTRICAL
- ☐ All outlets and lights per plan.
- ☐ Nail plates in place.
- ☐ Insulation not too close to recessed light fixtures.
- ☐ Ceiling fixtures roughed in, proper location.
- ☐ Rough-in boxes correctly set for drywall hanging, doors, trim, etc.
- ☐ Wiring for security, telephone, smoke detector.
- ☐ Panel work completed.
- ☐ Electrical inspection completed.
- ☐ _____
- ☐ _____

PLUMBING
- ☐ All rough-ins per plan.
- ☐ Nail plates in place.
- ☐ Backing boards in place for wall-hung lavatories and accessories.
- ☐ Pipes insulated in crawl space, secured properly.
- ☐ Rough-in for diverter correct distance from 2x to work with tile.
- ☐ Plumbing inspection completed.
- ☐ Tub not chipped.
- ☐ Access panel roughed in.
- ☐ _____

HVAC
- ☐ All ductwork per plan.
- ☐ No conflict between diffusers and electric fixtures.
- ☐ Ducts insulated properly where indicated.
- ☐ Control wiring, thermostat(s) installed if included.
- ☐ All flues properly installed.
- ☐ Inspections completed for any wiring and gas piping required.
- ☐ _____
- ☐ _____

FINAL INSPECTION BEFORE PUNCHLIST WITH CUSTOMER

Job Name: _____

Job Address: _____

ELECTRICAL

- ☐ All outlets and switches work; wall plates are straight and level.
- ☐ All outlet wall plates are installed tight to drywall or finish surface.
- ☐ Electric panel labeled for new circuits.
- ☐ All light fixtures have lamps installed and are working properly.
- ☐ Batteries in smoke detector, if required.
- ☐ Final inspection completed.
- ☐ _____
- ☐ _____
- ☐ _____
- ☐ _____

COUNTERTOPS

- ☐ Countertops securely attached to base cabinets or means of support.
- ☐ Backsplash installed if required.
- ☐ Backsplash scribed to wall if irregular wall surface exists.
- ☐ Countertop caulked as required.
- ☐ Countertop free of surface scratches.
- ☐ Solid surface and stone countertops correctly finished.
- ☐ Countertop joints fit tightly and are sealed.
- ☐ _____
- ☐ _____

PLUMBING

- ☐ All fixtures working properly.
- ☐ Fixtures are not chipped or showing signs of finish damage.
- ☐ Fixtures are secure to wall, floor, or countertop surface.
- ☐ Tub and shower are caulked, including at floor.
- ☐ Aerators and escutcheon plates are installed.
- ☐ All gas connections working properly.
- ☐ Final inspection completed.
- ☐ _____
- ☐ _____
- ☐ _____
- ☐ _____

QUALITY CONTROL
PRE-COMPLETION PUNCHLIST

Sheet _____ of _____

Owner _____

Address _____

City, State, Zip_____

Telephone _____

Job Location

_____

_____

Job No._____ Date _____

List of items to be completed prior to final payment of $_____:

_____

_____

_____

_____

_____

_____

_____

_____

_____

_____

_____

_____

_____

_____

_____

_____

_____

_____

Amount to be retained in escrow pending completion of above items $_____

It is agreed that when the above list of items is completed, approval for final payment will be authorized. Any omitted or defective items noted after final payment will be covered by the warranty.

_____   _____
Submitted by (Installer):   Date   Owner   Date

_____   _____
Dealer/Designer   Date   Owner   Date

TIME CARD

JOB NO.	JOB NAME	DESCRIPTION OF WORK	CATEGORY NO.	S	M	T	W	T	F	S	TOTAL HOURS	RATE	TOTAL EARNINGS

NAME | DATE | WEEK ENDING | 19

TOTAL REGULAR TIME

TOTAL OVERTIME

TOTAL GROSS EARNINGS

PAYROLL DEDUCTIONS

	FICA	FED. INC. TAX	STATE TAX	HEALTH INS.	OTHER

CORRECT:

EMPLOYEE

FOREMAN

TOTAL NET EARNINGS

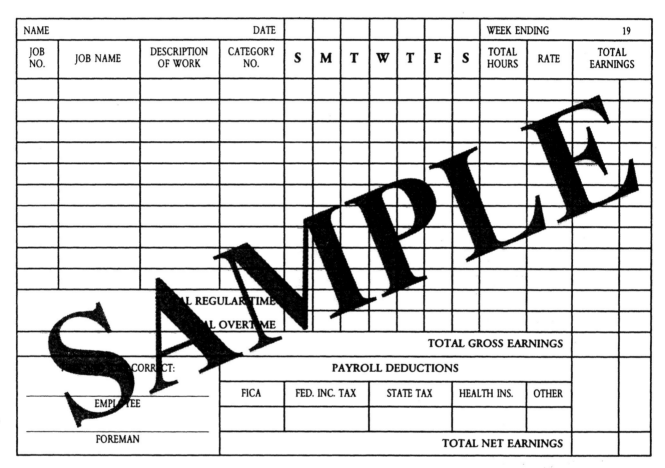

© 1995 NKBA IMF-4020

INDUSTRY FEEDBACK
RESPONSE FORM

To: _____

    _____

    _____

□ Manufacturer □ Distributor □ Retailer

□ Dealer □ K/B Designer □ Interior Designer

□ Architect □ Installer □ Plumber □ Electrician

From: _____

     _____

     _____

□ Manufacturer □ Distributor □ Retailer

□ Dealer □ K/B Designer □ Interior Designer

□ Architect □ Installer □ Plumber □ Electrician

Customer/Job Name: _____ Date: _____

City/State: _____ Date of Installation: _____

Brief Description of Problem: _____

_____

_____

List of Possible Causes: _____

_____

_____

_____

Description of Facts: _____

_____

_____

_____

_____

Who is in the best position to solve this problem? _____

List of All Possible Solutions: _____

_____

_____

_____

ON-SITE JOB
COMMUNICATION FORM

MESSAGE	REPLY
Date: Message No.	Date:
To:	To:
From:	From:
By:	By:
Signature or Initials of Addressor	Signature or Initials of Addressee

1. Addressor write message and leave on pad without removing copy
2. Addressee write reply and detach yellow copy for records
3. Addressor, after receiving reply, detach pink copy for records

UNIVERSAL BATHROOM PLANNING CLIENT SURVEY

NKBA *The Finest Professionals in the Kitchen & Bath Industry*
National Kitchen & Bath Association℠

Name: _____ Date: _____

Address: _____

City, State, Zip: _____

Phone: _____ Work: _____

Jobsite Address: _____

City, State, Zip: _____

Directions: _____

_____

Appointment: _____

Date: _____ Address: _____

Time: _____ City/State/Zip: _____

Comment: _____ Phone: _____

_____

Allied Professional: _____

_____

_____

Pertinent Information: _____

_____

_____

The Universal Bathroom Planning Client Survey Is a 9-page form that provides a complete physical profile of the user/s of the planned bathroom, including details of reach and grasp.

Manufacturers and Associations Named in Text:

American National Standards Institute (ANSI), 1430 Broadway, New York NY 10018.

American Society of Heating, Refrigerating and Air Conditioning Engineers (ASHRAE), 1791 Tullie Circle NE, Atlanta GA 30329.

American Standard, Inc., 1 Centennial Plaza, Piscataway NJ 08855-6820. (908) 980-3000. FAX (908) 980-3335.

Avonite, Inc. 1945 Hwy. 304, Belen NM 87003. (800) 428-6648. FAX (505) 864-7790.

Broan Manufacturing Co., 926 W. State St., Hartford WI 53027. (800) 548-0790. FAX (414) 673-8709.

Council of American Building Officials (CABO), 2233 Wisconsin Av. NW, Washington DC 20007.

Domtar Inc., 6300 Atlantic Blvd., Norcross GA 30071. (800) 241-4915. FAX (404) 448-5140.

Dornbracht, distributed by Santile International, 6687 Jimmy Carter Blvd., Norcross GA 30071. (404) 416-6224. FAX (404) 416-6239.

DuPont Corian Products, Barley Mill Products Bldg. 10-1283, Wilmington DE 19880. (302) 992-4373.

Eljer Plumbingware, 17120 Dallas Pkwy., Dallas TX 75248. (800) 435-5372. FAX (214) 407-2789)

Epánel, 145 Rte. 31 N., Suite 21, Pennington NJ 08534. (609) 466-1172. FAX (609) 466-0773.

Formica Corp., 10155 Reading Rd., Cincinnati OH 45241-5729. (513) 786-3533. FAX (513) 786-3024.

General Electric Lighting Div., 1975 Noble Rd., Nela Park, Cleveland OH 44112-6300. (216) 266-6675. FAX (216) 266-3433.

Georgia Pacific Corp., 133 Peachtree St. NE, Atlanta GA 30303. (404) 521-4000.

Grohe America, 241 Covington Dr., Bloomingdale IL 60108. (708) 582-7711. FAX (708) 582-7722.

Heritage Custom Kitchens, 215 Diller Av., New Holland PA 17578. (717) 354-4011. FAX (717) 355-0198.

Home Ventilating Institute, 30 W. University Dr., Arlington Hts. IL 60004. (708) 394-0150. FAX (708) 253-0088.

Kohler Co., 444 Highland Dr., Kohler WI 53044. (414) 457-4441. FAX (414) 457-1271.

Lippert Corp., Box 1030, Menomonee Falls WI 53052-1030. (414) 255-2350. FAX (414) 255-2304.

Marble Institute of America, 33505 State St., Farmington MI 48335. (810) 476-5558. FAX (810) 476-1630.

Merillat Industries, Box 1946, Adrian MI 49221. (517) 263-0771. FAX (517) 263-4792.

Nevamar Div., International Paper, 8339 Telegraph Rd., Odenton MD 21113. (410) 551-5000. FAX (410) 551-0357.

NuTone, Inc., Madison & Red Bank Rd., Cincinnati OH 45227-1599. (800) 543-8687. FAX (513) 527-5177.

Robern Inc., 1648 Winchester Rd., Bensalem PA 19020. (800) 877-2376. FAX (215) 245-5067.

Surface Imagery, 130 New Highway, Amityville NY 11701. (800) 852-0087. FAX (516) 842-7239.

Swan Corporation, One City Centre, St. Louis MO 63101. (314) 231-8148.

VT Industries, 1000 Industrial Park, Holstein IA 51025. (712) 368-4381.

Wilsonart International, 600 S. General Bruce Dr., Temple TX 76504. (800) 433-3222. FAX (817) 770-2384.

Index

Appendix F:
Graphics and Presentation Standards

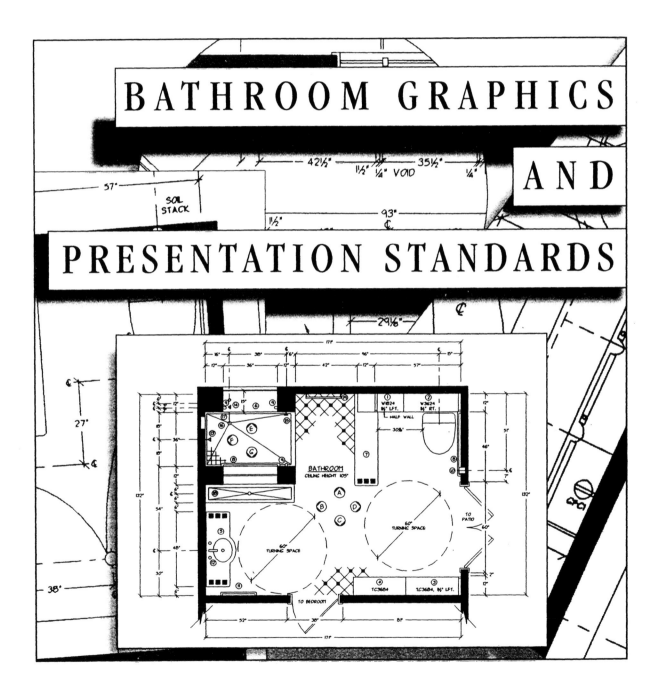

Table of Contents

Purpose

By standardizing floor plans and presentation drawings, Bathroom Designers will:

- Limit errors caused by misinterpreting the floor plans.

- Avoid misreading dimensions, which can result in costly errors.

- Prevent cluttering floor plans and drawings with secondary information, which often make the documents difficult to interpret.

- Create a clear understanding of the scope of the project for all persons involved in the job.

- Present a professional image to the client.

- Permit faster processing of orders.

- Simplify estimating and specification preparation.

- Help in the standardization of uniform nomenclature and symbols.

General Provisions Using Imperial Dimensions

I. Use of Standards

The use of these *National Kitchen & Bath Association Graphics and Presentation Standards* is strongly recommended. They contain a specific set of criteria which when applied by the Bathroom Specialist produce a series of project documents that include the following:

- The Floor Plan

- The Construction Plan

- The Mechanical Plan

- The Interpretive Drawings

    1) Elevations
    2) Perspective Drawings
    3) Oblique, Dimetric, Isometric and Trimetric
    4) Sketches

- Specifications

- Design Statement

- Contracts

Two sample sets of project documents for your review can be found in this publication, one uses imperial dimensions and the other is a metric conversion.

Paper: The acceptable paper for the original drawings of the floor plan, construction plan, mechanical plan, and interpretive drawings is set at a **minimum size of 11" x 17"**. Translucent vellum tracing paper, imprinted with a black border and appropriate space available for the insertion of pertinent information is strongly recommended. Copies of original drawings should appear in blue or black ink only on white paper. Ozalid or photocopy prints are acceptable.

The use of lined yellow note paper, typing paper, scored graph paper or scored quadrille paper **is not acceptable.**

NKBA Drawing Aid #6002

II. The Floor Plan

1) **Size and Scope of Floor Plan Drawings:** Bathroom floor plans should be drawn to a scale of 1/2 inch equals 1 foot (1/2" = 1'0"). * *For metric dimensioning, see Use of Standards beginning on page 35.*

- All base cabinetry should be depicted using a dashed line (— — —) while countertops are depicted using a solid line.

- The floor plan should depict the entire room when possible. When the entire room cannot be depicted, it must show the area where cabinetry and appliances are permanently installed.

- Floor plans must show all major structural elements such as walls, door swings, door openings, partitions, windows, archways and equipment.

- When the entire room cannot be depicted, the room must be divided by *"break lines"* (—⟋⟍—) and must show all major structural elements with adjoining areas indicated and labeled.

- Finished interior dimensions are used on all project documents to denote available space for cabinetry and/or other types of equipment. If the bathroom specialist is responsible for specifying the exact method of wall construction, finish and/or partition placement, the specialist should include partition center lines on the construction plan, as well as the finished interior dimensions.

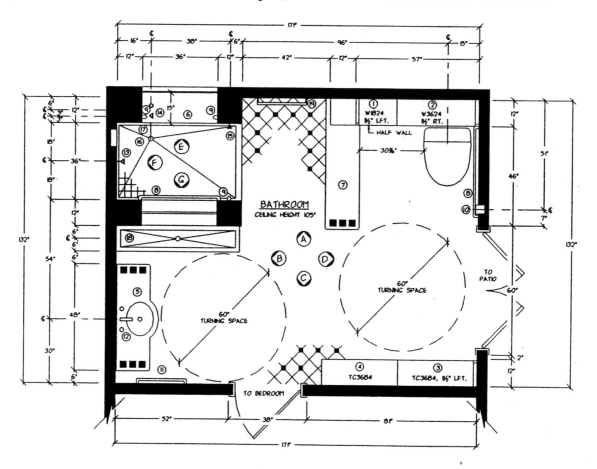

2) **Centerline (℄) dimensions:** must be given for equipment in two directions when possible.

- Mechanicals requiring centerlines include: lavatories, bathtubs/showers, toilets/bidets, fan units, light fixtures, heating and air conditioning ducts and radiators.

- Dimensions should be pulled from return walls or from the face of cabinets/fixtures/equipment opposite the mechanical element.

- Centerlines on the mechanical plan will be indicated by the symbol (℄) followed by a **long-short-long broken line** that extends into the floor area.

- When the centerline dimension line is outside the floor area, it is typically shown as the second (and, if required, the third) line following the dimension line which identifies the individual wall segments.

3) **Dimensioning of Floor Plan:** All drawing dimensions used on bathroom floor plans must be given in **Inches and Fractions of Inches <u>ONLY</u>,** (ie. 124 1/4").

- Combining dimensions listed in feet and inches or the exclusive use of dimensions listed in feet and inches, 10' 4 1/4" **<u>is not acceptable</u>** and should not be used under any circumstances. Again, this would also apply to the metric equivalent, do not combine meters and centimeters.

NOTE:

- Each set of dimensions should be at least 3/16" apart on separate dimension lines which are to intersect with witness lines. These intersecting points should be indicated by dimension arrows, dots, or slashes.

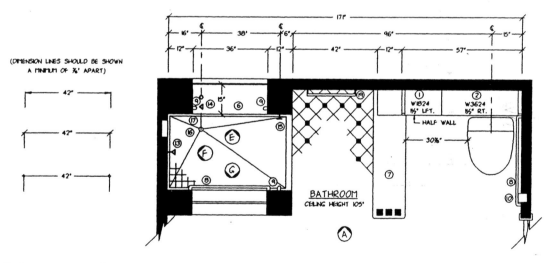

- All dimensions, whenever possible, should be shown **<u>OUTSIDE</u>** the wall lines.

- All lettering should be listed parallel to the title block at the bottom of the vellum paper and break the dimension line near its mid-point. This mechanical drafting technique eliminates errors in reading dimensions.

- An acceptable alternative is to draw all dimensions and lettering so that it is readable from the bottom edge or the right side of the plans with lettering on top of each dimension line.

The following dimensions **MUST** be shown on every floor plan as minimum requirements.

- Overall length of wall areas to receive cabinets, countertops, fixtures, or any equipment occupying floor and/or wall space. This dimension should always be the outside line.

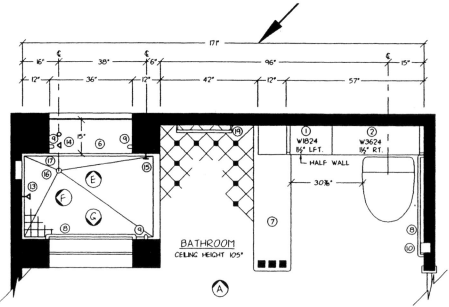

- Each wall opening, (windows, arches, doors and major appliances) and fixed structures (chimneys, wall protrusions and partitions) must be individually dimensioned. Dimensions are shown from outside trim. Trim size must be noted in the specification list. Fixtures such as radiators remaining in place must be outlined on the floor plan. These critical dimensions should be the first dimension line.

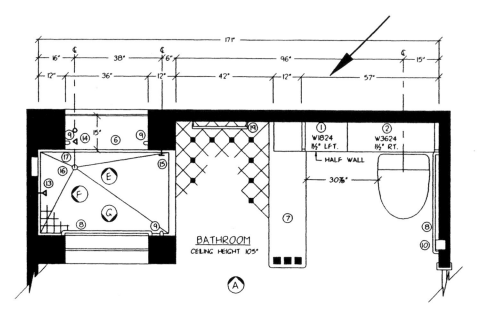

- Ceiling heights should appear on the floor plan. A separate plan for soffits is required when the soffit is a different depth than the wall or tall cabinet below. A separate soffit plan is recommended when the soffit is to be installed **PRIOR** to the wall or tall cabinet installation.

- Additional notes must be included for any deviation from standard height, width and depth. (cabinets, countertops, etc.)

- The exact opening must be given in height, width and depth for areas to be left open to receive equipment, cabinets and fixtures at a future date.

- Items such as island/peninsula vanities and bathtub platforms, must be shown with the overall dimensions given from countertop edge to opposite countertop edge, tall cabinet or wall. The exact location of the structure must be identified by dimensions which position it from two directions; from return walls or from the face of cabinets/equipment opposite the structure.

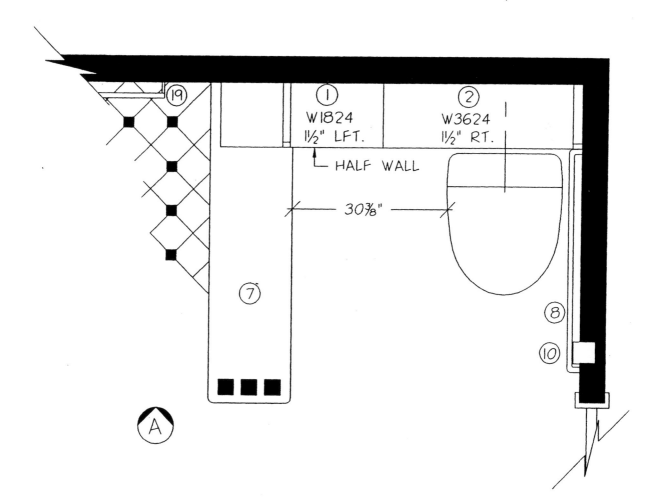

4) Cabinets/Fixtures and Equipment Nomenclature and Designation on Floor Plans:

- Cabinets should be designated and identified by manufacturer nomenclature inside the area indicating their position. Cabinet system trim and finish items are designated outside their area, with an arrow clarifying exactly where the trim piece is located.

- To insure clarity, some design firms prefer to number and call out all the cabinet nomenclature in the Floor Plan specification listing.

- Equally acceptable is the use of a circled reference number to designate each cabinet on the Floor Plan and Elevations with the cabinet code listed within the individual unit width on the elevations or in a separate cross-reference list on the elevations.

- **Regardless of which cabinet designation system is selected from above, additional information for supplementary fixtures/equipment and special provisions pertaining to the cabinets must be indicated within the cabinet or equipment area by a reference number in a circle. This additional information should then be registered in a cross-referenced specifications listing on the same sheet.**

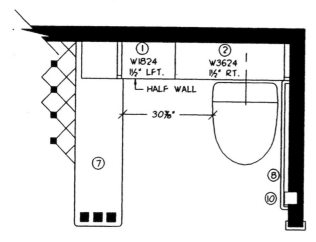

FLOOR PLAN
SPECIFICATIONS

① W1824, 1½" EXT. LEFT, UNDER CABINET LIGHT, DOOR 1½" LONGER THAN CASE TO CONCEAL LTS.

② W3624, 1½" EXT. RIGHT, UNDER CABINET LIGHTS, DOORS 1½" LONGER THAN CASE TO CONCEAL LTS.

- Special order materials or custom design features, angled cabinets, unusual tops, molding, trim details, etc., should be shown in a section view, (sometimes referred to as a *"cut view"*), a plan view in a scale larger than (1/2" = 1') (a metric equivalent is acceptable), or in elevation view.

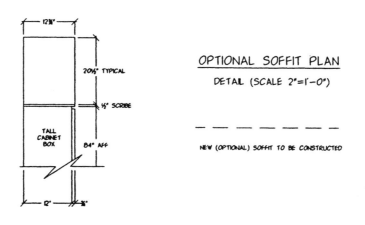

OPTIONAL SOFFIT PLAN
DETAIL (SCALE 2"=1'-0")

— — — — — — — —

NEW (OPTIONAL) SOFFIT TO BE CONSTRUCTED

Graphics and Presentation Standards for Bathroom Design

III. The Construction Plan

1) The purpose of the construction plan is to show the relationship of the existing space with that of the new design. The construction plan is detailed separately so that it does not clutter the floor plan. However, if construction changes are minimal it is acceptable to combine the construction plan with either the floor plan or mechanical plan.

2) **Construction Plan Symbols:**

- Existing walls are shown with solid lines or hollowed out lines at their full thickness.

- Wall sections to be removed are shown with an outline of broken lines.

- New walls show the material symbols applicable to the type of construction or use a symbol which is identified in the legend in order to distinguish them from existing partitions.

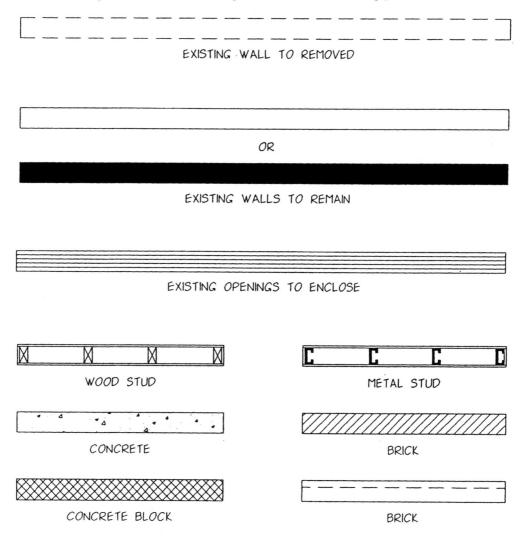

EXISTING WALL TO REMOVED

OR

EXISTING WALLS TO REMAIN

EXISTING OPENINGS TO ENCLOSE

WOOD STUD

METAL STUD

CONCRETE

BRICK

CONCRETE BLOCK

BRICK

NEW WALLS TO BE CONSTRUCTED

* Symbols adapted from Architectural Graphic Standards, 9th Edition

An Example of a Construction Plan:

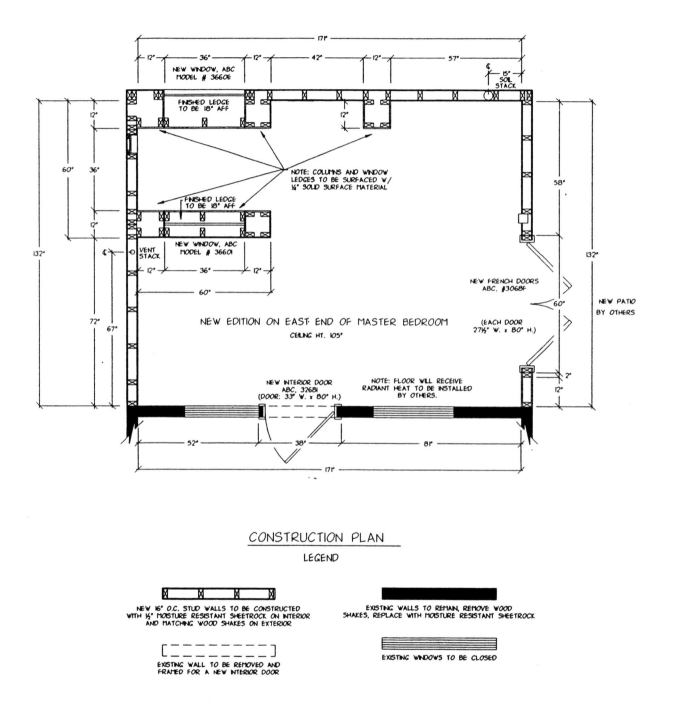

CONSTRUCTION PLAN

LEGEND

NEW 16" O.C. STUD WALLS TO BE CONSTRUCTED WITH ½" MOISTURE RESISTANT SHEETROCK ON INTERIOR AND MATCHING WOOD SHAKES ON EXTERIOR

EXISTING WALLS TO REMAIN, REMOVE WOOD SHAKES, REPLACE WITH MOISTURE RESISTANT SHEETROCK

EXISTING WALL TO BE REMOVED AND FRAMED FOR A NEW INTERIOR DOOR

EXISTING WINDOWS TO BE CLOSED

Graphics and Presentation Standards for Bathroom Design

IV. The Mechanical Plan

- By detailing separate plans for the mechanicals and/or construction, it will help to clearly identify such work without cluttering the bathroom floor plan.

- The mechanical plan should show an outline of the cabinets, countertops and fixtures without nomenclature.

- The mechanicals should be placed in the proper location with the proper symbols.

- All overall room dimensions should be listed.

1) The mechanical plan will consist of the Electrical/Lighting, Plumbing, Heating, Air Conditioning and Ventilation systems. If any minor wall/door construction changes are part of the plan, they should also be detailed on the mechanical plan.

2) A mechanical legend should be prepared on the plan. This legend will be used to describe what each symbol for special purpose outlets, fixtures or equipment means.

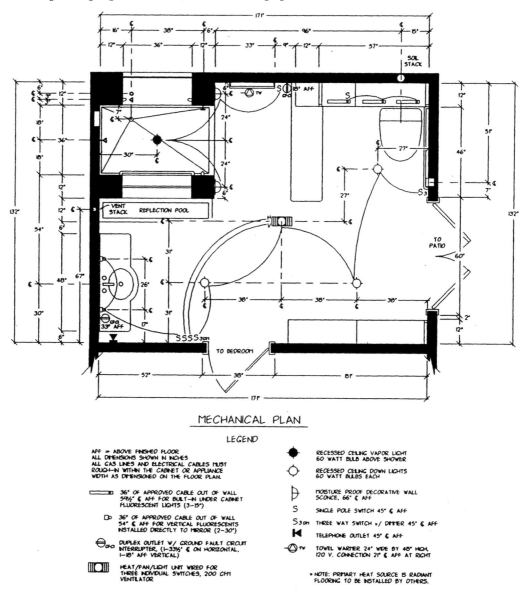

MECHANICAL PLAN

LEGEND

AFF = ABOVE FINISHED FLOOR
ALL DIMENSIONS SHOWN IN INCHES
ALL GAS LINES AND ELECTRICAL CABLES MUST
ROUGH-IN WITHIN THE CABINET OR APPLIANCE
WIDTH AS DIMENSIONED ON THE FLOOR PLAN.

36" OF APPROVED CABLE OUT OF WALL
59½" ℄ AFF FOR BUILT-IN UNDER CABINET
FLUORESCENT LIGHTS (3-15")

36" OF APPROVED CABLE OUT OF WALL
54" ℄ AFF FOR VERTICAL FLUORESCENTS
INSTALLED DIRECTLY TO MIRROR (2-30")

DUPLEX OUTLET W/ GROUND FAULT CIRCUIT
INTERRUPTER (1-33½" ℄ ON HORIZONTAL,
1-18" AFF VERTICAL)

HEAT/FAN/LIGHT UNIT WIRED FOR
THREE INDIVIDUAL SWITCHES, 200 CFM
VENTILATOR

RECESSED CEILING VAPOR LIGHT
60 WATT BULB ABOVE SHOWER

RECESSED CEILING DOWN LIGHTS
60 WATT BULBS EACH

MOISTURE PROOF DECORATIVE WALL
SCONCE, 66" ℄ AFF

S   SINGLE POLE SWITCH 45" ℄ AFF

S₃DM THREE WAY SWITCH W/ DIMMER 45" ℄ AFF

TELEPHONE OUTLET 45" ℄ AFF

TV   TOWEL WARMER 24" WIDE BY 48" HIGH,
120 V. CONNECTION 21" ℄ AFF AT RIGHT

• NOTE: PRIMARY HEAT SOURCE IS RADIANT
FLOORING TO BE INSTALLED BY OTHERS.

3) Centerline (℄) dimensions must be given for all equipment in two directions when possible.

- Mechanicals requiring centerlines include: lavatories, bathtubs/showers, toilets/bidets, fan units, light fixtures, heating and air conditioning ducts and radiators.

- Centerline dimensions should be pulled from return walls or from the face of cabinets/equipment opposite the mechanical element.

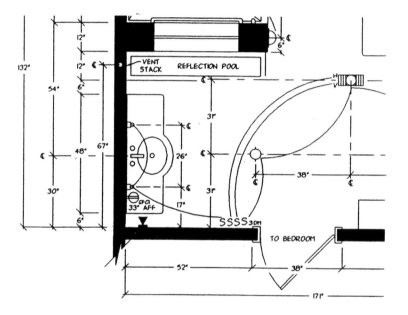

Centerlines on the mechanical plan will be indicated by the symbol (℄) followed by a **long-short-long broken line** that extends into the floor area.

℄ ————— — ———— — ———— — ———— — ————

Graphics and Presentation Standards for Bathroom Design

4) Mechanical Plan Symbols:

S	SINGLE POLE SWITCH
S_2	DOUBLE POLE SWITCH
S_3	THREE WAY SWITCH
S_4	FOUR WAY SWITCH
S_{DM}	SINGLE POLE SWITCH v/ DIMMER
S_{3DM}	THREE WAY SWITCH v/ DIMMER
S_{LM}	MASTER SWITCH FOR LOW VOLTAGE SWITCHING SYSTEM
S_L	SWITCH FOR LOW VOLTAGE SWITCHING SYSTEM
S_{WP}	WEATHERPROOF SWITCH
S_{RC}	REMOTE CONTROL SWITCH
S_D	AUTOMATIC DOOR SWITCH
S_P	SWITCH AND PILOT LAMP
S_K	KEY OPERATED SWITCH
S_F	FUSED SWITCH
S_T	TIME SWITCH
(S)	CEILING PULL SWITCH
	DUPLEX OUTLET
$_{GFCI}$	DUPLEX OUTLET WITH GROUND FAULT CIRCUIT INTERRUPTER
$_S$	SWITCH AND SINGLE RECEPTACLE OUTLET
$_S$	SWITCH AND DUPLEX OUTLET
(B)	BLANKED OUTLET
(J)	JUNCTION BOX
(L)	OUTLET CONTROLLED BY LOW VOLTAGE SWITCHING WHEN RELAY IS INSTALLED IN OUTLET BOX
	SINGLE RECEPTACLE OULET
	TRIPLEX RECEPTACLE OULET
	QUADRUPLEX RECEPTACLE OULET
	DUPLEX RECEPTACLE OUTLET–SPLIT WIRED
	TRIPLEX RECEPTACLE OUTLET–SPLIT WIRED
(C)	CLOCK HANGER RECEPTACLE
(F)	FAN HANGER RECEPTACLE
	INTERCOM
	TELEPHONE OUTLET
(T)	THERMOSTAT
	SMOKE DETECTOR

TV	TELEVISION OUTLET
C	CABLE OUTLET
T_L	LOW VOLTAGE TRANSFORMER
	HANGING CEILING FIXTURE
	HEAT LAMP
	HEAT/LIGHT UNIT
	HEAT/FAN LIGHT W/ 000 CFM VENT
	RECESSED CEILING DOWN LIGHTING
	RECESSED CEILING VAPOR LIGHT
	BUILT-IN LOW VOLTAGE TASK LIGHT
	BUILT-IN FLUORESCENT LIGHT
	CONTINUOUS ROW FLUORESCENT LIGHTS
	SURFACE MOUNTED FLUORESCENT LIGHT
	WALL SCONCE
$_{DW}$	DISHWASHER
$_{GD}$	FOOD WASTE DISPOSAL
$_{TC}$	TRASH COMPACTOR
$_R$	REFRIGERATOR OUTLET
$_H$	HOOD W/ 000 CFM VENTILATOR
$_M$	MICROWAVE OVEN
$_R$	ELECTRIC RANGE/COOKTOP
$_{WO}$	ELECTRIC SINGLE/DOUBLE OVEN
$_G$	GAS SUPPLY
$_{CT}$	GAS COOKTOP
$_{WO}$	GAS SINGLE/DOUBLE OVEN
$_{CW}$	CLOTHES WASHER
$_{CD}$	CLOTHES DRYER
$_{SA}$	SAUNA
$_{ST}$	STEAM
$_{WP}$	WHIRLPOOL
$_{TW}$	TOWEL WARMER
	HEAT REGISTER

ANY STANDARD SYMBOL GIVEN ABOVE W/ THE ADDITION OF LOWERCASE SUBSCRIPT LETTERING MAY BE USED TO DESIGNATE A VARIATION OF STANDARD EQUIPMENT.

WHEN USED THEY MUST BE LISTED IN THE LEGEND OF THE MECHANICAL PLAN.

Symbols adapted from Architectural Graphic Standards, 9th Edition

V. Interpretive Drawings

Elevations and perspective renderings are considered interpretive drawings and are used as an explanatory means of understanding the floor plans.

- Under no circumstances should the interpretive drawings be used as a substitute for floor plans.

- In cases of dispute, the floor plans are the legally binding document.

- Because perspective drawings are not dimensioned to scale, many Bathroom Specialists include a disclaimer on their rendering such as this:

> This drawing is an artistic interpretation of the general appearance of the floor plan. It is not meant to be an exact rendition.

1) **Elevation:** Elevations must show a front view of all wall areas receiving cabinets and equipment as shown on the floor plan.

   Elevations should dimension all cabinets, counters, fixtures and equipment in the elevation as follows:

- Cabinets with toekick and finished height.

- A portion of the cabinet doors and drawer front should indicate style and, when applicable, placement of handles/pulls.

- Countertops indicate thickness and show backsplash

- All doors, windows or other openings in walls which will receive equipment. The window/door casing or trim will be listed within the overall opening dimensions.

- All permanent fixtures such as radiators, etc.

- All main structural elements and protrusions such as chimneys, partitions, etc.

- Centerlines for all mechanical equipment.

Graphics and Presentation Standards for Bathroom Design

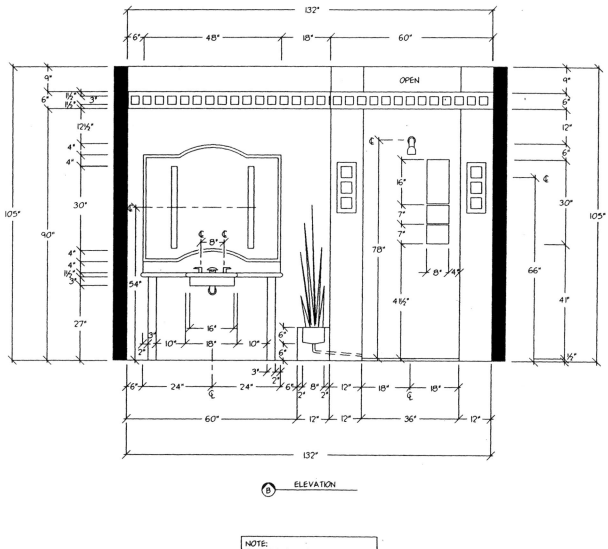

ELEVATION

NOTE:
DIMENSIONS MUST ACCURATELY
REPRESENT PRODUCTS USED.

2) **Perspective Drawings:** Perspectives are **not drawn to scale.** Grids, which are available through the **National Kitchen & Bath Association**, can be used as an underlay for tracing paper to accurately portray a perspective rendering. Two such grids are displayed on pages 17 and 18 for your reference.

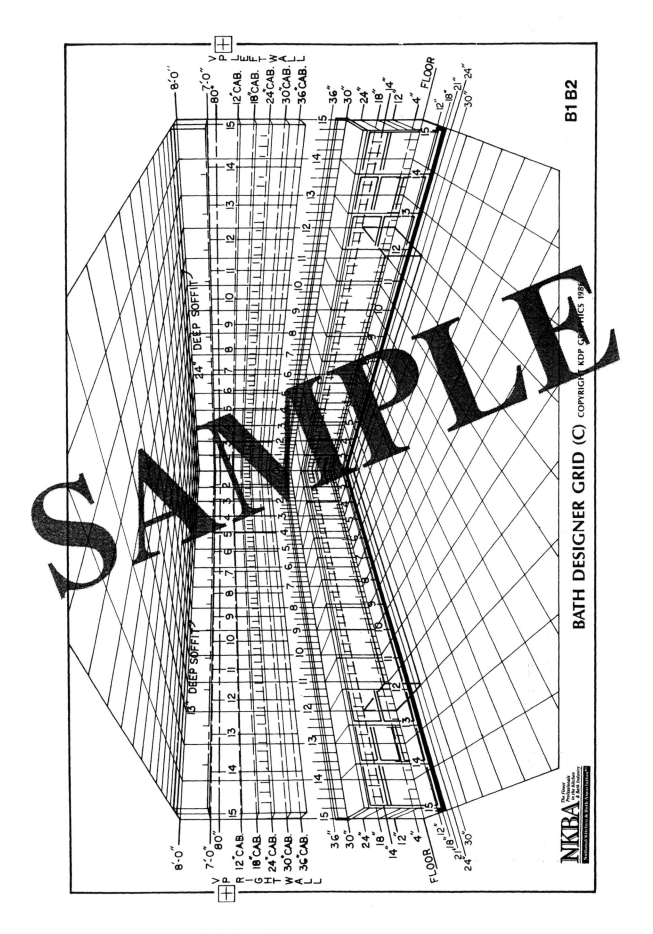

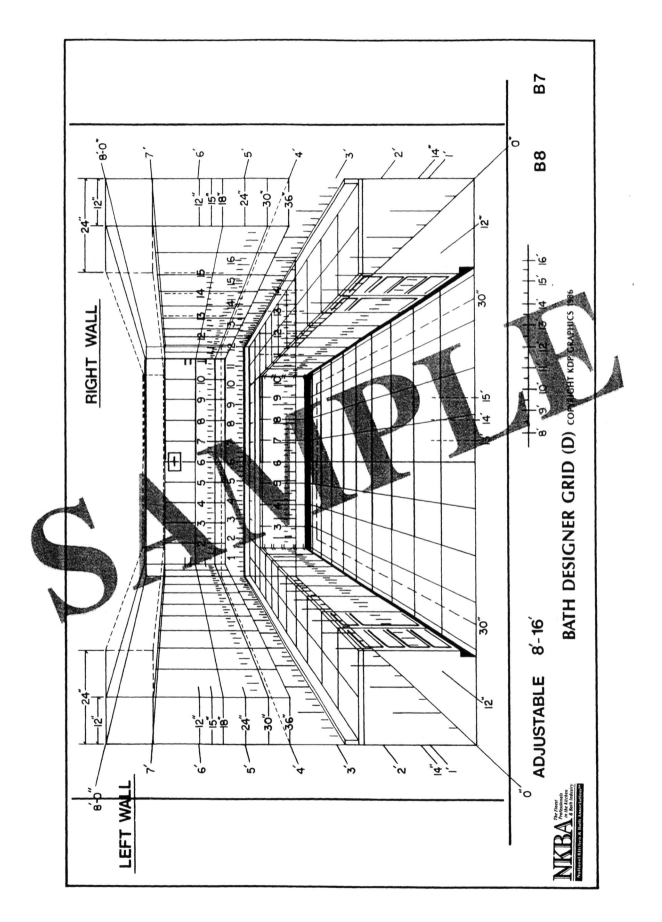

Designers have the option of preparing a one-point or two-point perspective, with or without the use of a grid.

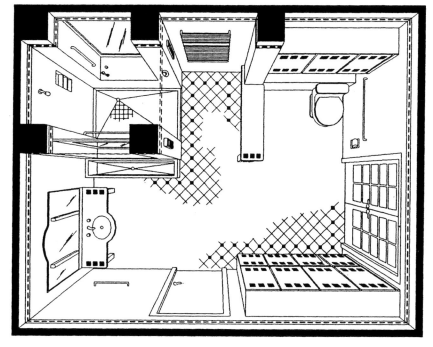

"Birds-Eye View" One Point Perspective

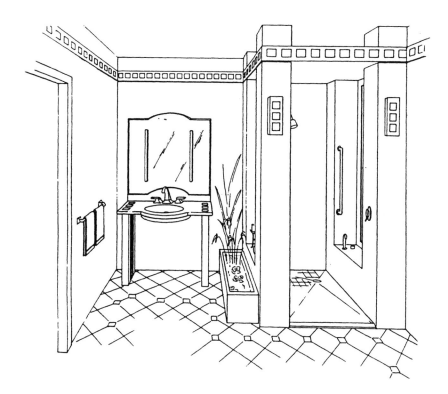

One Point Perspective

- The minimum requirement for perspectives shall be the reasonably correct representation of the longest cabinet or fixture run, or the most important area in terms of usage.

- Perspectives need not show the complete bathroom.

- Separate sectional views of significant areas or features are considered acceptable.

Two Point Perspective

Graphics and Presentation Standards for Bathroom Design

3) **Oblique, Dimetric, Isometric and Trimetric:** Several types of interpretive drawings can be used to illustrate special cabinets and equipment, such as countertops or special order cabinets, where mechanical representation and dimensions are important. These drawings give a simple way to illustrate an object in three-dimensional views.

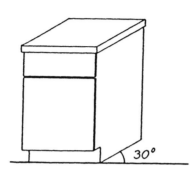

30° OBLIQUE

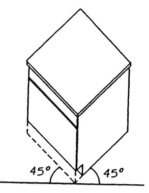

45° DIMETRIC

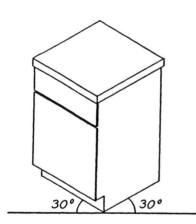

30° ISOMETRIC

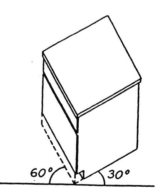

TRIMETRIC

4) **Sketches:** The use of sketches is a quick way to achieve a total picture of the bathroom without exact details in scaled dimensions. This quick freehand sketch can be studied, adjusted and sketched over, as the designer and client attempt to arrive at the most satisfactory layout for the bathroom. The quick sketch then can serve as a guide for drawing an exact plan of the bathroom.

Perspective Sketch

Graphics and Presentation Standards for Bathroom Design

VI. Sample Bathroom Project Drawings

The following set of sample project drawings have been prepared by a Certified Bathroom Designer under the direction of the **National Kitchen & Bath Association.** These sample drawings include:

- Floor Plan

- Construction Plan

- Mechanical Plan

- Countertop Plan *

- Soffit Plan *

- Elevations

- Perspectives

* It is recommended to prepare countertop and soffit plan drawings to further clarify project requirements.

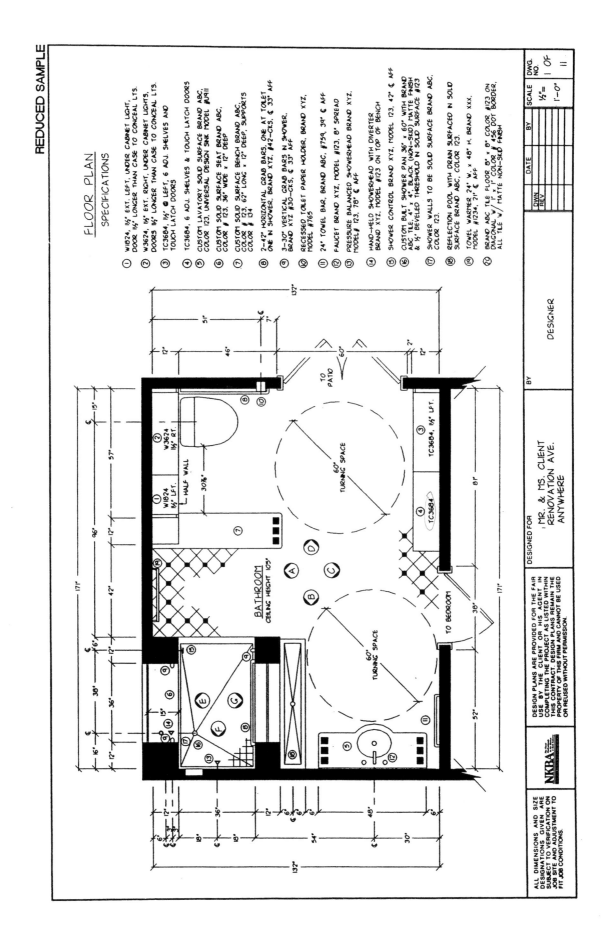

FLOOR PLAN

SPECIFICATIONS

1. W1824, 1½" EXT. LEFT, UNDER CABINET LIGHT, DOOR 1½" LONGER THAN CASE TO CONCEAL LTS.

2. W3624, 1½" EXT. RIGHT, UNDER CABINET LIGHTS, DOORS 1½" LONGER THAN CASE TO CONCEAL LTS.

3. TC3684, 1½" @ LEFT, 6 ADJ. SHELVES AND TOUCH LATCH DOORS

4. TC3684, 6 ADJ. SHELVES & TOUCH LATCH DOORS

5. CUSTOM LAVATORY SOLID SURFACE BRAND ABC, COLOR 123, UNIVERSAL DESIGN SINK MODEL #1411

6. CUSTOM SOLID SURFACE SEAT BRAND ABC, COLOR #123, 36" WIDE x 12" DEEP

7. CUSTOM SOLID SURFACE BENCH BRAND ABC, COLOR #123, 62" LONG x 12" DEEP, SUPPORTS COLOR 134

8. 2-42" HORIZONTAL GRAB BARS, ONE AT SHOWER, ONE AT TOILET BRAND XYZ, #42-CKS, @ 33" AFF

9. 3-30" VERTICAL GRAB BARS IN SHOWER, BRAND XYZ #30-CKS, @ 33" AFF

10. RECESSED TOILET PAPER HOLDER, BRAND XYZ, MODEL #765

11. 24" TOWEL BAR, BRAND ABC, #759, 39" @ AFF

12. FAUCET BRAND XYZ, MODEL #123, 8" SPREAD

13. PRESSURE BALANCED SHOWERHEAD BRAND XYZ, MODEL #123, 78" @ AFF

14. HAND-HELD SHOWERHEAD WITH DIVERTER BRAND XYZ, MODEL #123 ON TOP OF BENCH

15. SHOWER CONTROL BRAND XYZ, MODEL 123, 42" AFF

16. CUSTOM BUILT SHOWER PAN 36" x 60" WITH BRAND ABC TILE. 4" x 4", BLACK (NON-SKID) MATTE FINISH & ½" BEVELED THRESHOLD IN SOLID SURFACE BRAND #123

17. SHOWER WALLS TO BE SOLID SURFACE BRAND ABC. COLOR 123.

18. REFLECTION POOL WITH DRAIN SURFACED IN SOLID SURFACE BRAND ABC, COLOR 123.

19. TOWEL WARMER 24" W. x 48" H. BRAND XXX, MODEL #1234, 21" @ AFF

20. BRAND ABC TILE FLOOR 8" x 8" COLOR #123 ON DIAGONAL W/ 1" x 1" COLOR # 456 DOT BORDER, ALL TILE W/ MATTE NON-SKID FINISH

DESIGNED FOR

MR. & MS. CLIENT
RENOVATION AVE.
ANYWHERE

DESIGNER

| DWN | DATE | BY |
| REV | | |

SCALE ½" = 1'-0"

DWG. NO. 1 OF 11

NKBA

BATHROOM
CEILING HEIGHT 105"

TO PATIO

TO BEDROOM

60" TURNING SPACE

60" TURNING SPACE

HALF WALL

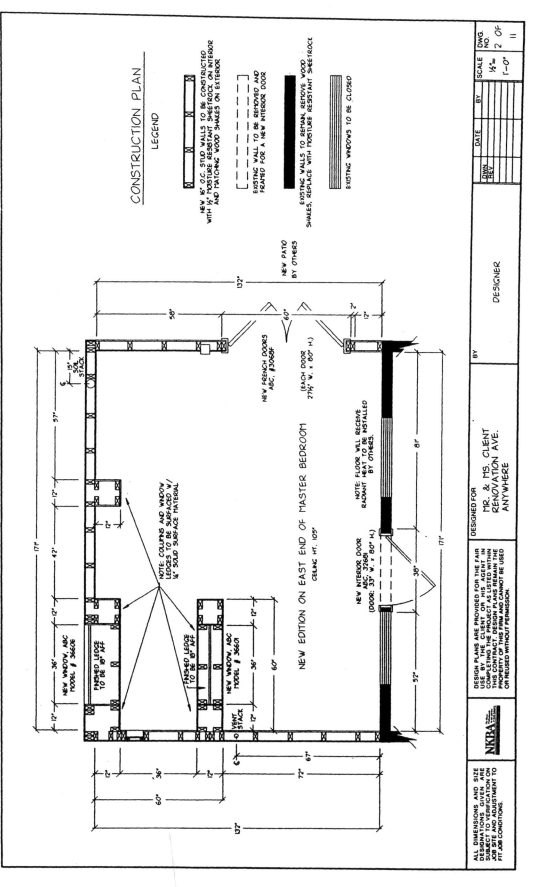

CONSTRUCTION PLAN
LEGEND

NEW 16" O.C. STUD WALLS TO BE CONSTRUCTED WITH ½" MOISTURE RESISTANT SHEETROCK ON INTERIOR AND MATCHING WOOD SHAKES ON EXTERIOR

EXISTING WALL TO BE REMOVED AND FRAMED FOR A NEW INTERIOR DOOR

EXISTING WALLS TO REMAIN, REMOVE WOOD SHAKES, REPLACE WITH MOISTURE RESISTANT SHEETROCK

EXISTING WINDOWS TO BE CLOSED

NEW EDITION ON EAST END OF MASTER BEDROOM
CEILING HT. 105"

NOTE: COLUMNS AND WINDOW LEDGES TO BE SURFACED W/ ¼" SOLID SURFACE MATERIAL

NEW WINDOW, ABC MODEL # 3660E

FINISHED LEDGE TO BE 18" AFF

FINISHED LEDGE TO BE 18" AFF

NEW WINDOW, ABC MODEL # 3660I

VENT STACK

NEW FRENCH DOORS ABC, #3068F
(EACH DOOR 27¾" W. x 80" H.)

NEW PATIO BY OTHERS

NEW INTERIOR DOOR ABC, 3768I
(DOOR: 33" W. x 80" H.)

NOTE: FLOOR WILL RECEIVE RADIANT HEAT TO BE INSTALLED BY OTHERS.

DESIGNED FOR
MR. & MS. CLIENT
RENOVATION AVE.
ANYWHERE

DESIGN PLANS ARE PROVIDED FOR THE FAIR USE BY THE CLIENT OR HIS AGENT IN COMPLETING THE PROJECT AS LISTED WITHIN THIS CONTRACT. DESIGN PLANS REMAIN THE PROPERTY OF THIS FIRM AND CANNOT BE USED OR REUSED WITHOUT PERMISSION.

ALL DIMENSIONS AND SIZE DESIGNATIONS GIVEN ARE SUBJECT TO VERIFICATION ON JOB SITE AND ADJUSTMENT TO FIT JOB CONDITIONS.

DESIGNER

DATE	BY	SCALE	DWG. NO.
DWN		½"= 1'-0"	2 OF
REV			11

NKBA

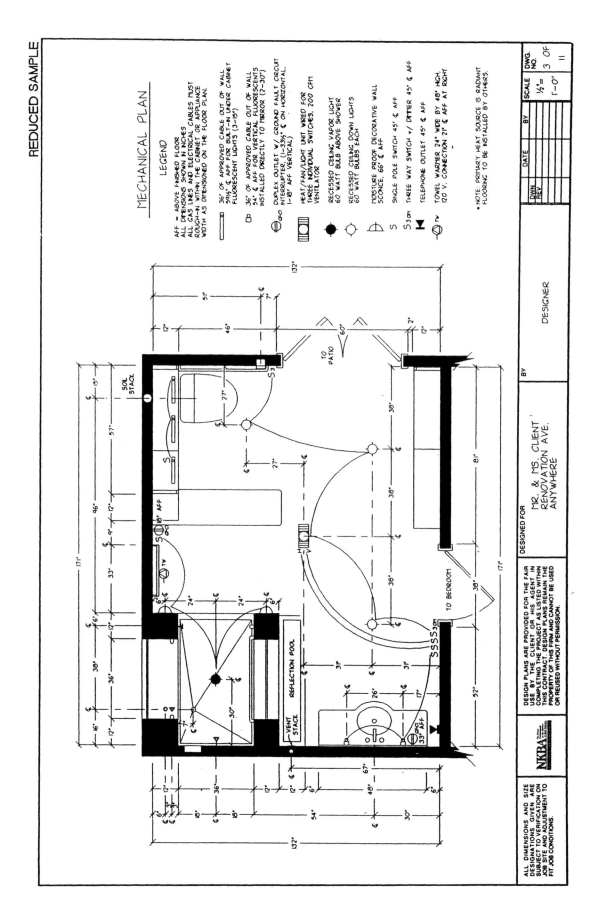

MECHANICAL PLAN

LEGEND

AFF = ABOVE FINISHED FLOOR
ALL DIMENSIONS SHOWN IN INCHES
ALL GAS LINES AND ELECTRICAL CABLES MUST
ROUGH-IN WITHIN THE CABINET OR APPLIANCE
WIDTH AS DIMENSIONED ON THE FLOOR PLAN.

36" OF APPROVED CABLE OUT OF WALL
59¾" ℄ AFF FOR BUILT-IN UNDER CABINET
FLUORESCENT LIGHTS (3-15")

36" OF APPROVED CABLE OUT OF WALL
54" ℄ AFF FOR VERTICAL FLUORESCENTS
INSTALLED DIRECTLY TO MIRROR (2-30")

DUPLEX OUTLET W/ GROUND FAULT CIRCUIT
INTERRUPTER, (1-33¾" ℄ ON HORIZONTAL,
1-18" AFF VERTICAL)

HEAT/FAN/LIGHT UNIT WIRED FOR
THREE INDIVIDUAL SWITCHES, 200 CFM
VENTILATOR

RECESSED CEILING VAPOR LIGHT
60 WATT BULB ABOVE SHOWER

RECESSED CEILING DOWN LIGHTS
60 WATT BULBS EACH

MOISTURE PROOF DECORATIVE WALL
SCONCE, 66" ℄ AFF

S   SINGLE POLE SWITCH 45" ℄ AFF

S₃ₘ THREE WAY SWITCH w/ DIMMER 45" ℄ AFF

TELEPHONE OUTLET 45" ℄ AFF

TOWEL WARMER 24" WIDE BY 48" HIGH.
120 V. CONNECTION 21" ℄ AFF AT RIGHT

• NOTE: PRIMARY HEAT SOURCE IS RADIANT
FLOORING TO BE INSTALLED BY OTHERS.

DWG. NO.   3 OF 11

SCALE ½"=1'-0"

BY

DATE

DWN
REV

DESIGNER

BY

DESIGNED FOR
MR. & MS. CLIENT
RENOVATION AVE.
ANYWHERE

DESIGN PLANS ARE PROVIDED FOR THE FAIR
USE BY THE CLIENT OR HIS AGENT IN
COMPLETING THE PROJECT AS LISTED WITHIN
THIS CONTRACT. DESIGN PLANS REMAIN THE
PROPERTY OF THIS FIRM AND CANNOT BE USED
OR REUSED WITHOUT PERMISSION.

ALL DIMENSIONS AND SIZE
DESIGNATIONS GIVEN ARE
SUBJECT TO VERIFICATION ON
JOB SITE AND ADJUSTMENT TO
FIT JOB CONDITIONS.

NKBA

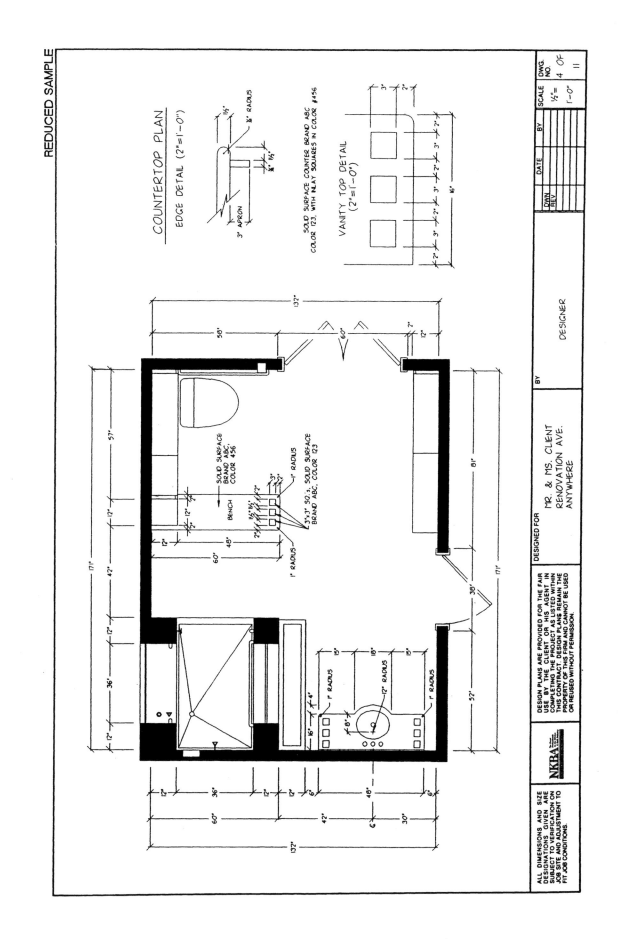

COUNTERTOP PLAN

EDGE DETAIL (2"=1'-0")

SOLID SURFACE COUNTER BRAND ABC
COLOR 123, WITH INLAY SQUARES IN COLOR #456

VANITY TOP DETAIL
(2"=1'-0")

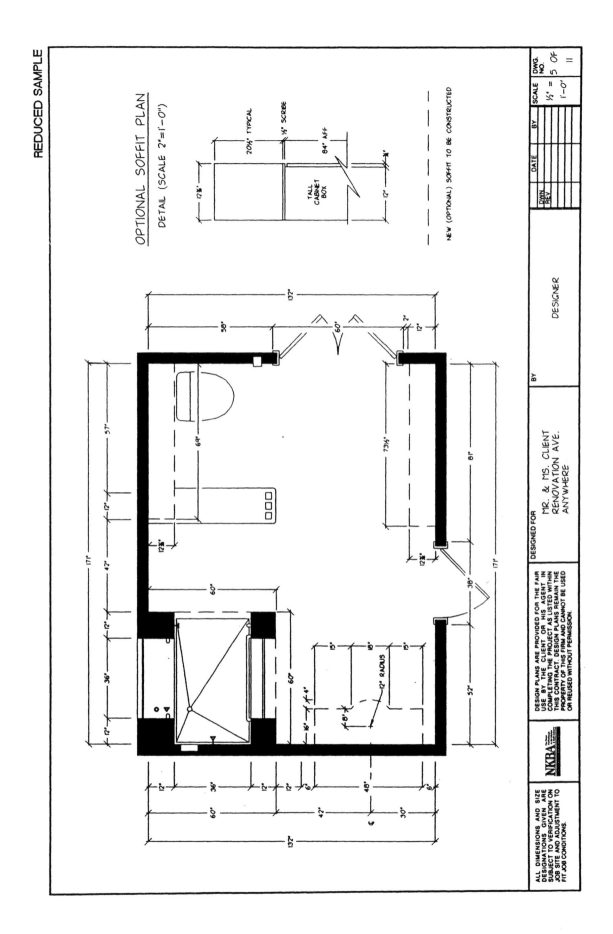

OPTIONAL SOFFIT PLAN

DETAIL (SCALE 2"=1'-0")

20¼" TYPICAL

¼" SCRIBE

84" AFF

TALL CABINET BOX

NEW (OPTIONAL) SOFFIT TO BE CONSTRUCTED

DESIGNER

DWN REV

DATE   BY

SCALE ½' = 1'-0"

DWG. NO. 5 OF 11

BY

DESIGNED FOR

MR. & MS. CLIENT
RENOVATION AVE.
ANYWHERE

DESIGN PLANS ARE PROVIDED FOR THE FAIR USE BY THE CLIENT OR HIS AGENT IN COMPLETING THE PROJECT AS LISTED WITHIN THIS CONTRACT. DESIGN PLANS REMAIN THE PROPERTY OF THIS FIRM AND CANNOT BE USED OR REUSED WITHOUT PERMISSION.

ALL DIMENSIONS AND SIZE DESIGNATIONS GIVEN ARE SUBJECT TO VERIFICATION ON JOB SITE AND ADJUSTMENT TO FIT JOB CONDITIONS.

NKBA

Graphics and Presentation Standards for Bathroom Design

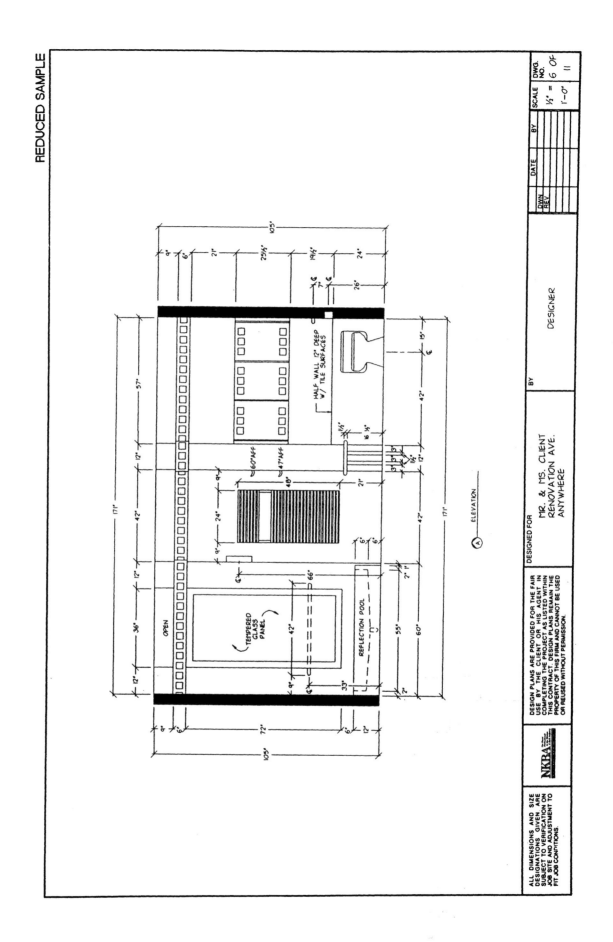

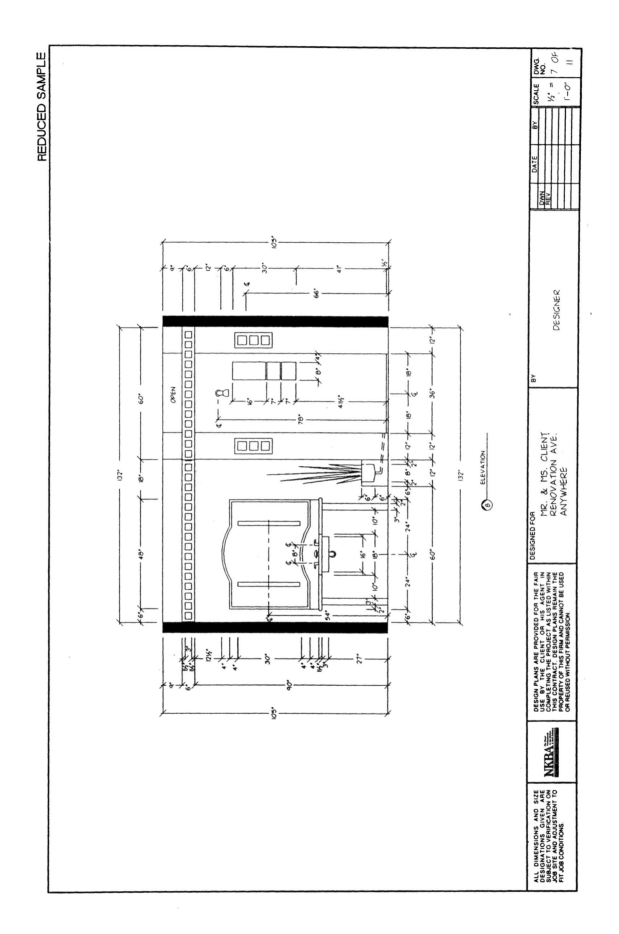

ELEVATION

DESIGNED FOR

MR. & MS. CLIENT
RENOVATION AVE.
ANYWHERE

BY

DESIGNER

DWN	DATE	BY	SCALE	DWG. NO.
REV			½" = 1'-0"	7 OF 11

NKBA

Graphics and Presentation Standards for Bathroom Design

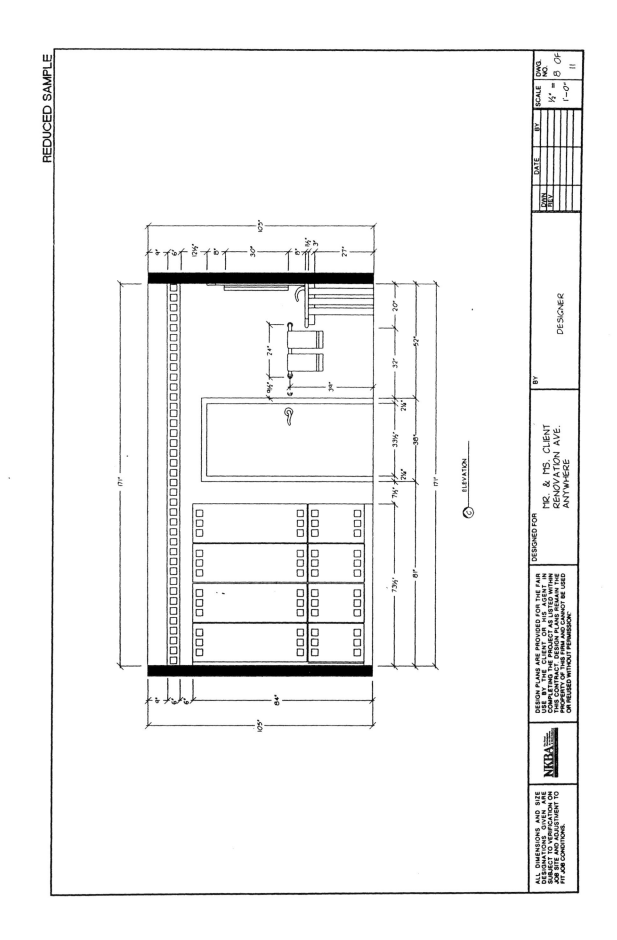

ELEVATION

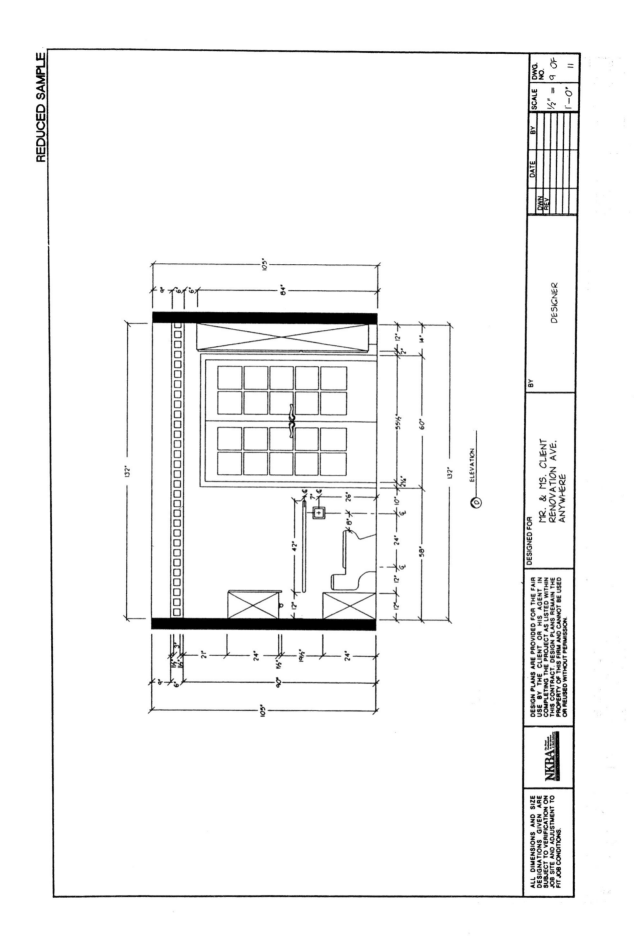

ELEVATION

DESIGNED FOR

MR. & MS. CLIENT
RENOVATION AVE.
ANYWHERE

BY

DESIGNER

ALL DIMENSIONS AND SIZE DESIGNATIONS GIVEN ARE SUBJECT TO VERIFICATION ON JOB SITE AND ADJUSTMENT TO FIT JOB CONDITIONS.

NKBA

DWN	DATE	BY	SCALE	DWG. NO.
REV			½" = 1'-0"	9 OF 11

Graphics and Presentation Standards for Bathroom Design

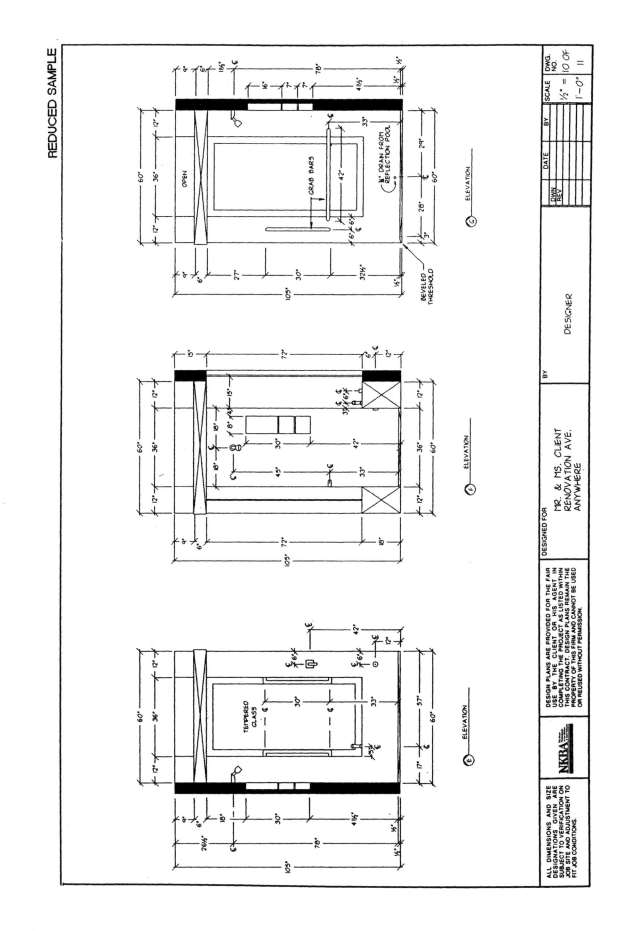

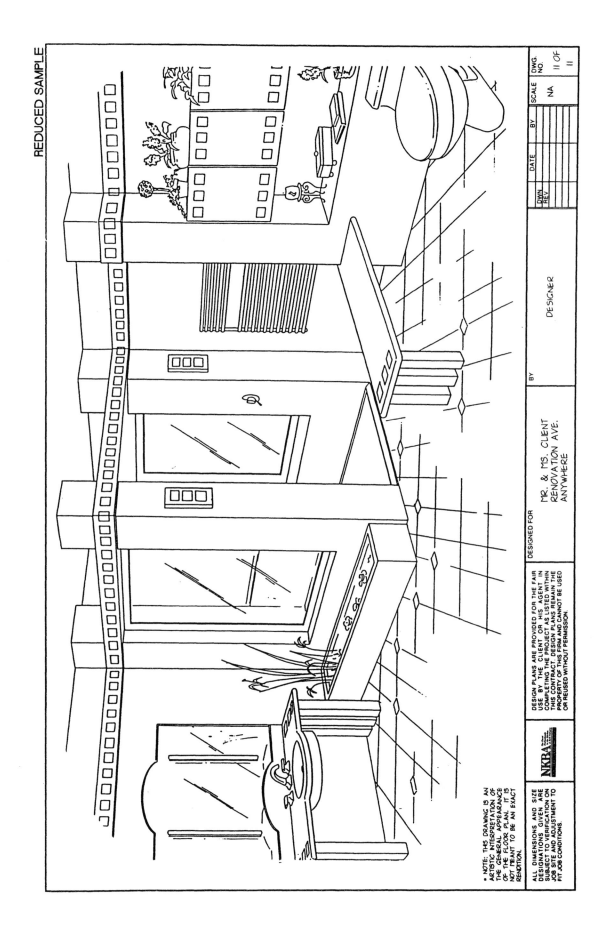

Graphics and Presentation Standards for Bathroom Design

General Provisions Using Metric Dimensions

I. Use of Standards

The use of these *National Kitchen & Bath Association Graphics and Presentation Standards* is strongly recommended. They contain a specific set of criteria which when applied by the Bathroom Specialist produce a series of project documents that include the following:

- The Floor Plan

- The Construction Plan

- The Mechanical Plan

- The Interpretive Drawings

    1) Elevations
    2) Perspective Drawings
    3) Oblique, Dimetric, Isometric and Trimetric
    4) Sketches

- Specifications

- Design Statement

- Contracts

Two sample sets of project documents for your review can be found in this publication, one uses imperial dimensions and the other is a metric conversion.

Paper: The acceptable paper for the original drawings of the floor plan, construction plan, mechanical plan, and interpretive drawings is set at a **minimum size of 28cm x 43cm.** Translucent vellum tracing paper, imprinted with a black border and appropriate space available for the insertion of pertinent information is strongly recommended. Copies of original drawings should appear in blue or black ink only on white paper. Ozalid or photocopy prints are acceptable.

The use of lined yellow note paper, typing paper, scored graph paper or scored quadrille paper **is not acceptable.**

NKBA Drawing Aid #6002

II. The Floor Plan

1) **Size and Scope of Floor Plan Drawings:** Bathroom floor plans should be drawn to a scale of 1 to 20 (ie. 1cm = 20cm). When the designer has a room dimensioned in imperial inches and wants to use a metric based cabinet brand, the industry norm is to use a 1:24 metric ratio as equal to a 1/2 inch scale. ** For imperial dimensions, see Use of Standards beginning on page 3.*

- All base cabinetry should be depicted using a dashed line ($- - -$) while countertops are depicted using a solid line.

- The floor plan should depict the entire room when possible. When the entire room cannot be depicted, it must show the area where cabinetry and appliances are permanently installed.

- Floor plans must show all major structural elements such as walls, door swings, door openings, partitions, windows, archways and equipment.

- When the entire room cannot be depicted, the room must be divided by *"break lines"* ($\diagdown$) and must show all major structural elements with adjoining areas indicated and labeled.

Finished interior dimensions are used on all project documents to denote available space for cabinetry and/or other types of equipment. If the bathroom specialist is responsible for specifying the exact method of wall construction, finish and/or partition placement, the specialist should include partition center lines on the construction plan, as well as the finished interior dimensions.

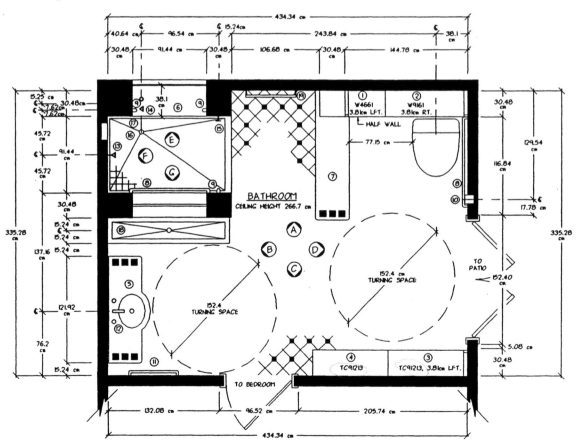

2) Centerline (℄) dimensions: must be given for equipment in two directions when possible.

- Mechanicals requiring centerlines include: lavatories, bathtubs/showers, toilets/bidets, fan units, light fixtures, heating and air conditioning ducts and radiators.

- Dimensions should be pulled from return walls or from the face of cabinets/fixtures/equipment opposite the mechanical element.

- Centerlines on the mechanical plan will be indicated by the symbol (℄) followed by a **long-short-long broken line** that extends into the floor area.

- When the centerline dimension line is outside the floor area, it is typically shown as the second (and, if required, the third) line following the dimension line which identifies the individual wall segments.

3) Dimensioning of Floor Plan: When using metric dimensions, some designers also list all wall dimensions in inches. This double sizing helps all parties involved clearly understand the plans.

An example of Time Saving Formulas to convert between metrics would be as follows:

Inches to Centimeters, multiply the total number of inches by 2.54
Centimeters to Inches, multiply the total number of centimeters by .3937

NOTE:

- Each set of dimensions should be at least .5cm apart on separate dimension lines which are to intersect with witness lines. These intersecting points should be indicated by dimension arrows, dots, or slashes.

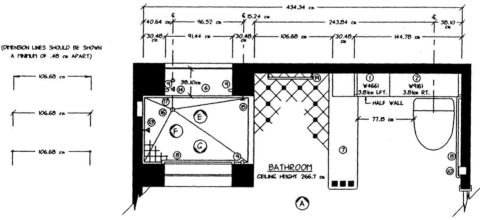

- All dimensions, whenever possible, should be shown **OUTSIDE** the wall lines.

- All lettering should be listed parallel to the title block at the bottom of the vellum paper and break the dimension line near its mid-point. This mechanical drafting technique eliminates errors in reading dimensions.

- An acceptable alternative is to draw all dimensions and lettering so that it is readable from the bottom edge or the right side of the plans with lettering on top of each dimension line.

The following dimensions **MUST** be shown on every floor plan as minimum requirements.

- Overall length of wall areas to receive cabinets, countertops, fixtures, or any equipment occupying floor and/or wall space. This dimension should always be the outside line.

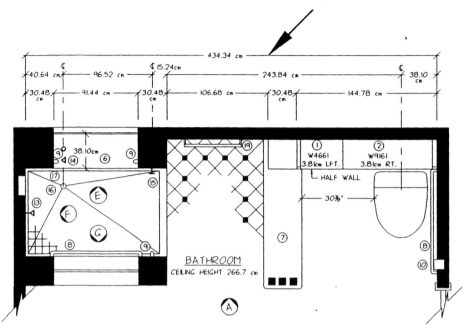

- Each wall opening, (windows, arches, doors and major appliances) and fixed structures (chimneys, wall protrusions and partitions) must be individually dimensioned. Dimensions are shown from outside trim. Trim size must be noted in the specification list. Fixtures such as radiators remaining in place must be outlined on the floor plan. These critical dimensions should be the first dimension line.

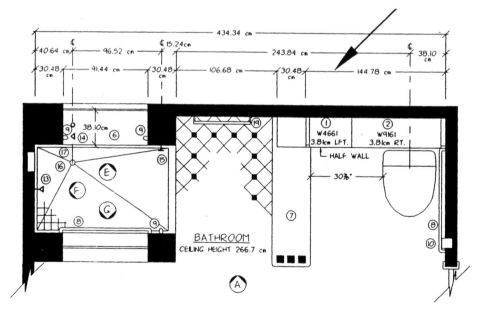

- Ceiling heights should appear on the floor plan. A separate plan for soffits is required when the soffit is a different depth than the wall or tall cabinet below. A separate soffit plan is recommended when the soffit is to be installed **PRIOR** to the wall or tall cabinet installation.

- Additional notes must be included for any deviation from standard height, width and depth. (cabinets, countertops, etc.)

- The exact opening must be given in height, width and depth for areas to be left open to receive cabinets and appliances at a future date.

- Items such as island/peninsula vanities and bathtub platforms, must be shown with the overall dimensions given from countertop edge to opposite countertop edge, tall cabinet or wall. The exact location of the structure must be identified by dimensions which position it from two directions; from return walls or from the face of cabinets/equipment opposite the structure.

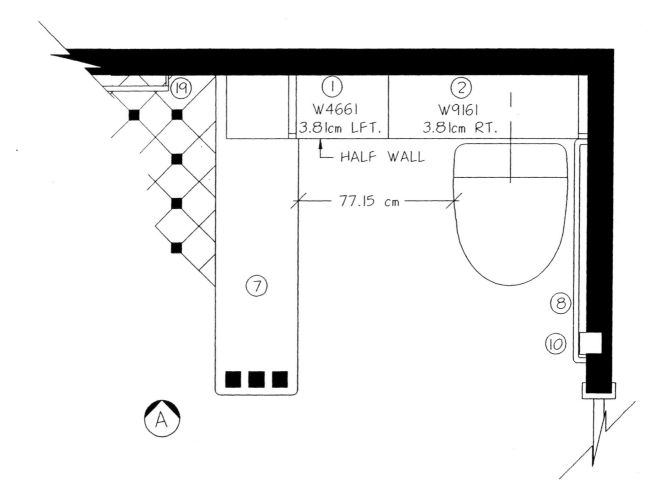

4) Cabinets/Fixtures and Equipment Nomenclature and Designation on Floor Plans:

- Cabinets should be designated and identified by manufacturer nomenclature inside the area indicating their position. Cabinet system trim and finish items are designated outside their area, with an arrow clarifying exactly where the trim piece is located.

- To insure clarity, some design firms prefer to number and call out all the cabinet nomenclature in the Floor Plan specification listing.

- Equally acceptable is the use of a circled reference number to designate each cabinet on the Floor Plan and Elevations with the cabinet code listed within the individual unit width on the elevations or in a separate cross-reference list on the elevations.

- **Regardless of which cabinet designation system is selected from above, additional information for supplementary fixtures/equipment and special provisions pertaining to the cabinets must be indicated within the cabinet or equipment area by a reference number in a circle. This additional information should then be registered in a cross-referenced specifications listing on the same sheet.**

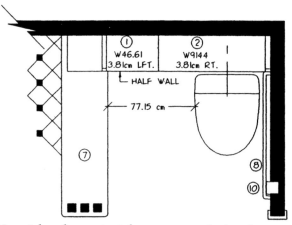

FLOOR PLAN
SPECIFICATIONS

① W4661, 3.81 cm EXT. LEFT, UNDER CABINET LIGHT, DOOR 3.81 cm LONGER THAN CASE TO CONCEAL LTS.

② W9161, 3.81cm EXT. RIGHT, UNDER CABINET LIGHTS, DOORS 3.81cm LONGER THAN CASE TO CONCEAL LTS.

- Special order materials or custom design features, angled cabinets, unusual tops, molding, trim details, etc., should be shown in a section view, (sometimes referred to as a *"cut view"*), a plan view in a scale larger than (1cm = 20cm), or in elevation view.

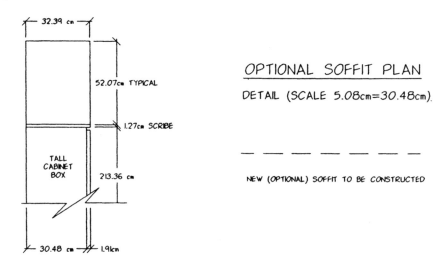

OPTIONAL SOFFIT PLAN

DETAIL (SCALE 5.08cm=30.48cm)

— — — — — — — —

NEW (OPTIONAL) SOFFIT TO BE CONSTRUCTED

III. The Construction Plan

1) The purpose of the construction plan is to show the relationship of the existing space with that of the new design. The construction plan is detailed separately so that it does not clutter the floor plan. However, if construction changes are minimal it is acceptable to combine the construction plan with either the floor plan or mechanical plan.

2) Construction Plan Symbols:

- Existing walls are shown with solid lines or hollowed out lines at their full thickness.

- Wall sections to be removed are shown with an outline of broken lines.

- New walls show the material symbols applicable to the type of construction or use a symbol which is identified in the legend in order to distinguish them from existing partitions.

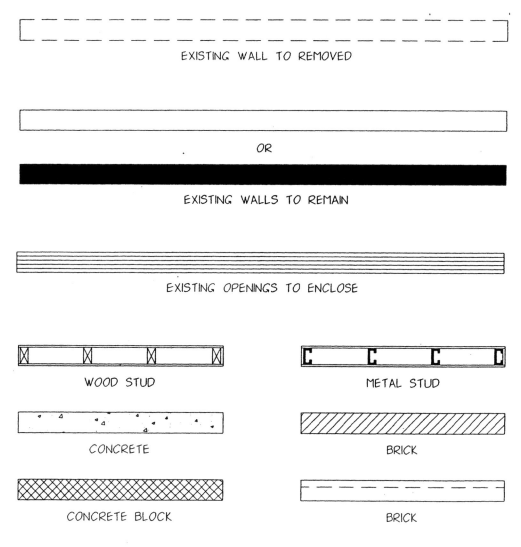

EXISTING WALL TO REMOVED

OR

EXISTING WALLS TO REMAIN

EXISTING OPENINGS TO ENCLOSE

WOOD STUD

METAL STUD

CONCRETE

BRICK

CONCRETE BLOCK

BRICK

NEW WALLS TO BE CONSTRUCTED

* Symbols adapted from Architectural Graphic Standards, 9th Edition

An Example of a Construction Plan:

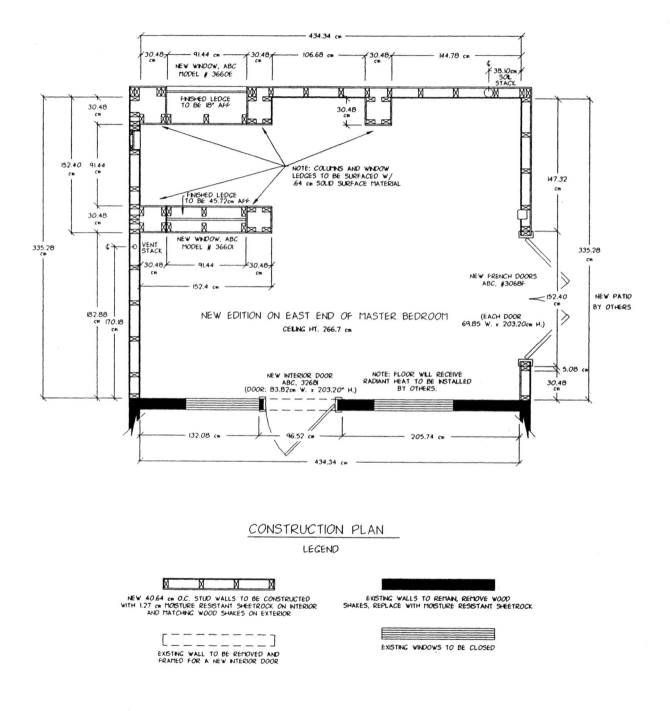

434.34 cm

30.48 cm 91.44 cm 30.48 cm 106.68 cm 30.48 cm 144.78 cm

NEW WINDOW, ABC MODEL # 3660E

38.10cm SOIL STACK

30.48 cm

FINISHED LEDGE TO BE 18" AFF

30.48 cm

NOTE: COLUMNS AND WINDOW LEDGES TO BE SURFACED W/ .64 cm SOLID SURFACE MATERIAL

152.40 cm 91.44 cm

147.32 cm

30.48 cm

FINISHED LEDGE TO BE 45.72cm AFF

335.28 cm

VENT STACK

NEW WINDOW, ABC MODEL # 3660I

335.28 cm

30.48 cm 91.44 cm 30.48 cm

NEW FRENCH DOORS ABC, #3068F

152.40 cm

152.4 cm

NEW PATIO BY OTHERS

182.88 cm 170.18 cm

NEW EDITION ON EAST END OF MASTER BEDROOM
CEILING HT. 266.7 cm

(EACH DOOR 69.85 W. x 203.20cm H.)

NEW INTERIOR DOOR ABC, 3268I
(DOOR: 83.82cm W. x 203.20" H.)

NOTE: FLOOR WILL RECEIVE RADIANT HEAT TO BE INSTALLED BY OTHERS.

5.08 cm

30.48 cm

132.08 cm 96.52 cm 205.74 cm

434.34 cm

CONSTRUCTION PLAN

LEGEND

NEW 40.64 cm O.C. STUD WALLS TO BE CONSTRUCTED WITH 1.27 cm MOISTURE RESISTANT SHEETROCK ON INTERIOR AND MATCHING WOOD SHAKES ON EXTERIOR

EXISTING WALLS TO REMAIN, REMOVE WOOD SHAKES, REPLACE WITH MOISTURE RESISTANT SHEETROCK

EXISTING WALL TO BE REMOVED AND FRAMED FOR A NEW INTERIOR DOOR

EXISTING WINDOWS TO BE CLOSED

IV. The Mechanical Plan

- By detailing separate plans for the mechanicals and/or construction, it will help to clearly identify such work without cluttering the bathroom floor plan.

- The mechanical plan should show an outline of the cabinets, countertops and fixtures without nomenclature.

- The mechanicals should be placed in the proper location with the proper symbols.

- All overall room dimensions should be listed.

1) The mechanical plan will consist of the Electrical/Lighting, Plumbing, Heating, Air Conditioning and Ventilation systems. If any minor wall/door construction changes are part of the plan, they should also be detailed on the mechanical plan.

2) A mechanical legend should be prepared on the plan. This legend will be used to describe what each symbol for special purpose outlets, fixtures or equipment means.

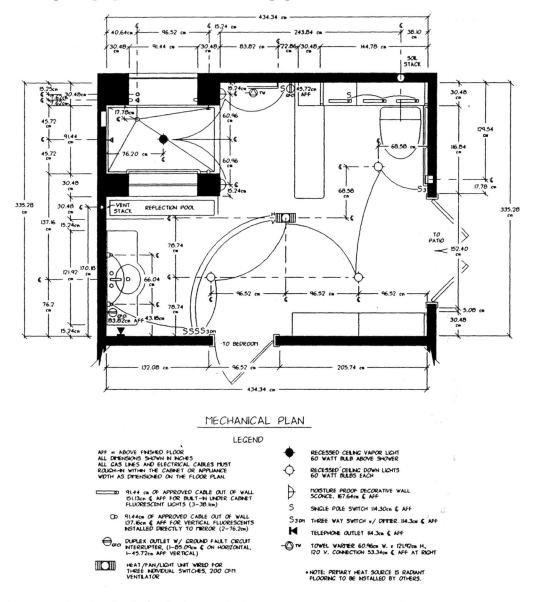

MECHANICAL PLAN

LEGEND

AFF = ABOVE FINISHED FLOOR
ALL DIMENSIONS SHOWN IN INCHES
ALL GAS LINES AND ELECTRICAL CABLES MUST
ROUGH-IN WITHIN THE CABINET OR APPLIANCE
WIDTH AS DIMENSIONED ON THE FLOOR PLAN.

91.44 cm OF APPROVED CABLE OUT OF WALL 151.13cm ℄ AFF FOR BUILT-IN UNDER CABINET FLUORESCENT LIGHTS (3-38.1cm)

91.44cm OF APPROVED CABLE OUT OF WALL 137.16cm ℄ AFF FOR VERTICAL FLUORESCENTS INSTALLED DIRECTLY TO MIRROR (2-76.2cm)

DUPLEX OUTLET W/ GROUND FAULT CIRCUIT INTERRUPTER, (1-85.09cm ℄ ON HORIZONTAL, 1-45.72cm AFF VERTICAL)

HEAT/FAN/LIGHT UNIT WIRED FOR THREE INDIVIDUAL SWITCHES, 200 CFM VENTILATOR

RECESSED CEILING VAPOR LIGHT 60 WATT BULB ABOVE SHOWER

RECESSED CEILING DOWN LIGHTS 60 WATT BULBS EACH

MOISTURE PROOF DECORATIVE WALL SCONCE, 167.64cm ℄ AFF

S   SINGLE POLE SWITCH 114.30cm ℄ AFF

S3cm THREE WAY SWITCH w/ DIMMER 114.3cm ℄ AFF

TELEPHONE OUTLET 114.3cm ℄ AFF

TV TOWEL WARMER 60.96cm W. x 121.92cm H., 120 V. CONNECTION 53.34cm ℄ AFF AT RIGHT

• NOTE: PRIMARY HEAT SOURCE IS RADIANT FLOORING TO BE INSTALLED BY OTHERS.

3) Centerline (₵) dimensions must be given for all equipment in two directions when possible.

- Mechanicals requiring centerlines include: lavatories, bathtubs/showers, toilets/bidets, fan units, light fixtures, heating and air conditioning ducts and radiators.

- Centerline dimensions should be pulled from return walls or from the face of cabinets/equipment opposite the mechanical element.

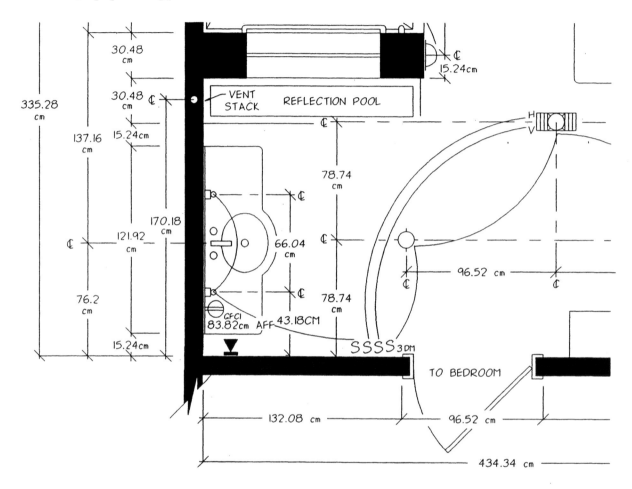

Centerlines on the mechanical plan will be indicated by the symbol (₵) followed by **a long-short-long broken line** that extends into the floor area.

4) Mechanical Plan Symbols:

S	SINGLE POLE SWITCH
S_2	DOUBLE POLE SWITCH
S_3	THREE WAY SWITCH
S_4	FOUR WAY SWITCH
S_{DM}	SINGLE POLE SWITCH v/ DIMMER
S_{3DM}	THREE WAY SWITCH v/ DIMMER
S_{LM}	MASTER SWITCH FOR LOW VOLTAGE SWITCHING SYSTEM
S_L	SWITCH FOR LOW VOLTAGE SWITCHING SYSTEM
S_{WP}	WEATHERPROOF SWITCH
S_{RC}	REMOTE CONTROL SWITCH
S_D	AUTOMATIC DOOR SWITCH
S_P	SWITCH AND PILOT LAMP
S_K	KEY OPERATED SWITCH
S_F	FUSED SWITCH
S_T	TIME SWITCH
Ⓢ	CEILING PULL SWITCH
	DUPLEX OUTLET
$_{GFCI}$	DUPLEX OUTLET WITH GROUND FAULT CIRCUIT INTERRUPTER
$_S$	SWITCH AND SINGLE RECEPTACLE OUTLET
$_S$	SWITCH AND DUPLEX OUTLET
Ⓑ	BLANKED OUTLET
Ⓙ	JUNCTION BOX
Ⓛ	OUTLET CONTROLLED BY LOW VOLTAGE SWITCHING WHEN RELAY IS INSTALLED IN OUTLET BOX
	SINGLE RECEPTACLE OULET
	TRIPLEX RECEPTACLE OULET
	QUADRUPLEX RECEPTACLE OULET
	DUPLEX RECEPTACLE OUTLET—SPLIT WIRED
	TRIPLEX RECEPTACLE OUTLET—SPLIT WIRED
Ⓒ	CLOCK HANGER RECEPTACLE
Ⓕ	FAN HANGER RECEPTACLE
	INTERCOM
	TELEPHONE OUTLET
Ⓣ	THERMOSTAT
	SMOKE DETECTOR

TV	TELEVISION OUTLET
C	CABLE OUTLET
T_L	LOW VOLTAGE TRANSFORMER
⊗	HANGING CEILING FIXTURE
	HEAT LAMP
	HEAT/LIGHT UNIT
	HEAT/FAN LIGHT W/ OOO CFM VENT.
	RECESSED CEILING DOWN LIGHTING
	RECESSED CEILING VAPOR LIGHT
	BUILT-IN LOW VOLTAGE TASK LIGHT
	BUILT-IN FLUORESCENT LIGHT
	CONTINUOUS ROW FLUORESCENT LIGHTS
	SURFACE MOUNTED FLUORESCENT LIGHT
	WALL SCONCE
$_{DW}$	DISHWASHER
$_{GD}$	FOOD WASTE DISPOSAL
$_{TC}$	TRASH COMPACTOR
$_R$	REFRIGERATOR OUTLET
$_H$	HOOD W/ OOO CFM VENTILATOR
$_M$	MICROWAVE OVEN
$_R$	ELECTRIC RANGE/COOKTOP
$_{WO}$	ELECTRIC SINGLE/DOUBLE OVEN
$_G$	GAS SUPPLY
$_{CT}$	GAS COOKTOP
$_{WO}$	GAS SINGLE/DOUBLE OVEN
$_{CW}$	CLOTHES WASHER
$_{CD}$	CLOTHES DRYER
$_{SA}$	SAUNA
$_{ST}$	STEAM
$_{WP}$	WHIRLPOOL
$_{TW}$	TOWEL WARMER
	HEAT REGISTER

ANY STANDARD SYMBOL GIVEN ABOVE W/ THE ADDITION OF LOWERCASE SUBSCRIPT LETTERING MAY BE USED TO DESIGNATE A VARIATION OF STANDARD EQUIPMENT.

WHEN USED THEY MUST BE LISTED IN THE LEGEND OF THE MECHANICAL PLAN.

*** Symbols adapted from Architectural Graphic Standards, 9th Edition**

V. Interpretive Drawings

Elevations and perspective renderings are considered interpretive drawings and are used as an explanatory means of understanding the floor plans.

- Under no circumstances should the interpretive drawings be used as a substitute for floor plans.

- In cases of dispute, the floor plans are the legally binding document.

- Because perspective drawings are not dimensioned to scale, many Bathroom Specialists include a disclaimer on their rendering such as this:

> This drawing is an artistic interpretation of the general appearance of the floor plan. It is not meant to be an exact rendition.

1) **Elevation:** Elevations must show a front view of all wall areas receiving cabinets/equipment as shown on the floor plan.

Elevations should dimension all cabinets, counters, fixtures and equipment in the elevation as follows:

- Cabinets with toekick and finished height.

- A portion of the cabinet doors and drawer front should indicate style and, when applicable, placement of handles/pulls.

- Countertops indicate thickness and show backsplash.

- All doors, windows or other openings in walls which will receive equipment. The window/door casing or trim will be listed within the overall opening dimensions.

- All permanent fixtures such as radiators, etc.

- All main structural elements and protrusions such as chimneys, partitions, etc.

- Centerlines for all mechanical equipment.

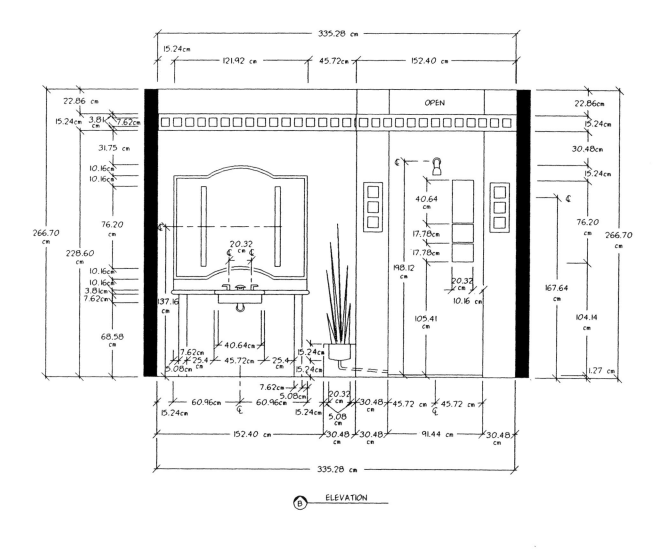

ELEVATION

NOTE:
DIMENSIONS MUST ACCURATELY
REPRESENT PRODUCTS USED.

2) **Perspective Drawings:** Perspectives are **not drawn to scale.** Grids, which are available through the **National Kitchen & Bath Association,** can be used as an underlay for tracing paper to accurately portray a perspective rendering. Two such grids are displayed on pages 48 and 49 for your reference.

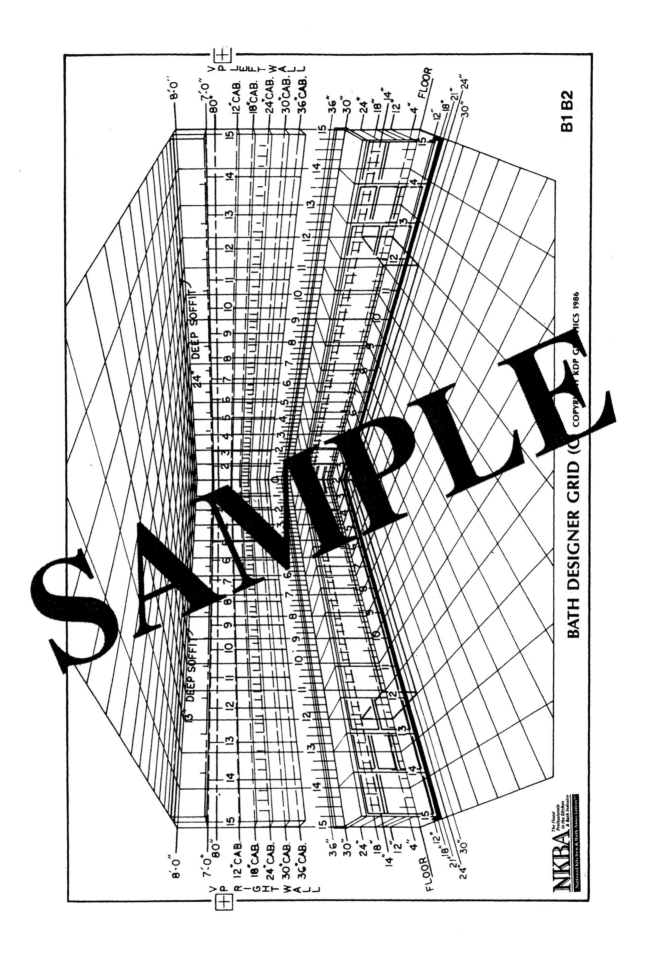

BATH DESIGNER GRID

B1 B2

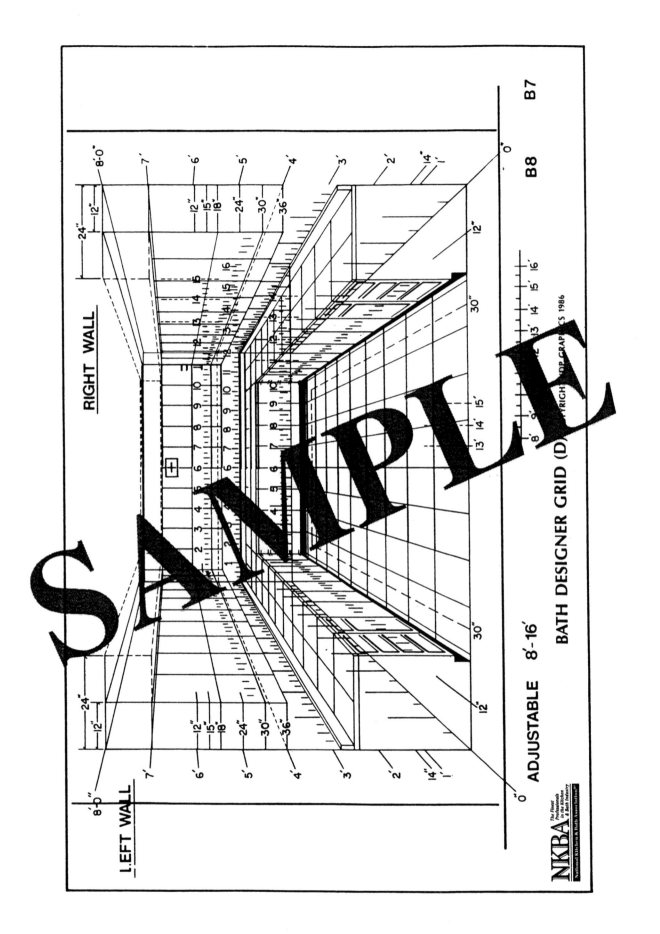

BATH DESIGNER GRID (D)

ADJUSTABLE 8'-16'

Designers have the option of preparing a one-point or two-point perspective, with or without the use of a grid.

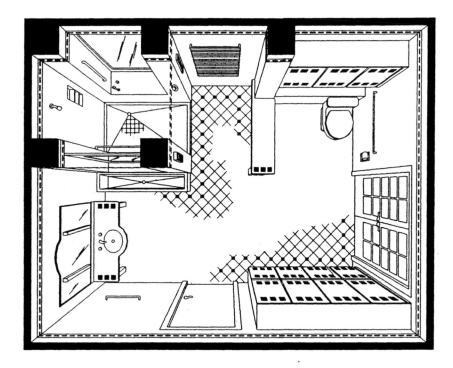

"Birds-Eye View" One Point Perspective

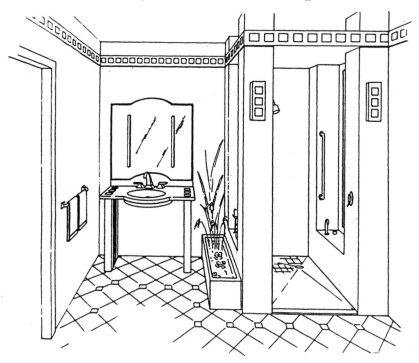

One Point Perspective

- The minimum requirement for perspectives shall be the reasonably correct representation of the longest cabinet or fixture run, or the most important area in terms of usage.

- Perspectives need not show the complete bathroom.

- Separate sectional views of significant areas or features are considered acceptable.

Two Point Perspective

3) Oblique, Dimetric, Isometric and Trimetric: Several types of interpretive drawings can be used to illustrate special cabinets and equipment, such as countertops or special order cabinets, where mechanical representation and dimensions are important. These drawings give a simple way to illustrate an object in three-dimensional views.

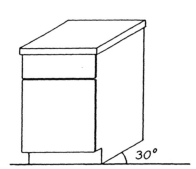

30° OBLIQUE

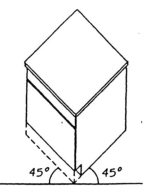

45° DIMETRIC

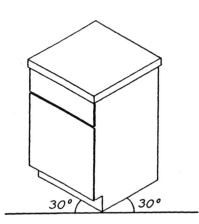

30° ISOMETRIC

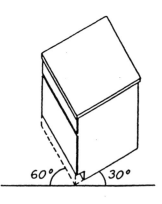

TRIMETRIC

4) Sketches: The use of sketches is a quick way to achieve a total picture of the bathroom without exact details in scaled dimensions. This quick freehand sketch can be studied, adjusted and sketched over, as the designer and client attempt to arrive at the most satisfactory layout for the bathroom. The quick sketch then can serve as a guide for drawing an exact plan of the bathroom.

Perspective Sketch

VI. Sample Bathroom Project Drawings

The following set of sample project drawings have been prepared by a Certified Bathroom Designer under the direction of the **National Kitchen & Bath Association.** These sample drawings include:

- Floor Plan

- Construction Plan

- Mechanical Plan

- Countertop Plan *

- Soffit Plan *

- Elevations

- Perspectives

* It is recommended to prepare countertop and soffit plan drawings to further clarify project requirements.

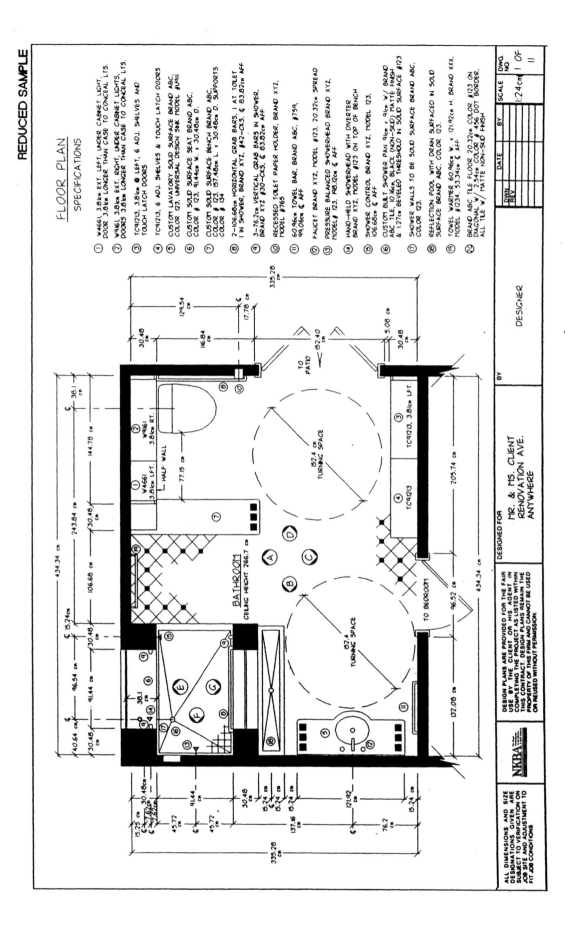

FLOOR PLAN
SPECIFICATIONS

1. W4661, 3.8cm EXT. LEFT, UNDER CABNET LIGHT. DOOR 3.8cm LONGER THAN CASE TO CONCEAL LTS.
2. W9161, 3.8cm EXT. RIGHT, UNDER CABNET LIGHTS. DOORS 3.8cm LONGER THAN CASE TO CONCEAL LTS.
3. TC91213, 3.8cm @ LEFT, 6 ADJ. SHELVES AND TOUCH LATCH DOORS
4. TC91213, 6 ADJ. SHELVES & TOUCH LATCH DOORS
5. CUSTOM LAVATORY SOLID SURFACE BRAND ABC, COLOR 123. UNIVERSAL DESIGN SINK MODEL #U411
6. CUSTOM SOLID SURFACE SEAT BRAND ABC, COLOR # 123. 91.44cm W. x 30.48cm D.
7. CUSTOM SOLID SURFACE BENCH BRAND ABC, COLOR # 123. 157.48cm L. x 30.48cm D. SUPPORTS COLOR # 134
8. 2—106.68cm HORIZONTAL GRAB BARS, 1 AT TOILET 1 IN SHOWER, BRAND XYZ, #42—CX5, @ 83.82cm AFF
9. 3—76.2cm VERTICAL GRAB BARS IN SHOWER, BRAND XYZ #30—CX5, @ 83.82cm AFF
10. RECESSED TOILET PAPER HOLDER, BRAND XYZ, MODEL #765
11. 60.96cm TOWEL BAR, BRAND ABC. #759, 99.06cm @ AFF
12. FAUCET BRAND XYZ, MODEL #123, 20.32cm SPREAD
13. PRESSURE BALANCED SHOWERHEAD BRAND XYZ, MODEL #123, @8.12cm @ AFF
14. HAND—HELD SHOWERHEAD WITH DIVERTER BRAND XYZ, MODEL #123 ON TOP OF BENCH
15. SHOWER CONTROL BRAND XYZ, MODEL 123, 106.68cm @ AFF
16. CUSTOM BUILT SHOWER PAN 9cm x 9cm W/ BRAND ABC TILE, 10.16cm, BLACK (NON—SKID) MATTE FINISH & 1.27cm BEVELED THRESHOLD IN SOLID SURFACE #123
17. SHOWER WALLS TO BE SOLID SURFACE BRAND ABC, COLOR 123.
18. REFLECTION POOL WITH DRAIN SURFACED IN SOLID SURFACE BRAND ABC. COLOR 123.
19. TOWEL WARMER 60.96cm W. x 121.92cm H. BRAND XXX. MODEL #234, 53.34cm @ AFF
20. BRAND ABC TILE FLOOR 20.32cm COLOR #123 ON DIAGONAL W/ 2.54cm COLOR # 456 DOT BORDER. ALL TILE W/ MATTE NON—SKID FINISH

BATHROOM
CELING HEIGHT 266.7 cm

TO PATIO

TO BEDROOM

TURNING SPACE 152.4 cm

TURNING SPACE 152.4 cm

HALF WALL

DESIGNED FOR
MR. & MS. CLIENT
RENOVATION AVE.
ANYWHERE

BY

DESIGNER

DATE | BY | SCALE 1:24cm | DWG. NO. 1 OF 11

DWN
REV

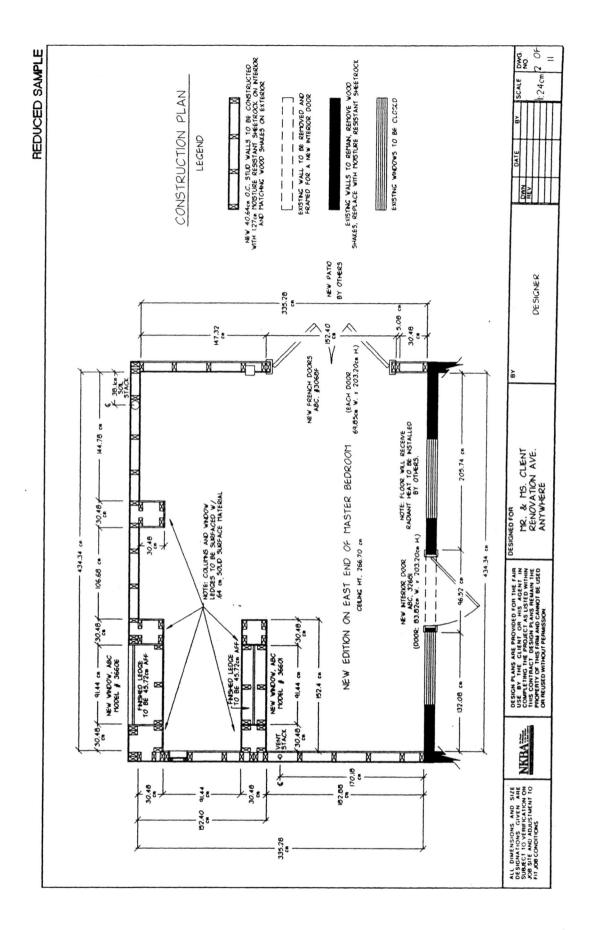

CONSTRUCTION PLAN
LEGEND

NEW 40.64cm O.C. STUD WALLS TO BE CONSTRUCTED WITH 1.27cm MOISTURE RESISTANT SHEETROCK ON INTERIOR AND MATCHING WOOD SHAKES ON EXTERIOR

EXISTING WALL TO BE REMOVED AND FRAMED FOR A NEW INTERIOR DOOR

EXISTING WALLS TO REMAIN, REMOVE WOOD SHAKES, REPLACE WITH MOISTURE RESISTANT SHEETROCK

EXISTING WINDOWS TO BE CLOSED

NEW EDITION ON EAST END OF MASTER BEDROOM
CEILING HT. 266.70 cm

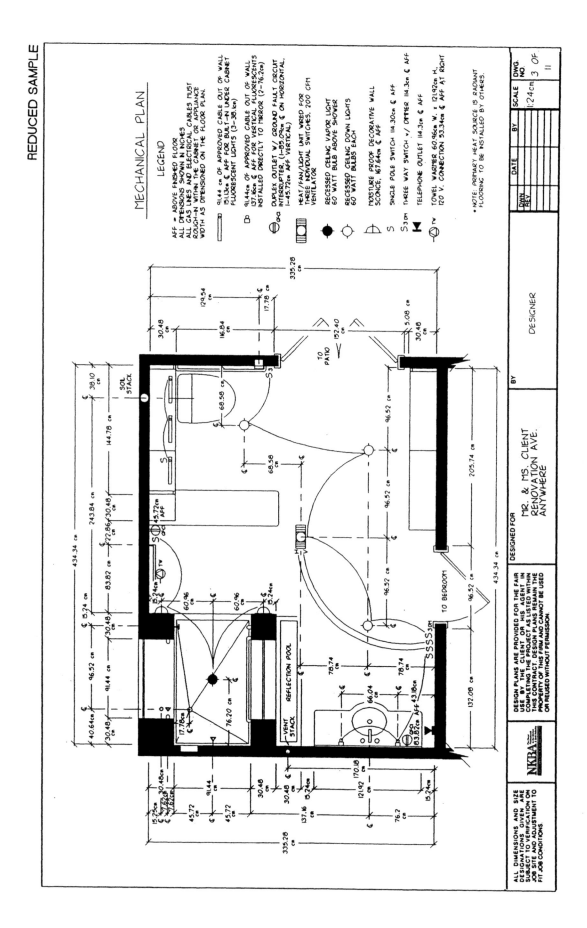

MECHANICAL PLAN

LEGEND

AFF = ABOVE FINISHED FLOOR
ALL DIMENSIONS SHOWN IN INCHES
ALL GAS LINES AND ELECTRICAL CABLES MUST
ROUGH-IN WITHIN THE CABINET OR APPLIANCE
WIDTH AS DIMENSIONED ON THE FLOOR PLAN.

91.44 cm OF APPROVED CABLE OUT OF WALL
151.13cm ℄ AFF FOR BUILT-IN UNDER CABINET
FLUORESCENT LIGHTS (3-30.kcm)

91.44cm OF APPROVED CABLE OUT OF WALL
137.16cm ℄ AFF FOR VERTICAL FLUORESCENTS
INSTALLED DIRECTLY TO MIRROR (2-76.2cm)

DUPLEX OUTLET W/ GROUND FAULT CIRCUIT
INTERRUPTER, (1-85.09cm ℄ ON HORIZONTAL,
1-45.72cm AFF VERTICAL)

HEAT/FAN/LIGHT UNIT WIRED FOR
THREE INDIVIDUAL SWITCHES, 200 CFM
VENTILATOR

RECESSED CEILING VAPOR LIGHT
60 WATT BULB ABOVE SHOWER

RECESSED CEILING DOWN LIGHTS
60 WATT BULBS EACH

MOISTURE PROOF DECORATIVE WALL
SCONCE, 167.64cm ℄ AFF

SINGLE POLE SWITCH 114.30cm ℄ AFF

THREE WAY SWITCH w/ DIMMER 114.3cm ℄ AFF

TELEPHONE OUTLET 114.3cm ℄ AFF AT RIGHT

TOWEL WARMER 60.96cm W. x 121.92cm H.
120 V. CONNECTION 53.34cm ℄ AFF AT RIGHT

* NOTE: PRIMARY HEAT SOURCE IS RADIANT
FLOORING TO BE INSTALLED BY OTHERS.

DESIGNER

DESIGNED FOR
MR. & MS. CLIENT
RENOVATION AVE.
ANYWHERE

DESIGN PLANS ARE PROVIDED FOR THE FAIR
USE BY THE CLIENT OR HIS AGENT IN
COMPLETING THE PROJECT AS LISTED WITHIN
THIS CONTRACT. DESIGN PLANS REMAIN THE
PROPERTY OF THIS FIRM AND CANNOT BE USED
OR REUSED WITHOUT PERMISSION.

ALL DIMENSIONS AND SIZE
DESIGNATIONS GIVEN ARE
SUBJECT TO VERIFICATION ON
JOB SITE AND ADJUSTMENT TO
FIT JOB CONDITIONS.

DATE	BY	SCALE	DWG. NO.
DWN		1:24cm	3 OF
REV			11

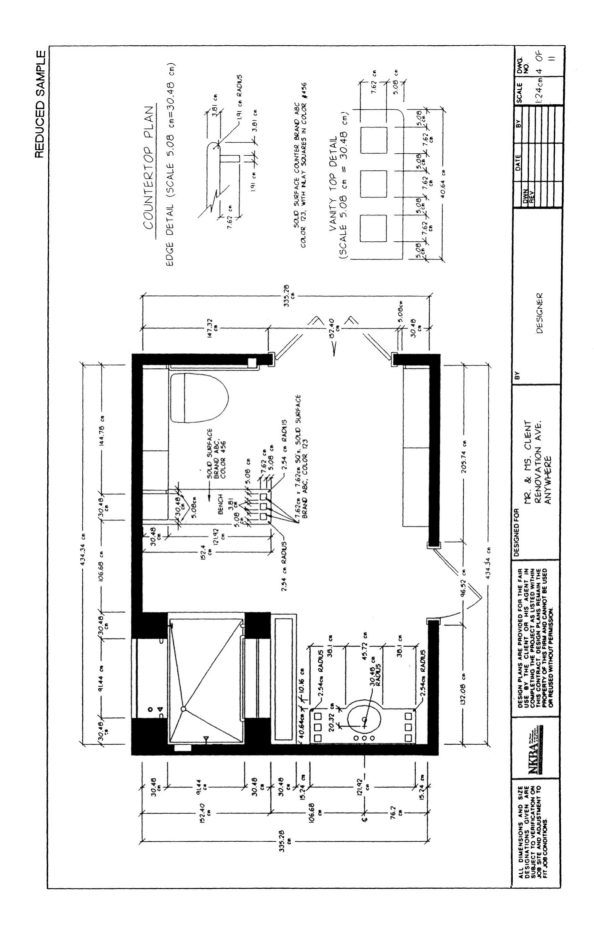

COUNTERTOP PLAN
EDGE DETAIL (SCALE 5.08 cm=30.48 cm)

SOLID SURFACE COUNTER BRAND ABC
COLOR 123, WITH INLAY SQUARES IN COLOR #456

VANITY TOP DETAIL
(SCALE 5.08 cm = 30.48 cm)

DESIGNED FOR

MR. & MS. CLIENT
RENOVATION AVE.
ANYWHERE

DESIGNER

BY

DATE   BY   SCALE   DWG. NO.
                   1:24cm 4 OF
DWN   11
REV

DESIGN PLANS ARE PROVIDED FOR THE FAIR USE BY THE CLIENT OR HIS AGENT IN COMPLETING THE PROJECT AS LISTED WITHIN THIS CONTRACT. DESIGN PLANS REMAIN THE PROPERTY OF THIS FIRM AND CANNOT BE USED OR REUSED WITHOUT PERMISSION.

ALL DIMENSIONS AND SIZE DESIGNATIONS GIVEN ARE SUBJECT TO VERIFICATION ON JOB SITE AND ADJUSTMENT TO FIT JOB CONDITIONS

NKBA

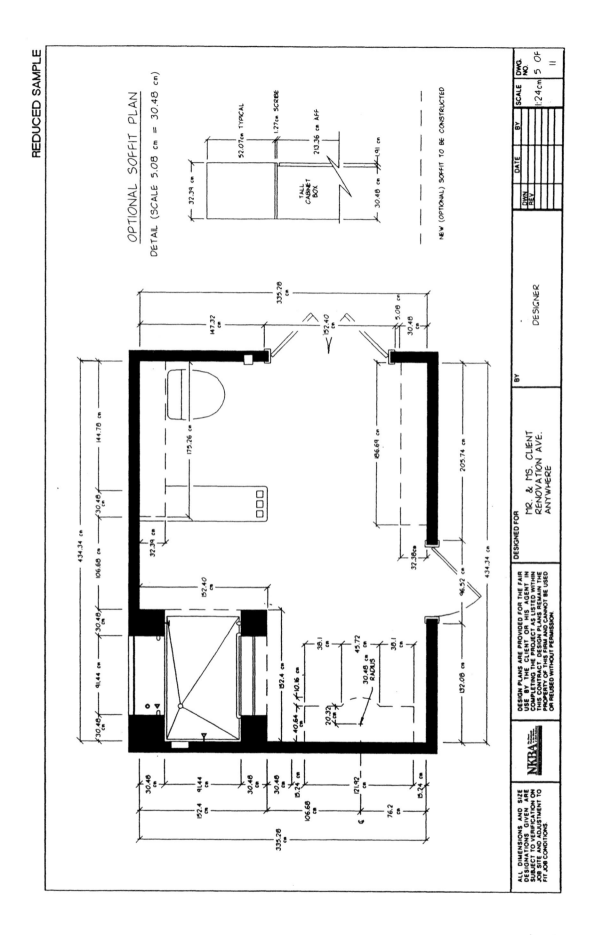

OPTIONAL SOFFIT PLAN
DETAIL (SCALE 5.08 cm = 30.48 cm)

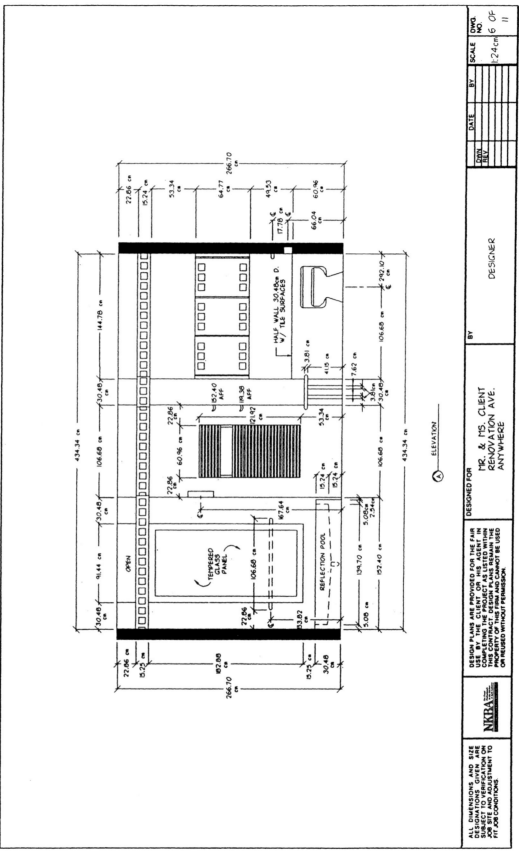

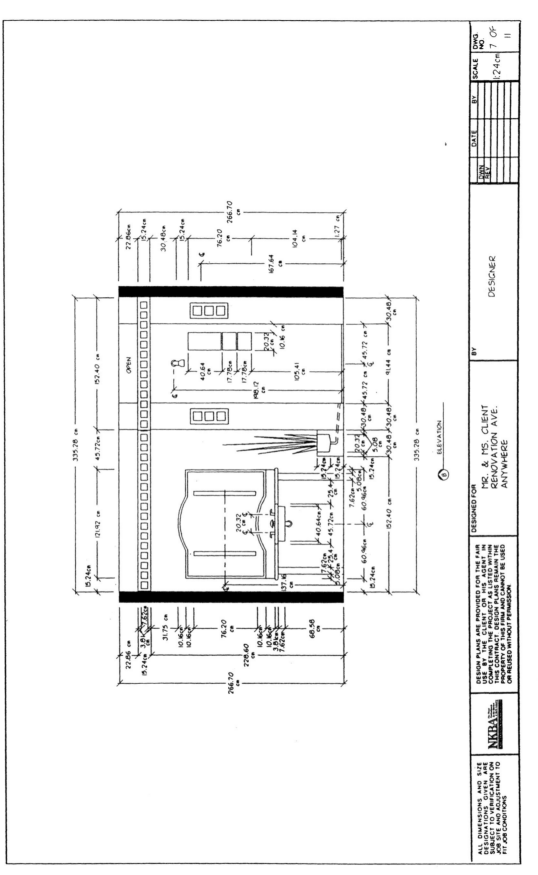

Graphics and Presentation Standards for Bathroom Design

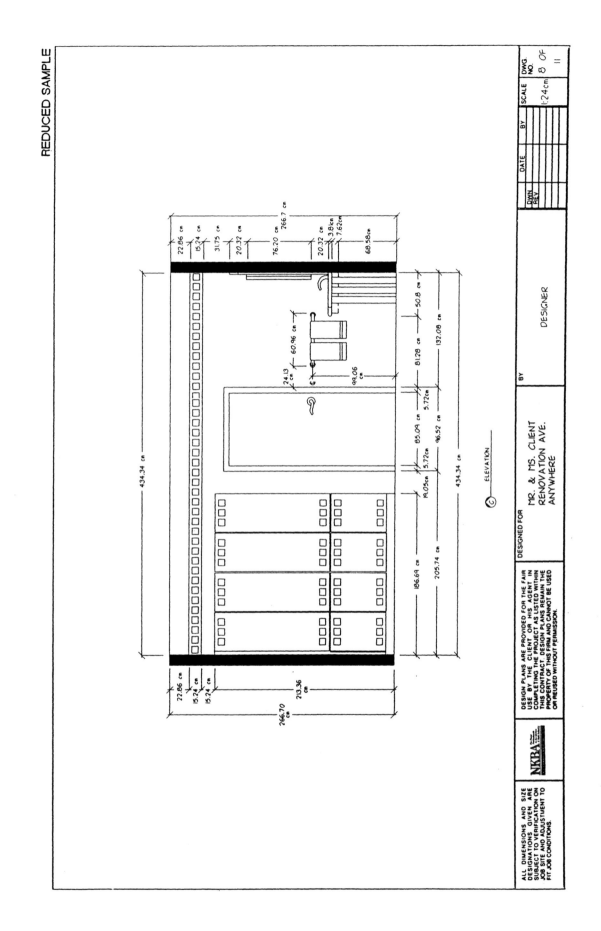

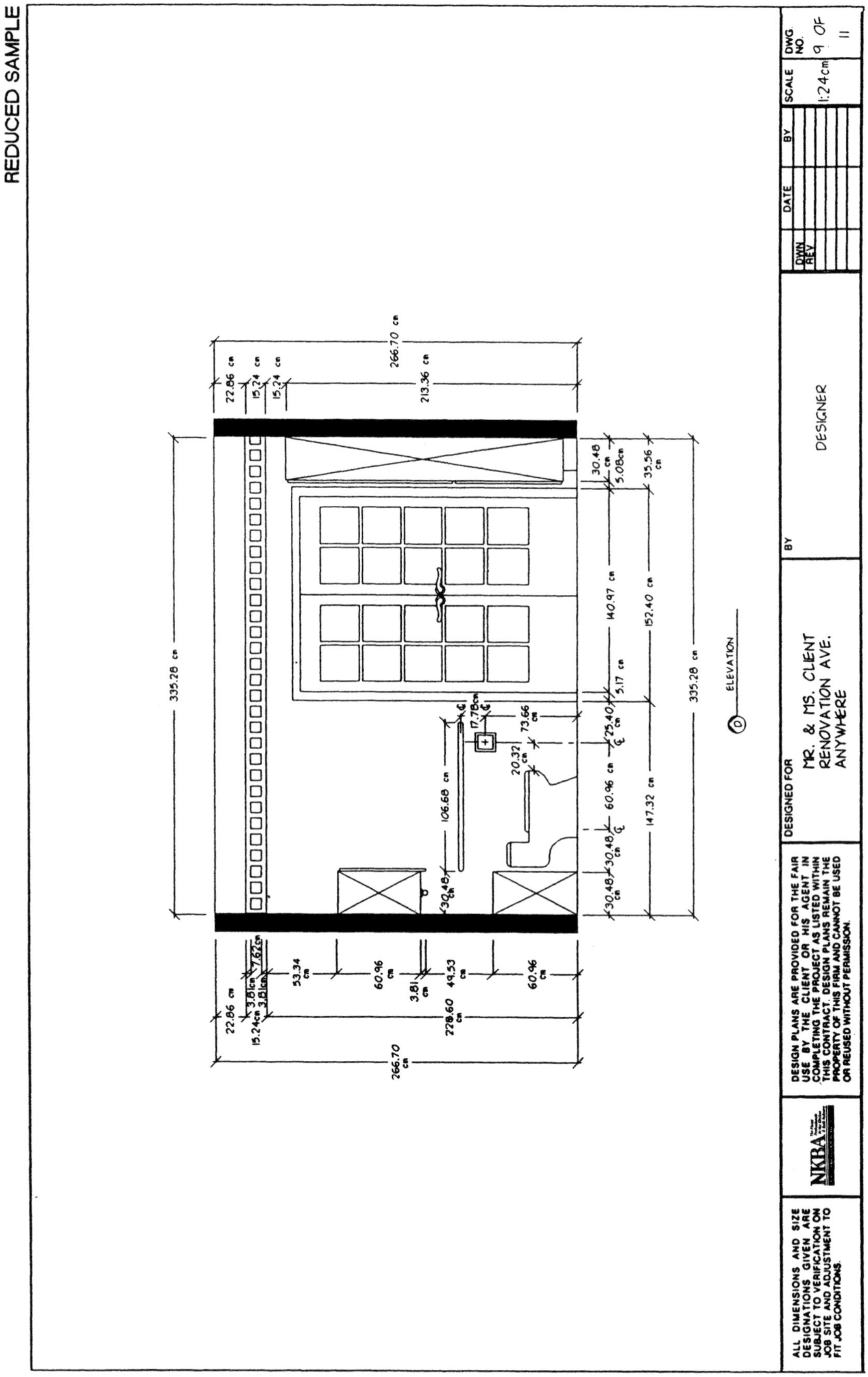

Graphics and Presentation Standards for Bathroom Design

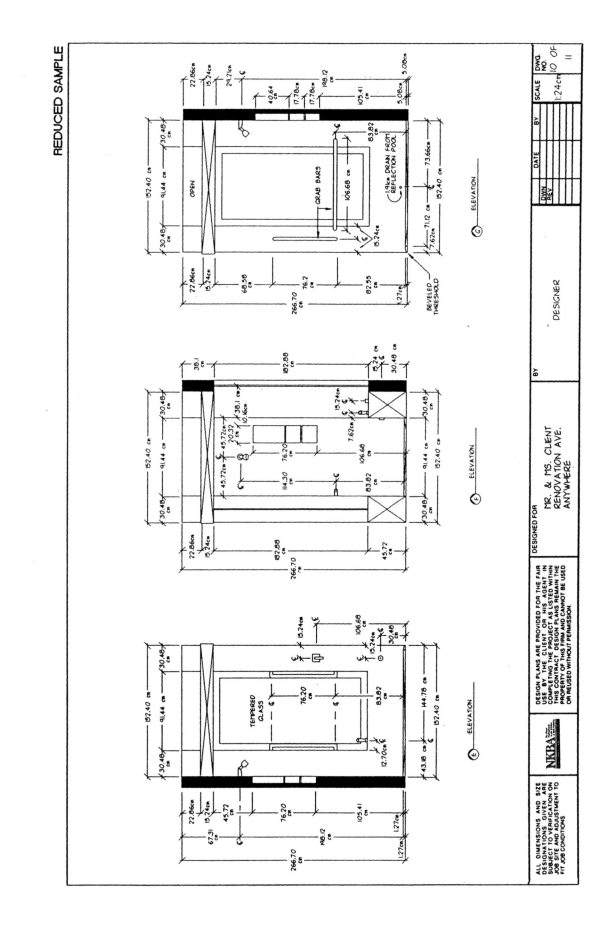

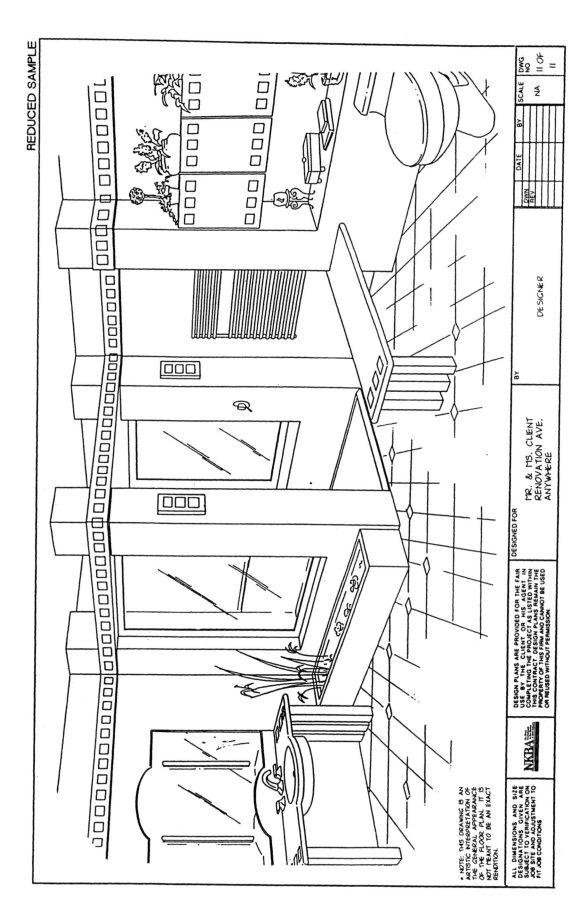

Graphics and Presentation Standards for Bathroom Design

Specifications

The purpose of the project specifications is to clearly define the details of the products listed and the scope and limits of the job. Specifications may be listed on a separate form, may be part of the working drawings or a combination of both.

- Project specifications define the area of responsibility between the Bathroom Specialist and the purchaser.

- They should clearly define all material and work affected by the job, either directly or indirectly.

- They must clearly indicate which individual has the ultimate responsibility for all or part of the above.

The following Delegation of Responsibilities shall apply: Bathroom Specialists are responsible for the accuracy of the dimensioned floor plans and the selections and designations of all cabinets/fixtures and equipment, if made or approved by them.

- Any equipment directly purchased by the Bathroom Specialist for resale, should be the responsibility of the Bathroom Specialist. Further, they must be responsible for supplying product installation instructions to the owner or the owner's agent.

- Any labor furnished by the Bathroom Specialist, whether by their own employees or through sub-contractors paid directly by them and working under their direction, should be the Bathroom Specialist's responsibility. **There should not be a Delegation of Total Responsibility to the Sub-Contractor Working Under these Conditions.**

- Any fixture/equipment purchased directly by the owner or the owner's agent from an outside source should be the responsibility of the owner or the owner's agent. The same applies to any sub-contractor, building contractor, or other labor directly hired and/or paid by the owner or the owner's agent.

- Specifications should contain descriptive references to all areas of work.

- All specification categories must be completed. If the job does not cover any given area, the words *"Not Applicable"*, *"N/A"*, or *"None"* should be inserted.

- In each area, the responsibility of either the Bathroom Specialist or the owner or the owner's agent must be assigned.

In all cases, the owner and the owner's agent must receive a completed copy of the project documents PRIOR to the commencement of any work.

STANDARD SPECIFICATIONS FOR BATHROOM DESIGN AND INSTALLATION

NKBA — *The Finest Professionals in the Kitchen & Bath Industry*
National Kitchen & Bath Association℠

Name: _CLIENT NAME_

Home Address: _CLIENT ADDRESS_

City: _____ State _____ Phone (Home) _(123) 456-7890_

(Office) _(123) 444-4561_

(Office) _(123) ___-6789_

(____) _(Same as Home)_

Jobsite Address _(Same as above)_

By

Hereafter called "Bathroom Specialist."

Bathroom Specialist will supply and deliver only such equipment and material as described in these specifications. Labor connected with this bathroom installation will be supplied by the Bathroom Specialist only as herein specified.

Any equipment, material and labor designated here as "Owner's responsibility" must be furnished and completed by the Owner, or the Owner's Agent in accordance with the work schedule established by the Bathroom Specialist.

Equipment, material and labor not included in these specifications can be supplied by the Bathroom Specialist at an additional cost for which authorization must be given in writing by the Owner, or the Owner's Agent.

All dimensions and cabinet designations shown on the floor plan, which are part of these specifications, are subject to adjustments dictated by job conditions.

All surfaces of walls, ceilings, windows and woodwork, except those of factory-made equipment, will be left unpainted or unfinished unless otherwise specified.

If specifications call for re-use of existing equipment, no responsibility on the part of the Bathroom Specialist for appearance, functioning or service shall be implied.

For factory-made equipment, the manufacturer's specifications for quality, design, dimensions, function and installation shall in any case take precedence over any others.

Cabinetry (as per approved drawing)

Manufacturer ABC

Cabinet Exterior   ☐ Wood   ☐ Steel   ☒ Decorative Laminate   ☐ Other

Cabinet Exterior Finish BRAND ABC, COLOR 123   Cabinet Interior Material MELAMINE   Finish WHITE

Door Style FULL OVERLAY, CUSTOM INLAY   Hardware HINGE # F0123

Special Cabinet Notes CUSTOM INLAY PATTERN @ TOP & BOTTOM OF ALL DOORS, COLOR 4560

Furnished By   ☒ Bathroom Specialist   ☐ Owner   ☐ Owner's Agent

Installation By   ☒ Bathroom Specialist   ☐ Owner   ☐ Owner's Agent

Countertops (as per approved drawing)

Manufacturer ABC   Material SOLID SURFACE

Design Details   Deck Thickness 3/4"   Color #123   Edging Thickness 1 1/2"   Color 123

Backsplash   Thickness 1/4"   Height 4"-8" Color #123   End Splash   Thickness —   Height —   Color —

Special Countertop Notes PATTERN INLAY #4560 @ RT. & LEFT ENDS OF VANITY AND ON END OF BENCH

Furnished By   ☒ Bathroom Specialist   ☐ Owner   ☐ Owner's Agent

Installation By   ☒ Bathroom Specialist   ☐ Owner   ☐ Owner's Agent

Fascia & Soffit (as per approved drawing) OPTIONAL

Construction   ☒ Flush   ☐ Extended   ☐ Recessed   ☐ N/A

Finish Material DRYWALL - PAINTED

Special Fascia/Soffit Notes 20 1/2" HIGH, 12 3/4" DEEP, 1/2" SCRIBE SPACE ABOVE CABINETS

Furnished By   ☒ Bathroom Specialist   ☐ Owner   ☐ Owner's Agent

Installation By   ☒ Bathroom Specialist   ☐ Owner   ☐ Owner's Agent

Lighting System

Description	Qty.	Model Number	Finish	Lamp Req.	Furnished By B.S.	Furnished By O/OA	Installed By B.S.	Installed By O/OA
RECESSED DOWN LTS.	3	R1234	WHITE	60W	X		X	
DEC. WALL SCONCE	2	S876	BLACK	2-25W	X		X	
RECESSED VAPOR LT.	1	V5678	WHITE	60W	X		X	
UNDER CAB. FLUORES.	3	F15	ALMOND	13	X		X	
VERTICAL FLUORES.	2	F30C	CHROME	13	X		X	
HEAT/LT./VENT UNIT	1	XY981	CHROME	60W	X		X	

Special Lighting System Notes

VERTICAL FLUORESCENT MOUNTED TO VANITY MIRROR 54" TO ℄.
SCONCE @ 66" ℄ AND UNDER CAB. LTS 55 1/2" TO ℄

KEY

B.S. = Bathroom Specialist   O = Owner   OA = Owner's Agent

Bath Fixtures, Fittings and Finishes

Item	Brand Name	Model	Finish	Furnished By B.S.	Furnished By O/OA	Installed By B.S.	Installed By O/OA	Hook Up By B.S.	Hook Up By O/OA
Water Closet	ABC	123	BLACK	X		X		X	
Seat	ABC	91	BLACK	X		X			
Fittings	ABC	L431	CHROME	X		X			
Stop and Supply	XYZ	987	"	X		X		X	
Miscellaneous									
Bidet	— NA —								
Fittings									
Stop and Supply									
Miscellaneous									
Urinal	—NA—								
Fittings									
Stop and Supply									
Miscellaneous									
Bathtub	—NA—								
Fittings									
Waste and Overflow									
Stop and Supply									
Enclosure									
Wall Surround									
Drapery Rod									
Bathtub Drapery									
Miscellaneous									
Whirlpool System	—NA—								
Fittings									
Miscellaneous									
Shower	CUSTOM:								
Fittings									
Drain	ABC	D3C	CHROME	X		X			
Showerhead 1	ABC pressure balanced	123A	CHROME	X		X		X	
Showerhead 2	ABC "	479	"	X		X		X	
Stop and Supply	XYZ	987	"	X		X		X	
Enclosure	—NA—								
Wall Surround	SOLID SURFACE	ABC	123	X		X			
Shower Floor	ABC TILE (NON-SKID)	—	4567	X		X			
Drapery Rod									
Shower Drapery									
Miscellaneous	BUILT-IN SHAMPOO HOLDER		SS123	X		X			
	" " SEAT		SS123	X		X			
	TEMPERED GL.	—	—	X		X			
	½" BEVELED THRESHOLD		SS123	X		X			

BMFF5

Bath Fixtures, Fittings and Finishes *(Continued)*

Item	Brand Name	Model	Finish	Furnished By		Installed By		Hook Up By	
				B.S.	O/OA	B.S.	O/OA	B.S.	O/OA
Lavatory 1	INTEGRAL SS	I-431	SS123	X		X			
Fittings	ABC	1234	CHROME	X		X		X	
Drilling Spread	8"								
Stop and Supply	XYZ	981	CHROME	X		X		X	
Pedestal Trap Cover									
Miscellaneous									
Lavatory 2	—NA—								
Fittings									
Drilling Spread									
Stop and Supply									
Pedestal Trap Cover									
Miscellaneous									
Steam Bath	—NA—								
Steam Enclosure									
Steam Generator									
Timer									
Miscellaneous									
Sauna	—NA—								
Interior									
Heater									
Timer									
Miscellaneous									
Spa/Hot Tub	—NA—								
Fittings									
Timer									
Heater									
Cover									
Skimmer									
Miscellaneous									
Exercise Equipment	—NA—								
Miscellaneous									
REFLECTION POOL	SOLID SURFACE	—	SS123	X		X			
- DRAIN	ABC	123	CHROME	X		X			
BENCH	SOLID SURFACE	—	SS123	X		X			
- SUPPORTS	"	—	SS456	X		X			
GRAB BARS (2)	XYZ 42"	42CKS	CHROME	X		X			
" (3)	XYZ 30"	30CKS	"	X		X			

Accessories (as per approved drawing)

Item	Brand Name	Model	Size	Finish	Furnished By B.S.	Furnished By O/OA	Installed By B.S.	Installed By O/OA	Hook Up By B.S.	Hook Up By O/OA
Mirror	CUSTOM (ELEV. B)	see dec. surfaces	48"w × 38"H	MIRROR	X		X			
Medicine Cabinet	—NA—									
Glass Shelves	—NA—									
Towel Bar(s)	ABC	759	24"	CHROME	X		X			
Hydronic (Electric)	XXX	1234	24"w × 48"H	"	X		X			
Towel Ring(s)	—NA—									
Robe Hook(s)	ABC	476H	LARGE	*SS123	X		X			
Tub Soap Dish(es)	—NA—									
Shower Soap Dish(es)	BUILT-IN SHOWER	ABC SOLID SUR.	8"w × 30"H	*SS123	X		X			
Bidet Soap Dish	—NA—									
Lavatory Soap Dish(es)	—NA—									
Grab Bars	XYZ (see misc. pt)	42/30CKS	42"/30"	CHROME	X		X			
Paper Holder	XYZ	K05	—	"	X		X			
Magazine Rack	—NA—									
Soap/Lotion Dispenser	—NA—									
Tumbler	—NA—									
Tissue Holder	—NA—									
Scale	—NA—									
Toothbrush Holder	—NA—									
Hamper	—NA—									
Other										

Closet Specifications —NA—

Item	Brand Name	Model	Size	Finish	Furnished By B.S.	Furnished By O/OA	Installed By B.S.	Installed By O/OA	Hook Up By B.S.	Hook Up By O/OA
Poles										
Shelf(ves)										
Drawers										
Shoe Racks										
Belt/Tie/Scarf Rack(s)										
Safe										
Ironing Board										
Miscellaneous										
Other Storage										

Graphics and Presentation Standards for Bathroom Design

Windows and Doors

Item	Brand Name	Model	Finish	Hardware	Furnished By B.S.	Furnished By O/OA	Installed By B.S.	Installed By O/OA
FIXED SHOWER WINDOW	ABC	3060E	—	—	X		X	
- SOLID SURFACE CASING	ABC		SS123		X		X	
FRENCH DOORS	ABC	3068F	UNFINISHED WOOD	1234	X		X	
INTERIOR DOOR	ABC	3268I	"	123	X		X	

Special Window and Door Notes:

ALL WINDOW & DOOR GLASS TEMPERED; ALL DOORS & THEIR CASEINGS PAINTED IVORY

Flooring

		Furnished By B.S.	Furnished By O/OA	Installed By B.S.	Installed By O/OA
Removal of Existing Floor Covering	— NA —				
Preparation of Floor for New Surface	BY OTHERS				X
Installation of Subfloor/Underlayment	5/8" PLYWOOD	X		X	
New Floor Covering Material Description:	CERAMIC TILE				X
Manufacturer ABC Pattern Name IVORY MARBLE (NON-SLIP)					
Pattern Number 1234 Pattern					
Floor Covering Installation SEE NOTE BELOW			X		X
Baseboard Material SOLID SURFACE W/ ABC, 123		X		X	
Transition Treatment THRESHOLD B.S. ABC, 123		X		X	
Remove and Repair Water Damaged Area — NA —					
Remove Unusable Closet — NA —					

Special Flooring Notes: RADIANT FLOORING INSTALLED BY OTHERS; TILE INSTALLED ON DIAGONAL WITH BORDER & 123 BLACK DOTS 2" X 2"

Decorative Surfaces (wall, ceiling, window materials)

Removal Work: Wall _X_ Ceiling _X_ Window —NA—   Preparation Work: Wall _X_ Ceiling _X_ Window _____

Description	Brand Name	Model	Finish	Material Quantity	Furnished By B.S.	Furnished By O/OA	Installed By B.S.	Installed By O/OA
DECORATIVE LAMINATE	ABC	BACKGR→123			X		X	
INLAY BORDER		INLAY→456			X		X	
WALL PAINT (IVORY)	DEF	—	EGGSHELL	2 GAL.	X		X	
CEILING PAINT (WHITE)	DEF	—	FLAT	1 GAL.	X		X	
CASINGS & DOORS (IVORY)	DEF	—	SEMIGLOSS	2 PT.	X		X	
PRIME ALL SURFACES	DEF	—	PRIMER	2 GAL.	X		X	

Special Decorative Surface Notes:

CUSTOM MIRROR W/ BLACK FRAME (SEE ELEV. B, PG 7 OF 11)

Electrical Work (except as described above in specific equipment sections)

	Furnished By		Installed By	
	B.S.	O/OA	B.S.	O/OA
Heating System Alteration NEW RADIANT FLOOR BY OTHRS		X		X
New Service Panel				
Code Update ALL OUTLETS GFCI	X		X	
Details				
TOWEL WARMER , 120V , 21" AFF	X		X	
ALL SWITCHES 45" TO ℄ AFF	X		X	
SEE MECHANICAL PLAN FOR DETAILS				
PG. 3 OF 11				

Plumbing (except as described above in specific equipment sections)

	Furnished By		Installed By	
	B.S.	O/OA	B.S.	O/OA
Heating System Alterations —NA—				
New Rough-in Requirements ALL NEW (SEE MECH. PLAN)				X
Modifications to Existing Lines —NA—				
Details				
SEE MECH. PLAN 3 OF 11 FOR DETAILS	X		X	
NEW VENT & SOIL STACK REQUIRED	X		X	

General Carpentry (except as described above in specific equipment sections)

	Furnished By		Installed By	
	B.S.	O/OA	B.S.	O/OA
Demolition REMOVE WOOD SHAKES FROM EAST WALL	X		X	
Existing Fixture and Equipment Removal —NA—				
Trash Removal ARRANGE FOR DUMPSTER	X			
Reconstruction Work (Except as Previously Stated)				
Windows FRAME PER CONST. PLAN (PG 2 OF 11)		X		X
Doors FRAME PER CONST. PLAN (PG 2 OF 11)		X		X
Interior Walls DRYWALL , 1/2" MOISTURE RESISTANT	X		X	
Exterior Walls MATCH EXISTING WOOD SHAKES & FINISH	X		X	
Details NEW ADDITION PER CONSTRUCTION PLAN				
BY LICENSED REMODELING FIRM		X		X

Graphics and Presentation Standards for Bathroom Design

Miscellaneous Work

	Responsibility	
	B.S.	O/OA
Trash Removal PILE IN DUMPSTER, EMPTY AS REQUIRED	X	
Jobsite/Room Cleanup DAILY PICK-UP, SPECIAL POST PROJECT CLEAN-UP	X	
Building Permit(s) AS REQUIRED	X	
Structural Engineering/Architectural Fees AS REQUIRED BY OTHERS		X
Inspection Fees AS REQUIRED	X	
Jobsite Delivery STORAGE IN GARAGE AVAILABLE	X	
Other		
SUPERVISE INSTALLATION WORK & SCHEDULE	X	

...ve read ... specifications and approve:

Accepted: _Client-1 Signature_

Accepted: _Client-2 Signature_

Date: 0/00/00

Authorized Company Representative

By: _Designer's Signature, CBD_

By: _____

Date: 0/00/00

Design Statement

The purpose of the design statement is to interpret the design problem and solution in order to substantiate the project to the client. Design statements may be verbal or written. Written statements maybe a separate document, may be part of the working drawings or a combination of both.

Design statements should clearly outline:

- design considerations and challenges of the project including, but not limited to: construction budget requirements, client needs and wants, special requests and lifestyle factors.

- how the designer arrived at their solution and addressed the design considerations and challenges for the project.

- aesthetic considerations such as use of principles and elements of design (ie. pattern repetition, finish/color/surface selections and other details).

It is important that a design statement be clear, concise and interesting to the reader. Written statements may be in either paragraph or bulleted/outline format. As a guideline, a design statement can be written in 250-500 words. Sample design statements follow, showing both acceptable formats.

Sample Design Statement - Paragraph Format

The primary design challenge in the bathroom design for Mr. and Ms. Client was to create a space that was functional for both Mr. Consumer who uses a wheelchair and Mrs. Consumer who stands 5' 3" tall. Additionally the consumers requested an environment that would feel like a sophisticated spa retreat and flow naturally with their bedroom decor, which is of contemporary Japanese influence. The space to be utilized was an addition which was added to the east end of the existing Master Bedroom.

The construction constraints required direct access to the bedroom somewhere along the east wall, as well as access to an exterior patio that would be built on the north wall. Other design requirements included an open roll-in shower with large seat, stool or bench area adjacent to shower, toilet with space for side transfer, lavatory with kneespace, storage closet and 60" wheelchair turning space.

The solution was derived methodically, first locating doors and then by dividing the remaining space into quarters by function. With the doors on the east and north walls, we placed the 60" diameter of floorspace required for turning in that corner. That left the other two walls for the plumbing fixtures. A custom 31 1/2" high pedestal sink was designed to accommodate both standing and sitting use and provide kneespace.

The shower was designated with four columns that framed the 36" wide seat and window areas. Controls were placed at the entrance and a hand-held showerhead was installed on the seat deck for easy access. All glass used was tempered for safety. The 1/2" curb height is easy to roll-over with a wheelchair. The 42" by 36" floorspace at the shower entrance provides the 90 degree turning space required for a wheelchair. The vertical towel warmer specified allows towels to be hung at a wide range of heights above the floor. A solid surface bench was designed opposite the shower for towel drying and aiding in transfer. Then, the remaining floorspace was utilized for the toilet and side transfer space. All corners were eased to eliminate any sharp edges and surfaces are of tile and solid surface for easy maintenance.

In order to provide the spa retreat feeling requested, a special reflecting pool for floating candles and potpourri was designed between the shower and lavatory. The semi-circular protrusion of the lavatory front was mirrored in the backsplash and mirror top. The square motif was picked-up from a shoji screen in the bedroom and used throughout the bathroom to create a unified theme. Squares are found in the molding, cabinet door style, lighting, floor and bench/lavatory supports. The neutral with black accent colors help to create a feeling of understated sophistication.

Sample Design Statement - Outline Format

The primary design challenge:

- Functional for Mr. Consumer who uses a wheelchair
- Functional for Mrs. Consumer who stands 5'3" tall
- Create an environment that would feel like a sophisticated spa retreat
- Flow naturally with their bedroom decor of Japanese influence

The construction constraints:

- Addition to east end of the existing Master Bedroom
- Direct access to the bedroom somewhere along the east wall
- Access to an exterior patio that would be built on the north wall

Other design requirements:

- Open roll-in shower with large seat
- Stool or bench area adjacent to shower
- Toilet with space for side transfer
- Lavatory with kneespace
- Storage closet
- 60" wheelchair turning space

The solution:

- Located 60" diameter floorspace directly adjacent to doors
- Custom 31 1/2" high pedestal sink accommodates seated and standing users
- Shower with 1/2" curb for roll-in access
- 36" wide shower seat with hand-held showerhead
- Controls placed at shower entrance for easy access
- All glass tempered for safety
- 42" by 36" floorspace at shower entrance for 90 degree turning
- Vertical towel warmer holds towels at multiple heights
- Solid surface bench opposite shower for towel drying and transfer
- Floorspace adjacent to toilet for side transfer
- All corners eased to eliminate any sharp edges
- Surfaces treatments of tile and solid surface for easy maintenance

Aesthetics:

- Special reflecting pool for floating candles and potpourri
- Curved protrusion of lavatory is mirrored in the backsplash and mirror top
- Square motif was picked-up from shoji screen in the bedroom
- Motif used in molding, cabinet door, lights, floor and bench/lavatory
- Neutral with black accent colors create understated sophistication

Graphics and Presentation Standards for Bathroom Design

Contracts

All contract forms used **must** be in strict compliance with Federal, State and Municipal Laws and Ordinances. Reference local codes for compliance standards. Laws do vary, therefore, you should be sure your contracts meet all local requirements.

STANDARD FORM OF AGREEMENT
FOR DESIGN AND INSTALLATION

Approved by the

NKBA *The Finest Professionals in the Kitchen & Bath Industry*
National Kitchen & Bath Association℠

National Kitchen & Bath Association

Between ....Purchaser

Home Address ....

City ....State................................Zip..........................

Phone Number...

Delivery Address...

And Seller

SAMPLE

The Seller agrees to furnish the materials and services set forth in the drawings (numbered...............................
and dated................................) and specifications annexed hereto.
The Purchaser agrees to make payment therefore in accordance with the schedule of payment.

Contract Price.. $ ....

Sales Tax (if applicable) .... $ ....

.... $ ....

Total Purchase Price.................................... $ ....

Schedule of Payment:

Upon signing of this agreement .... $ ....

Upon delivery of cabinets from manufacturer .... $ ....

Upon delivery of .... $ ....

Upon substantial installation of .... $ ....

This contract includes the terms and provisions as set forth herein. Please read and sign where indicated.

2. The standard form of warranty shall apply to the service and equipment furnished (except where other warranties of purchased products apply). The warranty shall become effective when signed by the Seller and delivered to the Purchaser. The warranty is for one year materials and labor.

3. The delivery date, when given, shall be deemed approximate and performance is subject to delays caused by strikes, fires, acts of God or other reasons not under the control of the Seller, as well as the availability of the product at the time of delivery.

4. The Purchaser agrees to accept delivery of the product or products when ready. The risk of loss, as to damage or destruction, shall be upon the Purchaser upon the delivery and receipt of the product.

5. The Purchaser understands that the products described are specially designed and custom built and that the Seller takes immediate steps upon execution of this Agreement to design, order and construct those items set forth herein; therefore, this Agreement is not subject to cancellation by the Purchaser for any reason.

6. No installation, plumbing, electrical, flooring, decorating or other construction work is to be provided unless specifically set forth herein. In the event the Seller is to perform the installation, it is understood that the price agreed upon herein does not include possible expense entailed in coping with hidden or unknown contingencies found at the job site. In the event such contingencies arise and the Seller is required to furnish labor or materials or otherwise perform work not provided for or contemplated by the Seller, the actual costs plus (   )% thereof will be paid for by the Purchaser. Contingencies include but are not limited to: inability to reuse existing water, vent, and waste pipes; air shafts, ducts, grilles, louvres and registers; the relocation of concealed pipes, risers, wiring or conduits, the presence of which cannot be determined until the work has started; or imperfections, rotting or decay in the structure or parts thereof necessitating replacement.

7. Title to the items sold pursuant to this Agreement shall not pass to the Purchaser until the full price as provided in this Agreement is paid to the Seller.

8. Delays in payment shall be subject to interest charges of (   )% per annum, and in no event higher than the interest rate provided by law. If the Seller is required to engage the services of a collection agency or an attorney, the Purchaser agrees to reimburse the Seller for any reasonable amounts expended in order to collect the unpaid balance.

9. If any provision of this Agreement is declared invalid by any tribunal, the remaining provisions of the Agreement shall not be affected thereby.

10. This Agreement sets forth the entire transaction between the parties; any and all prior Agreements, warranties or representations made by either party are superseded by this Agreement. All changes in this Agreement shall be made by a separate document and executed with the same formalities. No agent of the Seller, unless authorized in writing by the Seller, has any authority to waive, alter, or enlarge this contract, or to make any new or substituted or different contracts, representations, or warranties.

11. The Seller retains the right upon breach of this Agreement by the Purchaser to sell those items in the Seller's possession. In effecting any resale on breach of this Agreement by the Purchaser, the Seller shall be deemed to act in the capacity of agent for the Purchaser. The purchaser shall be liable for any net deficiency on resale.

12. The Seller agrees that it will perform this contract in conformity with customary industry practices. The Purchaser agrees that any claim for adjustment shall not be reason or cause for failure to make payment of the purchase price in full. Any unresolved controversy or claim arising from or under this contract shall be settled by arbitration and judgment upon the award rendered may be entered in any court of competent jurisdiction. The arbitration shall be held under the rules of the American Arbitration Association.

Accepted: ....
                                              Purchaser

Accepted: ....
                                              Purchaser

Date: ....

Titling Project Documents

Protecting Yourself

When you design a project for a client, you must protect yourself from liability when referring to the plans and drawings, and you must protect the plans themselves from being copied by your competitors.

When presenting the plans for a bathroom, **NKBA** recommends that you refer to the drawings as *"Bathroom Design Plans"* or *"Cabinet Plans"*. The design plans should have the following statement included on them in an obvious location in large or block letters.

> **DESIGN PLANS ARE NOT PROVIDED FOR ARCHITECTURAL OR ENGINEERING USE**

The individual drawings incorporated in the overall bathroom design presentation must also be carefully labeled. It is suggested that you refer to these other drawings as ***"Floor Plans", "Elevations", "Artist Renderings", and "Mechanical Plans"***.

With respect to the *"Artist Rendering"* , **NKBA** suggests that you include a notation on the drawings which reads:

> **THIS RENDERING IS AN ARTIST'S INTERPRETATION OF THE GENERAL APPEARANCE OF THE ROOM, IT IS NOT INTENDED TO BE A PRECISE DEPICTION**

The entire set of paperwork, which includes your design plans, specifications and contract, can be referred to as the **"Project Documents"**.

You should never refer to the design plan as an *"Architectural Drawing"*, or even as an "architectural-type drawing". **DO NOT USE THE WORDS** *"Architecture", "Architectural Design", "Architectural Phase", "Architectural Background"*, or any other use of the word *"Architectural"* in any of the project documents that you prepare, or in any of your business stationary, promotional information or any presentation materials. Any such reference to the work that you do or documents that you prepare may result in a violation of various state laws. A court may determine that your use of the word *"Architecture/Architectural"*, could reasonably lead a client to believe that you possess a level of expertise that you do not. Worse yet, a court may find you liable for fraud and/or misrepresentation.

Laws do vary per state, therefore, it is important that you consult with your own legal counsel to be sure that you are acting within the applicable statutes in your area. You must clearly understand what drawings you are legally allowed to prepare, and what drawings must be prepared under the auspices of a licensed architect or engineer.

Protecting your "Bathroom Design Plans"

After drafting the design plans for your client, you should insure that they will not be copied or used by a competitor. This may be done by copyrighting the design plan that you prepare.

Copyright is an International form of protection/exclusivity provided by law to authors of original works, despite whether the work is published or not. Original works of authorship include any literary, pictorial, graphic, or sculptured works, such as your design plans, provided they are original works done by you.

Copyright protection exists from the moment the work is created in its final form and will endure fifty years after your death.

Naturally, if two or more persons are authors of an original work, they will be deemed *co-owners* of its copyright. For example; if you as the Bathroom Specialist collaborate with an Interior Designer, you will both be co-owners of the design copyright.

An original work generated by two or more authors is referred to as a *"joint work"*. Generally, a *"joint work"* results if the authors collaborated on the work or if each prepared a segment of it with the knowledge and intent that it would be incorporated with the contributions submitted by other authors. Accordingly, a *"joint work"* will only be found when each co-author intended his respective contribution to be combined into a larger, integrated piece. There is no requirement that each of the co-authors work together or even be acquainted with one another.

A work created by an employee within the scope of his employment is regarded as *"work made for hire"*, and is normally owned by the employer, unless the parties explicitly stipulate in a written agreement, signed by both, that the copyright will be owned by the employee. If you are an independent contractor, the *"works made for hire"* statutes do not include architectural drawings or other design plans, therefore, the copyright in any bathroom design created by you will remain vested with you until you contractually agree to relinquish ownership.

To secure copyright protection for your plans, you are required to give notice of copyright on all publicly distributed copies. The use of the copyright notice is your responsibility as the copyright owner and does not require advance permission from, or registration with, the Copyright Office in Washington, DC.

Copyright © Notice

A proper copyright notice must include the following three items:

- 1. The symbol ©, or the word "Copyright", or the abbreviation "Copy";
  (© is considered as the International symbol for copyright)

- 2. The year of the first publication of the work; and

- 3. The name of the owner of the copyright in the work, or an abbreviation by which the name can be recognized, or a generally known alternative designation of the owner.

An example of a proper copyright notice would be:

Copyright © 1995 Joe Smith

The notice should be affixed to copies of your design plan in such a manner and location as to give reasonable notice of the claim of copyright.

As mentioned previously, you or your firm continue to retain copyright protection of your design plan even if the plan is given to the client after he has paid for it. Although the copyright ownership may be transferred, such transfer must be in writing and signed by you as the owner of the copyright conveyed. Normally, the transfer of a copyright is made by contract. In order to protect your exclusive rights, however, you should include a clause in your contract which reads:

Design plans are provided for the fair use by the client or his agent in completing the project as listed within this contract. Design plans remain the property of (your name) and cannot be used or reused without permission of (your name).

This clause should also be in any agreement between you and a client who requests that you prepare a design plan for his review. Such a design plan usually serves as the basis for a subsequent contract between you and the client for the actual installation of the kitchen. This type of agreement will prevent the client from obtaining a design plan from you and then taking that plan to a competitor who may simply copy your plan.

So long as you retain the copyright in the design plan, you will be able to sue any party who has copied your design plan for infringement.

Glossary - Graphic Terms

Architects Scale: A measuring tool used to draw at a determined unit of measure ratio accurately; ie. 1/2" = 1', in which each half inch represents one foot.

3/32" = 1'	1/4" = 1'	1" = 1'
3/16" = 1'	3/8" = 1'	1 1/2" = 1'
1/8" = 1'	3/4" = 1'	3" = 1'

It is equally acceptable to use the metric equivalents. (inches x 2.54)

Break Symbol: Indicated by (⟶⟋⟵) and used to end wall lines on a drawing which actually continue or to break off parts of the drawing.

Color: A visual sensation which is a result of light reflecting off objects and creating various wavelengths which when reaching the retina produces the appearance of various hues.

Copyright: Is an International form of protection/exclusivity provided by law to authors of original works, despite whether the work is published or not. Original works of authorship include any literary, pictorial, graphic, or sculptured works such as design plans that are your own original works. The symbol (©) is considered as the International symbol for copyright exclusivity.

Dimension Lines: Solid lines terminating with arrows, dots or slashes which run parallel with the object it represents and includes the actual length of the line written in inches or centimeters inside or on top of the line. Whenever possible, dimension lines should be located outside of the actual walls of the floor plan or elevation.

Dimetric: A dimetric drawing is similar to oblique, with the exception that the object is rotated so that only one of its corners touches the picture plane. The most frequently used angle for the projecting line is an equal division of 45° on either side of the leading edge. A 15° angle is sometimes used when it is less important to show the *"roof view"* of the object.

Elevation: A drawing representing a vertical view of a space taken from a preselected reference plane. There is no depth indicated in an elevation, rather everything appears very flat and is drawn in scale.

Floor Plan: A drawing representing a horizontal view of a space taken from a preselected reference plane (often the ceiling). There is no depth indicated in a floor plan, rather everything appears very flat and is drawn in a reduced scale.

Isometric:
The isometric, a special type of dimetric drawing, is the easiest and most popular paraline (three-dimensional) drawing. All axes of the object are simultaneously rotated away from the picture plane and kept at the same angle of projection (30° from the picture plane). All legs are equally distorted in length at a given scale and therefore maintain an exact proportion of 1:1:1.

Kroy Lettering Tape:
Translucent sticky backed tape, which after running it through a special typing machine, creates a stick on lettering ideal for labeling drawing title blocks.

Lead:
A graphite and clay mixture which is used for drawing and drafting in combination with a lead holder. Similar to a pencil without the wooden outer portion. Available in various degrees of hardness, providing various line weights.

Legend:
An explanatory list of the symbols and their descriptions as used on a mechanical plan or other graphic representation.

Matte Board:
A by product of wood pulp with a paper surface which has been chemically treated in order to be acid free and fade resistent. The use of matte board will protect drawings from fading, becoming brittle and bending or creasing.

Oblique:
In an oblique drawing one face (either plan or elevation) of the object is drawn directly on the picture plane. Projected lines are drawn at a 30° or 45° angle to the picture plane.

Owners Agent:
That person or persons responsible for mediating the clients requests with the designer and acting as the interpretor on any area the client is unsure of or in question on.

Ozalid Prints:
More commonly referred to as *"Blueprints"*, are a method of duplicating drawings in which special paper coated with light sensitive diazo is used. This paper with drawing on transparent paper, is exposed to ultra violet light creating a negative, then the print is exposed again to the developer which produces the *"blackline", "blueline"* or *"sepia print"* depending upon the paper used.

Perspective:
The art of representing a space in a drawing form which appears to have depth by indicating the relationship of various objects as they appear to the human eye or through the lens of a camera.

Photocopy:
A method of duplicating drawings in which light causes toner to adhere to paper of various sizes, typically *(8 1/2" x 11"), (11" x 14")* or *(11" x 17")*, producing prints in high contrast, which are similar to blackline ozalid prints.

Quadrille Paper:
White ledger paper base with blue, non-reproducible ruling lines which all carry the same weight. *** NOTE: This is not an acceptable type of drafting paper for project documentation.**

Section: Often referred to as *"cut-view"*, these drawings are defined as an imaginary cut made through an object and used to show construction details and materials which are not obvious in standard plan or elevational views.

Technical Rapidograph Pens: Provides for a smooth flow of ink with stainless steel points or *"Tungsten Carbide"* point of various sizes, again providing various line weights.

Tracing Paper: Thin semi-transparent paper used for sketching. Also called *"bumwad"* paper.

Transfer Type: Sometimes referred to as *"Press-Type"* or *"Rub-on-Type"*, is a translucent film with lettering or dot screen images which may be transferred to a drawing by rubbing the image after it is positioned on the drawing paper. When the film is lifted, the image remains on the drawing paper and the film is left blank.

Trimetric: The trimetric drawing is similar to the dimetric, except that the plan of the object is rotated so that the two exposed sides of the object are not at equal angles to the picture plane. The plan is usually positioned at 30/60° angle to the ground plane. The height of the object is reduced proportionately as illustrated (similar to the 45° dimetric).

Vellum: Rag stock which has been transparentized with synthetic resin resulting in medium weight transparent paper with a medium-fine grain or *"tooth"* which holds lead to the surface.

Witness Lines: Solid lines which run perpendicular to the dimension line and cross the dimension line at the exact location of its termination. These lines should begin approximately 1/16" outside of the walls of the floor plan and end approximately 1/16" beyond the dimension line.

Graphics and Presentation Standards for Bathroom Design

Imperial/Metric Comparison Chart

IMPERIAL / METRIC COMPARISON CHART

KITCHEN AND BATH FLOOR PLANS SHOULD BE DRAWN TO A
SCALE OF 1/2" EQUALS 1' FOOT (1/2" =1'- 0"). AN EQUALLY
ACCEPTABLE METRIC SCALE WOULD BE A RATIO OF 1 TO 20
(ie. 1 CM TO 20 CM)

	INCHES	MILLIMETERS	CENTIMETERS
◆ ACTUAL METRIC CONVERSION TO MILLIMETERS IS 1" = 25.4 MM .	1/8"	3 MM	.32 CM
TO FACILITATE CONVERSIONS	1/4"	6	.64
BETWEEN IMPERIAL + METRIC	1/2"	12	1.27
DIMENSIONING FOR CALCULATIONS	3/4"	18	1.91
UNDER 1", 24 MM IS USED.	1"	24	2.54
◆ TO FACILITATE CONVERSIONS BETWEEN IMPERIAL + METRIC FOR CALCULATIONS OVER 1", 25 MM IS TYPICALLY USED.	3"	75	7.62
	6"	150	15.24
◆ ACTUAL METRIC CONVERSION	9"	225	22.86
TO CENTIMETERS IS 1" = 2.54 CM.	12"	300	30.48
	15"	375	38.1
	18"	450	45.72
	21"	525	53.34
	24"	600	60.96
	27"	675	68.58
	30"	750	76.2
	33"	825	83.82
	36"	900	91.44
	39"	975	99.06
	42"	1050	106.68
	45"	1125	114.3
	48"	1200	121.92
	51"	1275	129.54
	54"	1350	137.16
	57"	1425	144.78
	60"	1500	152.4
	63"	1575	160.02
	66"	1650	167.64
	69"	1725	175.26
	72"	1800	182.88
	75"	1875	190.5
	78"	1950	198.12
	81"	2025	205.74
	84"	2100	213.36
	87"	2175	220.98
	90"	2250	228.6
	93"	2325	236.22
	96"	2400	243.84
	99"	2475	251.46
	102"	2475	259.08
	105"	2625	266.7
	108"	2700	274.32
	111"	2775	281.94
	114"	2850	289.56
	117"	2925	297.18
	120"	3000	304.8
	123"	3075	312.42
	126"	3150	320.04
	129"	3225	327.66
	132"	3300	335.28
	135"	3375	342.9
	138"	3450	350.52
	141"	3525	358.14
	144"	3600	365.76

Metric Conversion Chart

LENGTH

10 MILLIMETERS = 1 CENTIMETER (CM)
10 CENTIMETERS - 1 DECIMETER
10 DECIMETERS - 1 METER (M)
10 METERS - 1 DEKAMETER
100 METERS - 1 HECTOMETER
1,000 METERS - 1 KILOMETER

AREA

100 SQ. MILLIMETERS = 1 SQ. CENTIMETER
100 SQ. CENTIMETER = 1 SQ. DECIMETER
100 SQ. DECIMETERS = 1 SQ. METER
100 SQ. METERS - 1 ARE
10,000 SQ. METERS - 1 HECTARE
100 HECTARES - 1 SQ. KILOMETER

LINEAR DRAWING MEASUREMENTS

1 MILLIMETER (MM) - .03937"   1" = 25.4 MM   12" = 304.8 MM
1 CENTIMETER (CM) - .3937"   1" = 2.54 CM   12" = 30.48 CM
1 METER (M) - 39.37"   1" = .0254 M   12" = .3048 M

SQUARE MEASURE

1 SQ. INCH - 6.4516 SQ. CENTIMETERS
1 SQ. FOOT - 9.29034 SQ. DECIMETERS
1 SQ. YARD = .836131 SQ. METER
1 ACRE = .40469 HECTARE
1 SQ. MILE = 2.59 SQ. KILOMETERS

DRY MEASURE

1 PINT = .550599 LITER
1 QUART = 1.101197 LITER
1 PECK = 8.80958 LITER
1 BUSHEL = .35238 HECTOLITER

CUBIC MEASURE

1 CU. INCH - 16.3872 CU. CENTIMETERS
1 CU. FOOT - .028317 CU. METERS
1 CU. YARD - .76456 CU. METERS

LIQUID MEASURE

1 PINT - .473167 LITER
1 QUART - .946332 LITER
1 GALLON - 3.785329 LITER

LONG MEASURE

1 INCH = 25.4 MILLIMETERS
1 FOOT = .3 METER
1 YARD = .914401 METER
1 MILE = 1.609347 KILOMETERS

Graphics and Presentation Standards for Bathroom Design